ACTS

OF THE

ANTI-SLAVERY APOSTLES.

ACTS

OF THE

ANTI-SLAVERY APOSTLES.

BY

PARKER PILLSBURY.

"AND THEY WENT EVERYWHERE PREACHING THE
WORD."—Acts, viii : 4.

BOOKS FOR LIBRARIES PRESS
FREEPORT, NEW YORK

First Published 1883
Reprinted 1970

STANDARD BOOK NUMBER:
8369-5220-0

LIBRARY OF CONGRESS CATALOG CARD NUMBER:
71-107826

PRINTED IN THE UNITED STATES OF AMERICA

INTRODUCTION.

Some books, judged by their titles, are more remarkable for what they do not contain, than for what they
do. This work is only Acts, not *the* Acts of the Anti-
Slavery Apostles. It is only a small portion of a very
small part of those apostles.

There were many in the great west, as well as not a
few in the east, whose labors, sacrifices and sufferings
entitle them to volumes of well-written biography,
who can scarcely be mentioned here, even by name.

At this time of my life of nearly three score and
fourteen years, more than forty of which have been
spent in the field of moral, peaceful and religious agitation for the rights of humanity, it seemed presumption in me to attempt a labor of even this magnitude.
And it was only earnest, continued importunity on the
part of my very few surviving associates in the conflict, and their friends, that finally determined my
course. Truth only has been sought. Not the whole
truth ; for that were impossible. But strict truth and
exact justice, to the full extent of my time and space.

The present generation knows little of the terrible
mysteries and meanings of slavery or anti-slavery ;
the outrages and horrors of the former, or the desperate and deadly encounters with the monster by the
latter, long before the cannonade of Fort Sumpter, or
the dreadful war chorus of the subsequent rebellion.
And all which is now attempted is some disclosure of
those mysteries.

By anti-slavery apostles are meant those only whose
work was in the lecturing field ; who literally " went
everywhere preaching the word ; " often as with their

lives in their hands.   Nor will only few of them, however worthy and deserving, be mentioned even by
name.   This work will be rather pictures and sketches
than history.   It will hardly enter more than two
states, New Hampshire and Massachusetts ; never go
beyond New England.   But in New England every
type and phase of anti-slavery experience, doing,
suffering and triumphing was represented to the
fullest possible extent.   What was true there was true
everywhere in the country.   And the truth on slavery
and anti-slavery can be presented on .so small space,
and in time equally limited, as well as if the whole
country were included, and all the thirty years of the
moral and peaceful, and so, truly religious, agitation
of the mighty problem were covered and all the heroes
and . martyrs named.   The whole, as originally intended, would have comprised acts and experiences
of, some of those heroes, with brief personal sketches
of them, together with short biographical notices of
William Lloyd Garrison, of *The Liberator*, and Nathaniel Peabody Rogers, of the *Herald of Freedom*.

But, as the work of writing went on, articles began
to appear from our old opponents or their children,
not only declaring that they or their fathers abolished
the evil, but that it could have been sooner and more
easily done, " had Garrison and his small, but motley
following " been out of their way !   So some chapters
of acts of the *pro*-slavery apostles, became necessary,
at cost of both extending the volume, and also excluding some worthy names and noble deeds that had
earned good right to grace these pages.   These mis-
representations came mainly from the clergy, as did
most of our bitterest opposition while prosecuting our
anti-slavery labors, as will be hereafter shown beyond
all question or contradiction.

So now the order of the book will be : A chapter on Mr. Garrison ; a second, on Mr. Rogers ; a third on slavery—as it was ; then one on anti-slavery, what it was not, and what it was ; and then follow the acts of the anti-slavery apostles ; with acts of the pro-slavery apostles subjoined ; the latter generally telling their own story in their own words, works and ways, no cross-questioning ever entering into their truly judgment-day assizes, as will be made fully to appear to a surrounding world. And it scarcely need be added that the abundant testimony adduced, is only a small part of what the churches and their ministers have treasured. up against themselves, to be hereafter unfolded from their own archives, should occasion for it ever arise.

CONCORD, N. H., 1883.   P. P.

CONTENTS.

CHAPTER X.

CHAPTER XI.

CHAPTER XII.

CHAPTER XIII.

CHAPTER XIV.

CHAPTER XV.

CHAPTER XVI.

ACTS OF THE ANTI-SLAVERY APOSTLES.

CHAPTER I.

WILLIAM LLOYD GARRISON.

The Acts of the twelve apostles are not the history of Christianity. Nor will the Acts of the Anti-Slavery Apostles be a history of the anti-slavery movement in the United States. My own beginning in that sublime enterprise was in the year 1840, when, dating from the establishment of *The Liberator*, in Boston, by William Lloyd Garrison, it was about ten years old. At that time, so far as can be shown, was first announced the doctrine of immediate unconditional emancipation to every slave, without compensation to master or expatriation to the slave.

Most of my anti-slavery work was of the missionary character, as was that of the first Christian apostles, who "went everywhere preaching the word." And the purpose of this Scripture is to present a true record, as far as practicable, of what passed under my own immediate observation, and in which it was my honor to bear some humble part. My earliest associates, editors as well as lecturers, are mostly now no more, and some personal account of a part of them is also in my present contemplation. My first anti-slavery newspapers were *The Liberator*, *The Emancipator*, published in New York, organ and property of the American Anti-Slavery Society, and *Herald of*

Freedom, of Concord, New Hampshire. Through
some changes occurring in 1840, *The Emancipator*
passed out of the society's hands, but was immediately succeeded by the *National Anti-Slavery Standard*,
which continued with unswerving integrity till slavery
was abolished in the country by presidential proclamation, and the *male* slave at least was made secure in
his right of suffrage and citizenship. The first issue
of his *Liberator* by Mr. Garrison was on January 1,
1831. It was a most humble, unpretentious little sheet
of four pages, about fourteen inches by nine in
size, but charged with the destiny of a race of human
beings whose redemption from chattel, brutal bondage,
was one day to shake to its foundations the mightiest
republic ever yet existing on the globe. My first
introduction to Mr. Garrison was in the early spring
of 1839. I had just concluded to undertake a short
lecturing and financial agency for the Massachusetts Anti-Slavery Society, and was invited to a
meeting of its executive committee, to mature my
arrangements. It was an evening business session, in
West street, Boston, and at the close Mr. Garrison
invited me to his home, then of unassuming pretensions, in Seaver Place, to pass the night. The next
day was Saturday, and I went by stage to Fitchburg,
about fifty miles, and on Sunday evening delivered my
first address on slavery, as agent of my association.
And though I did in the course of that year, and the
beginning of 1840, accept and occupy the position of
a minister for a very small Congregational church and
society in an obscure New Hampshire town, it seems
on the whole more pertinent, proper and desirable, to
date the beginning of my life mission and labor from
that anti-slavery committee meeting in Boston and
introduction to Mr. Garrison, and first work as an anti-

slavery agent in Fitchburg and through the county of
Worcester in the spring of 1839.

Of the boyhood history of Mr. Garrison this may
not be the place to speak. Like many men of high
eminence, he commenced life among the lowly. Nor
was his native town, Newburyport, Massachusetts,
ever distinguished for any but most conservative ideas
in government, religion or social policy. His excellent
mother, a devout member of the Baptist church, early
sent him to learn the trade of a shoemaker.   Fortunately too early, for his knees could not support the
lap-stone, the anvil of the shoemaker of that day, and
he was soon discharged, and entered as an apprentice
to a cabinet maker. But neither was this a success. Nor
did he even approach nor tend to his future high calling, until, while still a youth, he entered a printing office.
That, as has been truly said, was to him high school,
college and university, from which he graduated with
honors, after long and faithful apprenticeship.

His first business enterprise was to establish a little
newspaper in his native town, which he characteristic-
ally named the *Free Press*. He soon learned, however, that the time for a *Free Press* was not yet.   But
the voice of his *genius* still said, Cry! and he responded next in Boston, with the *National Philanthropist*, devoted doctrinally and practically to entire
abstinence from all intoxicating drinks. His motto
was, "Moderate drinking, the down-hill road to
drunkenness." This undertaking was in the year
1827, when he was twenty-two years old. But the
Philanthropist, like the *Free Press*, proved a premature birth. In 1828, his powers of mind and heart
coming to be better appreciated, he had and accepted
a proposition to go to Bennington, Vermont, and
establish a political paper to be known as *The Journal*

of the Times, and to advocate the claims of John Quincy Adams to the Presidency of the United States. Here, again, was a failure, and this journal soon slept with its predecessors. However, the valiant, persevering young editor was still full of courage and hope, and held on his way. He soon made acquaintance with Benjamin Lundy, an early, brave and true-hearted Quaker anti-slavery man, though hardly yet a pronounced abolitionist. Of kindred spirit, in the main, the two men formed a partnership in the autumn of 1829, and together published the *Genius of Universal Emancipation.*

But though of one spirit, there was in *methods* between the two men a difference wide as earth and heaven. Mr. Lundy, in common with the highest humanities of the time, only demanded a *gradual* removal of slavery. Mr. Garrison, instead of gradual, almost stunned the nation with the new and more excellent evangel: "IMMEDIATE AND UNCONDITIONAL EMANCIPATION!"

Here, then, was a new problem to be solved, or reconciled. An organized existence with one heart, but two voices: one serene, quiet, such as men might hear but not fear; the other the seven unloosed Apocalyptic thunders that men should hear, and hearing, *tremble*, as had Thomas Jefferson already, even in anticipation, almost half a century before the terrible utterance was heard by mortal ear! But Friend Lundy's persuasion prevailed for the present. After long, honest consideration and discussion, he finally said to Mr. Garrison: "Well, thee may put thy initials to thy editorial articles and I will put my initials to mine."

But the stern logic of events soon showed that iron and clay could never be so welded together. This was in Baltimore, a slave-breeding, slave-trading, slave-holding city ; indeed, had already become a great shipping emporium of the domestic slave trade of the United States ! where, as has been said, slave pens flaunted their signs in open day on the principal streets, their rich owners the best city society and most devout worshippers in Christian churches. The wonder was that the *gradualism* of Lundy could be tolerated. And he soon learned who had struck at the great tap root of the deadly upas. Mr. Garrison wrote : " My demand for immediate emancipation so alarmed and excited the people everywhere, that where Friend Lundy would get one new subscriber I would knock off a dozen." And so the *Genius of Universal Emancipation* would undoubtedly have soon been buried in the tomb of its three predecessors who owed their paternity to Mr. Garrison. But his intrepidity and fidelity in denouncing the domestic slave trade and exposure of its great cruelty, in the action of a ship captain engaged in it from his own native town of Newburyport, led to his arrest on a charge of libel, and conviction, fine, and imprisonment in a Baltimore jail. Nor had he one friend in the city to prevent it, if even to deplore his fate.

Released from prison, his fine and court expenses being paid by Mr. Arthur Tappan of New York, and his partnership with Friend Lundy dissolved by mutual consent and in most cordial spirit, Mr. Garrison conceived the thought of establishing a paper at Washington, where the slave power and the domestic slave trade, in all their terrors, had established themselves under the sheltering wing and by direct authority of the Federal Government. Having in August, 1830, issued his prospectus, he visited the principal cities between Baltimore and Boston to test

the tone of the public feeling for such an enterprise.
But though he found Boston scarcely more friendly to
his doctrines and determinations against slavery than
even Baltimore itself, he finally concluded that it,
rather than Washington, was the ground whereon
The Liberator should be set up.

Writing, after his tour of observation, he said :

During my recent tour for the purpose of exciting
the minds of the people by a series of discourses on
the subject of slavery, every place I visited gave fresh
evidence of the fact that a greater revolution in public sentiment was to be effected in the Free States, and
particularly in New England, than at the South. I
found contempt more bitter, opposition more active,
detraction more relentless, prejudice more stubborn,
and apathy more frozen than among slave owners
themselves. Of course there were individual exceptions to the contrary. This state of things afflicted
but did not dishearten me. I determined at every
hazard to lift up the standard of emancipation in the
eyes of the nation within sight of Bunker Hill and in
the birth-place of liberty. That standard is now
unfurled, and long may it float, unhurt by the spoila-
tions of time or the missiles of a desperate foe, till
every chain be broken and every bondman set free !
Let Southern oppressors tremble. Let all the enemies of the persecuted blacks tremble ! Assenting to
the self-evident truth maintained in the Declaration
of Independence, that "all men are created equal and
endowed by their Creator with certain inalienable
rights, among which are life, liberty, and the pursuit
of happiness," I shall strenuously contend for the
immediate enfranchisement of our slave population.
In Park Street Church, on the fourth of July, 1829, in
an address on slavery, I unsuspectingly assented to
the popular but pernicious doctrine of *gradual* abolition. I seize this opportunity to make a full and unequivocal recantation, and thus publicly to ask pardon
of my God, of my country, and of the poor slaves,
for having uttered a sentiment so full of timidity,
injustice and absurdity. A similar recantation from

my pen was published in the *Genius of Universal Emancipation*, at Baltimore, in September, 1829. My conscience is now satisfied. I am aware that many object to the severity of my language. But is there not cause for severity? I will be as harsh as truth, and as uncompromising as justice. On this subject I do not wish to think, or speak, or write with moderation. No! No! Tell a man whose house is on fire to give a moderate alarm; tell him to moderately rescue his wife from the hands of the ravisher; tell the mother to gradually extricate her babe from the fire into which it has fallen; but urge me not to use moderation in a cause like the present! I am in earnest—I will not equivocate—I will not excuse—I will not retreat a single inch. And I WILL BE HEARD. The apathy of the people is enough to make every statue leap from its pedestal, and to hasten the resurrection of the dead!*

Thus, at last, had come the hour and the man. The great clock of the eternities struck the hour. And out of the dread silences came the prophetic word which was to finish the work of Washington and the Revolution, proclaiming " LIBERTY throughout all the land, to all the inhabitants thereof." In a Baltimore prison he had learned to "remember them that are in bonds, as bound with them;" and this was his self-consecration, in the earnest strains of Thomas Pringle :

> " Oppression! I have seen thee face to face,
> And met thy cruel eye and cloudy brow ;
> But thy soul-withering glance I fear not now—
> For dread to prouder feelings doth give place
> Of deep abhorrence! Scorning the disgrace
> Of slavish knees that at thy footstool bow,
> I also kneel; but with far other vow
> Do hail thee and thy herd of hirelings base ;—
> I swear, while life-blood warms my throbbing veins,
> Still to oppose and thwart, with heart and hand,
> Thy brutalizing sway—till Afric's chains
> Are burst, and Freedom rules the rescued land—
> Trampling Oppression and his iron rod :
> *Such is the vow I take :* SO HELP ME GOD !"

---

* *The Liberator*, Vol. 1, No. 1 : Saturday, January 1, 1831.

This was the man in his sixth and twentieth year.
His work and word, if not his name, was The Liberator. And to the end this was his motto : " My country is the world ; my countrymen are all mankind."

Of the philosophy and method of Mr. Garrison as
the acknowledged leader of the anti-slavery movement, a few words cannot here be out of place. In
scripture phrase it might be sufficient to say, "the
weapons of his warfare were not carnal." He was
ever pre-eminently a man of peace. At this time he
was a devout believer in the truest, best interpretation
of the New Testament, especially of the Sermon on
the Mount and the story of the Good Samaritan. He
held his mission to be a completion of the work begun
in the Revolutionary War ; but in magnitude, sublimity and solemnity, as well as in probable results on the
destiny of the world, as far transcending that, as
moral truth and right transcend physical force. All
war, he held to be inherently, intrinsically wrong.
And so he early declared all carnal weapons, even for
deliverance from bondage, contrary to the spirit of
Christ as well as of His teachings ; and even counselled the slaves earnestly against any resort to them
in achieving their liberty. And the Constitution of
the American Anti-Slavery Society, work of his hand,
contained such a provision.

In a " Declaration of Principles adopted by a convention assembled in Philadelphia to organize a
national anti - slavery association," are words like
these from the same brain, heart and hand :

The right to enjoy liberty is inalienable ; to invade
it is to usurp the prerogative of Jehovah. Every man
has a right to his own body, to the products of his
labor, to the protection of law, and to the common
advantages of society. It is piracy by our laws to
buy or steal a native African and subject him to servi-

tude : surely the sin is as great to enslave an American. Every American citizen who detains a human being in involuntary bondage is (according to Exodus 21:16,) a man stealer. The slaves ought instantly to be set free, and brought under the protection of law.

After much more in similar strain, follows this :

These are our views and principles—these our designs and measures. With entire confidence in the over-ruling justice of God, we plant ourselves upon the Declaration of our Independence and the truths of Divine Revelation as upon the Everlasting Rock. We shall send forth agents to lift up everywhere the voice of remonstrance, of warning, of entreaty and of rebuke.

We shall circulate unsparingly and extensively, anti-slavery tracts and periodicals.

We shall enlist the pulpit and the press in the cause of the suffering and the dumb.

We shall aim at a purification of the churches from all participation in the guilt of slavery.

We shall spare no exertions nor means to bring the whole nation to speedy repentance.

Our trust for victory is solely in God. *We* may be personally defeated, but our principles, never ! Truth, jnstice, reason, humanity, must and will gloriously triumph !

In youth, Garrison had been a pronounced politician of the conservative party, as were most of the leading men of his native town. It was the sound of the Greek revolution against Turkish despotism which first filled his ear, and fired his young soul with the spirit of freedom. The powerful appeals of Daniel Webster and Henry Clay in the American Senate fed the flame. Webster became to him the divinity of the forum. He even contemplated at one time a brief term at the West Point military school that he might take the field in person in the cause of the struggling Greeks. John Randolph had not yet told him and Webster and Clay that "the Greeks were at their own doors."

But as Mr. Garrison increased in wisdom and spiritual stature, and it became evident that he was to be the divinely constituted leader in the sublimest movement in behalf of liberty and humanity of many generations, his vision was so anointed that he saw clearly that, though he was indeed to wrestle with principalities and powers, and with *spiritual* wickedness in high places also, his weapons were to be drawn from no earthly magazines. The sword of the spirit of Truth only, was to be made mighty in his hands, to an extent such as had not been beheld before, from the day when an apostate Christianity in the person of Constantine the Great, mounted the throne of the Cæsars and most ingloriously proclaimed herself mistress of the world !

When the American Anti-Slavery Society was formed in Philadelphia, in 1833, Garrison was a New Testament Christian, as he understood the word, in all the word can rightly be made to mean. And most of all, did he reverence the doctrines of freedom and peace. Peace on earth, liberty and good-will to men, to all men, and all women, were then his proclamation and song. Human life he came to regard as sacred above all other things. And so capital punishment and war, as well as slavery, were to him an abhorrence. Hence, logically, he renounced all allegiance to human governments founded in military force, and openly proclaimed himself disciple of the Prince of Peace, in these memorable words :

O Jesus ! noblest of patriots, greatest of heroes, most glorious of martyrs ! Thine is the spirit of universal liberty and love, of uncompromising hostility to every form of injustice and wrong. But not with weapons of death dost thou assail thy enemies, that they may be vanquished or destroyed. For thou dost not wrestle against flesh and blood, but against principalities and powers, against the rulers of the darkness of this world, against spiritual wickedness in high places. Therefore hast thou put on the whole armor of God ; having thy loins girt about with truth, and having on the breast-plate of righteousness, and thy feet shod with the preparation of the gospel of peace ; going forth to battle with the shield of faith, the helmet of salvation, the sword of the spirit ! Worthy of all imitation art thou, in overcoming the evil that is in the world. For, by the shedding of thy own blood, but not the blood of thy bitterest foes even, shalt thou at last obtain a universal victory.

> The Christian's victory alone
> Hostility forever ends ;
> Erects an undisputed throne
> And turns his foes to friends.
>
> Ye great, ye mighty of the earth !
> Ye conquerers, learn this secret true !
> A secret of celestial birth—
> *By suffering to subdue!*
>
> —LETTER TO KOSSUTH.

The New England Non-Resistance Society was organized in 1838, and Mr. Garrison was elected corresponding secretary and member of the executive committee ; and many of its first official papers and records, besides breathing his spirit, bear unmistakable imprint of his brain and hand. A portion of the preamble to its constitution reads thus :

Whereas, The penal code of the first covenant has been abrogated by Jesus Christ ; and whereas our Savior has left man example that we should follow his steps in forbearance, submission to injury and non-resistance, even when life itself is at stake ; and whereas the weapons of a true Christian are not carnal but spiritual, and therefore mighty through God to the pulling down of strongholds ; and whereas we profess to belong to a kingdom not of this world, which is without local or geographical boundaries, in which there is no division of caste, nor inequality of sex ; therefore, we, the undersigned, etc., etc.

A part of Article II of the constitution reads :

The members of this society agree in the opinion that no man nor body of men, however constituted or by whatever name called, have right to take the life of man as penalty for transgression ; that no one who professes to have the spirit of Christ can consistently sue a man at law for redress of injuries, or thrust any evil-doer into prison ; or hold any office in which he would come under obligation to execute any penal enactments, or take any part in the military service ; or acknowledge allegiance to any human government. * * *

At this time it cannot be doubted that the belief of Mr. Garrison in both the inspiration and authority of the Bible, the Trinity and Atonement, but especially in all the teachings and precepts of Christ, was almost precisely such as was then, and still is professed, by the whole Evangelical church.   Among his many devout poetical effusions this will be found :

SONNET TO THE BIBLE.

O Book of books ! Though skepticism flout
Thy sacred origin, thy worth decry ;
Though trancendental folly give the lie
To what thou teachest : though the critic doubt
This fact ; that miracle ; and raise a shout
Of triumph o'er each incongruity
He in thy pages may perchance espy ;
As in his strength, the effulgent sun shines out,
Hiding innumerous stars, so dost thou shine,
With heavenly light all human works excelling.
Thy oracles are holy and divine,
Of free salvation through a Savior telling.
All truth, all excellence dost thou enshrine ;
The mists of sin and ignorance expelling.

Such was Mr. Garrison as a Christian, as a follower of the Christ of the New Testament.   And wondrously consistent with his faith were his spirit, his life, and his whole character.

At home or abroad ; in private or in public ; as writer or as speaker ; as husband, father, friend, neighbor, or in whatever relation ; after long, wide, and intimate acquaintance with men in pulpit, church, politics, and the world at large ; for the constant exercise of what we call the christian virtues and graces, I surely have seen few the peer, none the superior of William Lloyd Garrison.

And yet he was called an infidel by almost all the universal church of the nation, from the university and theological seminary down to the humblest village pastors, churches, and Sunday-schools. With a life pure and spotless as the white plumage of angels, his whole character and conduct unsullied by the slightest breath of reproach, blessing many temporally and spiritually with whom he had intercourse, gentle and patient with ignorance, forbearing and long-suffering with prejudice and perverseness, and yet bold and brave, unconcealing and uncompromising where oppression and iniquity, injustice and cruelty were to be exposed and rebuked, no matter in what high places entrenched—yet was he branded, blasted as infidel, even atheist, when those words were made to stand for, were presumed to stand for all that is to be dreaded, shunned, execrated and exterminated at whatever cost !

Revering the New Testament as law divine, he studied and respected its teachings. Did he read " Resist Not Evil ?" He observed the sacred requirement, preached it in his journal, *The Liberator*, and practiced it everywhere. Hence arose the Non-Resistance Society, as well as a great national anti-slavery movement, which, without proscription, rested substantially and was largely sustained on a similar foundation.

With him " love your enemies " never meant shoot them in war, nor hang nor imprison them in peace.

And so *The Liberator*, which was his own property from first to last, was not only a proclamation of peace, liberty and love on earth, but of general, universal unfolding, progressing and perfecting to all man and womankind.

But, joining himself to no religious sect nor party, chained down to no narrow, dogmatic ringbolt, he had ever eye and ear, as well as heart and hospitality, for whatever new truth might appear—in whatever book, science or ·religion it might be found. And what wonder if years of violent opposition and persecution from almost the whole American church and clergy on account of his fidelity to the christian doctrines of peace, purity and liberty as they were taught in the sermon on the mount, and the unswerving example of its great Author, should have clarified and quickened his vision mentally and spiritually! At any rate, he subsequently re-examined the faiths and formulas of the professedly evangelical sects in religion, including their avowed belief in plenary inspiration of Holy Scripture.

As one result of his farther investigations, he attended a convention at Hartford, Connecticut, in 1853, called especially to consider the claim and character of the Jewish and Christian Scriptures. The meeting was very large, having representatives, men and women, from east and west, continuing four days, with three long sessions each. In one of them Mr. Garrison offered and ably defended a series of resolutions, the first of which was to this purport:

Resolved, That the doctrines of the American church and priesthood, that the Bible is the word of God; that whatever it contains was given by divine inspiration, and that it is the only rule of faith and practice, is self-evidently absurd; is exceedingly injurious both to the intellect and the soul; is highly pernicious in its application, and a stumbling block in the way of human redemption.

And yet, to the end of life, no man more venerated or made wiser use of the Bible than did Mr. Garrison. A late testimonial of his reads thus :

I have lost my traditional and educational notions of the holiness of the Bible, but I have gained greatly, I think, in my estimation of it. * * * I am fully aware how grievously the priesthood have perverted it and wielded it as an instrument of spiritual despotism and in opposition to the sacred cause of humanity ; still to no other volume do I turn with so much interest ; no other do I consult or turn to so frequently ; to no other am I so indebted for light and strength ; no other is so identified with the growth of human freedom and progress. To no other have I appealed so effectively in aid of the various reformatory movements which I have espoused. And it embodies an amount of excellence so great as to make it, in my estimation, THE BOOK OF BOOKS.

Garrison early learned to doubt nothing only because it was new, and he accepted nothing unless he saw on it more than the mold and moss of age and time. He found the world, even its most enlightened people, dead in the trespasses and sins of intemperance, slavery, war, capital punishment, and woman's enslavement. He lived to set on foot, or largely and liberally co-operate in enterprises and instrumentalities for correcting all these abuses, for righting all these fearful wrongs.

But at last there came another stranger to his door. With characteristic hospitality that door was again opened. Francis Jackson, one of the noblest, bravest, most steadfast supporters of Mr. Garrison and his life work, once said with respect to sheltering and protecting the fugitive slave : "When I unfeelingly shut my door against a hunted, fleeing slave, may the God of compassion close the door of his mercy against me !"

So no slave, nor even stranger, ever appealed in vain to Garrison. The new guest was Spiritualism. That was a " sect everywhere spoken against " as fast as it grew in numbers—as anti-slavery had been in the generation preceding it. Even many of the best abolitionists, men and women who had bravely suffered persecution for and with the slave, treated it with contempt and scorn. Not so, never so, with Mr. Garrison. Many of his truest friends, some of them Quakers, as well as of other religious denominations, became early and devoted spiritualists, and that alone would have forever prevented him from dismissing, still less condemning, any stranger or defendant uncondemned, or even unheard.

And in finally giving the new and mysterious idea recognition, he found, and to the end of his life believed, that he had literally entertained angels, and angels not unawares.

Nor did he hesitate to make proclamation of the new and sublime Evangel. In *The Liberator* of March 3d, 1854, is an article from his pen, of which the following are but the opening paragraphs, giving a detailed account of a highly demonstrative seance he had just attended in New York, where writing, rapping, drumming, "drumming in admirable time and most spiritual manner," and other wondrous phenomena were witnessed. He wrote :

We are often privately asked what we think of the "spiritual manifestations," so called, and whether we have had any opportunities to investigate them.

When we first heard of the "Rochester knockings" we supposed (not personally knowing the persons implicated) that there might be some collusion in that particular case, or if not, that the phenomena would, ere long, elicit a satisfactory solution, independent of any spiritual agency. As the manifestations have spread from house to house, from city to city, from one part of the country to the other, across the Atlantic into Europe, till now the civilized world is compelled to acknowledge their reality, however diverse in accounting for them; as these manifestations continue to increase in variety and power, so that all suspicion of trick or imposture becomes simply absurd and preposterous; and as every attempt to find a solution for them in some physical theory relating to electricity, the odic force, clairvoyance, and the like, has thus far proved abortive—it becomes every intelligent mind to enter into an investigation of them with candor and fairness, as opportunity may offer, and to bear such testimony in regard to them as the facts may warrant; no matter what ridicule it may excite on the part of the uninformed or sceptical.

As for ourselves, most assuredly we have been in no haste to jump to a conclusion in regard to phenomena so universally diffused, and of so extraordinary a character. For the last three years, we have kept pace with nearly all that has been published on the subject; and we have witnessed, at various times, many surprising "manifestations;" and our conviction is that they cannot be accounted for on any other theory than that of spiritual agency. This theory, however is not unattended with discrepancies, difficulties, and trials. It is certain that, if it be true, there are many deceptive spirits, and that the apostolic injunction to "believe not every spirit," but to try them in every possible way, is specially to be regarded, or the consequences may prove very disastrous. We might write a long essay on what we have seen and heard touching the matter, but this we reserve for some other occasion.

At the burial of his friend Henry C. Wright, who died on the 16th of August, 1870, he made one of the most eloquent and impressive addresses of his whole life. Mr. Wright had been for several years a pronounced and active spiritualist, and this is the

tribute, or a portion of it, which Mr. Garrison paid to
that part of his life work :

I see it reproachfully stated in one newspaper at
least, that he was a spiritualist. What if he was?
That is simply a question of evidence. What has
been possible in any age of the world as to spiritual
phenomena, is possible in ours. And if we cannot
believe what transpires in our days, before our own
eyes, we certainly do not and cannot believe what is
merely reported to have taken place ages ago. What
shall be said of the intelligence or sincerity of those
who say they implicitly accept all the marvels and
miracles recorded as having taken place thousands of
years ago, with not a living witness to attest to any
one of them ; while they scout as arrant imposture
perfectly analogous wonders and revelations, though
these are confirmed by multitudes of living witnesses
whose faithfulness cannot be questioned, and whose
critical judgment and profound caution refute every
imputation of folly or ignorance.

When spiritualism was on trial at the bar of the
judgment of this world, some of Mr. Garrison's friends
saw with deep regret his hospitality and charity
towards it. There were those who even denied positively that he was, or was in any danger of becoming,
a spiritualist. So doutbtless his early political and
religious associates felt and reasoned, when they saw
his heart warmed, and his hand and voice were lifted
in behalf of the imbruted slave and his few devoted,
but despised and persecuted friends. With his shining talents and deep devotion to his then sincerely
cherished political and religious principles, both of
respectable and popular character, how could he ever
become an Abolitionist ?

But there's a Divinity that shapes our ends ; and
Garrison was a young man when he wrote :

> " I am an Abolitionist,
>   Oppression's deadly foe ;
>   In God's great name will I resist
>   And lay the monster low.
>   In God's great name do I demand
>   To all be Freedom given,
>   That peace and joy may fill the earth
>   And songs go up to heaven."

And spiritualism he yoked to his chariot of salvation
so soon as he espoused it in its fullness and conscious
truth, as had already his friend Henry C. Wright, a
few years before, and doubtless in the full faith and
hope of Lord Brougham, when he wrote : *"Even in
the most cloudless skies of Skepticism, I see a rain-cloud,
if it be no bigger than a man's hand, and its name is
Spiritualism."*

CHAPTER II.

NATHANIEL PEABODY ROGERS

When some discerning Romans saw how many statues were reared in their city to persons of only indifferent merit, while Cato, one of their wisest and best, had none, they wondered. But the great man had answered the question beforehand : " Better that posterity should ask why Cato has not a monument, than why he has."

In the cemeteries of Concord, New Hampshire, are many memorial stones. Some of great beauty and cost, with proportionally elaborate and, perhaps, appropriate inscriptions. But situated among them is one lot of the ordinary family size, protected by no iron railing, no granite embankment, and whose dead level surface would seem never to have been invaded for burial, agricultural or any other human purpose.

And yet to that hallowed spot I have conducted many devout pilgrims from east and west, both women and men. For there, since Sunday, the 18th day of October, 1846, exactly thirty-six years ago this very day, and almost hour, have slumbered the mortal remains of Nathaniel Peabody Rogers, surely one of the brightest, noblest, truest and every way most gifted sons, not only of the Granite state, but of any state of this union of states, departing at the early age of only fifty-two years.

And no visitor from near or remote, ever fails to ask, sometimes with almost stunning emphasis : " Why has Rogers no monument ?"

Should that sacred spot speak out from its silence of six and thirty years, doubtless its answer to the eminently pertinent inquiry would be, as was that of Cato, so well remembered, so much admired, so often repeated now, after more than two thousand years.

Such as was Rogers, never die. They need no monuments reared by other hands than their own. Time mows down all marble and granite, tramples out all inscriptions in bronze or brass. And so such registers are soon lost for evermore. It has been said of the immortal Senator Sumner and his humble tombstone at Mount Auburn, and lowly indeed it is :

> " The grass may grow o'er the lowly bed
> Where the noblest Roman hath laid his head ;
> But mind and thought, a nation's mind
> Embalm the lover of mankind."

And scarcely of any man departed or still visible to mortal sight, could this be sung more appropriately than of the subject of this chapter ; and for some seven years editor of the *Herald of Freedom*, published in Concord, New Hampshire, ten or twelve years.

Mr. Rogers was born at Plymouth, on the 3d of June, 1794, and was one of the tenth generation from him who is so well, widely and honorably known as " Rev. John Rogers," the first in that blessed company of martyrs who suffered in the reign of the bigoted and bloody Mary, in the year 1555. And surely the blood of the martyr, literally and spiritually, flowed in the veins of his remote descendant, answering " heart to heart," as well as " face to face." For those who have been privileged to see both our departed editor in the flesh and form, and a singularly well preserved portrait of the martyr in the American Antiquarian Society hall at Worcester, Massachusetts, have wondered at the remarkable resemblance in the

shape of head and face, in complexion, color of eye
and hair, and the whole general expression of the two
memorable men.   He graduated with honors at Dartmouth college, in the year 1816.   He studied law with
the distinguished Richard Fletcher, and then settled
down to its practice in his native town, marrying a
daughter of Hon. Daniel Farrand, of Burlington, Vermont.   He conducted a flourishing and successful law
practice in Plymouth for about twenty years before
moving to Concord to take charge of the *Herald of
Freedom.*

As student in general literature, especially in history and poetry, none of his day were before him.
Few ever heard Shakespeare, Scott, Byron and Burns
read more beautifully, more thrillingly, than at his
fireside, surrounded by his estimable wife and seven
children, with sometimes a few invited friends.   But
general reading and home delights never detracted
from the duties of his profession.   When he died, an
intimate friend, who had known him long and well,
wrote that so accurate was his knowledge of law, and
so industrious was he in business, that the success of
a client was always confidently expected from the
moment his assistance was secured.   His life mission,
however, was neither literature nor law.   He was in
due time ordained, consecrated as a high priest in
the great fellowship of humanity, and wondrously,
divinely did he magnify his office in the ten or twelve
last years of his earthly life.

In the year 1835, he made acquaintance with
Garrison, and soon placed himself at his side as the
hated, hunted, persecuted champion of the American
slave, as by this time Garrison was known to be.   And
from that time, too, Rogers was ever found the firm,
unshaken, uncompromising friend and advocate of not

only the anti-slavery enterprise, but of the causes of temperance, peace, rights of woman, abolition of the gallows and halter, and other social and moral reforms.

Here may be the place to say what certainly should be said at some time and place, a few words on the early religious character of Mr. Rogers. For it is neither known to this generation nor presumed what manner of men and women were most of those who early espoused the cause of the American slave ; especially in their relations to the popular and prevailing religion of their time. Both Mr. and Mrs. Rogers were active and honored members in the Congregational church at Plymouth, when they espoused the cause of the slave. And they naturally looked, as did other anti-slavery christians, to the church and pulpit as the divinely appointed instrumentality for emancipating the bondmen, especially of their own country, enslaved, too, by laws of their own enactment and religious sanction and approval.

Perhaps a few excerpts from an early editorial in the *Herald of Freedom* will illustrate the quality of the religious sentiment and opinion of the editor, as well as the tone and temper of his heart and spirit. The whole article is in the *Herald* of August 11, 1838, and is a review of a contribution to the *Christian Examiner*, entitled " The Presence of God." The *Examiner* was a Unitarian journal, the sect at that time quite alien to the more evangelical views of Mr. Rogers :

We wander a moment from our technical anti-slavery sphere, to say, with permission of our readers, a word or two on a beautiful article in the *Christian Examiner*. It is from the pen of one of our gifted fellow citizens, to whom ·the unhappy subjects of insanity in this state owe so much for the public charity now contemplated in their behalf. It is written with great eloquence, perspicuity and force of style ; and what is more, it seems scarcely to want that spirit of heart-broken Christianity so apt to be missing in the peaceful speculation of reviews, and may we not say in the speculations of the elegant corps among whom the writer of the article is here found. We will find briefly what fault we can with the article. Its beauties need not be pointed out. They lie scattered profusely over its face. It is an article on "The Presence of God," and treats of our relations to Him. But does it set forth that relation as involving our need of the Lord Jesus Christ, in order that we may be able to stand in it ? For ourselves we cannot contemplate God, and dare not look towards Him unconnected with Christ. Our writer seems boldly to look upon Him as the strong-eyed eagle gazes into the sun. God is of purer eyes than to behold iniquity. He cannot look upon sin but with abhorrence. We have sinned ; therefore we fear to behold him. In Christ alone is He our Father in heaven, and we His reconciled children. In Christ we dare take hold of His hand, and of the skirts of His almighty garments. The Lord Jesus Christ and Him crucified is the medium through whom alone we dare look upon God, in His works, His providence, or His grace. Sinless man might, without this medium. Fallen man may not.   *   *   *   The writer contemplated God in His works—but he seems, though awed, elevated and delighted at their grandeur, beauty and wisdom, to feel still baffled of the great end in their contemplation. Does he not, we would ask him, feel the absence of some link in the chain of communication with this ineffable being, which might, if not interrupted, anchor his soul securely within the veil, which after all continues to shroud him from communion and sight ? Can he, in sight of the works of God, speak out and sing in the strains of the Singer of Israel ?   *   *   *   The writer speaks of the communion of God with our minds. This he seems to regard with chief interest. He speaks of "the need of having attention," meaning intellectual attention, "waked up to these old truths." "Listlessness of mind," he continues, "an inveterate habit of inattention to the existence of the Eternal Spirit, needs to be broken in upon. We need to help each other to escape a fatuity of mind on this subject that we may feel that God's ark still rides o'er the world's waves, and that the burning bush has not gone out." There is an "inattention," it is true, but it is of the heart, not merely of the mind, of the nature and not of "habit" merely ; a spiritual inattention, or rather alienation from God, which must be broken in upon. It is not the creature of habit. Adam felt it in all its force on the very day of his first transgression. He heard the voice of God, which, in his innocency, he had hailed with joy, beyond all he felt at the beauties of Paradise ; heard it walking in the garden in the cool of the day, and he hid himself from the presence of the Lord God among the trees of the garden. His wife also hid herself, for she, too, had transgressed, and we, their moral heirs, hide ourselves so to this day. They could walk in the garden in sight of the beautiful works of God, perhaps admire the splendors of Eden, but when they heard His voice, they hid themselves. Not from *habit* surely, that not being the creature of a day. There was "inveteracy," not of habit, but of fallen nature. It is that which must be "broken in upon" before we shall incline to come out from among the trees to welcome the presence of God. It may be there is a figurative meaning in this hiding among the trees from the presence of Him who made those trees. And may we not deceive ourselves in supposing we contemplate God in His works, when, in truth, we are seeking to hide ourselves from His presence among the glorious trees of this earth's garden?   *   *   *   We have revolted from God. We are born universally in a state of alienation from Him. The Scriptures and all experience teach this. We do not more certainly inherit the transmitted form of our fallen first-parents, than their descended nature. We are born with the need of being "born again." Of this we are sure. We cannot evade it. It is our fate in the wisdom of God. We cannot escape it any more than the Old World could the deluge.   *   *   *   We have an ark of safety, to be sure, capacious enough to save the entire race of man. It will save only those who will enter it. And the time of entering, as it was at the flood, is before the sky of probation is overcast. The door is that now, as then, before the falling of the first great drops of the eternal thunder shower. The ark of safety, we need not say, is Christ. He is the Way, the Truth and the Life. No man can come to the Father but by Him. Whoever hath seen Him hath seen the Father. And by Him is the only manifestation of the presence of God. The presence of His power may be seen in all objects around us. But His strong love to the children of men, cannot be seen but through Christ.

   *   *   But we are forgetting that our *Herald* is a small sheet. We have not space to notice the exquisite beauties of our writer's production as a composition merely ; or the argument it draws of God's presence from his works ; and as it purports to notice merely this evidence of his presence, we will not here express our regret that the name of Christ is not mentioned in the article. May the gifted writer, if he be out of the ark of safety, not delay to enter in. Let him not tarry without to gaze with the eye of elegant curiosity on the scenery of this Sodom world —but bow his neck, "and enter while there's room." And as we bespeak his immediate heed to "the one thing needful," so we demand his pen, voice, influence, prayer and action and open coöperation in the deliverance of his fellow countrymen from the CHAIN OF SLAVERY.

Thus loyal was the editor of the *Herald* to the religious doctrine and teaching of his time in the church of his choice. The church of his fathers through nine generations. Thus diligently had he studied and considered them; and thus eloquently and faithfully, though tenderly and affectionately, did he present, recommend and enforce them, whenever and wherever he had opportunity.

In 1838 he removed from Plymouth to Concord, and became sole editor of the *Herald of Freedom.*

He had, from its establishment in 1834, furnished many most brilliant and trenchant articles for its columns. To the readers of the paper, now alas! the most of them, with its editor, no more, nothing need be said of his power with his pen. Only a single duodecimo volume of three hundred and eighty pages of his editorial writings has been reprinted and preserved, and that long ago disappeared from the market. Ten dollars, it is said, have been offered for a single copy ; though that perhaps might have been before most of the early readers had passed away. Some of its descriptive articles have been pronounced as unsurpassed in life and vigor, brilliancy and beauty, as were their rebukes of slave holders and their abettors and accomplices, scathing, withering, but always eminently just.

His " Jaunt to the White Mountains " with Garrison in the year 1841, was copied from the *Herald* columns into a neat tract and was a capital contribution to the tourist literature of that period. Its length precludes possibility of insertion here ; but one of less volume and of scarcely less power entitled Ailsa Craig, may not so reasonably be rejected. For the world never knew the sublimely gifted writer as it should have known him, and doubtless would, but for his too early removal to higher spheres. Young readers will surely pardon a page or two when they have read them, introduced here for their profit as well as pleasure, showing not only the power of the writer, but also giving them a description of one of the most remarkable as well as interesting spots in the British realm. It is from the *Herald of Freedom* of April 30, 1841:

AILSA CRAIG.

This famous rock in the Irish Sea, we meant to have said something about when we saw it, long before this time. But anti-slavery makes us omit and forget the wonders of the Old World. We passed it on a trip from Scotland to Ireland. We left Glasgow on the twenty-eighth of July, 1840, at ten in the morning, for Dublin. William Lloyd Garrison in company, our fellow passenger to the Irish Capital. *   *   * We went on board a steamer and rode down the ship-thronged Clyde. Nothing can exceed its beauty below the great city of Glasgow. To be sure, they have robbed it of its native banks,— and commerce has substituted for the green slope, a sloping wall of neat and firm stone masonry on each side, and straightened its once indented shores. But the utility of the metamorphosis is so mighty, and so palpable, making this narrow stream, far away inland, the highway for the commerce of one of the great ports of Britain ; of a city as large as New York or Liverpool, where the largest ships may ride as freely as in the ocean for depth of water, that it gives it a most imposing, singular, and interesting appearance. It is hardly broader than some of the widest streets of London. Our little steamer elbowed its way among the keels that thronged it like "the full tide of human existence," along the slippery pavements and broad side-walks of Cheapside, or Glasgow's Broadway, the swarming Irongate. It was amusing to see the ploughed up water roll along the stone banks, half way up their slopes, in waves that coiled and convolved like the folds of the sea serpent. The walls were a good deal higher than the natural shores, which were wet and low. They had filled in behind them with earth, and made high, wide and level land on either side which was now covered with old verdure, and planted with stately trees :—and the promenader might take his rural walk there, side by side with the winged commerce of every quarter of the globe :—the "white sail gliding by the tree," and the smoky plumage of the steamers streaming off over among the glorious woodlands. We made our way steadily, though not rapidly down the widening channel, and came to where the "bonnie" Vale of Leven, came upon the Clyde from Loch Lomond and its enclosing mountains which we could descry in the misty distance, up the Vale.

All abolitionists have heard of the Vale of Leven, and remember its Remonstrance to the Women of America, sent over here some four years ago, and unfurled over the heads of thousands in Broadway Tabernacle at an anti-slavery anniversary. The four thousand Scottish women who signed it, dwelt in the Vale of Leven. We saw John Summerville, the minister who obtained their signatures. What would induce one of our clergy, with any "weight of influence" to be seen going about for *women's* signatures to an *abolition* petition? Where Leven Vale meets the Clyde rises a tremendous rock, in the clefts of which lodges the grim old fortress of Dumbarton Castle, famous in the history of Sir William Wallace.

The river soon broadened into a frith, as the Scotch call their bays. The mountains retreated from each other, and sails were to be seen here and there at anchor in the coves and harbors of the wide waters near their bases. We met a naval horse race on the frith of eight beautiful little vessels at the very top of their speed. They were running the heats, in a wide circle, and leaning down hard to the sea close on each other's heels; all sail crowded they made the water foam white about their prows. It was quite an animating sight, with none of the painful sensations at seeing poor *quadruped* horses scourged and pressed beyond their powers. There was no *distress*, nor faltering of wind, in these graceful little racers, as they swept the frith of Clyde.

A Mr. McTear had come aboard the steamer at Greenock for Dublin. He was a Greenock merchant. We were talking with him on the deck when we spied a conical rock, as it seemed, rising out of the water some distance ahead. It appeared through the thin mists like a hay stack, and about as large. We spoke of it to Mr. McTear, and he told us it was Ailsa Craig. We remembered mention of it by Scott, in the Lord of the Isles, where he calls it *rock* instead of *craig*, in the mouth of Robert Bruce:

> " Lord of the Isles, my trust in thee
> Is firm as Ailsa *rock !* "

We had supposed it was in the Forth on the other
side of Scotland. As we were looking at it,
Mr. McTear asked us to guess the distance to it.
Strangers he said, were apt to greatly mistake the
distance. We looked at the rock along the interven-
ing water. We could get no aid from the shores
which were at great distance, quite out of sight on one
hand. We supposed of course, we should underrate
the distance. So we stretched it liberally, as we
thought, and guessed two miles, though it did not
look like that distance. You have made the common
mistake, he said ; it is over twenty. We could hardly
credit it ; but he told us we should see it was śo, for
we would be over two hours getting to it and were
going at ten knots. And over two hours it was ; and
such was the deceptive character of the way, that
when we thought we were coming right upon it, and
wanting our friend Garrison, who was asleep below,
to see it, we went down and told him to hurry up and
see "Ailsa Rock." It proved, to the amazement of us
both, that we were then nearly ten miles from it.
And the little prominence, that looked so like a hay
stack, or a hay cock, when we descried it first, grew
as we neared it, a mighty mountain, nine hundred and
eighty feet high, rising abruptly out of the sea, and
two miles about the base.

He had been himself governor of the Craig some
years before, and had great sport and some danger in
killing the birds. His way of killing them was with a
club, and he told us how many thousands, we dare
not say how many he had killed in a single day of a
famous kind of goose. He had let himself down to a
quarter of the cliffs where they hunted to get the
young and eggs, and the old ones attacked him and
he fought them with his club till he was covered with
blood, theirs and his own. He had a good mind, he
said, to give them one gun, just to let us see them fly,
as we were strangers. As he had been the Marquis's
governor, he said, he would venture that he would
overlook it in him. He ordered his boy to bring the
musket. The boy returned and said it was left
behind at Glasgow. "Load up the swivel then," said

the captain. " It will be all the better. It will make quite a flight, ye'll find. Load her up pretty well." The steamer meanwhile kept nearing the giant craig, which was a bare rock from summit to sea, and all of a dull, chalky whiteness, occasioned, as the captain said, by the excrement of the birds. We saw caves in the sides of the mountain and down by the water ; the retreats, our informant told us, in former times, of the smugglers who used to frequent the craig and carry on an extensive trade from these places of concealment. We had got so near as to see the white birds flitting across the entrances to the caverns like bees about the hive. With the spy-glass we could see them distinctly and in very considerable numbers ; and at length approached so that we could see them on the ledges all over the sides of the mountain. We had passed the skirt of the craig, and were within a half mile, or less, of its base. With the glass we could now see the entire mountain side peopled with the sea fowl, and could hear their whimpering, household cry as they moved about, or nestled in domestic snugness on the ten thousand ledges. The air, too, about the precipices, seemed to be alive with them. Still we had not the slightest conception of their frightful multitude. We got about the center of the mountain, when the swivel was fired. The shot went point blank against it and struck the stupendous precipice, as from top to bottom with a reverberation like the discharge of a hundred cannon.

And what a sight followed ! They rose up from that mountain, the countless myriads and millions of sea birds, in a universal, overwhelming cloud that covered the whole heavens, and their cry was like the cry of an alarmed nation. Up they went, millions upon millions, ascending like the smoke of a furnace ; countless as the sands on the sea shore ; awful, dreadful for multitude, as if the whole mountain were dissolving into life and light, and with an unearthly kind of lament, took up their line of march in every direction off to sea.

The sight startled the people on board the steamer, who had often witnessed it before, and for some

minutes there ensued a general silence.   For our own
part, we were quite amazed and overawed at the
spectacle.   We had seen nothing like it before.   We
had seen White Mountain Notches and Niagara Falls
in our own land, and the vastness of the wide and
deep ocean, which was separating us from it.   We had
seen something of art's magnificence in the old world;
its cloud-capped towers, gorgeous palaces and solemn
temples, but we had never witnessed sublimity to be
compared to that rising of sea-birds from Ailsa Craig.
They were of countless varieties in kind and size,
from the largest goose to the smallest marsh bird, and
of every conceivable variety of dismal note.   Off they
moved in wild and alarmed route, like a people going
into exile, filling the air far and wide, with their
reproachful lament at the wanton cruelty that had
broken them up and driven them into captivity.   We
really felt remorse at it ; and the thought might have
occurred to us how easy it would have been for them,
if they had known that the little, smoking speck that
was laboring along the sea-surface beneath them had
been the cause of their banishment, to have settled
down upon it and engulfed it out of sight forever.

We felt astonished that we had never heard before
of this wonderful haunt of sea-fowl, and that no one
had ever written a book upon it.   It struck us really
as one of the wonders of the world.   And not us
alone.   Others, not at all given to the marvellous,
declared it surpassed everything they had ever before
witnessed.   We supposed the mountain must have
been quite deserted from the myriads that had flown
away ; but lifting the glass to it, as we were
leaving its border, we were appalled to find it
still alive with the myriads that were left behind.
They kept leaving and leaving until our steamer
got far beyond the Craig, and till we could no
longer discern their departure with the tele-
scope.   And it was miles off into the dusky Irish
Sea, before we saw the ebbing of their mighty movement, and that they were beginning to return.   We
felt relieved to see them going back. . It had scarcely
occurred to us in our surprise, that they were not

leaving their native cliffs forever. Slowly and sadly they seemed to return, while the eye sought in vain to ken the outskirts of their mighty caravan. And Ailsa Craig had sunk far into our rear, and quite sensibly diminished in the distance, before the rearmost of the feathered host had disappeared from our sight.

The excitement occasioned us considerable depression of spirits, from which we were not entirely relieved until night came down upon the St. George's Channel, and the protracted northern twilight could no longer disclose objects to our wearied vision. Then after refreshing ourselves with some substantial confectionery, with which dear George Thompson had kindly stuffed our pockets from a shop at Greenock, before leaving "the land of cakes," our beloved fellow-passenger and ourself, after sundry fond remembrances of the other side of the ocean, some expectations of next day's greeting in Dublin, and some grateful sense, as we trust, of the goodness that had not forgotten us amid all our dangers by sea and land, we forgot what we had seen, and whereabouts we were, in the arms of oblivious sleep."

To do justice to the memory of Nathaniel Peabody Rogers, to his character and work, would require genius and inspiration like his own. Nor, perhaps, would this cheap age even then understand nor comprehend it. It manufactures sham and shoddy at too many of its mills, political, literary, social, moral and religious. It quotes Pope and Burns about an "honest man," but seems not to know him when he comes. It celebrated the birthday of Robert Burns with much pomp and demonstration in less than one month after it hung John Brown for a heroism and devotion to freedom and humanity, which began, rekindled with divine fervor, where the zeal of LaFayette for a white man's liberty paled out of human sight. And socially, morally and religiously it had hung Rogers long before, in the same

4

persecuting spirit that burned his illustrious ancestor
in the Smithfield pyre. In the true spirit of martyrdom did Rogers, like John Brown, join the anti-
slavery movement in an hour of peril. Garrison had
been mobbed in Boston, as was said, "in broad day,
by Boston's best men in broadcloth, gentlemen of
property and standing;" driven from a female
anti-slavery concert of prayer which he had been
invited to attend and address. Mr. Garrison said of
the spectacle when all the streets near the place of
meeting were thronged with a mob burning with
murderous intent : "It was an awful, sublime and
soul-thrilling scene—enough, one would suppose, to
melt adamantine hearts, and make even fiends of
darkness stagger and retreat. Indeed the clear,
untremulous voice of that christian heroine, Miss
Parker, in prayer occasionally awed the ruffians into
silence, and she was heard distinctly, even in the
midst of their hisses and yells and curses." Garrison withdrew from the prayer meeting and the mayor
entered in obedience to the wishes of the fiendish
crew, and dispersed it. Then the cry, the shriek,
the yell was, "we must have Garrison." "Out with
him ! Lynch him !" Some of the rioters discovered
and seized him. They drew him furiously to a
window and were about to thrust him out, when one
of them relented and said, "Let us not kill him outright." But they coiled a rope about his body, nearly
stripped him of his clothing, then dragged him
through the streets till he was finally rescued by *posse
comitatus* and at frightful peril was at length got to
the mayor's office. There he was provided with
clothing and from thence sent to jail, as "a disturber
of the peace," the mayor and his advisers declaring
that "the only way to preserve his life." In Alton,

Rev. Elijah Parish Lovejoy, too, another anti-slavery editor, had been shot and killed by a mob, five bullets being taken from his body, three from his breast, and that, too, in 1837, only a few months before Mr. Rogers removed with his family to Concord to conduct the *Herald of Freedom*. So that in assuming such position, he also, as might be said, "took his life in his hand." For Concord itself was no stranger to the mob at that time and for years afterward was the consecrated guardian of slavery.

As a member of the Plymouth Congregational church, both Mr. and Mrs. Rogers had coöperated earnestly, faithfully in works of religious benevolence and charity. But when they demanded that those in bonds in their own country should be remembered even "as bound with them," they were repulsed as disorderly, contumacious disturbers of the peace of the church and its minister, who, at that time, was among the most virulent opposers of the whole anti-slavery enterprise. But they did not withdraw from their church connection till they saw that southern slaveholders were more welcome to the pulpit and sacramental table, than were faithful, devoted abolitionists, whose moral and religious integrity of character, as well as soundness of opinion, were above reproach or suspicion. Rogers, beyond most public men, ever had unshaken faith in the people, though conservative while a politician, and orthodox in his religious faith. When he left the church he investigated its character anew and for himself. The claims of the clergy to prerogative in things temporal as well as spiritual, he soon learned to hold in profound disesteem. To no one man then living, or who has appeared since, does the world owe more than to him for exposing and rebuking the

arrogance and insolence, not to say down-right fraud
and dishonesty, of a ministry whose ruling, directing
power in all the great popular demonstrations of the
land, north as well as south, was exerted in support
and sanctification of slavery. The exceptions to this
charge were too few to change the result, as will
appear in the progress of this work.

Mr. Rogers never doubted for a moment that the
people, well and wisely taught, would abolish slavery
and cease to oppress one another. And so like the
Great Emancipator of Nazareth, he directed all his
sternest strokes and rebukes at the priests and
rulers, who really " bound the heavy burdens and laid
them on men's shoulders," as in Judea, two thousand
years ago. He and his associates of the Garrison
school of abolitionists relied solely on the power of
moral and spiritual truth to rescue the slave as well
as to redeem and save the world. They formed, they
joined no political party. They abjured the ballot
altogether as a reforming or restoring agency, as
much as they did the bullet, the only specie redemption of the ballot, in every government of force.
Both Mr. and Mrs. Rogers were members and officers
of the New England Non-Resistance Society. And
none ever more highly adorned the doctrine of their
profession than they.

As one with vision anointed to perceive all moral
and spiritual truth, Rogers seemed to stand almost
alone. His editorial writings are witness to this, and
will be to more than the next generation. It were
well for man and womankind, if whole volumes of
them, judiciously selected, could be reproduced and
scattered everywhere, like the shining constellation
among the dimmer stars. His words to-day are,
many of them, wondrously fresh and new.

The temperance cause had no firmer or more consistent friend. The peace societies had best of reasons to be proud of his support, in word and deed. To him human life was sacred as the life of God. Once, at a grand Peace gathering, it was strenuously argued by most of the members who spoke, that human life could and should be taken by divine command. And the president of the society himself made an argument in defence of all the slaughters of the Canaanites and other tribes and peoples, men, women and children, by Moses, Joshua and their destroying hosts, because perpetrated by command of God. It was at one of the last meetings Rogers ever attended, and he was then too feeble to bear an active part in the deliberations. But after listening a good while to scripture text and learned logic under Levitical law, he rose to his feet and in low voice asked : " Does our brother yonder say that if God commanded him, he would take a sword and use it in slaying human beings, and innocent, helpless human beings ? " Yes, if God commanded," was the answer. "Well, I wouldn't," responded Rogers, and sank back into his seat, amid loud cheers of evident approval and admiration.

Woman, to him, was in all rights, privileges and prerogatives, the full equal of man. He was a christian in the divinest, sublimest sense of that still mysterious and much abused word. And as such his kingdom was not of this world. And so he could neither vote in, nor ask others to vote in nor to fight for any government based on military power.

As husband and father, none ever knew one in whom his family were more supremely felicitated. As companion and friend, blessed and happy were all those who enjoyed his confidence and esteem. Gentle, simple, tender, kind, ready to sacrifice his own comfort; sharing on occasion, like General Washington, his room and bed with a colored man, and yet always discriminating in high degree; with tastes most refined; ever ready to criticise, even censure a friend, however dear, when he deemed it just and demanded; firm as his own Ailsa Craig, whenever or wherever, or however a moral principal was in jeopardy; running over with music, poetry, and culture of every kind, he was a man, the like of whom the world has seldom seen—may not soon see again.

CHAPTER III.

SLAVERY—AS IT WAS.

Everybody now is anti-slavery. It is honorable now to be a child of the man who "cast the first anti-slavery vote in our town;" or called "our first anti-slavery meeting;" or first entertained Garrison as guest, or Abby Kelley, or Frederick Douglass; or rescued Stephen Foster or Lucy Stone from the hands of a ferocious mob; or raised, or commanded the first company of colored troops in the war of Rebellion, at the time when not a musical band could be found in the whole city of New York to play for a colored regiment, as it marched from the New Haven Railway station to the steamer at the foot of Canal street to embark for the seat of war! *"Paid pipers,"* the venerable Dr. Tyng with withering scorn called them all on the same evening in Cooper Institute, where he presided at a lecture by George William Curtis. "Paid pipers," with wind too immaculate to blow away in escort of a gallant battalion of our country's saviors, when there was no other name under heaven given among men," whereby the nationality could be saved but the *negro name*; despised as he was and rejected of men; "a man of sorrows" and acquainted all his dreary life with grief! Everybody now is an abolitionist, or son, or grandson of an anti-slavery parentage, and so all seem to claim equal honor, so far as honor is due, for ridding the world of the sublimest scourge and curse that ever afflicted the human race.

Few now, however, have much conception of what slavery was; or what was genuine, effective anti-slavery, when slavery sat supreme "on its throne of skulls," and ruled the whole nation, state, church and school, literature, trade, commerce, manufactures and agriculture, as with rod of iron! And its first command, great command, only command was, "Thou shalt have no god but me." Not, as from Mount Sinai, "no other *gods* before me," but no other *god*. Not "no other gods *before* me," but "no other gods *with*, or *above* or *below* me!" So it was. Anti-slavery then, was more than a name; more than pro-fession; or denomination in religion; or party in the government. So Christianity had mighty meanings when the great apostle to the Gentiles wrote: "I am not ashamed of the gospel of Christ." And "I deter-mined to know nothing among you save Jesus Christ and him crucified." It had fearful meanings when the gardens of Nero were illumined with the burning bodies of martyred saints, both men and women, young and old! When to name the Christ of God was death in lingering torments—when crucifixions were so multiplied that, as in grim epigram it was said, "space was wanted for crosses, and crosses for chris-tians." And yet so sublime was christian heroism at that hour, that it could have well been added, but christains are never wanting for crosses.

But what was our slave system, that so many now proudly claim to have aided to destroy? And whose fathers and mothers were those who really did bear active, effective part in the thirty years moral and peaceful conflict, inaugurated by Garrison with "sword of the spirit;" whose only weapons were

" The mild arms of truth and love,
Made mighty through the living God?"

Or whose sons and brothers rushed at last to the field of mortal combat, and fought the bloodiest, mightiest, everyway, most frightful war, that has shaken the earth and darkened the skies in all the christian years? Slavery! What is it? What was it on the American plantation? "Peculiar Institution," some called it. "Patriarchal Institution," others! But what was it? All language pales and is silent in its dread presence. Slave-holding! "Deed without a name!" In cant phrase we said slavery degrades man to the brute, sinks woman to the dead level of the horse. And then who knows the height and depth, the length and breadth of those stunning words; insulting blasphemies against the Holy Spirit of Humanity! Let one advertisement, distributed by large handbills, as well as published in the daily newspapers of New Orleans, aid the imagination:

RAFFLE. MR. JOSEPH JENNINGS respectfully informs his friends and the public that, at the request of many acquaintances, he has been induced to purchase from Mr. Osborne, of Missouri, the celebrated DARK BAY HORSE, "STAR," aged five years, square trotter and warranted sound; with a new, light Trotting Buggy and Harness: Also the dark, stout Mulatto Girl, "Sarah," aged about twenty years, general house servant, valued at *nine hundred dollars*, and guaranteed: and will be RAFFLED for at four o'clock P. M., February first, at the selection hotel of the subscribers. The above is as represented, and those persons who may wish to engage in the usual practice of raffling will, I assure them, be perfectly satisfied with their destiny in this affair.

The whole is valued at its just worth, fifteen hundred dollars; fifteen hundred CHANCES at One Dollar each. The Raffle will be conducted by gentlemen selected by the interested subscribers present. Five nights will be allowed to complete the Raffle. Both of the above described can be seen at my store, No. 78 Common street, second door from Camp, at from nine o'clock, A. M., to two P. M.

Highest throw to take the first choice; the lowest throw the remaining prize, and the fortunate winners will pay Twenty Dollars each for the refreshments furnished on the occasion.

N. B. No chances recognized unless paid for previous to the commencement.   JOSEPH JENNINGS.

In the light of a spectacle like this, it is possible to fancy slightly what should be understood when it is said that slavery degrades human beings to the plane of brute beasts.

Or reverse the order of illustration, if we dare, and imagine a brute beast raised to the dignity and honor, the privilege and prerogative of a man, an immortal being.   History or fable tells us of a Roman Sovereign who made a favorite horse first Consul of the Empire. Such mockery might have been.   But suppose in a christian country, in a christian sanctuary, it were proposed to admit, not a horse, but some dogs into full fellowship and communion with the church.   It is on a delightful Sunday of early summer, in a pleasant New England country town.   The village gardens are already abloom with early flowers, the orchards are white with prophecy of abundant fruit, and every tree is an orchestra of cheerful birds, whose worship-notes almost charm the Sabbath silence into sweet accord with the songs of paradise.   All the village and the districts around assemble at their, to them, "house of God."   At the appointed hour, the baptized communicants of the accepted faith are invited to seats at the sacramental board.   The unregenerate of the congregation retire to the outer seats, paying silent but respectful attention.   The first scene in the solemn service is admission of new members, who are invited forward to the altar.   There, in presence of the congregation, they listen and bow silent assent to the Articles of Faith and the Covenant Vows, and receive the seal of baptism, in the name of the triune God. Solemn and impressive as this may be, it may excite no unusual emotions, being neither new nor infrequent.   But slavery, we used to say with lip only, "degrades man and woman to a level with the brutes ;" puts the "bay horse, Star," and the "Mulatto girl, Sarah," into the same raffle, or on the same auction-block.   Now change the order.   Elevate the brutes to the place of immortal beings at the baptismal font and sacramental table.   Whistle up two or three dogs and solemnly read over to them the creed and

covenant, and sprinkle them with the holy drops of
baptism, calling them by their appropriate brute
names, "Lion, I baptize thee in the name of the
Father, and of the Son, and of the Holy Ghost. Tiger,
I baptize thee in the name of the Father, and of the
Son, and of the Holy Ghost." And let the third be a
female : "Topsy, I baptize thee in the name of the
Father, and of the Son, and of the Holy Ghost.
Amen."

Let such a spectacle be enacted on a delightful
summer Sunday afternoon, in a beautiful New England village, in its pleasant white meeting-house, and
at the memorial supper of that crucified Redeemer in
whom the church and its pastor devoutly believed,
and through whom they humbly hoped for salvation.
Can the effect on the beholders of such a daring spectacle be described, or even imagined? As well, but
no better, attempt a description of that slavery which
truly did degrade human beings to a level with horses
and with dogs. This whole scene was once supposed
as illustration, in the days of slavery, in just such town
and house of worship as here described, and not only
that town, but the pulpit and religious press of both
the hemispheres almost shrieked as with holy horror at
what they called so audacious, so diabolical blasphemy.
And the cry came up from near and far for immediate punishment of him who had so illumined slavery,
to the fullest demand of the statute, which was long
confinement, it was held, in the State prison ! But
one thing was made clear. The words, Slavery
degrades man to a level with beasts, were seen and
felt as perhaps never before. The congregation where
the illustration was presented saw and solemnly felt
that from beasts up to men—to men exalted to angelic
heights—was no farther than those deeps down which

immortal man is plunged, to reach the level of the beasts that perish.   And that frightful pit was reached by every chattel slave ever born.

But the question, What was American slavery? is not yet answered. To call it robbery, by only our dictionary definition, would pay it high compliment. Its fell work began where all ordinary robbery leaves off. John Wesley saw it and pronounced it, "Sum of all villainies." And if he did not pronounce the slave holder sum of all villains, he did address him in words like these :

What I have said to slave-traders, equally concerns all slave-holders, of whatever rank and degree, seeing man-buyers are exactly on a level with man-stealers. You say, I pay honestly for my goods, and am not concerned to know they are honestly come by. Nay, but you are. * * * You know they are not honestly come by ; you know they are procured by means nothing near so innocent as picking pockets, house-breaking, or robbery on the highway. You know they are procured by a deliberate species of more complicated villainy, of fraud, robbery and murder, than was ever practiced by Mohammedans or Pagans ; in particular, by murders of all kinds ; by the blood of the innocent poured upon the ground like water. Now it is *your* money that pays the African butcher. *You*, therefore, are principally guilty of all these frauds, robberies and murders. *You* are the spring that puts all the rest in motion. They would not stir a step without *you :* therefore the blood of all these wretches who die before their time lies upon *your* head.   " The blood of thy brother crieth against thee from the earth." O, whatever it costs, put a stop to its cry before it be too late ; instantly, at any price, were it the half of your goods, deliver thyself from blood-guiltiness ! Thy hands, thy bed, thy furniture, thy house, and thy lands, at present are stained with blood. Surely it is enough ; accumulate no more guilt ; spill no more the blood of the innocent. Do not hire another to shed blood ; do not pay him for doing it. Whether you are a Christian or not, show yourself a man! Be not more savage than a lion or a bear.

Slavery is not robbery therefore, because it is so much more, and worse. Indeed, to rob man of manhood, and beastialize him down with not only animals, but the dead matter on which brutes feed and tread, makes any farther spoliation simply impossible.

Or shall we pronounce American slavery adultery, wholesale, unblushing adultery? If not, it must be because, as with robbery, it was something so much worse. For, first, what is adultery but setting aside all rights, privileges and responsibilities, human and divine, of both the marriage and parental relations? Slavery knew no more of marriage and parentage among slaves than among swine. Logically, as well as legally, it could not. And the statutes and court decisions so declared.

But such abomination had not only state sanction, but church sanctification as well. Judge Birney, of Kentucky, once a slave-holder, in his memorable tract entitled : "The American Churches the Bulwarks of American Slavery," second edition, revised by the author, cites this instance :

In 1835 the following query referring to slaves was presented to the Savannah River Baptist Association of Ministers : "Whether in case of involuntary separation of such a character as to preclude all prospect of future intercourse, the parties ought to be allowed to marry again."

The following was the answer :

* * * Such separation among persons situated as are our slaves, is civilly a separation by death. And we believe that in the sight of God, it would be so viewed ! * * * The slaves are not free agents, and a dissolution by death is not more entirely without their consent and beyond their control than by such separation.

James G. Birney was at one time a slave-holder as well as judge in the courts, and a ruling elder in the Presbyterian church. He was induced to emancipate his slaves, as well as to provide for their future support, taking them over into the free state of Ohio for that purpose, by the faithful and earnest argument and appeal of Theodore D. Weld, an early, eloquent and everyway most efficient apostle and laborer in the anti-slavery field. Washing his own hands from the blood and guilt of slave holding, Judge Birney set himself to the work of abolishing the foul system. Among his first endeavors was an attempt to purify the churches, beginning with his own. But neither his official standing in both state and church, nor his high consequent social status availed to shield him from every possible indignity and outrage at the hands of infuriated mobs, composed largely sometimes of members of the churches. Driven from 'Kentucky he removed to Ohio. His descent on Cincinnati, where he had now become known, was a signal to waken all the vengeance of both church and state against him. Meetings were at once called, "to see if the people will permit abolition papers to be published in this city." At the first meeting the postmaster, who was also a minister, presided. A committee of thirteen, all eminent citizens, and eight of them church members, was appointed to wait on Mr. Birney and assure him that his paper must stop, or the meeting would not be responsible for the consequences of its continuance. The chairman of the committee declared that " if the paper were not promptly suspended, a mob, unusual in numbers, determined in purpose, and desolating in its ravages, would be inevitable !" All of which proved true, for the paper did not stop. In the darkness of midnight the mob entered and carried press, types and all else of contents and sunk them in the Ohio river. And twice afterwards was the same outrage perpetrated. No wonder Mr. Burney entitled his memorable tract. published at the time, "The American Churches the Bulwarks of American Slavery." For the title was more than justified on every subsequent page, as will hereafter be made to appear. And the word of divine truth uttered by Mr. Weld, and the baptism of fire and water three times administered by the fiendish mob, with full approval of state, church and pulpit, were sufficient consecration of the author of the memorable tract to his subsequent anti-slavery ministry and apostleship.

But returning to the argument. Not only was slavery adultery, as sanctified and committed by the churches, in thus sundering all marriage rights and responsibilities ; it was legally and in solemn compact annihilation of human marriage and parentage. The court decisions contained sentiments such as these : "With consent of their masters, slaves may marry ; but in a state of slavery it can produce no *civil* effect, because slaves are deprived of all civil rights." [*Judge Matthews, of Louisiana.*] Attorney-General Delany, of Maryland, held that slaves would not be admonished for incontinence, or punished for adultery or fornication ; or prosecuted for petty treason, or for killing a husband, being a slave. The code of Louisiana declared, "a slave could not contract matrimony. Tne association which takes place among slaves, and is called marriage, being properly designated *contubernium*, a relation without sanctity, and to which no civil rights adhere." So the plain, unquestionable fact was, slavery was wholesale, legalized, sanctified concubinage, or adultery, from first to last. Our government was based on the prostrate bodies, souls and civil,

social, marital, parental, educational, moral and religious rights of half a million of immortal beings. In
three-quarters of a century their numbers multiplied till
at the downfall of the institution there were four millions, and not one legal marriage ever existed in all
their generations ! And yet, compelled by law thus
to live and herd like brute beasts, hundreds of thousands of them were admitted to baptism and sacramental communion and fellowship in all the great evangelical denominations in the land !

One other attribute of the dreadful system remains
to be exposed, and that was *murder*. Under the written law of slavery, more than seventy offences, when
committed by slaves, were punishable with death. One
law read, " if any slave shall presume to strike any
white person, such slave may be lawfully killed." Of
course killed on the spot. A woman or girl would
have been killed (undoubtedly many were killed) for
defending her person against the lustful attack of her
overseer or other white assailant.

Special laws existed for recapturing escaped slaves
at any cost of life to the victims, by first proclaiming
them outlaws. The following legal instrument with
its accompaniments will suffice to show the way :

STATE OF NORTH CAROLINA, }
Lenoir County. }

Whereas, complaint hath been this day made to us, two of the Justices
of the Peace for the said county, by William D. Cobb, of Jones county,
that two negro slaves belonging to him, named Ben (commonly known by
the name of Ben Fox) and Rigdon, have absented themselves from their
said master's service, and are lurking about in the counties of Lenoir and
Jones, committing acts of felony ;—these are, in the name of the State, to
command the said slaves forthwith to surrender themselves, and return
home to their said master. And we do hereby, by virtue of an act of the
Assembly of this State, concerning servants and slaves, intimate and declare, if the said slaves do not surrender themselves and return home to
their master immediately after the publication of these presents, *that any
person may kill and destroy said slaves by such means as he or they think
fit, without accusation or impeachment of any crime or offence for so
doing, or without incurring any penalty or forfeiture thereby.*
Given under our hands and seals, this 12th day of November, 1836.

B. COLEMAN, J. P. [Seal.]
JAMES JONES, J. P. [Seal.]

Two Hundred Dollars Reward.—Ran away from the subscriber, a certain negro man named Ben, (commonly known by the name of Ben Fox). Also, one other negro, by the name of Rigdon, who ran away on the 8th of this month.

I will give the reward of one hundred dollars for each of the above negroes, to be delivered to me or confined in the jail of Lenoir or Jones county, or *for the killing of them, so that I can see them.*

November 12, 1836. **W. D. COBB.**

Another advertisement, from the Sumpter County (Alabama) *Whig,* will illustrate the methods of slave hunting in other States besides North Carolina :

NEGRO DOGS.—The undersigned having bought the entire pack of NEGRO DOGS of the Hay & Allen stock, he now proposes to *catch runaway negroes.* His charge will be three dollars a day for *hunting,* and fifteen dollars for *catching* a runaway. He resides three and one-half miles north of Livingston, near the lower Jones' Bluff road.

November 6, 1845. **WM. GAMBEL.**

The New York *Commercial-Advertiser* of June 8th, 1827, contained the following item of news, not uncommon at that time, as the irresponsibility of slave-holders over the lives of their slaves had hardly been questioned :

HUNTING MEN WITH DOGS.—A negro who had absconded from his master, and for whom a reward of a hundred dollars was offered, has been apprehended and committed to prison in Savannah.

The editor who states the fact adds, with as much coolness as though there were no barbarity in the matter, that he did not surrender till he was considerably maimed by the dogs that had been set on him— desperately fighting them, and badly. cutting one of them with a sword.

The St. Francisville (La.) *Chronicle* of February 1st, 1839, reports a slave-hunt after this sort :

Two or three days ago a *gentleman* of this parish, in hunting runaway negroes, came upon a camp of them in the swamp on Cat Island. He succeeded in arresting two of them, but the third made fight. On being shot in the shoulder, he fled to a sluice, where the dogs succeeded in drowning him before assistance could arrive.

Had "*assistance* arrived," would it have been tendered to the dogs or their victim? is a question, to

5

this day. But calling off the dogs altogether, let the subject be illumined a little farther with lights like this, from the Charleston (S. C.) *Courier*, in 1825.

TWENTY DOLLARS REWARD.—Ran away from the subscriber, on the 14th instant, a negro girl named Molly. She is 16 or 17 years of age, slim made, lately BRANDED ON HER LEFT CHEEK, THUS, " R," AND A PIECE IS TAKEN OFF HER EAR ON THE SAME SIDE; THE SAME LETTER IS BRANDED ON THE INSIDE OF BOTH HER LEGS.

ABNER ROSS, Fairfield District, S. C.

True, the *killing* is here omitted, possibly by accident, but if such an atrocity does not involve murder, sublimated, what shall be said of this from the Wilmington (N. C.) *Advertiser* of July 13th, 1838?

RANAWAY—MY NEGRO MAN, RICHARD.—A reward of twenty-five dollars will be paid for his apprehension, DEAD OR ALIVE! Satisfactory proof will only be required of his *being killed*. He has with him, in all probability, his wife, Eliza, who ran away from Colonel Thompson, now a resident of Alabama.

But no more such evidences of the murderous spirit of slavery can be needed; though the last advertisement suggests an incident in South Carolina, so late as 1844, which is too instructive and assuring not to be given.

That "wife, Eliza, who ran away from Colonel Thompson," possibly might have a tale unfolded, whose lightest word would have harrowed up the soul. There were many such tales. A young man in South Carolina was seen walking with a young woman, a slave, to whom it was known he was tenderly attached, and whom, it was farther shown, he married and aided to escape from slavery. That was his crime. He was arrested, tried, and found guilty. Sentence of death was pronounced upon him by Judge J. B. O'Neale, in word and spirit as now reproduced:

JOHN L. BROWN—It is my duty to announce to you the consequences of the conviction which you heard at Winnsboro', and of the opinion you have just heard read, refusing your two-fold motion in arrest of judgment for a new trial.

You are to die! To die an ignominious death— the death on the gallows! This announcement is, to

you, I know, most appalling.   Little did you dream of
it when you stepped into the bar with an air as if you
thought it was a fine frolic.   But the consequences of
crime are just such as you are realizing.   Punishment
often comes when it is least expected.   Let me
entreat you to take the present opportunity to commence the work of reformation.   Time will be furnished you to prepare for the great change just before
you.   Of your past life I know nothing, except what
your trial furnished.   That told me that the crime for
which you are to suffer was the consequence of a
want of attention on your part to the duties of life.
The strange woman snared you.   She flattered you
with her words, and you became her victim.   The
consequence was, that, led on by a desire to serve her,
you committed the offense of aiding a slave to run
away and depart from her master's service ; and now,
for it you are to die !

You are a young man, and I fear you have been
dissolute ; and if so, these kindred vices have contributed a full measure to your ruin.   Reflect on your
past life, and make the only useful devotion of the
remnant of your days in preparing for death.

Remember now thy Creator in the days of thy
youth, is the language of inspired wisdom.   This
comes home appropriately to you in this trying moment.

You are young ; quite too young to be where you
are.   If you had remembered your Creator in your past
days, you would not now be in a felon's place, to receive
a felon's judgment.   Still, it is not too late to remember your Creator.   He calls early, and He calls late.
He stretches out the arms of a Father's love to you—
to the vilest sinner—and says : "Come unto me and
be saved."   You can perhaps, read.   If so, read the
Scriptures ; read them without note, and without comment ; and pray to God for His assistance ; and you
will be able to say when you pass from prison to execution, as a poor slave said under similar circumstances : "I am glad my Friday has come."   If you
cannot read the Scriptures, the ministers of our holy
religion will be ready to aid you.   They will read and

explain to you until you will be able to understand ;
and understanding, to call upon the only One who
can help you and save you—Jesus Christ, the Lamb
of God, who taketh away the sin of the world.   To
Him I commend you.   And through Him may y
have that opening of the Day-Spring of mercy from
on high, which shall bless you here, and crown you as
a saint in an everlasting world, forever and ever.

The sentence of the law is that you be taken hence
to the place from whence you came last ; thence to
the jail of Fairfield District ; and that there you be
closely and securely confined until Friday, the 26th
day of April next ; on which day, between the hours
of ten in the forenoon and two in the afternoon, you
will be taken to the place of public execution, and
there be hanged by the neck till your body be dead.
And may God have mercy on your soul !

No event in anti-slavery history up to that time so
stirred the two hemispheres as did this frightful sentence of Judge O'Neale.   Even in the British House of
Lords, two illustrious members, Brougham and Den-
man, gave it pathetic and powerful consideration.
One London journal said: "The dreadful case of
John L. Brown has created throughout Great Britain,
a sensation of deepest and most painful character.
Addresses to the churches in South Carolina have
been extensively signed by the independent churches
in England and Scotland."

The Glasgow *Argus*, among the most important
journals of Scotland, twice published the *Charge* on
account of its fearful character, and said of it, "we
know of nothing more atrocious in the judicial annals
of modern times.   *   *   And what are we
to think of a judge, who in passing sentence for what
in our country, our land of Freedom, would be looked
upon as a praiseworthy act, invokes the sacred name
of Deity and the Holy Book of Inspiration as lending
sanction to the atrocity about to be committed!"

But perhaps the most imposing movement in Great Britain, on this terrible perversion of all justice, as well as outrage on all decency, humanity and charity, was a "Memorial addressed to the Churches of Christ in South Carolina, as representing those of other states," signed by more than thirteen hundred ministers and office-holders in the churches and other benevolent associations of London, and other portions of the kingdom, in solemn protest against it. But it need hardly be told, that all the sympathy felt, all the effort made, all the appeals and memorials sent, eloquent, tender, pathetic, devout as many, if not all of them were, seemed almost wholly thrown away on the press, pulpit, and vast majority of the people of the United States, even though South Carolina did yield to foreign pressure at last, and commuted the sentence to fifty lashes on the bare back; and even they were said to have been remitted on condition that the young man quit the state forever.

But this account though already extended, would not be complete unless the feelings excited in the hearts of the American Abolitionists, in view of the whole scene, could have utterance. Let then their favorite and faithful poet, Whittier, be their oracle :

ON THE SENTENCE OF JOHN L. BROWN.

Ho! thou who seekest late and long
    A License from the Holy Book
For brutal lust and hellish wrong,
    Man of the Pulpit, look!
Lift up those cold and atheist eyes,
    This ripe fruit of thy teaching see;
And tell us how to heaven will rise
    The incense of this sacrifice—
This blossom of the gallows tree!

Search out for slavery's hour of need
    Some fitting text of sacred writ;
Give heaven the credit of a deed
    Which shames the nether pit.

Kneel, smooth blasphemer, unto Him
   Whose truth is on thy lips a lie— .
Ask that His bright winged cherubim
   May bend around that scaffold grim
To guard and bless and sanctify.

Ho ! champion of the people's cause—
   Suspend thy loud and vain rebuke
Of foreign wrong and Old World's laws—
   Man of the Senate, look !
Was *this* the promise of the free,
   The great hope of our early time—
That slavery's poison vine should be
   Upborne by Freedom's prayer-nurs'd tree
O'erclustered with such fruits of crime ?

Send out the summons East and West,
   And South and North, let all be there
Where he who pitied the oppressed
   Swings out in sun and air.
Let not a Democratic hand
   The grisly hangman's task refuse ;
There let each loyal patriot stand,
   Awaiting slavery's command,
To twist the rope and draw the noose !

But vain is irony—unmeet
   Its cold rebuke for deeds which start
In fiery and indignant beat
   The pulses of the heart.
Leave studied wit and guarded phrase
   For those who think but do not feel—
Let MEN speak out in words which raise
   Where'er they fall, an answering blaze
Like flints which strike the fire from steel.

Still let a mousing priesthood ply
   Their garbled text and gloss of sin,
And make the lettered scroll deny
   Its living soul within :
Still let the place-fed, titled knave
   Plead robbery's right with purchased lips,
And tell us that our fathers gave
   For Freedom's pedestal, a slave,
The frieze and moulding, chains and whips !

But ye who own that Higher Law
   Whose tablets in the heart are set,
Speak out in words of power and awe
   THAT GOD IS LIVING YET !
Breathe forth once more those tones sublime
   Which thrilled the burdened prophet's lyre,

And in a dark and evil time
  Smote down on Israel's fast of crime
And gift of blood, A RAIN OF FIRE !

Oh, not for us the graceful lay
  To whose soft measures lightly move
The Dryad and the woodland fay,
  O'er-locked by mirth and love !
But such a stern and startling strain
  As Britain's hunted bards flung down
From Snowden to the conquered plain,
  Where harshly clanked the Saxon chain,
On trampled field and smoking town.

By Liberty's dishonored name,
  By man's lost hope and failing trust,
By words and deeds which bow with shame
  Our foreheads to the dust ;
By the exulting Tyrant's sneer,
  Borne to us from the Old World's thrones,
And by his victims' griefs who hear,
  In sunless mines and dungeons drear,
How Freedom's land her faith disowns !

Speak out in ACTS, the time for words
  Has passed ; and DEEDS alone suffice ;
In the loud clang of meeting swords
  The softer music dies !
Act—act in God's name, while ye may !
  Smite from the CHURCH, her leprous limb !
Throw open to the light of day
  The bondman's cell, and break away
The chains the STATE has bound on him !

Ho ! every true and living soul,
  To Freedom's perilled altar bear
The Freeman's and the Christian's whole
  Tongue, pen, and vote, and prayer !
One last, great battle for the right—
  One short, sharp struggle to be free !
To do is to succeed—our fight
  Is waged in Heaven's approving sight ;
The smile of God is Victory."

Severity of punishments inflicted on slaves short of
death, were often a thousand times more cruel than
death by the halter ; not unfrequently terminating in
death, though only by whipping. But hanging was
not always severe enough, as witness a law of Maryland, enacted in 1729 :   " The slave shall first have the

right hand cut off, then be hanged in the usual manner ; the head be severed from the body, the body divided into four quarters, and the head and quarters be set up in the most public places of the county where such act was committed." And this horrible barbarity could be inflicted by a simple justice's court.

But it may be said this legislation was before the foundations of this republic were laid. That is true. But in the year 1836, in the city of St. Louis, Missouri, an act was perpetrated, of which the following was the accepted newspaper account, on the spot and over the country :

On the 28th of April, 1836, in the city of St. Louis, a black man named McIntosh, who had stabbed an officer who had arrested him, was seized by the multitude, fastened to a tree in the midst of the city, wood piled around him, in open day, and in the presence of an immense throng of citizens, he was burned to death. The Alton *Telegraph* thus describes a part of the scene :

All was silent as death while the executioners were piling the wood around the victim. He said not a word till he felt that the flames had seized him. He then uttered an awful howl, attempting to sing and pray, then hung his head and suffered in silence. After the flames had surrounded their prey, his eyes burned out of his head, and his mouth apparently parched to a cinder, some one in the crowd more compassionate than the rest, proposed to end his misery by shooting him. But it was replied that he was already out of his pain. " No, no," cried the wretch, " I am not. I am suffering as much as ever. Shoot me ! Shoot me !" " No," exclaimed one of the fiends standing by the roasting sacrifice, " no, he shall not be shot. I would sooner slack the fire if that would increase his misery !"

A St. Louis correspondent of a New York paper sent an account of the diabolical deed, of which this is an excerpt :

The shrieks and groans of the victim were loud and piercing, and to observe one limb after another drop into the fire, was awful indeed. In dying, he was about fifteen minutes. I visited the place this morning and saw the body, or the remains of it, burned to a crump. The legs and arms were gone, and only a part of the head and body was remaining.

A subsequent judicial decision by judge Luke E. Lawless, of the Circuit Court of Missouri, made at a session of court in St. Louis, was, that as the burning of McIntosh was the act, directly or indirectly, by countenance of a majority of the citizens, it is a case which transcends the jurisdiction of the grand jury !

And so the dreadful sacrament was sanctified and solemnized by high judicial decision. And as such atrocities were common while slavery lasted, why need the law of Maryland be shorn of its odium and terror in the popular apprehension, only because it was older than the Declaration of American Independence ?

Assuming that nations are not better than their laws, or that laws are never made till needed, what shall be said of legislation like this? A law of North Carolina provided that :

If any person shall wilfully kill his own slave, or of any other person, every such offender shall, on conviction, forfeit and pay the sum of seven hundred pounds, and shall forever be rendered incapable of holding or exercising any office.

And this law was not repealed till the year 1821, if ever. Another section of the same act provided :

If any person shall, in sudden heat of passion, or by undue correction, kill his own slave, or the slave of any other person, he shall forfeit the sum of three hundred and fifty pounds.

A still further provision of the same act read thus :

If any person shall wilfully cut out the tongue, put out the eye, castrate, or cruelly scald or burn any slave, or deprive any slave of any limb or member, or shall inflict any other cruel punishment, other than by whipping or beating with a switch, horse-whip or cow-skin, or by putting on irons, or imprisoning such slave, such person, for every such offence, shall forfeit and pay one hundred pounds.

Judge Stroud, in his carefully prepared "Sketch of Laws Relating to Slavery," says in his latest edition, (1856) : "This, *so far as I can learn*, has been suffered to disgrace the statute book to the present hour. Amid all the mutations which Christianity has effected within the last century, she has not been able to conquer the spirit which dictated this law."

And not to speak of the shameful outrage, so denounced in Deuteronomy, xxiii ; 1st, what must be thought of the decency, humanity, not to say religion, of a people that enacts, supports, sanctifies a law which beats without limit, without mercy, with horse-whip, cowskin or other missile, a human being, man, woman, child, unrebuked, unless the last stroke should produce immediate death ?

With one more well authenticated fact and one other witness, and he none other than Thomas Jefferson himself, the question as to the character of slavery shall be submitted to readers, to history, to posterity. The outrage to be described was witnessed by John James Appleton, Esq., whom Hon. David Lee Child and his illustrious wife, Mrs. Lydia Maria Child, endorse as "a gentleman of high attainments and accomplishments," a secretary of legation at Rio Janeiro, Madrid and the Hague, commissioner at Naples and charge d'affaires at Stockholm. Mr. Appleton was present at the burial of a female slave in Mississippi, who had been whipped to death by her master, for being gone longer on an errand than was thought necessary. She protested under the terrible torture that she was ill and had to rest in the fields. To complete the climax of horror, she was delivered of a dead child while undergoing the punishment!! Is it strange that she had to rest by the way? But we will hasten to our last witness.

To-day as I write, the Democratic party, party of Thomas Jefferson, is celebrating here in Massachusetts, a political success, almost unexampled under the circumstances, in state elections, since the party was first inaugurated. The tribes of Israel never claimed Abraham as their father with more devout pride and filial reverence, than have the Democrats of this nation Thomas Jefferson as theirs, since their party first learned to lisp his name.

And those tribes crying, "Crucify Him, crucify Him," in the court-room of Pilate, or mocking their victim as he climbed Mount Calvary, bearing his cross in sweating agony, did not more dishonor their patriarchal father and founder than did the Democratic party and their Whig accomplices on the plains of Texas, murdering the Mexicans in a bloody war to reinstate slavery where the Mexican government, with its Roman Catholic religion, had not many years before, abolished it, as all humanity hoped, forever. That was almost forty years ago. Undoubtedly, devotion to slavery sent the old Whig party to a scarcely too early grave. Worship of the same unclean and bloody Moloch, stove down democratic rule, from the kindled wrath of the Infinite Justice around Fort Sumter, until the victories won yesterday in so many States of this Union, and proudly celebrated to-day, give sign almost unmistakable, of its probable return at the next presidential election.

And now the next and last witness as to the whole quality and character of slavery, even as he saw it and himself embraced it, is the patriarchal American Democrat, Thomas Jefferson himself.

His memorable "Notes on the State of Virginia," so often cited in the past, so greatly disregarded while slavery continued, were revised and published in 1787, when the problem of slavery was shaking the new republic to its foundation.

The section relating to slavery contains so many general observations on human relations and obligations, individual as well as collective, social as well as civil and governmental, with a profoundly reverent recognition of higher authority than any man-made institutions, or constitutions, that it surely is not too much to declare that a return of the Democratic party to power will be a blessing or scourge and curse, exactly in proportion as it shall follow, or reject the doctrines and counsels of its justly venerated founder and progenitor, as laid down in the passage from his "Notes on the State of Virginia," here reproduced :

There must doubtless be an unhappy influence on the manners of our people, produced by the existence of *Slavery* among us. The whole commerce between master and slave is a perpetual exercise of the most boisterous passions, the most unremitting despotism on the one part, and degrading submission on the other. Our children see this and learn to imitate it ; for man is an imitative animal. This quality in him is the germ of all education. From his cradle to his grave, he is learning to do what he sees others do. If a parent could find no motive, either in his philanthropy or his self-love, for restraining the intemperance of passion toward his slave, it should always be a sufficient one that his child is present. But generally it is not sufficient. The parent storms, the child looks on, catches the lineaments of wrath, puts on the same airs in the circle of smaller slaves, gives a loose to the worst of passions, and thus nursed and educated, and daily exercised in tyranny, cannot but be stamped by it with odious peculiarities. The man must be a prodigy who can retain his manners and morals unde-praved by such circumstances.

And with what execration should the statesman be loaded, who, permitting one-half the citizens thus to trample on the rights of the other, transforms those into despots, and these into enemies, destroys the morals of one part and the *amor patriæ* of the other! For if a slave can have a country in this world, it must be any other in preference to that in which he is born to live and labor for another ; in which he must lock up the faculties of his nature ; contribute, as far as depends on his individual endeavors, to the evan-ishment of the human race, or entail his own miser-able condition on the endless generations proceeding from him.

With the morals of the people, their industry also is destroyed. For in a warm climate no man will labor for himself who can make another labor for him. This is so true, that of the proprietors of slaves, a very small proportion indeed are ever seen to labor. And can the liberties of a nation be thought secure when we have removed their only firm basis—a conviction in the minds of the people that these liberties are the gift of God? That they are not to be violated but with his wrath ? Indeed, I tremble for my country when I reflect that God is just : that his justice can-not sleep forever : that considering numbers, and natural means only, a revolution of the wheel of For-tune, an exchange of situation is among possible events : that it may become probable by supernatural interference ! The Almighty has no attribute which can take sides with us in such a contest ! But it is impossible to be temperate and pursue this subject through the various considerations of policy, of mor-als, of history, natural and civil. We must be con-tented to hope they will force their way into every mind. I think a change already perceptible since the origin of the present revolution. The spirit of the master is abating ; that of the slave rising from the dust ; his condition molifying ; the way I hope pre-paring, under the auspices of heaven, for a total emancipation. And that this is disposed, in the order of events, to be with the consent of the masters, rather than by their extirpation.

Such was American slavery. Jefferson proved its historian as well as prophet, to wondrous extent. Happy for the nation, had it heeded his wise and timely counsels. Happy for it would it even now learn to regard them.

When, before or since our slave system, did governments ever punish with death for seventy offences, and then forbid, under penalties almost as severe as death, to teach one of the victims of such tyranny to read one law of man or God, in any book, the Bible not excepted? It may have been. But when, or where? What but cold-blooded murder must such governing have been! To rid the land of such a plague, no wonder it required an army on our side only, of more than two million seven hundred thousand men, half a million of whom never returned! And then, as a crowning, sealing sacrifice, an idolized president massacred, murdered, and his tall form stretched across their premature graves, while not this nation only, but foreign peoples stood aghast! All this, not to speak of moneyed cost and loss; nor counting the sighs and tears, bereavements and mournings of mothers, sisters, widows and orphans! All this, not reckoning moral and spiritual, as well as financial impoverishment and desolation, not to be restored perhaps till our third and fourth generations! Such was part of the price paid to redeem the land from its uncommon curse. Men called the war of sword and bayonet, *Rebellion*. It might have been rebellion on the part of slavery and the South. But to the North it was *Retribution*. The South claimed as property, the slave. But the North, by the terms of the Federal

Union, held him pinned down to the earth as with the point of the bayonet. From the torture-chambers of the imprisoned slave our guilt ascended, by silent but sure evaporation, until it hung in threatening clouds over all the sky, waiting the dread hour when the Infinite Patience could endure it no longer!

At last the command was given, and the tempest and thunder shook the very heavens, saying to the North, "Give up;" to the South, "Keep not back." No lightning-rod shielded either; and Slavery, with all its reeking, shrieking altars, and ghastly paraphernalia of whips, fetters, blood-hounds and red-hot branding-irons, was swept away in cataclysms of blood and fire!

CHAPTER IV.

ANTI-SLAVERY — WHAT IT WAS NOT,
AND WHAT IT WAS.

Such account could slavery give of itself, "Peculiar Institution" it was often called. But it was not peculiar to the southern states. Fortunes were made by the African slave trade, even in little Rhode Island. The history of slavery and slave trading in Massachusetts is one of the most surprising volumes ever issued by the American press. New Hampshire held slaves. General Washington himself, while President of the United States, hunted a slave woman and her child all the way into that then remote state. Vermont, had a fugitive slave case in 1808. But the brave Judge Harrington stunned the remorseless claimant with his decision that " nothing less than a bill of sale from the Almighty could establish ownership" in his victim. And he, too, returned home despoiled and shamed.

Slavery was the sin and crime of north as well as south. It was sustained by the government, it was sanctified by almost the whole religion of the nation. I have read that even the Quakers gravely considered the question, not whether it was right to hold slaves, but whether it was proper to brand them with red hot marking irons. To the credit of that sect, however, it should be told that it was among the first, if not the very first, to cast the accursed thing forever out of its fellowship.

Three clauses in the federal constitution were so interpreted as to brand the whole nation as slave-holders, slave-hunters and slave-traders ; and one of

those clauses was in two words, "suppress insur-
rections." And another was in this apparently innocent, inoffensive period :

No person held to service or labor in one state
under the laws thereof, escaping into another, shall,
in consequence of any law or regulation therein, be
discharged from such service or labor ; but shall be
delivered up on claim of the party to whom such
service or labor may be due.

And under that guarantee, which, as president, he
was solemnly sworn to execute, did George Washington himself pursue a slave mother and her child from
the Potomac to the Piscatauqua as remorselessly as
though they had been a sheep and her lamb. Fortunately, however, for the victims, they escaped and
lived and died in the old Granite State.

Our African slave trade was a piracy that paled all
ordinary buccaneering into innocence. That traffic,
with all its nameless terrors and tortures, was secured
to the United States and positively protected by this
specious and apparently inoffensive phrase in the
ninth section of Article I in the federal constitution :

The migration or importation of such persons as
any of the states now existing shall think proper to
admit, shall not be prohibited by the Congress prior to
the year one thousand eight hundred and eight, but a
tax or duty may be imposed on such importations,
not exceeding ten dollars for each person.

And Mr. Madison, afterwards president, declared,
and it is part of our history, that "the southern states
would not have entered the union without the temporary permission of that trade."

The first fugitive slave law was enacted in 1793.
But as anti-slavery sentiment increased, through the
faithful and persistent labors of the uncompromising
Abolitionists, "underground railroads," as they

were called, multiplied, and Judge Harrington's
decisions became more frequent. Underground railroads were only lines of travel through the northern
states to Canada, over which, under cover of night,
great numbers of slaves were conveyed, sometimes
in whole families; one anti-slavery man hurrying them
from his town to the next, or farther, if necessary, and
then another taking them in charge, and so on till
they were safely landed in Canada, beyond reach of
further pursuit or danger. "Uncle Tom's Cabin"
has no more interesting chapter than that in which
"Senator Bird's" adventure is described with his
night express train over that memorable but dark and
dangerous highway out of democratic despotism to
freedom in a land of kings and queens. And large
numbers escaped with greater security, as their friends
multiplied along the way, by their own unaided
efforts.

So another and severer fugitive law was demanded,
and in 1850 enacted. That law, in the first place,
made every inch of our country, and the deck of
every vessel, on sea, lake or river, hunting ground for
slave-holder and kidnapper. And whoever refused
to aid in the bloody, brutal business of chasing,
seizing and holding the human prey, when called into
the service, or harbored or concealed the victims so
that they escaped, was punished " by fine not exceeding six thousand dollars, and imprisonment not exceeding six months." And, moreover, could be then held
in an action for damages to the slave claimant, for
one thousand dollars for every slave lost through
refusal to obey that most shameful as well as unrighteous and inhuman edict. And many of the best
families in the land were beggared only for religiously
observing the Golden Rule and remembering and

regarding them who were in bonds as bound with them.

As early as the year 1840, efforts began to be made by some anti-slavery men, who had faith or hope in political action against slavery, to change the inter-pretations of the constitution and decisions of the Supreme Court so as to make not only the clauses just now cited, but the whole instrument a proclamation and protection of universal liberty. Foremost among these men was Mr. Gerrit Smith, of New York. A third political party was inaugurated, and James G. Birney, whose name has already had honorable men-tion in these pages, was the first nominated anti-slavery candidate for the presidency, and whose first anti-slavery works, as a repentant slave-holder, entitled him to such distinction. But his name was with-drawn after his first vote was given in 1844, and John P. Hale of New Hampshire, succeeded him. He also was superseded in the candidacy for one who undoubtedly might control a larger vote, Martin Van Buren, but whose anti-slavery reputation was surely of most questionable character. But the popular sentiment, press, pulpit, everything, everywhere pre-vailed over all such innovation till the election of Abraham Lincoln, who in his inaugural address on March 4th, 1861, declared for slave-holding and slave-hunting in these strange, but surely ever memor-able words :

I understand a proposed amendment, which amend-ment I have not seen, has passed Congress, to the effect that the federal government shall never inter-fere with the domestic institutions of the states, including that of persons held to service. To avoid misconstruction of what I have said, I now depart from my purpose not to speak of particular amend-ments, so far as to say, that holding such a provision to be now implied constitutional law, I have no objection to its being made express and irrevocable.

Mark the words, "express and irrevocable." Express : not implied ; not doubtful. Irrevocable : not to be revoked ; more than statute of Medes and Persians.

Thus to slave-breeding as well as slave-working ; to slave-buying, selling, holding and hunting, was the whole nation and government committed under the presidency, not of a southern, but a northern man ; not of the Democratic, but the Republican party, and, as was claimed, the very best of that party. And the whole national domain was made human hunting ground, from Plymouth Rock and Bunker Hill, to the wilds of Alaska, and the Golden Gate. And by the fugitive slave law, every man and woman was held to the bloodhound business of hunting slaves, when required by the officers, under heavy fines and cruel imprisonments. Such, in the Christian year one thousand eight hundred and sixty-one, was the culmination of all anti-slavery political parties.

The American Anti-Slavery Society had also a constitution. Its declared aim was, "to convince all our fellow-citizens, by arguments addressed to the understanding and conscience, that slave-holding is a heinous crime in the sight of God ; and that the duty, safety and best interests of all concerned, require its immediate abandonment, without expatriation." Another declaration was this: "The society will never in any way countenance the oppressed in vindicating their rights by resorting to physical force."

A declaration of sentiment, issued at the inauguration of the society, spoke thus :

Our trust for victory is solely in God. We may be personally defeated, but our principles never. Truth, justice, reason, humanity, must and will gloriously

triumph.   *   *   *   We shall send forth agents
to lift up the voice of remonstrance and warning.
We shall circulate unsparingly, anti-slavery tracts and
periodicals.   We shall enlist the pulpit and the press.

And faithfully, consistently, persistently, without
concealment, without compromise, did the true abolitionists continue so to act to the end.   In an
enterprise solely moral and religious, as well as
philanthropic, the first, most earnest appeal was to the
church and pulpit.   A more devoutly religious man
than was Mr. Garrison at the outset, or more soundly
orthodox and evangelical in sentiment, could not be
found.   That has already been sufficiently shown.
And his strongest, kindest, most affectionate appeals
in behalf of the enslaved were first made to the
ministers and churches of Boston, the then venerable
Dr. Beecher being most eminent among them.

I was a very humble unordained minister in a little
New Hampshire town, where I was preaching as a
candidate for settlement, when my first official testimony was asked and cheerfully given in relation to
the crime and curse of slavery.   The county anti-
slavery society where I was, issued, through a committee whose chairman was the afterwards well and
widely known Stephen S. Foster, a Circular to all the
ministers of the county, respectfully asking their
several answers to the following questions, relative to
the duty of the church and clergy of the country on
the subject of slavery :

1. Do you, or do you not believe that a man's right
to liberty is derived from God, and is therefore
inalienable ?

2. Do you regard slave-holding, under all circumstances, as a sin against God, and an immorality ?

3. Do you approve and support the principles and
measures of the American Anti-Slavery Society and
kindred organizations ?

4. Do you allow the claims of the Anti-Slavery Society the same prominence in the pulpit exercises of the Sabbath as those of other benevolent institutions ?

5. Are the slave-owners excluded from the communion of the church to which you minister, and slave-owning ministers from the pulpit ?

6. Are you in favor of withdrawing all Christian fellowship from slave-owners ?

7. Are you in favor of supporting such benevolent institutions as admit slave-owners to participate in their management, and knowingly receive into their treasuries the avails of the unrequited toil of the slave, and the human-flesh auctions of the south ?

Readers, young and old, can see by these crucial questions what stern demands were made on the abolitionists at that day, who would keep their hands clean, their garments unspotted from the guilt of slavery, whose victims then numbered two and a half millions.

Many ministers, to whom the letter of inquiry was sent, paid no attention to it. Some answered cautiously and prudently, having in their churches and societies influential men whose political party ties, if not their own personal opinions, bound them as with iron bands, to the accursed institution. A very few ventured as far in testimony or protest against the system as possible without periling their denominational position and fellowship. Perhaps the only satisfactory response in all respects to the questions propounded, was in part as given below :

Your sixth question is : "Are you in favor of withdrawing all Christian fellowship from slave-owners ?"

A step so important as this should not be rashly taken. * * * And yet to those who would be separate from all sin, who would " have no fellowship with the unfruitful works of darkness," what question could be of easier solution? With those fell demons of darkness, whose awful cruelties are equalled only by their shameless and unblushing licentiousness, none should expect me to hold "Christian fellowship." But shall I with the more humane and outwardly moral? For my part, I can conceive of no possible circumstances where one person can claim property in another, under our slave system, without being guilty of iniquity and oppression, and of giving countenance and sanction to whatever abuses may result from that system. I might own a slave, and so far as simple treatment is concerned, do him no injustice. I might feed, blanket, bed and house him as tenderly as I do my horse. I might give him mental and moral instruction so far as the laws regulating slavery allowed; and, were it possible, make him as happy as the angels before the heavenly throne. * * * But what then? If I own him under the slave system of this nation, I lend my influence, countenance, sanction and sanctification to all the atrocities connected with that system. Not one pain nor pang could be inflicted on the tortured slave, by cart-whip or cat-hauling; the poison tooth of blood-hound, the murderous rifle-bullet, or red hot branding-iron, or the soul-crushing agonies of the mother torn from her helpless babes and sold on the auction block, forever from their sight, not one of these, nor any other of the nameless and horrible outrages and cruelties of the accursed plague, might not be justly chargeable to my account! My very virtues as a slave-holder might do more to perpetuate the system than all the vices which cluster around it, till I might indeed be the most wicked slave-holder in the land. What better palliation could the average slave-holder plead than that such a man as I was a breeder and holder of slaves? * * * In my own opinion, the most guilty of all among the slave-holders are those whose professions are loudest and strongest in favor of morality and religion; the minister, the elder, the deacon and private member of the church. In one word, as Judge Birney, a ruling elder in the Presbyterian church, has already proclaimed and proved: "The American Churches are the Bulwarks

of American Slavery." Did not their influence, sanctify slavery, its own odiousness would be its overthrow.
And must I commune in sacramental fellowship with
those who of all others are guiltiest in relation to the
most daring system of iniquity that ever cursed the
earth or scourged the inhabitants thereof? O,. my
soul, come not thou into their secret ; unto their assembly, mine honor, be not thou united !

To-day, when everyone is, or would be thought an
abolitionist, or the descendant of an abolitionist, such
sentiments seem only reasonable and right ; only logical and consistent ; slavery being everywhere and
always a heinous sin and crime. But in 1840, when
slavery had yet before it almost a quarter of a century
in which to plague us, it was not so. Slave-holders
were welcomed to the pulpits and sacramental suppers
of the churches in every state and county, if not in
every single town, where churches existed. And the
faithful and devout abolitionists, however evangelical
in sentiment, were as universally cast out. There
were exceptions, but so rare as rather to affirm and
confirm than impeach the rule.

And the political test of the time was not less stern
and severe. The great political parties vied with
each other in zeal and devotion to the demands of the
national idol. Louisiana and Florida had already
been purchased by the government, in obedience to
its behest, though in avowed violation of the federal
constitution. All the Indian tribes in the southern
seaboard states had been driven from their homes,
their churches and school-houses, their printing presses
and the graves of their ancestors, with unheard of
haste and cruelty, that their coveted lands might be
seized and doomed to slave-holding, the Seminoles in
Florida only excepted. And General Taylor, with
government troops, supplemented by imported Cuban

blood-hounds, was soon to complete the bloody business by exterminating such as presumed to resist, and capturing and banishing the rest to the western wilds, then unexplored and almost unknown. Arrangements were making, secret and open, to seize Texas from Mexico, at whatever cost of national dishonor and war, to reinstate slavery, which Roman Catholic Mexico had abolished almost twenty years before, and then annex it to the United States. Both the whig and democratic parties were emulating each other in their zeal and devotion to so vile an object by such unhallowed means. And so the anti-slavery demand on the parties, as well as on the churches, was to come out of them. No religious or theological opinions were questioned, no political party preferences were challenged, Baptist, Congregationalist, Methodist or Presbyterian might remain true to their chosen creed, only treat slavery in the church as other robbery, adultery, and murder. So whig and democrat, only let the equalty of all men, as announced in the Declaration of Independence, be solemnly observed and applied, might remain whig and democrat forever.

For themselves, the American Anti-Slavery Society abolitionists, at their national anniversary in 1844, adopted the resolution below, to which they adhered till the slave-holders' rebellion made sure the end of slavery :

Resolved, That secession from the present United States government is the duty of every abolitionist ; since no one can take office or cast a vote for another to hold office under the United States constitution, without violating his anti-slavery principles, and rendering himself an abettor of the slave-holder in his sin.

To expect to find editors, missionaries and apostles able, ready, willing to adopt, inculcate and defend doctrines and measures thus uncompromising and extreme,

was to pay high compliment to human nature, courage
and character. But such appeared, both women and
men. Indeed, long before this time, the slave power
had revealed itself in almost every possible way, both
in state and church, as ready to execute terrible vengeance on any who dared refuse quick obedience to
its behests, or even to question its right to reign
supreme. At the opening of the anti-slavery apocalypse by Garrison in 1830, the whole nation—state,
church, government, religion, education, trade, commerce,—all were held subservient to its sovereign will
and pleasure. Every conceivable human interest,
nearly every distinguished clergyman, politician, office-
seeker as well as office-holder, bowed reverently in
our temple of Moloch, humbly exclaiming, "Not my
will, but thine be done." Already had Garrison been
heavily fined, and imprisoned in Baltimore, only for
exposing in a newspaper an atrocious instance of
cruelty in our *coastwise* slave trade. In Boston he had
been mobbed, stripped nearly naked, dragged by a
rope through the streets till rescued by the authorities
and shut in the strongest jail, to save his imperilled
life. A worthy minister in New Hampshire, engaged to
give an anti-slavery lecture, was arrested as a "common brawler," jerked from his knees and pulpit to
trial as he was offering his opening prayer. Churches,
school-houses, orphan asylums and dwellings of colored
people, in Providence, New York, Philadelphia and
Cincinnati, had been mobbed, sacked, burned down ;
twelve in New York and one church ; more than forty
in Philadelphia and two churches ; and one church
and many dwellings in Cincinnati. And many colored
men were severely injured in their persons, and girls
and women grossly outraged by their diabolical assailants. So were they hated for their color ; and because

millions of their kindred were slaves to democratic,
republican and christian masters. Pennsylvania Hall,
in Philadelphia, was ereqted at cost of forty thousand
dollars, wholly for anti-slavery and other philanthro-
phic purposes. During an anti-slavery convention, in
1838, that spacious and beautiful structure was
mobbed, set on fire, and burned to ashes, with all its
contents. A valuable library and much other property
were consumed in the flames. Nor did the city
authorities, from mayor and aldermen to sheriff and
police, utter a protest ; still less proffer any protection,
or word of sympathy to the innocent and peaceful
sufferers. Rev. Elijah Parish Lovejoy, native of
Maine, graduate of Waterville College, and brother of
Owen Lovejoy, afterwards member of Congress, perished in an attempt to protect his press and printing
office from the fate of Pennsylvania Hall. It was in
Alton, Illinois, north of St. Louis, on the opposite
bank of the Mississippi, that the most heart-rending
and horrible instance of burning a slave to death over
a slow fire in St. Louis in the year 1837, had just been
made public, as has been already described. The
St. Louis newspapers, though generally approving the
devilish deed, stirred the civilized world with their
account of it. Of course the editorial pen of Lovejoy
was hot with hallowed fire at the awful recital. His
office and life were soon threatened. He appealed to
the authorities for protection. He might as well have
looked to the murderers of the poor slave. His
friends counselled him to flee. He answered : " I
dare not flee away from Alton. The crisis has come
and I have counted the cost. Should I attempt to
flee I should feel that the Angel of the Lord was pursuing me with flaming sword, wherever I went. And
it is because I fear God, that I am not afraid of all

who oppose me in this wicked city!" This was the fourth printing press he had set up. All the others had been ruthlessly destroyed by the same mob violence that now assailed this. Refused all municipal protection, he and a few brave friends entered the building alone. They fearlessly faced the mob till the building was in flames. As they came out, Lovejoy received five bullets and fell dead. Three of the bullets were taken out of his breast. He was but thirty-two and left a young wife and babes. When his mother read the account of his death, she said: "It is well; I had rather he died defending his principles, than that he should have forsaken them!" So it became all who entered the conflict to count well the cost.

CHAPTER V

My first intimate acquaintance and companion in travel in the missionary field, was Stephen Symonds Foster. To him was largely due my first and best lessons in anti-slavery work. My preparation for the Congregational Ministry was all made in less than four years from the reaper and the plough. The three years regular theological course was at Gilmanton, New Hampshire, where attempt was made to stretch the charter of an accademical institution to cover an entire theological department. The enterprise failed, though in those years, the little, remote hamlet of "Gilmanton Corner," aspired and strove hard to become famous as the seat of *Gilmanton Theological Seminary*. I was first to enter the new department, and for several days one professor, and he not inaugurated nor installed, and one student, were all that were visible of that "School of the Prophets." But during my three years, the usual three regular classes were formed, though with small numbers, and two professors were elected and inaugurated. Some good and useful men were graduated, but in a few years, "Gilmanton Theological Seminary" ceased to be, and was known no more. My own three years' course seemed to me so short, preceded as it had been by neither collegiate nor academical study, that I determined on a year at Andover. It continued, however, only through the long fall and winter term;

and then, after a short anti-slavery traveling agency, I commenced the work of a parish minister in a small New Hampshire town, but without ordination. My religious sentiments were of the true Gilmanton and Andover complexion. The creed of both was the same, though my printed copy was the *Andover*, a pamphlet of thirty pages octavo. A few extracts may be interesting to readers in these stirring theological times :

Every person appointed or elected a professor in this seminary shall, on the day of his inauguration into office, and in presence of the trustees, publicly make and subscribe the following declarations :

I believe that there is one, and but one, living and true God ; that the word of God contained in the scriptures of the Old and New Testament, is the only perfect rule of faith and practice;   *   *   *
that in the Godhead are three Persons : The Father, the Son and the Holy Ghost ; that these three are one God, the same in substance, equal in power and glory ; that Adam, the federal head and representative of the human race, was placed in a state of probation, and that, in consequence of his disobedience, all his descendants were constituted sinners ; that by nature every man is personally depraved, destitute of holiness, unlike, and opposed to God, and that previously to the renewing agency of the Divine Spirit, all his moral actions are adverse to the character of God ; that being morally incapable of recovering the image of his Creator which was lost in Adam, every man is justly exposed to eternal damnation;   *   *   *
that God of his mere good pleasure elected some to everlasting life ; and that he entered into a covenant of grace to deliver them out of this state of sin and misery by a Redeemer ; that the only Redeemer of the elect is the eternal Son of God ;   *   *   *
that the souls of believers are at their death made perfect in holiness and do immediately pass into glory ; that their bodies, being still united to Christ, will at the resurrection, be raised up to glory ; and

that the saints will be made perfectly blessed in the
full enjoyment of God to all eternity ; but that the
wicked will awake to shame and everlasting contempt,
and with devils, will be plunged into the lake that
burneth with fire and brimstone forever and ever.
*   *   *   I moreover believe that God, according to the counsel of His own will, and for His own
glory, hath foreordained whatsoever comes to pass ;.
*   *   *   that God's decrees perfectly consist
with human liberty, God's universal agency with the
agency of man, and man's dependence with his ac-
countability.   *   *   *   And, furthermore, I
do solemnly promise that I will open and explain the
Scriptures to my pupils with integrity and faithfulness ;
that I will maintain and inculcate the Christian faith
as expressed in the creed by me now repeated, together
with all the other doctrines and duties of our holy religion so far as may appertain to my office, according
to the best light God shall give me ; and in opposition
not only to Atheists and Infidels, but to Jews, Mahom-
etans, Arians, Pelagians, Antinomians, Arminians,
Socinians, Unitarians and Universalists.   *   *   *
The preceding declaration shall be repeated by every
professor in the seminary, in the presence of the trustees, at the expiration of every successive period of
five years ; and no man shall be continued as president or professor in this institution who shall not
continue to approve himself to the satisfaction of the
trustees, a man of sound and orthodox principles in
divinity, agreeably to the system of evangelical doctrines contained in the said Westminster Shorter
Catechism, and more concisely delineated in the aforesaid Creed.

These extracts are copied from the *Laws of the
Theological Institution in Andover,* printed at Andover
by Gould & Newman, in 1837, one year before my
entrance there.   Nor had I openly dissented from any
of these doctrines, as I understood them, when I left
the Congregational church and its pulpit for the divine
ministry of freedom, humanity and holiness.

My anti-slavery apostleship commenced as a life-work in New Hampshire in 1840. In that year was held in London the memorable World's anti-slavery convention, made memorable most of all by its rejection of several American commissioned delegates, one of them being Mrs. Lucretia Mott, because they were women. "British usage," was the only plea in justification, in a realm that had had women at the head of state and church, parliament, army, navy, the whole nation, many times, all down the centuries from Boadicea to Queen Victoria. Mr. Garrison, of the *Liberator*, and Mr. Rogers, of the *Herald of Freedom*, on seeing the credentials of their associate delegates thus dishonored, retired to the gallery and did not enroll themselves as members of the convention ; a course which was not only approved but admired by the great body of their constituents.

My first work as an agent in New Hampshire was to conduct the *Herald of Freedom* during the absence of the editor abroad. When he returned to his editorial post in autumn I entered the lecturing field, with full resolve to see the overthrow of the Southern slave system or perish in the conflict. The doctrine of the American society was moral, peaceful, religious agitation, in the strain of the poet Whittier :

> " With the mild arms of truth and love,
>   Made mighty through the living God."

And as my leaders and teachers, Garrison and Rogers, relied only on truth, reason and argument for success, so not less did I. My first lecturing tour was in northern New Hampshire, extending to but few towns and occupying only a few days. I went as substitute for Rev. John W. Lewis, a very large and unusually black Baptist minister — my companion, John R. French, afterward printer of the *Herald of Freedom*. He had been advertised in the *Herald* to accompany Mr. Lewis, neither of them, nor myself either, ever having been in that part of the State. Sudden illness kept Mr. Lewis at home, and I was deputed by the Board of Managers his substitute, perhaps as near to a colored man as could then conveniently be found. This circumstance led to many amusing incidents, as most of the towns we visited had never seen any person of African descent ; and so curiosity to see a specimen of the "connecting link" sometimes added many to our audiences. Nor did we always, at the outset, disabuse the people, and more than once I was introduced with becoming grace as "Rev. John W. Lewis, who will now address us." In one instance, we accompanied an excellent old gentleman home to tea, between our afternoon and evening meetings. It was quite dark when we arrived, and there was not time for ceremony nor explanation, and I was immediately introduced as Rev. Mr. Lewis, and my companion as "our young brother, French." We had reached the tea-table before we revealed our secret. The only unpleasant circumstance attending was that it was then such reproach, almost crime, to wear a colored skin, that the family felt called upon to make to me humble apologies for the affront, if not outrage, they had put upon me. But I justified them satisfactorily, on two or three grounds. They had read and accepted the advertisement in the *Herald ;* nor had we explained to the contrary ; nor was my own color really so light as to entitle me to any special respect on its account. " No," said the good old man, quite earnestly, "nor so dark as to be suspected as a negro ; for I told some of my friends after the meeting that as you sat there by Nat Allen, while brother French was speaking, I looked at you both, and couldn't see but that Nat was quite as black as you."

7

Had I been Mr. Lewis, he would have noted a difference, as he was one of the tallest, largest and darkest of his race.

Nat Allen, while he lived, was one of the noblest,
truest of the anti-slavery host ; and as good at home
as abroad. A humble, hard-working harness maker,
and poor as well as radical and outspoken, he was still
everywhere respected. I drove at that time a small
but very pretty nag I bought of my father, and Mr.
Rogers had loaned me an old wagon and harness, the
latter much too large for my little mare. This, our
faithful friend Allen saw ; and before we had completed our work in Littleton and neighboring towns,
he had cut out and made a handsome harness which
exactly fitted my dapple Tunbridge—name I gave her
from her Morgan sire, and by which in after years she
became well known to New England Abolitionists.
Under the circumstances, a more generous gift was
never bestowed. And more than once was the generous giver cruelly imprisoned for his fidelity to the
cause of the more cruelly imprisoned slave. Readers
may hear from Nat Allen again.

At this time my severed connection with the church
and pulpit had not been formal ; so occasionally I
was asked to preach on Sunday, and especially where
a liberal heresy had begun to assert itself. This happened in Littleton, where some wealthy Unitarians had
aided in building a handsome Congregational church,
on one condition. There were only one or two families, and they seldom or never asked for the house,
unless once or twice in summer, when a liberal clergyman might chance to be at the White Mountains, perhaps arriving late in the week. It need not be said
here that forty and more years ago the mountains
were no such resort as at present ; nor were bronchitis

and hay-fever such sore judgments of the pulpit as to-day.   So it was not difficult to obtain of those build-ing the Littleton church a pledge that the Unitarians should have an occasional use of it at the shortest notice.

It chanced that the Unitarian families were not hostile to anti-slavery, and when I arrived in town on Saturday afternoon, my friend Allen and others asked their Unitarian neighbors to invite me to preach for them on the following day.   There was no objection, but it was questioned whether I, being a Congrega-tionalist, could properly ask to be admitted to the pulpit as such.   To this there could be but one answer, and my friend Allen went with me to call on the minister.   For some reason we did not see him till Sunday morning.   When we called in the morning we were shown into the library, and soon the minister entered, attended by his father, also a clergy-man, well and widely known, but retired from regular service.   We were coolly greeted and denied admis-sion to the pulpit for any cause.   My editorial con-nection with the *Herald of Freedom*, then just termin-ated, probably had not increased my ministerial pop-ularity and any argument or appeal was only wasted. We were simply reminded that we had our answer and that it was getting late for church.   I think we had risen to our feet before friend Allen began his part of our mission.   In his usual serene and mild manner he said : " I am very sorry Mr. Pillsbury is refused access to the pulpit to-day in such an unchristian manner ; but I am instructed to say by the Unitarian trustees that, in case of such refusal, they shall occupy the meeting-house to-day, and that Mr. Pills-bury will be their preacher."   Which at once changed the whole face of affairs.   Both father and

son saw and felt that the failure was with them. But
the end of the interview was not quite come. I do
not remember what was said by, but only to our two
opponents. I told the minister he had not in the
least disappointed me, but that I should now probably, disappoint him. Your congregation, I said, are
already assembling ; they are coming to hear you ;
expect to hear you—have a right so to expect ; and it
is not in me nor my friend Allen to wish to disappoint
them. So go now and attend your morning service
as usual ; and only be so kind as to give notice that
I will preach this afternoon and lecture on slavery
this evening at seven o'clock. My proposal was
accepted, but by no means in the spirit with which it
was made. However, it resulted admirably. For
Littleton soon became one of our very best anti-
slavery towns, as the volumes of the *Herald of Freedom* of subsequent years most fully show, and so
remained till slavery was abolished.

Another incident of this campaign and with which
another congregational minister was connected, was
in Campton, one of the approaches to the now well
known " Franconia Notch " and rock-ribbed throne
of the "Old man of the Mountain." The minister was
Thomas Parnell Beach. His small but well instructed
congregation were most of them already abolitionists.
Arriving at his house by invitation, on Saturday
evening, my companion and myself found that
arrangements were made for us to occupy the church
next day, provided I would give the morning and
afternoon sermons. The proposal was accepted and
with results, near and remote, of which none of us that
night dreamed. But an interest was awakened which,
in less than one year, led Mr. Beach to withdraw from
his sectarian pulpit and denomination, generally at

that time apparently indifferent, or incorrigibly pro-slavery, and to reconsecrate himself unreservedly to the ministry of the gospel of humanity.

On the pleasant August afternoon when Mr. Beach delivered his formal and affecting valedictory discourse to his congregation, Mr. Rogers of the *Herald of Freedom* was present and sent a brief report to his readers in the next paper, as given below in his own glowing words :

Not returning home so soon as I expected, I send for editorial what I may throw off in a few minutes before the departure of the Concord stage. I shall attempt briefly a sketch of the most interesting and important Sunday meeting I ever witnessed, yesterday at Campton. I went up there to hear our persecuted and hunted brother, Beach. * * * He has set an example for the age. His yesterday's work in the little meeting house at Campton will constitute, I apprehend, an important point of remembrance—a land-mark in the history of the mighty reformation now going on for the deliverance of mankind and the overthrow of the usurped dominion of the sectarian clergy here and in other parts of christendom. Forenoon, he preached from the text ; "The foxes have holes and the birds of the air have nests, but the Son of Man hath not where to lay his head." He illustrated the character of the modern church and clergy in the light of his text—set forth their love of the world, of popularity, ease and comfort, and the poverty and destitution of the Savior and his disciples * *
It was unmitigated, unadulterated gospel preaching— a terrible sermon, and I thought while hearing it, that it contained more of faithful, uncompromising gospel preaching than I ever before heard. The auditory was made up mostly of his warm friends and his persecuting, exasperated enemies. In relation to his stay among them, they are divided. A portion of them, including the *new-organized* abolitionists, are ransacking the land to find petty faults on which to found his expulsion by a pro-slavery council. They have had

one, headed by Andrew Rankin, that found nothing in
him worthy of death or excommunication. Their
infamous partiality and hypocritical procedure went
far to complete the opening of the eyes of Brother
Beach to the anti-christian character of the 'whole
sectarian machinery. And on Sunday he came out in
all the confidence of simple faith in God and in the
majesty of truth, and renounced the whole of it to an
extent and in a manner', which, perfectly prepared as
I was to second, I was not prepared to witness, and
which was truly overwhelming.

Afternoon he took his stand on the floor of the
house, in front of the poor little abdicated pulpit,
which looked utterly insignificant and heathenish when
thus pointedly abandoned. He held a memorandum
in his hand, and his text was, "Have faith in God."
He spoke of the character of faith, not like a hired
clergyman writing on his contract to preach, but as a
man experiencing what he was saying. It was brief,
full, clear, convincing, convicting. No sound mind
could doubt his meaning or its truth. He said if a man
had faith he would know it, and that if he had it not
he would know it ; and that if he had it he would act
upon it, and if he did not act upon it he was not a
Christian. He denied that the gospel could be preached
in faith on a contract for a salary. He said the preacher
who relied on his contract for support, did not rely on
God, and had not faith. He renounced his own contract with the people to whom he was preaching, and
released them from it. He declared himself bound
to preach to them at the calling and mission of Christ ;
and his obligation to rely on God for support. He
released the people from all obligation they were under
to pay him or sustain him for future preaching during
the year, or for what they owed him for past preaching. He released them from a two hundred dollar
obligation and a forty dollar promissory note which
they owed him, and declared them null and void,
leaving the people to act on their consciences in regard to the whole of it. He renounced his human
license to preach and his ordination by men. He renounced sectarian organization, and expressed his

regret that he ever entered into any covenant with a church corporation, or added anything to his covenant made with Christ at the surrender of his heart to Him. He renounced all profession of religion but that of *Christian life* and conversation—renounced the pulpit as a consecrated elevation, and planted himself on a level with his hearers ; renounced his titled ministership, and declared he should henceforth go on his mission from Christ among his equal fellow men and women. He declared he should hold no more meetings which were not open to all to speak freely as himself. He renounced all sermon writing as a mode of preaching the gospel. * * * In short, he swept the board of all the mummeries of human invention which had crept in upon the simplicity of Christ, and he did it all with a calmness, order and ability which filled me with admiration. I can give no account of it. To be appreciated it must have been witnessed. Thomas Parnell Beach stands now " redeemed, regenerated and disenthralled," a plain and simple preacher of Christ.

The subsequent labors of Mr. Beach were of most devoted and heroic, and sometimes suffering, description, but not of long continuance, for he survived less than five years after his withdrawal from the sectarian ministry. He died in Sharon, Ohio, on the thirtieth of May, 1846. He was born in Canada, Vermont, in 1808, graduated at Bowdoin Collge, married in 1837 Miss Sarah Barker, of Bethel, Maine, and settled soon after in Wolfboro', N. H., as Congregational minister and Preceptor of the Academy, from which he afterwards removed to Campton, where the anti-slavery cause discovered him in the autumn of 1840.

Not very much was ever written concerning him, and few at this day probably remember him. But before this anti-slavery scripture is finished, he may be recurred to again in manner, it is hoped, not unbecoming his memory.

In Whitefield, one of my Gilmanton classmates was the Congregational minister. He received us cordially, invited me to his pulpit on Sunday morning, and to his sacramental supper afterwards, and we held our subsequent anti-slavery meetings in his meeting-house.

Rev. Mr. Fleming, of Haverhill, asked me to preach for him, he having been absent the past week and not being prepared to preach himself. But at the close of the morning service, he told the congregation what he had done, and then, turning to me, he said if the afternoon discourse was to be like this just heard, he must decline it. I assured him it could not be less objectionable, in plain speaking, and he then announced that he should preach in the afternoon himself. Which he did, and gave a very feeble discourse to a small and not interested audience. My companion, Mr. French, and myself sat directly before him and near the pulpit, evidently much to his embarrassment. Undoubtedly his refusal to permit my preaching in the afternoon was both damage to himself and advantage to me. The small, uninterested audience who heard him was surely a happy contrast, and most significant, too, measured by our large and quite spirited and attentive house in the evening.

At that period the anti-slavery agents were accustomed to call early on the ministers when they entered a town, particularly in all country towns and parishes, to confer with them and solicit their coöperation in anti-slavery work. It soon became apparent, however, that very little aid was to be expected in that quarter. A formal division in the ranks of professed abolitionists had already been made, and the evangelical churches and their ministers had, with wondrous unanimity, so far as they were anti-slavery at all,

joined themselves to the "new organization."   Grievous charges were preferred against Mr. Garrison for
heresy and infidelity, and the American anti-slavery
society, at its anniversary in 1840, committed the unpardonable sin of insisting that on their platform,
however it might be in the church or elsewhere, there
should be no high nor low, rich nor poor, great nor
small, male nor female.   It was solemnly asked :

> " Shall we behold, unheeding,
>   Life's holiest feelings crushed ?
> When woman's heart is bleeding,
>   Shall woman's voice be hushed ?"

Already had the eloquence of Sarah and Angelina
Grimke, Abby Kelley, and other noble women begun
to thrill the hearts of women and men, even ministers,
all over the land, as they tenderly but fearlessly
pleaded the cause of the slave woman under the lash
and red-hot branding-iron or on the auction-block with
her children, she sold one way, they in other ways,
sundered forever, but all exposed alike to the cruel
and merciless outrages of the slave system !   At the
final separation the *woman question* was urged most
vehemently as reason for breaking with the original
American society, especially by the clergy.   In New
Hampshire the Methodists and Free Will Baptists
were quite numerous, and had always encouraged, if
not even demanded that their church members should
bear active, equal part, men and women, in all social
if not more public meetings for worship.   But the
more dignified denominations there, and not more
there than in every state, deemed such usage a pro-
fanation and abomination.   The Hopkinton Association of Congregational divines doubtless spoke the
general sentiment of Congregationalism, Presbyterian-
ism, and all the sects held in highest esteem in all the

states, as well as New Hampshire, in a solemn decree unanimously and promptly enacted, the declarative portion of which was to this effect :

Not that women may not bear a part in the songs of the church, because this is an established part of public worship, and is not prohibited to women as public teaching and praying are ; publicly to sing God's praise, under men as leaders, is, by implication, enjoined upon women, as is the celebration of the holy supper, and of the Savior's resurrection, by keeping the first day of the week as holy time. Nor does the prohibition deprive females of any of the privileges of the Bible class, or religious conference, in which they are indulged with *perfect freedom of speech, in answering the questions which their pastors, leaders, or catechists put to them.* But, as to leading men, either in instruction, or devotion, and as to any interruption, or disorder, in religious meetings, " Let your women keep silence in the churches ;" not merely let them be silent, but let them keep or preserve silence. Not, that they may not preach, or pray, or exhort merely, but they may not open their lips, to utter any sounds audibly. Let not your women, in promiscuous religious meetings, preach or pray, audibly, or exhort audibly, or sigh, or groan, or say Amen, or utter the precious words, " Bless the Lord ;" or the enchanting sounds, "Glory ! Glory !"

The resolution to sustain the equal right of women on the anti-slavery platform with man, was adopted in the American Society at the annual meeting in New York in 1840, by majority of 557 to 440 ; the test question at the time being simply the placing of a woman on one of the committees. But the new organization forthwith sprang out of it, known for a time as the American and Foreign Anti-Slavery Society.

The annual meeting of the New Hampshire Anti-Slavery Society was held in Concord, less than a month afterward and with result much the same, only that the opposition was less in numbers, though by no means in spirit. The test vote, admitting or excluding women as members of the convention, was on an amendment substituting the word *gentlemen* for *persons* as originally submitted. The amendment was lost, 197 to 58 ; and the original resolution was adopted nearly unanimously, and with much enthusiasm. But a new organization society was immediately attempted, though with but indifferent success, excepting for political purposes, though carrying with it nearly all the ministers and most of the church members who made any pretentions to anti-slavery in the state.

The Connecticut Anti-Slavery Society went over to the new organization almost in a body, with maledictions on the doctrine of woman's equality anywhere. The Hartford *Congregationalist* also declared that the women's anti-slavery *Fair* had to be taken from New Haven because no place in that city could be obtained in which to hold it. The meeting at which the society set its terrible ban on women was held there and would have been held in a Congregational church, but both minister and church, the *man* part of it, declared it should not be opened without a pledge given that women should neither speak nor vote in the meetings ! That same minister presided at the opening of the meeting, when and where it was held and declared with indignant warmth : "I will not sit in a chair where women bear rule ; I will not sit in a meeting where the sorcery of woman's tongue is thrown around my heart ; Women shall not speak in our meetings. I will not submit to petticoat government, here, nor anywhere else. I had enough of that in my childhood. Now I am a man, I will not submit to it even in my own house. No woman shall lord it over me. I am major-domo in my own house." Some one responded in the audience: "A strange spirit has risen up among us ; " and he immediately called him to order ; adding, " I think I have the spirit of God. I am a Christian ! " This, and the Haverhill and Littleton ministers already described, with the Hopkinton association of divines, were only true representatives of the great majority of the popular New England clergy of that day. Their plainness of speech well accorded with the rest. And besides, much larger bodies than the Hopkinton association, were alike audacious in utterance, as well.

That campaign in northern New Hampshire, made in the autumn after the society secessions, separations and new organizations, fully convinced me, had other hopes been entertained before, that the church and its ministry would be found in very deed the "bulwarks," if not at last "the forlorn hope of slavery," in complete confirmation of the declarations of Hon. James G. Birney.

It was no less plain, too, that very few of the abolitionists themselves were aware of the terrible contest before them ; as many later withdrawals from their always scanty ranks proved.   In a subsequent account rendered to the society through their paper, the *Herald*, I hazarded the prediction, that "before the fell demon of slavery should be cast out, there would be contortions, foamings and wallowings to rend our civil, social, and ecclesiastical organizations, in so much that many would say, ' They are dead.'   For it is of a kind that goeth not out but by prayer and fasting.   Other foul spirits, too, will be discovered ; their very name, legion.   All the foundations of the great deep will be broken up.   On earth must be perplexity and distress of nations ; the sea and the waves roaring, and the hearts of men failing them for fear, and for looking at the things that are coming on the earth ; for the powers of heaven shall be shaken."

If our thirty years war of moral and peaceful agitation failed to fulfill all these prophecies, what shall be said of the subsequent four years war of rebellion, with all their frightful costs of blood and treasure? War, whose thunders shook the land, the sea, the skies! Whose reverberations still go sounding down towards the night of the nineteenth century !

CHAPTER VI.

CONVENTIONS AND MEETINGS WITH MR. ROGERS
AND MR. FOSTER—DIGRESSION ON
NEW ORGANIZATION.

New Hampshire continued my field of operations through 1840. Following the Grafton county campaign were two or three quite notable anti-slavery conventions, the best everyway, perhaps, at Milford, when all parts of Hillsboro' county had representation. Mr. Garrison, Mr. Rogers, Mr. Foster, and some others were present to assist in the proceedings.

The genius and spirit of our movement at that time may be gathered somewhat from the Resolutions generally, most thoroughly considered and usually adopted with few, if any, dissenting voices. At Milford the following passed after a searching and able discussion:

Resolved, That slavery is a national, not a local, institution, and the whole people are involved in all its guilt, evils and dangers.

Resolved, That the churches, rebuked by anti-slavery and pronounced unworthy the name of christian, and the clergymen whom it declares unworthy of support as religious teachers, are those, and only those, who connive at the existence of American slavery, or refuse to bear faithful, public testimony against it.

Resolved, That the anti-slavery society was originally constituted on principles of perfect equality and justice, and any attempt to change that construction, and to *new organize it*, is a departure from those principles and a practical betrayal of the cause of the slave.

Milford was early an anti-slavery town. With such resolutions most ably discussed, and almost unanimously adopted by a large congregation, the meeting was everyway a success. It commenced on Thanksgiving evening, with an opening address by Mr. Garrison, in the spacious and then new Congregational meeting-house, the minister, Mr. Warner, another Gilmanton classmate of mine. Himself and church, however, were already far on the road to new organization. Those who remained faithful to the anti-slavery cause soon after withdrew from the church, and were henceforth known as *come-outers*, infidels, non-resistants, Garrisonians, or whatever other name, honorable or opprobrious, was fastened upon them and others like them.

It may be worthy of mention that the Concord attendants drove over to Milford in two open carriages, leaving home early on Thanksgiving morning, in a cold November rain, from which umbrellas were a poor protection. But the joyous greeting and reception which awaited us at our half-way house, the hospitable and sumptuous home of the farmers, Luther and Lucinda Melendy, on Chestnut hill, in Amherst, very soon dispelled all memory of outside storms, or other exposure or inconvenience. Rogers, in his *Herald* account of the convention, said of this incident:

We were received at the Melendys with the welcome which compensates for months of pro-slavery scowling round about our path of life. Cordiality and brotherly love adorned the face of the household— the bounties of the season, the hospitable board ; and the Bible, the *Liberator*, *Herald of Freedom*, and *National Anti-Slavery Standard* the reading table. Here were the circumstances and conditions of genuine anti-slavery.   *   *   *   We were obliged to leave the interesting spot too soon. We reached Milford, brother and sister Melendy in company, just as friend Warner's meeting-house was lighted up for a lecture from Garrison. It rained with all the dismalness of a November night.

But our Milford reception cleared the sky of every cloud, and hung rainbows of beauty and joy in every direction. Those early anti-slavery friendships surely were akin to heaven itself, growing brighter, too, and more beautiful, as the subsequent tempests of proscription, ostracism and persecution rose in all their terrors over us. The triple power of society, the state and the church, conspired against the rising tide of humanity and liberty ; determined, apparently, to rivet on, fast and forever, the fetters of the slave, in the name of, and with sanction of our democratic republicanism and Protestant Christian religion. At that hour all our hearts seemed to beat as one—all anointed vision to see eye to eye. Garrison and Rogers had not met before since their arrival in Boston from their foreign tour, not many weeks previously, and they greeted each other as David and Jonathan, when their loves " passed the love of women ! " At that convention, almost all exclaimed, " It is good for us to be here." We reached Concord from the Milford convention on Saturday night, glad and thankful for one day of change, if not of rest, after our Thanksgiving week's work.

On Monday, Stephen Foster and myself had engagements in Canterbury. Our valiant friend Rogers, desirous to extend his acquaintance among the abolitionists of the state, volunteered to accompany us and to continue with us another week. Canterbury and last of November continued for us cold and most inhospitable receptions. The meeting-house was closed altogether, and the town-hall was as dirty and disagreeable, everyway, as it was dilapidated and cold. But we got into it. Pretty soon the meeting-house was unlocked, and a few came, among others the Congregational minister, Rev. Mr. Patrick.   Our friend Foster, and most of his quite numerous family connections, were, or had been, members of his church ; and as Foster reasoned of righteousness, temperance and judgment to come, his minister trembled.   In great excitement he rose to his feet as if to speak. He stood a moment, as though deliberating whether to speak or retire.   But for some reason he did neither, and soon sat down, though much agitated at what he had to hear, and the truth of which he well knew could not be questioned.   The evening meeting was better attended, and excellent work was done, with results not yet wholly effaced ; as the generous and high moral and progressive sentiment of the thriving little town has always shown.

Our next gathering was at Sanbornton Bridge, and in the very meeting-house out of whose pulpit, a few years before, Rev. George Storrs had been violently jerked, as, on his knees, he was preceding an anti-slavery address with prayer.   He was arraigned as *a common brawler* before a magistrate, and tried as such.

How we and our mission might be estimated in such society, was shown in the fact that as it was presumed we should occupy the pulpit, the cushions were thoroughly plastered over with well crushed but most deplorably *un*-merchantable eggs.   Had the young priests of such an unholy anointing only known us a very little better, they might have been spared such an offering to their idol.   We had a good while before proved most of the pulpits to be but cowards' castles, or despots' thrones, even without the baptism of bad eggs, and shunned the whole of them accordingly. The afternoon meeting was small, numerically, but not so the evening, for the heroes of the pulpit-

8

cushion and addled eggs attended in person, and rendered speaking most difficult by their *boys*-trous proceedings. Still, our work resulted beyond expectation. We were handsomely and hospitably entertained by Dr. Ladd and others ; and as we were then raising the means to discharge a debt of two thousand dollars owed by our society, we were much cheered by our success in that direction.

From the valley of Sanbornton Bridge we ascended next day to the heights of Sanbornton Square. We had not heard that even new organization had dared invade it, so well and widely was its hostility to the anti-slavery, temperance, and other reforms understood. At the Bridge we did discover tracks of a new organized agent, a minister who had done his best and worst, there and elsewhere, to blast the fair fame of the old society and all its instrumentalities, though, as we saw, more to his own harm than ours. But how we sped at the Square can best be told by the editor of the *Herald of Freedom* himself. In the number of December 4th, 1840, some editorial correspondence read as below :

After dinner, Wednesday, we rode to Sanbornton Square, calling on Richard Lane. Mrs. Lane seemed an abolitionist. Her husband was absent, but they had received no notice of an anti-slavery meeting. Came soon to the sightly and commanding Square, superb with prospect. Tavern kept by Mr. Lane. It is the *Lane* that leads to the chambers of death—a broad one, and numbers throng it. Had occasion to go into it. Many smoking their pipes in the bar-room. One respectable looking elderly gentleman at the end of a cigar. All smoking away, and the air three-quarters tobacco. Asked the landlord if any appointments had been given out Sunday before of an anti-slavery meeting, taking for granted if there had he would have heard of it, the rum tavern being in some

places on good terms with the meeting-house.   None
that he knew of.   Brother Pillsbury had gone up to
the neighborhood of the academy to find a Mr.
Webster, said to be an abolitionist.   Resolved to go
there ; felt utterly desolate in the smoky rum tavern
and the heartless pro-slavery square.   Homesick to
find one anti-slavery house.   Went to Mr. Webster's ;
told Mrs. W. (husband not in) that she must, if convenient, receive us as travelers at their temperance
tavern.   Our request was readily granted.   Called out
with brother Pillsbury to see about a meeting.   Met
the Rev. Mr. Bodwell, Congregational minister, in
company with a distinguished Colonizationist, Dr.
Webster, of Hill.   Rev. Mr. Bodwell said he had
received no notice · of the meeting.   Ascertained of
him there was to be a prayer meeting at the academy
that evening.   Proposed to him, if perfectly agreeable
to him, to have our anti-slavery meeting instead, and
at the academy, if he thought best ; not otherwise, he
having remarked just before that if we had an anti-
slavery meeting in the neighborhood there would be
probably few at the prayer meeting.   He was not
opposed to us, he was not in favor of us ; he stood
neutral, and he wished to be so considered.   · He did
not wish to be considered as having been called on in
relation to the meeting ; could not say whether he
would be present or not ; told us Esquire Lane,
Colonel Sanborn and himself were the committee in
charge of the academy ; did not wish himself to give
permission to use the academy for a meeting ; wished
us to consult Esquire L. and Colonel S., and did not
wish to be considered as having been consulted at all
in relation to the academy.   We remarked to him that
it did not seem to us he could possibly take a neutral
position, but he must judge for himself.   In the course
of our talk, Dr. Webster remarked that he objected to
the abolitionists for their opposition to colonization ;
that he did not see as they need quarrel with that, or
why both could not go on harmoniously together.
Mr. Bodwell said he could not, and that he had no
objection to abolition if it did not oppose colonization,
and he thought both might go on together.   We told

him if that were possible he might, for aught we could
see, be an abolitionist, whether we liked colonizing the
colored people or not.   He need not oppose abolishing
slavery because we opposed colonizing the free colored
people.   It was bleak talking on the cold hill side,
and we parted, Mr. Bodwell to his snug parsonage
and we down to find Esquire Lane.   We found him
accidently at the bar room of the tavern, and asked
him for the academy, telling him of the *non entity*
position of Rev. Mr. Bodwell, not assenting nor denying, nor doing neither, neither doing anything nor
nothing at all.   Esquire L. said at once he had no
objection, though he did not countenance the meeting.
He said we were all slaves here.   We told him we were
afraid so.   He said he was opposed to using force
against us—force had been used but he never countenanced it ; thought it only promoted our object, the
way was to keep away from us.   The subject he thought
ought not to be agitated here *where we had no slaves.*
We told him men differed as to the propriety of agitating here, and that that was a fair matter of discussion, and asked him if it were not.   He admitted that
it was, and that we had the right to discuss, but he
should not come near us.   We told him we should be
glad to have him attend, and if we were wrong put us
right.   Barroom by this time pretty full.   Esquire
Caleb Kimball, among others, considerably excited by
opposition to anti-slavery, or some other cause, said he
knew us and was a friend, but had no opinion of this
nigger question ; we had no right to be stirring it up
here ; if anybody wanted a black wife, he might
have one for all him.   (A laugh.)   He had as lief we
should get pelted with rotten eggs as any way, though
he did not approve of mobs.   He was far from approving mobs ; he would not be catched in one.   The
constitution, he thought, guaranteed slavery to the
states, and the north no business to interfere ; had no
business with it any way ; we had no more right to
take away their property than they had to come and
take away our cattle.   The company gathered around
and we carried on the talk under a thick cloud of
tobacco smoke mixed with the breath of the tavern

bar. We did not deny Esquire Kimball's opinion, but contended that we and he had the right of discussion and liberty of speech about any subject we pleased. We were one of the people as much as he was, and had a right to our opinions, and meant to have just what opinions we pleased, and to speak our sentiments out anywhere and everywhere, and at all times, and for all of anybody, and everybody else had the same right, and we did not believe there was a man in the room who would deny it. We were going to have a meeting if we could get a place, and should be glad to have every friend present attend it and speak his mind freely, and we believed that if they could hear us every man would say that we were right. We said slavery was an abominable thing ; it was in the country and we had a right to talk about it, to talk against it, and we meant to, and had got to ; and if we did not and run it down, it would run us down, and eat us out of house and home ; had nearly done it already ; had made us nearly all slaves here, as Esquire Lane had just said ; that it had got us so low that we did not dare to speak about it or allow our neighbors to ; that Esquire Kimball had just said he thought we ought to be pelted with rotten eggs if we did not keep still about it. The 'squire said he was no friend to mobs. Yes, but said we, you said you had as lief we should be pelted with rotten eggs as not if we stirred up this slavery question here ; and if we did you would have to mob us. Slavery, we said, would demand it of you, and you would have to. The 'squire said his father was one that helped to adopt the constitution, and he remembered all about it, and about slavery ; it was in the constitution, he said. We contended that the constitution was a free one, and was always called so, and a glorious free one, and the like. And so we went on discussing, and the very rum-drinkers and tobacco-eaters and smokers heard us with a patience the Rev. Mr. Bodwell could not in his meeting-house; reminding us, as we thought of it, of the Savior's comparison of the publicans and harlots with the clergy of Jerusalem. We could convince the tavern haunters, by the way, if the property

and standing would only allow us a chance, we could
make abolitionists of them much easier than of the
better classes, civil, military or ecclesiastical. * * *
* * * A tall substantial-looking farmer came in
and listened awhile to our discussion as we were talking of slavery's effect on the north. He said emphat-
ically that it was as bad to enslave black people as
white ; and that if you enslave any it enslaves everybody else ; and if you allow slavery in the country
you can't keep liberty. Give us the blue-frocked
farmers for anti-slavery. * * * On the whole, we
had a grand meeting, and wish we had continued it
there in the evening ; we should have had an attentive auditory, and we don't believe Mr. Lane would
have sold a drop the whole evening. We went out
with brother Pillsbury, after getting leave to have the
academy, and called at every house and notified the
people of our meeting, and brother Foster drove in his
sulky out of the neighborhood to do the same. The
hour arrived ; we resorted to the literary institution.
It was a steeple edifice—meeting-house and town-
house (church and state) hard by all in a row ; all
steepled and painted as white as so many "whited
sepulchres." No light gleamed from the academy
windows ; all dark as "the people covered with gross
darkness." We entered it ; not a spark of fire nor a
soul there. We consulted what to do. Four little
boys came in, then one man, Deacon Lane, and a
woman, then two young women, academy scholars,
boarders at our friend Webster's, one more man, and
lastly, friend Webster himself, the abolitionist of Sanbornton Square, and our assembly was complete.
Brother Pillsbury found the bell rope and pulled it
till the sound rang clear and loud all over Sanbornton
hills. It agitated the cold night air, but not the colder
hearts of the people. Brother Bodwell must have
heard it like a knell in his study. Nobody else came
near. Brother Pillsbury went to a store and bought a
candle and *lighted the house*, wrapping a bit of newspaper round it and setting it in a corner of the desk.
It threw its beams round upon the empty seats and
the "darkness visible" of the "Woodman Sanbornton

Academy," the title, we believe, of this *Liberal* institution. We held a season of prayer, not with the full
formalities of a meeting. We felt the desolate condition of the unfortunate people and their minister, and
we prayed for them. Brother Foster followed. When
we rose from our knees he opened his mouth to
the handful present in a most impressive and striking
exhortation, addressing them as " the entire humanity
of the place," told them that on them, in the providence of God, had devolved the responsibility of
awakening that people and minister ; told them the
slave's case and of the judgment, and bore an appalling testimony against the place. Brother Pillsbury
and myself followed with similar appeal and testimony.
Friend Webster spoke with feeling for the cause and
sorrow for the state of the people, and we separated,
chilled by sitting without fire. Brothers Foster and
Pillsbury went to see Mr. Bodwell, and from what
they said, did their duty to him faithfully.

Could the editor of the *Herald of Freedom* have accompanied Mr. Foster and myself through the state,
during that cold and dreary winter, he would have
found many Sanbornton Squares, and some even more
benighted and morally desolate. Even at the tavern
there, we met several persons who, spite of rum, tobacco,
blasphemy and negro hate, spoke many kindly words,
and thought we were honest in our belief and work,
and entitled to better treatment than we were receiving. And the generous, even heroic, hospitality of
Mr. Josiah Webster and his excellent wife (father and
mother of our Concord fellow-citizen, Calvin Webster,
then a boy of thirteen) won our admiration, as well as
gratitude, for in those days it was often perilous to
harbor and entertain an abolitionist. Mr. Webster
had a brother, Rev. John Calvin Webster, who was
also well known as an abolitionist, and, for a clergyman, of best and truest type, away beyond and above
most of his clerical brethren.

Leaving Sanbornton we crossed over to Gilmanton, then seat of the Theological seminary from which I emerged a licensed Congregational minister two years before, one of a class of eleven, the first graduating class, most of us professing to be earnest, outspoken abolitionists. Our reception at Gilmanton, but for one family, must have been as dreary and cheerless as Sanbornton Square would have been without its Websters.. And we had begun to say that every Sodom seemed to have a Lot, and every Sahara at least one oasis. And in the spacious, hospitable home of Mr. Clark, we were like Bunyan's pilgrims on the " Delectable mountains."

But alas for our cause ! The Congregational meeting-house was opened, warmed and lighted for us, afternoon and evening, and the minister had given notice of our coming from the pulpit. The Theological seminary and academy were close at hand, the latter with its preceptor and pupils ; the former with its three professors and as many classes. In the village were a Methodist and Quaker, as well as Congregational meeting-house, and all open on Sunday for worship. The day was not unfavorable, the traveling for the season was remarkably good. At the appointed hour we entered the meeting-house. It was empty and void as chaos before the eternal fiat had gone forth, " Let there be light." The Clarks came in good time. Next three women, then two theological students and one other man. The Baptist minister, Rev. Mr. Boswell, had ridden over some miles of Gilmanton hills to be present, and remained through the evening, giving friendly and approving testimony, and late and last Mr. Lancaster, Congregational minister. He came to both meetings, but spoke no word. In the evening the numbers were less by two or three, the only woman present, Mrs. Lancaster, wife of the minister.   Nor was there but one theological student. Three years before had the like of Rogers and Foster come there to speak on slavery, my whole class of eleven would surely have attended, with possibly one or two exceptions, and though most of us were working our passage into the pulpit, the dollar or half dollar of each would have helped on the collection.   But at that time the torpedo touch of new organization had not done its fell work ; and many of the younger ministers, as well as theological students, were earnest and devoted abolitionists.   While slavery was regarded only as an evil, and at the distant south, no tell-tale telegraph nor lightning express trains, nor even "under-ground railroad" between, discussion of it might be tolerated.   But when Garrison proclaimed it a sin and crime, always and everywhere, the pulpit began to be alarmed.   And when next we began to resolve and re-resolve that no slave-holder could be a christian ; and later that his northern abettor and apologist was as bad as himself ; and that a slave-holding religion was essentially anti-Christ ; a slave-holding church a synagogue of Satan, and a slave-holding ministry and all the fellow communicants a brotherhood of thieves, of man-stealers. the battle was joined in deadly earnest.

Our next encounter was Pittsfield.   The Congregationalist minister, Mr. Curtis, was a pioneer in the new organization, and in various ways we felt his baneful influence.   The Free-will Baptist minister and one or two of his congregation showed us some hospitality, especially Mr. and Mrs. McCrillis of his church. We had an audience of a dozen, but two young men of them had come with us all the ten hilly miles from Gilmanton.   Pittsfield was a flourishing cotton factory village, and Mr. Curtis had at one time been an able anti-slavery apostle ; nor did he apostatize till the axe was laid at the root of the deadly tree of slavery, the church and its pulpit. He was president of the New Hampshire anti-slavery society at the time of secession, but he had been conspiring with his clerical brethren all the previous year, 1839, to seize the helm of the society and bring it under clerical and congregational control. At the anniversary of that year, he exhibited much sectarian bitterness and new organization predilection, more than once ruling Stephen Foster out of order while speaking, and once even calling our invited guest, Mr. Garrison, down for what he termed irrelevancy. Still he was next day re-elected president, the society wishing to avoid the very appearance of proscription.

In the following autumn, the Deerfield Association of Ministers, Mr. Curtis a leading member, issued a call for a convention of Congregational and Presbyterian ministers and churches, for the purpose as was declared, of correcting a mistake existing *at the south*, relative to the position of the New Hampshire churches on the subject of slavery. The convention met in Concord and sat two days and then quite portentously adjourned to meet in Concord on the day preceding the next anniversary day of the state society. The motive for such adjournment could not be mistaken ; Mr. Curtis was president of that convention, and as such, was careful and prompt to have seasonable notice given of the adjourned meeting. At the same time he sent to the congregational organ of New Hampshire, then *The Panoply*, a call over his own name, addressed "to the sound, judicious and enlightened abolitionists of New Hampshire," summoning them to attend the meeting of the state anti-slavery society, and save it from being perverted to unworthy purposes. And a request accompanied this call, that when the *Panoply* had copied it, it be sent to the *Herald of Freedom*.

The call to the Concord convention of ministers and churches, issued by the Deerfield Association, included the editor of the *Herald*, and Stephen Foster, both of whom were still church members. Early in the second session, Mr. Rogers offered this resolution :

Resolved, That this convention cordially approve of the American Anti-Slavery Society and kindred organizations ; and the direct and proper way of assuring our southern brethren that we are not in favor of slavery, is to unite with these organizations for its overthrow.

That resolution was laid on the table. The resolution limiting membership to the convention to ministers and *male* church members, excluding women, was adopted. Mr. Foster asked for the yeas and nays, and the vote stood forty to twenty-six against women membership. So when the roll was called, the names of women were passed over. Late on the second day of the convention, the resolution of Mr. Rogers was taken from the table, amended and passed.

But the editor of the *Panoply*, Rev. David Kimball, himself a member of the convention, in his leading editorial, published with the convention proceedings, declared that more than half the members were gone when the resolution of Mr. Rogers was taken up, and so there was not a fair expression of the minds of the convention. Which was doubtless true. And another thing was also true. Only a very small number of the Congregational and Presbyterian ministers of the state cared enough about the anti-slavery cause to attend the convention as friends or foes. Less than forty-five of the two hundred and thirty towns in the state had any representation, and more than half of them, probably, were represented only by *laymen*, though several sent women, only to be rejected. And another fact is as patent as, and more significant than, the rest. Only the very best of the clergy, those who had shown most friendliness toward the anti-slavery movement, were present at all. And some of them soon became, and so continued, our most inveterate enemies. The last resolution which the convention adopted unanimously read:

Resolved, That as long as ministers and church members continue in the sin of slave-holding, we feel it our duty to withhold from them christian fellowship and commuion.

What that resolution implied shall be referred to Rev. Mr. Curtis, who was president of that convention, and at that time of the New Hampshire anti-slavery society, to explain and declare. He had for some years been active in measures for a pretended severance of church fellowship between the north and south, through the missionary, Bible and other similar coöperating organizations, including also the General Assembly of the Presbyterian church, and the Congregational churches of New England. What kind of separation he intended is seen by an extract of a letter of his own in the *Congregational Journal* at the time, to this effect:

My advice was, to dissolve all connection with the General Assembly, as a body, while they, as a body, sanction slavery. I do not perceive that such a measure need at all decide the question, or make it doubtful, whether individual Congregational and Presbyterian churches should continue in the kindest fellowship towards one another, when neither *professes* any sympathy for slavery. Let the individual fellowship of the churches be left to their own regulation, as it must be left.

That was the kind of excision contemplated by Mr.
Curtis, who represented the most radical anti-slavery
wing of the New Hamsphire and of the New England Congregational pulpit and church.   Cut off the
General assembly as such, refuse coöperation with
Bible and missionary societies as such, but retain sacramental and other communion with the "individual
Congregational and Presbyterian churches" composing
them as before! A surgical operation never contemplated at the school of Salerno, nor any other medical institution since.   But even such action was not
taken.   The advice of Mr. Curtis was never accepted
nor respected to any observable extent.   The fellowship continued as before.

But readers may have forgotten that this episode of
explanatory history commenced back in the town of
Pittsfield, where the anti-slavery lecturers and the
editor of the *Herald* encountered in an unusual degree
the baneful influence of a professing anti-slavery minister. Mr. Bodwell, of Sanbornton Square, made no anti-
slavery pretentions ; nor did Mr. Corser at the Bridge,
where the pulpit cushions were "daubed with such
untempered mortar," as if typifying the quality of the
gospel preached there.   But the sacramental fellowship was as real and constant with them as with the
most radical anti-slavery church members and ministers in the land   And the same christian embrace was
extended to all the individual churches and clergy
composing the General assembly of the Presbyterian
church as well.

Our Pittsfield meeting was held in the basement
vestry of the Free Will Baptist church, the only building in the town to which uncompromising anti-slavery
could be admitted.   The Free Will minister, Rev. Mr.
Cilley, attended, as did a very few members of his

church ; Mr. and Mrs. McCrillis, who kindly entertained us while in town, of course among them. Rev.
Mr. Curtis and his new organized church and society
kept carefully aloof. The account given of our reception and experiences there by the editor of the *Herald*,
might be too long to reproduce here, but a few
excerpts can hardly be spared. And the more because
Pittsfield was pre-eminently a representative town,
anti-slaverywise, under the newly organized type of
the doctrine, and Mr. Curtis and his church and people
of the very best membership, as well in New York
and New England as New Hampshire. So in what
follows, Mr. Rogers spoke really of the whole Congregational and Presbyterian churches of the northern
states :

We groped our way to the underground meeting,
where we found assembled anti-slavery's accustomed
numbers—a full dozen of the surviving heart of Pittsfield. Brother Cilley was among them. Brother
Curtis came not also among us. He was said to have
been at a school exhibition in the town, and in uncommon flow of spirits ; as merry, according to the
account, he must have been as Herod the night of
John's beheading, and as regardless of the despised
and infidel meeting going on in the little Free Will
vestry as that festive monarch was of the scenes in the
prison of the Baptist. * * * We wondered if
brother Curtis did not now and then think of our
anti-slavery meeting, amid the gay festivities of his
exhibition. And when he went home to his evening
devotions, did not that meeting intrude into his solemn
fancy ? And when he laid his head upon his pillow
that night, did not that meeting occur again to his
unquiet remembrance ? Nay, in his night visions did
it not usurp the place of that joyous exhibition ? And
in the morning when he went through his reverend
services at the altar, did not that intrusive meeting
interrupt the even tenor of his solemnities, and more
than once occur during his "long prayer?" He

knows.   Sundry women were in our meeting, and some
others of brethren.   We could scarcely have fallen
short of a dozen.   We took up the comparative claims
of the anti-slavery and new organization societies,
mainly for the sake of brother Cilley (not yet quite new
organized) ; read over the creed of new organization,
as set forth in the New Hampshire Abolition Society
constitution, and found it extremely *extraneous*.   We
were astonished at its impudent charges against anti-
slavery, and its open and shameless commission of the
very offences it had falsely charged upon us.   Brother
Cilley seemed hardly satisfied after all on " the woman
question."   The propriety of woman's acting on committees seemed to worry his mind.   We had supposed
that in the Free Will church woman's sphere was as
broad as man's, and that that order thought it no
shame for a woman to speak in a meeting, but an
honor rather and a duty.   Brother Cilley had scruples,
however, as to the propriety.   * * *   Anti-slavery
leaves woman and man and child free to equal action.
Freewillism *obliges* woman to speak, while it only
expects man, thus maintaining the darling masculine
prerogative and superiority.   Sister McCrillis rose at
length, after the evening was well nigh spent, and she
had not once opened her lips, and very significantly
asked permission to go home.   Her question seemed a
poser to brother Cilley's queries as to the proprieties,
and we thought at once relieved him of them all.   The
noble woman and her female fellow-attendants went
out, leaving us quite ashamed of the idea of questioning the right or the propriety of woman's doing in an
anti-slavery meeting as she thinks best.

What is exactly true of the connection of the northern Congregational, Presbyterian, and other large
evangelical christian bodies, acting together as Bible,
missionary and tract societies and associations, is, there
never was any real separation ; in the large bodies
they all acted together.   Individual churches sometimes for themselves, made protest and even a feeble
form of separation.   But Mr. Curtis, one of the most

anti-slavery ministers among them all, told us to what purpose. " Let the individual fellowship of the churches be left to themselves," he said after cutting connexion with the larger ecclesiastical bodies. But even that to any effective extent, was never done.

In 1842, Judge Birney revised and made more conclusive the argument in his work entitled " The American Churches the Bulwarks of American Slavery;" himself a leading member and ruling elder of the Presbyterian church when the book was written. In 1844, appeared, "The Brotherhood of Thieves; or a True Picture of the American Church and Clergy," taking up the argument where Mr. Birney had left off, besides greatly strengthening his, by multiplied proofs from the same sources.

In 1847, " The Church as It Is ; the Forlorn Hope of *Slavery*," appeared, bringing the action of the churches and clergy on the slavery question down to that time. A peculiarity of all these books was, the churches and ministers furnished the testimony, so that they were judged by their own words and works. · A division occurred in the general conference of the Methodist church. But the south, not the north, separated. And there still remained seven or eight annual conferences in the northern division, the boundaries distinctly discribed in the *Book of Discipline*. And on slavery the books of north and south read exactly alike, and it was shown clearly by Methodist testimony that there were still thousands of slave-holders and many thousand slaves in the northern general conference. The one unquestionable fact was, that though there were exceptions to the fearful charge, the system of slavery was supported by the government and sanctified by the religion of the nation, till the Infinite Patience could bear it no longer. The

trump of the avenging angel first sounded at Fort
Sumter, summoning north and south to their judgment
day. Nor could the dread call be resisted. At the
memorable field of Bull Run the two armies met face
to face. It was on a beautiful summer Sunday morning. The northern and the southern states, regiments
of Baptists, Congregationalists, Methodists, Presbyterians, Episcopalians, from Maine to Michigan ; regiments of the same denominations were up to meet
them from the shores of the Mexican gulf to Mason
and Dixon's line. Many of both armies must have
sometime sat together at the sacramental supper-tables
of the same denominational faith. But now their
hour had come. Now the warnings, entreaties and
expostulations of the faithful abolitionists were ended,
and their terrible predictions were to be fulfilled. On
that bright Sunday the two armies met in battle array.
Avenging Justice beheld them, and seizing the one in
His right hand the other in His left, dashed them together, dashed them in pieces, and gave frightful
multitudes of them their last sacrament ; not any more
in the blood of slaves sold for wine of communion,
but in the steaming battle blood of each other !

For days both sides claimed a victory. The rebel
commander-in-chief sent to his congress at Richmond
forthwith dispatches dated Sunday night, and commencing thus : "The night has closed upon a hard
fought field. The enemy were routed, and precipi-
tately fled, abandoning a large amount of arms, knap-
sacks and baggage. The ground was strewn for miles
with those killed, and the farm-houses and grounds
around were filled with the wounded. Pursuit was
continued along several routes till darkness covered
the fugitives."

Let readers mark those words, "the fugitives." New England, Boston even, had many noble sons in that fight ; and only a little while before New England, and even Boston, was returning *fugitive slaves* to their masters.   Who was He who once said, "With what measure ye meet, it shall be measured to you again ?" And what the Boston pulpit, what Andover Theological Seminary said, what nearly every evangelical doctor of divinity taught on the duty of returning fugitive slaves, shall be shown in some future chapter of these fearful chronicles.

CHAPTER VII.

ACTS CONTINUED, WITH PERSONAL SKETCH OF STEPHEN SYMONDS FOSTER.

The last chapter contained an account of a sally into the lecturing field in which Mr. Foster and myself were accompanied by our inestimable coadjutor, Mr. Rogers, of the *Herald of Freedom*. My next campaign was with Foster alone, and as some account of Mr. Garrison and Mr. Rogers has been given, it may be proper to advert briefly to some of the more general incidents in the early life of Stephen S. Foster. It has been already intimated that in this work only the acts of a small number of the anti-slavery apostles can be even named. There were many, both men and women, whose separate faithful labors, patient endurance of privations, perils, sacrifices and sufferings, earned for each one a volume larger and abler than this can possibly be. Men and women whose very names should only be spoken by those of cleanest lips and purest hearts.

Mr. Foster was born in Canterbury, New Hampshire, in November, 1809, son of Colonel Asa Foster, of revolutionary days. He was the ninth child of a family of thirteen.

The old Foster homestead is in the north part of Canterbury, on a beautiful hillside, overlooking a long stretch of the Merrimack river valley, including Concord, and a wide view east and west, as well as south. It includes several hundred acres, and is still owned by one of the Foster brothers.

Stephen left it early and learned the trade of a carpenter and builder.   In that, however, he did not come to his life occupation.   His parents were most devout and exemplary members of the Congregational church, to which he also was joined in youthful years.   At that time the call for ministers and missionaries, especially to occupy the new opening field at the west, called then " the great valley of the Mississippi," was loud and earnest.   At twenty-two he heard and heeded it, and immediately entered on a course of collegiate study to that end, and it is only just to say that a more consistent, conscientious, divinely consecrated spirit never set itself to prepare for that then counted holiest of callings.   Though assenting to the creed and covenant of his denomination, his whole rule of practical life and work was the " Sermon on the Mount," as interpreted and illustrated in the life and death of its author.

With him " Love your enemies" was more than words, and " Resist not evil" was not returning evil, nor inflicting penalties under human enactments.   And he went early to prison for non-appearance at military parade, armed with weapons of death.

In Dartmouth College he was called to perform military service.   On christian principles he declined, and was arrested and dragged away to jail.   So bad were the roads that a part of the way the sheriff was compelled to ask him to leave the carriage and walk. He would cheerfully have walked all the way, as once did George Fox, good naturedly telling the officer, " Thee need not go thyself ; send thy boy, I know the way ;" for Foster feared no prison cells.   He had earnest work in hand which led through many of them in subsequent years.

Eternal Goodness might have had objects in view in sending him to Haverhill, for he found the jail in a condition to demand the hand of a Hercules, as in the "Augæan" stables for its cleansing. His companions there were poor debtors, as well as thieves, murderers, and lesser felons. One man so gained his confidence as to whisper in his ear that on his hands was the blood of murder, though none knew it but himself. Another poor wretch had been so long confined by illness to his miserable bed, that it literally swarmed with vermin, crawling from his putrid sores.

Foster wrote and sent to the world such a letter as few but he could write, awakening general horror and indignation wherever it was read, and a cleansing operation was forthwith instituted. The filth on the floor was found so deep and so hard trodden, that strong men had to come with pick-axes and dig it up. And that jail was not only revolutionized, but the whole prison system of the state from that time began to be reformed ; and imprisonment for debt was soon heard of here no more.

His college studies closed, he entered, for a theological course, the Union Seminary in New York. Soon afterward there was threatened war between our country and Great Britain, over a short stretch of the northeastern boundary line, about which the two nations had disputed for half a century. Wholly opposed to war as was he, for any cause, he and a few of his friends proposed a meeting for prayer and conference, in relation to it as then menaced. Foster asked for the use of a lecture room for their purpose, but was surprised as much as grieved to find the seminary faculty not only opposed to granting the use of the room, but sternly against the holding of any such meeting.

That refusal, probably more than any other one event, determined his whole future course. For while in college he had had many serious doubts and misgivings as to the claim of the great body of the American church and clergy to the christian name and character ; not only because of their supporting war and approval of his incarceration for peace principles, but also for their persistent countenance of slaveholding and fellowship of even slave-breeders and slave-holders, as christians and christian ministers.

In 1839, Mr. Foster abandoned all hope of the Congregational ministry, and entered the anti-slavery service, side by side with Garrison, of the Boston *Liberator*, and Nathaniel Peabody Rogers, of the New Hampshire *Herald of Freedom*. And from that time onward till slavery was abolished, and indeed to the day of his death, the cause of freedom and humanity, justice and truth, had no more faithful, few if any more able champions.

In the autumn of 1845, he married Miss Abby Kelley, of Worcester, Massachusetts, then a well and widely - known lecturer on anti-slavery, temperance, peace, and other subjects pertaining to the rights and the welfare of man and womankind. She and a daughter, their only child, survive him. The daughter graduated first at Vassar College, then entered Cornell University, which she left at the end of the year, with the degree of Master of Arts.

I first saw Stephen Foster in the autumn of 1834. We were commencing teaching schools in adjoining districts of a small country town. A "revival of religion" soon appeared in the town, and was eminently powerful in his school, if, indeed, it did not commence there. His school was much larger than mine, and many of the parents were members, and some of them officers, of the Congregational church. They found in Mr. Foster a teacher, or at any rate a leader in religion, as well as in the literature of their school. And though most satisfactory progress was made in all the branches, and the discipline of the school was deemed throughout of the very best, nearly every scholar of or above fifteen years old was converted and joined the Congregational church ; and then their teacher and some of themselves came over as missionaries into my more remote and benighted district, and quite a work was accomplished there. The venerable minister of the town thought, and from the standpoint, and in the light of that day, thought truly, that, "with young Mr. Foster, evidently, was 'the secret of the Lord!'" And that same characteristic faithfulness he brought with him into the anti-slavery cause. And soon learning where was the great, deep, tap-root of the deadly upas, he laid the axe at the root of the tree.

His encounters with the church and ministry, the frequency with which his meetings had been and were still broken up by brutal mobs, not unfrequently justified by the pulpit and religious press, had made him a disciple to the Birney doctrine, "The American Churches the Bulwarks of American Slavery," long before this startling tract had come before the public.

Mr. Birney's experiences with the same power suggested his title ; but a few years later, another pamphlet appeared from Foster's own pen, entitled, "The Brotherhood of Thieves ; or a True Picture of the American Church and Clergy." Mr. Birney had already proved the pertinence and propriety of such a title in his little work ; but in a ringing book, of more than seventy pages, Foster showed, by super-abundant testimony, and every single witness furnished by the church itself, that if slavery were *man stealing*, as the Presbyterian church had declared it forty years before, and "*the highest kind of theft*," then surely the whole southern church was indeed a vast "*Brotherhood of Thieves!*" with their northern baptized brethren, who fellowshiped them as christians, their not less guilty accomplices!

Mr. Foster therefore made the popular, prevailing religions his main point of attack. What could he have done otherwise? The churches of the north were opened to southern slave-breeders, slave-traders, slave-hunters, and slave-holders, if members of the same, and often even of widely different denominations, both for preaching, baptizing and sacramental supper occasions and purposes. There were a few exceptions; but not enough to affect the general charge. Northern academies, colleges, universities, and theological seminaries, toned down their whole curriculum of moral and religious training and teaching to suit the depraved demand and taste of the whole brotherhood of southern slave-holders. And with most rare exceptions, the northern press attuned itself to the same key.

The religious public soon learned to dread Mr. Foster's presence or approach. Convicted of the most malignant pro-slaveryism, and by its own public records and reports of proceedings of ecclesiastical bodies and associations, from general assemblies, general conferences, and American Bible, missionary and tract societies, to state and county conferences and consociations, they had good reason to fear such a judgment-day before the time.

So there was a conspiracy among all classes of the people to conquer the abolitionists, "*by letting them severely alone.*" And in some states the clergy went so far as to issue pastoral letters to the churches, declaring that anti-slavery lecturers had no right to invade a people who had chosen a pastor and regularly inducted him into office ; nor had such a people any right to permit it.   A Massachusetts clerical mandate, duly published in the religious papers, signed by two congregational ministers, contained this paragraph :

When a people have chosen a pastor, and he has been regularly inducted into office, they have so far surrendered up to him the right to discharge the appropriate duties of his office in the parish over which he is settled, that they themselves can not send another to discharge those duties, *all or any part of them*, against his wishes, without an evident invasion of his territory.   Whoever comes before a parish under these circumstances is an intruder.   And equally so is he who, after being admitted by the pastor, sets up his judgment in matter that falls properly under the pastor's control.   These are both acts of trespass, and the perpetrators of them are or should be liable to ecclesiastical censure.   *The unfaithfulness or incapacity of the pastor is no apology for the offence.*

Nor was this law a dead letter in any place where it could possibly be enforced, whether in Massachusetts or anywhere in the north or west.

But the brave faithfulness of Mr. Foster to the enslaved and to his own solemn convictions, soon triumphed over such religious despotism.   He conceived the idea of entering the meeting houses on Sunday, and at the hour of sermon, respectfully rising and claiming the right to be heard then and there, on the duties and obligations of the church to those who were in bonds at the south.

This measure he first adopted in the old North church, at Concord, in September, 1841.   He was immediately seized by "three young gentlemen, one a southerner from Alabama, and the other two, guards at the state prison, thrust along the broad aisle and violently pushed out of the house." A full account of the transaction was published in the *Herald of Freedom* on the following Friday, 17th of the same month. But Mr. Foster could not be deterred from his purpose. And the measure proved so effective as a means of awakening the public attention to the importance of the anti-slavery enterprise, that others were led to adopt it. Of course it led to ·persecution, and some were imprisoned for the offence—Mr. Foster as many as ten or twelve times, in New Hampshire and Massachusetts. Perhaps his most memorable experience at the hands of the civil law, at the time, was in Concord, in June, 1842. On Sunday, the twelfth of that month, being in Concord, he went to the South church, and at the time for sermon he rose in a pew at the side of the pulpit, and commenced speaking in his usual solemn and deeply impressive manner. He evidently would have been heard, and with deep attention, too, for many in the house not only knew him well, but knew that this was a course not unusual with him, and one in the rightfulness of which he conscientiously believed, and, besides, was sometimes able to make most useful and effective. Even the Concord Unitarian society, one Sunday, gave respectful hearing ; the minister, Rev. Mr. Tilden, inviting him to speak.

But at the South church, it was not so. There he was seized by the then Secretary of State, others assisting, and forthwith carried by main force out of the house. The editor of the *Herald of Freedom* was present and saw the whole transaction, and in his next paper, gave a remarkably clear and full report of it. It is well worth reading and even study, by any who would understand the spirit and temper of those turbulent times.

As the whole affair was conducted, and as it finally resulted, it was not inappropriately called in the *Herald*, a mob. "A mob in the sanctuary called the South church. House ostentatiously dedicated to the worship of God. A mob begun in the pulpit by the anointed embassador of 'the prince of peace,' in midst of professed christian worship!"

At the close of the long prayer of morning service, during which, in those days, the congregation all reverently rose and stood, Foster remained standing and when the people were seated, he commenced in low, solemn and devout manner to say that he wished to speak a few words in behalf of two and a half millions of our kidnapped and enslaved countrymen. Nearly all appeared deeply attentive, and the scene was profoundly serious and impressive, as became the hour, the place and the theme.

But instantly, the minister from the pulpit called out with much anger, "Mr. Foster, we must not be disturbed in our worship!" At the same time a man high in authority, stalked across the house in front of the pulpit and seized him by the arm. But he had laid violent hand on no brawling disturber of the peace, nor of worship, but the equal in every way of the minister, and morally and spiritually, vastly his superior, as every moment demonstrated more and more. He was perfectly serene, gentle, orderly and respectful ; and that seemed the more to waken the pulpit indignation. He mildly asked the officer, who as yet confronted him alone, if such conduct as his became a christian, and if Jesus Christ ever interrupted respectful speaking in such a way, or forced anybody out of the house only for speaking? But the people

must not be permitted to hear him ; and as no one yet
had come to the rescue with the officer, he called up to
the choir to set the music going to silence him. Foster responded that he hoped the choir would not resort
to such means to silence his voice ; or if they should,
they could not repress the truth. But before this was
all uttered, the music was set going in full diapason
with all the spite of the vilest mob.

The music, of course, blasphemously silenced Foster ; but while it was performing, the officer, in true
posse comitatus manner and spirit, ordered up the sexton and several others, chiefly church members, if not
wholly, and some of them new organized abolitionists,
and seizing hold of him, carried him by main brute
force out of the house, he making no resistance nor
proffering any resistance by using his own strength or
limbs.

It was said in defense of the infamous act :
" They carried him gently out !" To that Mr. Rogers
responded the same week in the *Herald of Freedom* to
this effect :

Yes, very *gently*. They did not use a particle of
brute force, beyond what was necessary to effect their
brute purpose. But remember they laid hands on a
man and put him out of a house before all of the congregation, against his will, in contempt of his right of
speech, and in the deepest intended dishonor of his
person. The officer would have struck any man dead
who had thus profaned his official person. So would
that reverend minister. I thought the officer might
refrain from Foster while he remained silent. All was
hush, save the *devout* music ; that had restored the
interrupted worship and it was solemnly going on.
But they feared Foster might speak by and by, and so
thought they would put him out by anticipation.
* * * They laid hold of Foster when he was standing perfectly still (whether he had a right to speak or
no right), when all was hushed but the clamor in the

gallery, and lawlessly conveyed him out of the house of God. He meekly submitted to the infamous indignity. The minister looked on with all clerical complacency, from his curtained elevation. Nero would hardly have looked on with more when he fiddled at the burning of Rome. They laid their sacrilegious hands on Foster. I care not that they handled him *gently.* The outrage is that they handled him at all. It was an outrage most abhorrent to human feelings. The very law abhors it, sprung, as it was, from the dark ages of feudal England, and punishes its slightest touch of a man. But ecclesiastical supremacy knows no law. They trampled law under foot; and had they been outraging a man wicked as themselves, he would visit it upon them. But Foster is a christian, and they are safe. It was a flagrant breach of the peace, and a highly gross assault and battery, aggravated by outrage of the right of speech. * * * I saw Foster in their hands. It was an unusual sight. It was an abhorrent, unnatural sight. It was as a lamb in the hands of wolves. His countenance beamed with magnanimous christian expression. Several of the congregation indignantly left the house; I was among the number. At the bottom of the entrance stairs I found the abductors in a state of guilty agitation, on the verge of furious excitement. The officers hard breathing and most vivaciously at work shutting the folding doors and fastening them. * * * I could not help exclaiming, shame on you friends; shame on you for your conduct! "Do you want to go out or stay in, Mr. Rogers," said the excited officer. Go out, of course, said I, out of such a house as this. They shut all the doors and bolted them behind them with most cowardly care. We walked away pondering on the spirit of the worship we had left. Some women who came out after us found 'the doors locked, and had to go out through a round-about-way to a postern which was also locked from terror of Foster.

All this transpired at the morning service. In the afternoon, Mr. Foster felt constrained to enter the church again and attempt to speak a few words before the services commenced. All of his friends discouraged the attempt ; even Mr. Rogers counselled against it. He said he would no more go into that South church with those murderous stone stairs at the outlet, than he would walk into the Spanish inquisition. But Foster answered in the very spirit of the heroic apostle, Paul, when he asked his less brave brethren, " What mean ye to weep and to break my heart, for I am ready not to be bound only, but also to die for the name of the Lord Jesus." And he went again in the afternoon up those same " murderous stone stairs."

He commenced speaking as soon as he entered, and before the performances had begun. Immediately some young men, without order or authority even from the pulpit, most ferociously seized him, dragged him down the aisle and cast him down as far as the broad stairs of the ascent, from which he was forthwith, in the very spirit of most malignant murder, hurled down the entire stairway ; and then with kicks, hair-pulling and other indignities, thrown out on the ground. By this time the whole entrance was thronged with a violent vociferating mob, furiously, and some profanely, defending the sacredness of the meeting-house. Foster, pale, faint and disabled, lay on the ground, still at the mercy of the mob. Some of us took him up and tenderly assisted him to the then hospitable home near by, of Amos and Louisa Wood. Mr. Wood soon arrived and told us that after the outrage on Mr. Foster, he had risen in his pew to protest against such proceedings, and that the same officer who conducted the attack in the morning rushed upon him, and with others thrust him also, although a member of the church, out of the house.

Mr. Foster appeared so seriously injured that we

deemed it advisable to summon a physician. So it
fell on me to return and venture up the broad aisle of
that same perilous sanctuary, and call a doctor from
the base of the pulpit itself. No bones were broken
nor dislocated; but bruises and sprains rendered
walking difficult and painful for several weeks.

But only the tragic portion of this wondrous spectacle has yet been told. A farce followed more remarkable still, for the church and pulpit counted their
grievance so great as even to appeal to the civil courts
for redress. They well knew their victims were non-
resistants, both Mr. Wood and Mr. Foster, whose
rights they had so atrociously infringed, not to speak
of bodily ills inflicted, especially on Foster. Both
were christians in the sense and meaning of the Sermon on the Mount.   Both suffered imprisonment in
our then loathsome jails, rather than perform military
service or pay fines in money for non-appearance on
the murder-meaning, murder-breeding muster field.
So a suit at law would be perfectly safe at the worst.
And a suit was commenced on Monday afternoon.
Foster, only able to move about on a cane, was
arrested at the house of Mr. Amos Wood, where we
had taken him after his injury at the hands of the pulpit, the church and their then only too willing outside
defenders. Several of us had been informed that the
arrest was to be made, and had gathered there to witness the doing of it.

The sheriff was a most kind hearted man, and
appeared to appreciate properly the quality of the
business then in hand. Entering the room where we
were sitting, Mr. Foster in an invalid chair, he approached him, warrant in hand, and said : " Mr. Foster, I have authority here to take you before Judge
Badger, to answer to a charge of disturbing public

worship." Probably these are not the exact words spoken, but Foster, in the mildest manner possible, responded : " I do not know of any business between me and friend Badger requiring my attendance to-day, and must decline to answer to your call." Of course the sheriff insisted, as in duty bound, but in manner and spirit that contrasted strangely with the truly mob demeanor of the meeting-house on the day before. When he saw that if Foster went he must be carried, literally, he asked some of us present if we would be kind enough to assist him in bearing him out to his carriage, which we naturally declined. Then he said he should have to call in other aid. Foster good naturedly suggested that the minister and his aids of yesterday would be the proper persons on whom to call. The news of what was transpiring by this time was on many tongues and in many ears, and the excitement on the street was not small. It did not prove an easy matter to summon the *posse comitatus*. But finally one member of the church, and a working man not of the church, came in with the officer, and taking Foster gently in their hands and arms bore him bare headed to the door and placed him on the carriage seat. Foster, Rogers and others asked the non-church member why he didn't let the church do her own dirty work ? And the sheriff himself instead of arresting us, some of us being women, too, for thus attempting to obstruct the purposes of justice, only answered that it was " *a very unpleasant* duty to perform," which, knowing the man as we did, we well understood before. A crowd followed the prisoner to the judgment hall. It was on the second story, and the stairway being narrow it was truly a ludicrous operation for the officer and his posse to climb it with so unseemly a burden. Foster said afterwards himself that he felt rather serious than otherwise, till ascending the stairs, feet foremost high above his head, and yet handled with utmost caution, he could not help laughing outright, and did not recover his gravity again through the whole farcical trial.

As the editor of the *Herald of Freedom* was a lawyer and witnessed the court proceedings, probably readers would prefer his account in his own words. And in this they shall be gratified, copied literally, a few names omitted, from his columns of the same week :

The court room was thronged. Esquire Badger took his seat and read over the complaint in the hearing of Foster, charging him with "rude and indecent behavior," etc., "force and arms," etc., in the usual rigmarole of a criminal process, and asked him : "What say you, Mr. Foster, are you guilty or not guilty ?" Foster replied : "Friend Badger, I do not recognize you as my judge, nor shall I answer before you as a culprit. I am not your subject, and owe you no allegiance. As a brother man and equal I am willing to talk with you, on this or any other subject, but not as a magistrate." Friend Badger said the answer was not such as he wished. He wished him to say whether he was guilty or not guilty. Foster replied that he had his answer, and must put such construction on it as he saw fit.

The first witness was called and put on oath to tell the truth. It did not use to strike me so absurdly to hear a man sworn to tell the truth. He, the witness, said he was in the meeting house, saw Mr. Foster rise to speak, and Esquire S. immediately go to him and stop him, and take him out of the house. When asked if he did not interrupt the meeting by rude and indecent behavior, etc., he replied that he did not hear what he said. This was the substance, as I remember, of his testimony.

Capt. A. M. next presented himself as a witness. He is a member of the church that dragged Stephen out, and the same captain who shut Amos Wood up in the Black Hole at Hopkington, winter before last, for not being willing to train. Captain M. S.'s testimony was in effect the same as Captain S., who preceded. He didn't hear a word Foster said in the meeting. I think he gave it *as his opinion* that he interrupted, or disturbed the meeting by speaking, but did not tell what he said. When Captain M. retired, Captain W. came forward. Captain W. was also of the South church. He was sworn. He seemed competent to give all necessary testimony, within his knowledge, and not unreasonably backward to furnish it. He sat close by Foster, he said, in the meeting house, saw him stand up, and heard him speak, and thought what he said was a great disturbance of the meeting, etc., could not tell, however, what he said ; not a single word of it. He was asked if Foster behaved in a rude and indecent manner. Captain W. thought he disturbed the meeting very much, and that his speaking was contrary to the regulations of the South church. Foster asked him if speaking itself was contrary to the regulations, and when he said not, asked him who had a right to speak there? The captain answered, nobody but the minister. Foster asked him if it would be contrary to the regulations of the South church if he should come in during service time and give an alarm of fire? The captain replied in a grave manner that he did not choose to enter into that kind of conversation. But you are a witness, said Foster, and must answer all proper questions. He, however, did not answer. I will ask another question, said Foster : If your child should be kidnapped and carried off to the south, and I should learn of it in service time of the South church, and should come in and give the alarm, would you think that an interruption? The captain appealed to the court, and I think he was told he must answer ; for he did, and as I understood him said he should not think that an interruption. Suppose then, continued Foster, that two and a half millions of my countrymen should be kidnapped and sold into slavery, and I should come in in time of service and give the alarm, would that be violating the regulations of the South church? The

audience manifested great satisfaction at Foster's
questions.   The captain said thereupon, "These questions are asked for sport."   The testimony here closed
—not a word being sworn to of what Foster said, nor
any evidence given of rude or indecent behavior on
the part of anybody but the minister and the officer
who first laid hands on Foster.   One spectator said,
" Discharge him ; " another, as he left the room, said,
" This is a farcical piece of business ; " a third said,
" There isn't a particle of evidence against Foster ; "
still another asked me, "What will the court do?"
Convict, I answered.   "On what ground?" he asked :
I said :   I cannot tell on what ground, I only think he
will convict him.

Early in the trial Esquire Whipple, (the prosecutor)
read the law on which the complaint was founded.
Toward the close of the examination, Foster glanced
his eye over it and discovered that it was not in force,
that it had been repealed.   He observed to the court
pleasantly, that he did not wish to interfere in their
proceedings, but he believed they were trying him
upon a statute that was not in force.   He did not wish
them to be at the trouble of going over the business
twice, he said, and he had not the time to spare himself.   He had had occasion in his dealings with other
churches to look at the law, and told them what it was
and where they would find it.   Hereupon a burst of
applause broke from all parts of the audience, which
lasted considerable time.   Esquire Whipple looked
amused and Esquire Badger a little *put to it*.   However, Foster set them on the right track as to the law,
and after awhile all went on again.   Come to read the
law through, it was plain as noon-day to every one
that it contemplated no such case as Foster's.   So
they had no law against him, and no facts.

Friend Badger then went out and was gone some
minutes.   I thought it might be to consult higher
authorities as to the course to be taken with a criminal
against whom there was neither law nor proof.   Still,
I had a presentiment he would convict.   He returned
and resumed his seat.   He asked Mr. Foster if he had
anything to say in his defense.   Foster replied,

he made no defense, that what he said was not
said to the court, but to the audience. I am in
your power I know — you can fine me or imprison
me. You know I have done no wrong. No one has
said aught against me. One witness gave his opinion
that I had interrupted the meeting ; but he had no
right to give opinions, he was a witness, he should
give facts. You know I have done nothing amiss. If
I had, why was not Daniel Noyes, the minister, here to
testify against me ? He sat where he could see all
that I did. I have done no wrong. He and Stevens
and those who violated my rights of speech and of
person, why do you not prosecute them instead of
me ? It is not my duty said Friend Badger. It is your
duty upon your own principles, replied Foster. I cannot prosecute. It is contrary to my principles. You can,
and are bound to. The injury is not against me. It
is against the State, and you know their guilt and are
bound to prosecute them. But do with me as you
please.

Esquire Badger then gave sentence. He would
protect an anti-slavery meeting, he said, as soon as any
other meeting, if it was disturbed. He would do
justice to Mr. Foster as soon as to anybody else.
(Thought I, Friend Badger, you had better not give
reasons, but convict and say nothing.) He went on to
say "The complaint was broad enough to cover the
case." Sure enough ; but then, there was no evidence to sustain it. He said nothing about any evidence. The complaint is broad enough he said to
cover the case, and he declared Foster guilty, and
fined him five dollars and the costs ! ! An expression
of disapprobation, amounting pretty near to sovereign
contempt, manifested itself throughout the court
room ! The champions of the church had already
sneaked off. A man like Nathan Stickney must have
been ashamed of the decision. T. C., who was about,
(looking sheepishly enough,) hither and thither during the trial, exerting what malign influence he could
covertly, would not be so scrupulous as to the kind of
victory, or mode of obtaining it. He looked as though
he would enjoy a sentence against Stephen Foster to

that pestilential dungeon at Hopkinton for twenty years, for the quiet of the South church.   And he is an *anti-slavery man!*   He is, I believe, secretary of New Hampshire new organization.

As soon as the magnificent sentence was pronounced, the friends of humanity present (not abolitionists neither, professedly, though nearer being so than they are aware of) rushed to the table and threw down the money to pay it.   I would give their honored names, but it adds nothing, *yet*, to any man's reputation with the world to be commended in the *Herald of Freedom*. They are well known here.   They make no sectarian profession, but if not in the kingdom of heaven, they are nearer to it infinitely, than the miserable pro-slavery devotees of the meeting-house.   Foster thanked them in the fullness of a grateful heart, but protested respectfully against their paying.   It will be better for the cause, said he, that I suffer.   I can go to their jail, seeing they have unlawfully doomed me there.   Others are there now.   But no heed was paid to his remonstrance.   Everybody felt deeply that he was a persecuted, injured, innocent and faithful man ; and entertained the profoundest contempt and indignation at the hypocritical priest and the mobocratic official of the State, who had outraged and injured him.

The tide of humanity ran too strong for the *legal* opinions of friend Badger.   He seemed to find he had mistaken the current.   He had fined an innocent man, prosecuted by the church, five dollars, and the PEOPLE were against it.   He had not anticipated that.   The church minions had slunk away.   The table was covered with more money than was wanted.   Friend Badger caught the general feeling and *remitted* the fine.   The friends immediately passed the money over to Foster, who told them he would spend it in the anti-slavery cause.

The whole article, from which this account is but an extract, fills more than seven solid columns of the *Herald of Freedom*, and the names and titles of persons are given in full, and especially those most prominent in the shameful transaction.   Perhaps it were

better that they had been all given in the same manner and continued in this extract.   Almost all the
parties, official and unofficial, are now dead ; many of
them died long ago, even those who led the mob outrages at the church door where Foster received his
bodily injuries.   The court room during the trial,
which lasted through the most of an afternoon, was
crowded with an audience whose sympathies at the
beginning were doubtless quite evenly divided, for
Concord was at that time by no means an anti-slavery
town.   But when the complaint was read, solemnly
charging the accused, who was a well-known, consistent peace man and non-resistant, with "force and
arms," and "rude and indecent behavior," the whole
scene assumed a ludicrous aspect only.   As the trial
proceeded, however, it soon became manifest that
malice and spite instigated the arrest, and that summary vengeance was to be inflicted, however unjust.
Then when Foster so serenely corrected the court in
its knowledge of law, telling just when the law was
repealed, and where, and at whose desire, and exactly
for what purpose the law then existing to protect
public religious meetings was enacted, all of which he
showed to the full satisfaction of the court, the burst
of admiring applause was as general and hearty as it
was long continued.   Not was there any attempt to
suppress it.   That was the verdict of humanity and
justice, instinctively rendered, with voice and power
irresistible.

And when Judge Badger remitted the fine, which
doubtless gave him great pleasure, though he trans-
cended his authority in doing so, there was another
demonstration of delight, at which Sheriff Pettingill
stepped forward and told him he would remit his fees
with the fine, and take nothing for his services.   To

which the judge good naturedly responded that he would not be outdone in magnanimity, and would throw in his charges with the rest, and Mr. Foster might be discharged. The demonstration which succeeded needs no description, no report.

But there was yet one more incident worthy of mention. Judge Badger beholding the generous pile of silver which had been tossed on his table, asked, "What shall be done with all this money?" "Give it to Foster, give it to Foster," was shouted out from all over the yet crowded room. Carried by acclamation. It was done. Sheriff Pettingill then gave Foster his hand and said, "Now if you will step into my carriage I will be very happy to take you back to your lodgings." The offer was cordially and gratefully accepted by our weary and suffering friend, and thus ended the day with its strange and wondrous disclosures and deeds.

But perhaps narration should not close without a brief mention of two or three meetings held immediately, to consider the right and propriety of so liberal construction of the rights of speech and worship, as were attempted by Mr. Foster and countenanced by Mr. Wood. Both being members of the state anti-slavery executive committee, that committee united with them in a formal call for such expression. And a committee was appointed to extend a special invitation to the clergy of the town to attend and participate in the deliberations. But the clergy did not come, though the people did, in number and quality, too, much to their surprise. Mr. Foster vindicated himself in the course he pursued, by the example of Jesus Christ and his apostles, who were both dragged out of the synagogues by the church and clergy of their time. He showed that Christ enjoined on his disciples to enter those places, and assured them that they would be scourged in the synagogues and dragged out, and that there would come a time when whosoever should kill them, would think he did God service. He showed that the modern synagogue was even more intolerant and persecuting than the ancient Jewish. For there Christ and His apostles were even invited to speak, and never were disturbed for speaking, but only for what they spoke. But he said you drag me out of your christian houses of worship only for attempting in a respectful and christian manner, to be heard, not knowing what I would say. And you haul me before the magistrates and thrust me into prisons, and may yet kill me for only attempting to do what Christ and His apostles could and did do, unmolested, in all the places for worship of their time. It was only when they rebuked the hypocrisy and wickedness of the worshippers, that they were accused of disturbing the worship, and thrust out accordingly. Mr. Foster was just recovering from the severe injuries he had suffered at the hands of the South church, and perhaps never in his life spoke with more pathos and power. And the whole sympathy, if not sentiment, of his crowded audience was with him. The following resolution was on the table for discussion :

Resolved, That the conduct of Stephen S. Foster and Amos Wood, in attempting to speak in behalf of our enslaved countrymen, in the South church on Sunday last, without leave of the minister, was a gross and flagrant outrage on the prerogatives of the clergy and the rights of the people, and should be most unequivocally condemned by every friend of good order and lover of liberty.

The editor of the *Herald* in his report, said : " Only one voice answered in favor of the resolution, and that was an abortive, faint remanded *yea*, taken back in its very birth and sounding ludicrously with the thundering *no*, which followed upon it.   This must have been gratifying to our lame and suffering brother Foster, who was still undergoing great pain from the *christian handling* of the church.   Though it would not have shaken his faith, his own firm faith, had the response or the responses of all men, been the other way."

Most of the leading abolitionists, including Mr. Garrison, Wendell Phillips, and others in Massachusetts, doubted the wisdom of Mr. Foster's course in thus entering the Sunday congregations, where only the stated minister was expected to speak.   But none who knew him intimately ever doubted his entire honesty, indeed deep, solemn conviction of religious duty, in what he did, and in all that he did.   The clergy were not behind the most depraved politicians in their determination to prevent the people, both in and outside the churches, from learning the truth on a problem which every abolitionist knew full well involved the national preservation or destruction, accordingly as it might be solved.   The whole nation came to understand it rightly at last ; but not till its eyesight had been washed and clarified in blood and tears.

Mr. Foster, having adopted and proved the great utility of his new method, persisted in it until it was demonstrated that no other had ever subserved so good a purpose in arousing the whole nation to its duty and danger.   Nothing like or unlike it, before or afterward, so stirred the whole people, until John Brown, with his twenty heroes, marched on Harper's Ferry and challenged the supporters of slavery to mortal combat.

One reason that Foster often gave for his extreme action, as well as utterance, was, that ends sometimes

justified any means, He would say, "should I see
your house on fire, and yourselves and families in
danger of instant death in the flames, must I go and
gently knock and wait till you come and unlock the
door before notifying you of your peril? Or, suppose
I saw a church full of worshipers, with the roof all
ablaze, would they be likely to drag me out should I
rush in, unbidden, and shout, fire, fire, at the top of
my voice?" And then he would say, "your whole
country is in extremest peril. Your whole country is
on fire. Every one of you should tremble, like
Thomas Jefferson, *'remembering that God is just, and
that His justice cannot sleep forever !'*" But as we now
know, he was not believed; though his words could
not have been more true, had they been in very deed
inspired by the Holy Ghost.

Another argument he often urged with great pertinency and force, based on christian scripture, too,
and the practice of the Apostolic church :

The great apostle, Paul, gave direction for conducting worship ; and at this time neither Paul nor Jesus
had a more devout disciple than Foster ; nor the Congregational church a more holy, conscientious and
consistent member. The apostolic injunction simply
was, that order be preserved, though every one, having psalm, doctrine, interpretation or revelation, should
be heard, each in turn. And then, to close, is
added, "For ye may all prophesy one by one ; that all
may learn and all be comforted." So, too, the example and practice of Jesus Christ in the Jewish synagogues, he would cite, as already shown, with much
point and power. "True," he would say, "the people
sometimes dragged him out as you do me. But it was
not because he spoke ; it was for what he said." It
was always his claim, as with both Christ and Paul,

that, "where the spirit of the Lord is, there is liberty," and liberty of speech preëminently.

When the people came to his meetings he never went to theirs. If the ministry kept away, and, as they generally did in those days, endeavored to keep the people away, he went to them as frequently as possible, at whatever cost. If imprisoned, as many times he was, he comforted himself that he not only " remembered them that were in bonds *as* bound with them," but that he actually *was bound with them*, and for their sake ; and verily, he had in it great reward.

Whoever attended his meetings always had the largest liberty of speech, no matter how widely they differed from him. He asked only two things of an opponent : first, that good temper and spirit be kept, and second, that both parties keep strictly to the question in hand. And sometimes he would hold his audiences till midnight.

Probably he encountered more mob opposition and violence than any other agent ever in the anti-slavery lecturing field. But almost always he would in some way obtain control of his opponents. There were exceptions. Once he had four meetings broken up in a single week. Though in Portland he suffered more by violent hands than in the South church at Concord, he was finally rescued and borne off in triumph by a band of noble and heroic women. Not, however, till he had suffered much bodily harm and the loss of his hat and other parts of his clothing. His traveling companion, Rev. John Murray Spear, was worse handled than he. He was carried to his home at the hospitable house of an anti-slavery family, and confined to his chamber for a number of weeks. There was suffering as well as heroism, in those days.

On the island of Nantucket, mob violence became such that a course of lectures Foster had commenced was cut short, and he was advised to leave the place by his friends, which he did, though before he left they desired him to write a letter at his earliest convenience, explanatory of his course, and in further illustration and proof of some of his positions.   His answer to that reasonable request was, *The Brotherhood of Thieves: or, a True Picture of the American Church and Clergy ;* in some respects the most remarkable pamphlet of seventy-two closely-printed pages that the anti-slavery, or any other enterprise of reform has ever produced.   It was published in 1843.   It defied contradiction, both as to doctrine and declaration.   It passed through many editions, and went everywhere, east and west.   And no matter who, or what power and influence abolished slavery, that work stands unrefuted and unrefutable ; and shall stand a monument to the moral and material heroism, ability, fidelity, and disinterestedness of its author, till time shall be no more.

Distinguished abolitionists were often called men of one idea.   Anti-slavery, in its immeasurable importance to all the interests of the country, material, mental, moral, and social, as well as religious, and political, was one idea far too great for ordinary minds, even without any other.   But the sturdy symmetry and consistency of Mr. Foster's character were as wonderful as were his vigor and power in any one direction. Earliest and bravest among the temperance reformers, when even that cause was almost as odious as anti-slavery became afterward ; a radical advocate of peace from the standpoint of the Sermon on the Mount, "Resist not Evil," seconded by the apostolic injunction, "Avenge not yourselves ;" a champion in the woman suffrage enterprise from its inception ; an intelligent, earnest advocate of the rights of labor, and deeply interested in all the educational and moral, social and philanthropic associations for the advancement and improvement of the city and neigh- borhood where he lived, he left behind him a record and a memory to grow brighter as the years sweep on; and his virtues becoming more and more luminous, shall be the better appreciated by multitudes who learn to profit by them.

The beauty and harmony of his home were unsur- passed. It was sacred to peace and love. Its unosten- tatious but elegant and generous hospitality was the admiration of all who ever enjoyed it, by day or night. At almost seventy-two, he passed away on the 8th of September, 1881, deeply lamented by many true and devoted friends, whose respect, admiration and affection he had won by a long life intensely devoted to the highest interests of man and womankind.

But it is time for Mr. Foster and myself to return to the lecturing field.

On a cold, cloudy afternoon in early winter, we left Concord for a short campaign, to commence in that part of Pembroke now known as Suncook. At that time it was a neighborhood of a dozen houses, mostly small, one store, a tavern of the class then known as "Meadow-hay taverns," and a brick school-house, elbowed a little to one side, and in which we were to hold our meeting. The road was rough and hard frozen, the day was cold, and my old open wagon unfurnished with buffalo robes. But we were young and tolerably vigorous, and cared little for such trifles, well warmed within with an earnest purpose, we could resist a good deal of wind and weather. We intended to reach an anti-slavery family on our way, in time for

tea and then go on with them to the meeting, a mile
or two beyond. But when we arrived, tea was done
and nothing was said about it, though a ride of some
miles over a frozen, rough road, after a busy afternoon
of preparation for the tour, seemed to argue strongly
in favor of some refreshment, the prospective evening
work emphasizing the necessity. So we fasted, and
my patient pony, Tunbridge, communed meantime with
the stone hitching-post at the gate. In due season, we
started for the meeting, the family carriage leading
the way. The people were gathering in goodly numbers and, tying Tunbridge to a tree and covering her
well in her warm blanket, we entered the school-house
and were soon at our wonted business. Our meetings
were always open to, and often lively and late with
free discussion. So it proved on that evening ; and
when we did close, it was after ten o'clock, and Foster
and myself found ourselves left entirely alone in the
house, and our horse and wagon outside, fastened to
a tree.

For special reasons it should be told here that when
we entered the service of the State Society, we found
it in debt to the editor and publishers of the *Herald
of Freedom*, two thousand dollars ; nor did it own any
printing-press, type, nor other office appointments.
Our first business then seemed to be of a financial
character, and Mr. Foster entered into it with his
characteristic energy and fidelity. Most of the debt
was due to the editor, contracted while patiently performing work of unsurpassed ability, fidelity and
devotion to the cause of liberty and humanity. Foster conceived the plan of funding the debt and dividing it into shares of five dollars each, in all amounting
to four hundred shares. Any individual might take
one share or more according to ability or inclination,

and two persons could unite in taking one share. No payment was to be required till all the shares were secured, and to the lasting honor and credit of Mr. Rogers, it should be told that his own subscription to the shares amounted to almost half the sum due him.   To dispose of these shares was, of course, an important part of the business of our meetings where there was prospect of any success ; and our own compensation by a general collection, was never named till all the shares possible, were secured.   And my own salary that year was exactly three hundred and four dollars and forty-eight cents, and that not all collected in cash.   And Foster certainly was not better paid.   Whether at that Pembroke meeting we passed round the hat for ourselves I do not remember, but we did secure a few shares to the debt.   At all events, when the meeting closed, we were left entirely alone.

Our only recourse was the " Meadow-hay tavern," down in the village.   No reproach to the then keeper of the house that such were sometimes so misnamed. I had met him before and knew him as a worthy man. We drove down, but found the house closed and the family all in bed.   But the hostler, as was then universal custom, slept in a " bunk," as it was called, in the barroom.   Not quite Goldsmith's :

* * * " bed by night and chest of drawers by day,"

but still subserving some such purpose.   With not much difficulty we waked the hostler and he appeared and let us in.   We told him we were sorry to disturb him but we were strangers and wished accommodation for ourselves and horse over night.   He said he could feed our horse but that he could do nothing for us, beyond giving us a bed.   So I went with him to the stable, saw our Tunbridge well fed and cared for, and the wagon placed under cover, and at eleven o'clock, we went supperless to our bed. That, we shared together, as the best our *vice* landlord could do for us at that hour of the night.

Our next engagement was away across the country at Epsom, a long drive over rough and hilly roads, and we were to commence at one o'clock. Before sunrise I was at the stable with the hostler attending to my mare. When Foster appeared, we went into a store opposite, and invested four cents in baker's biscuits, and four more in raisins ; and sitting down by the stove, we made our supper of the previous night and our breakfast for that morning out of our purchase. And, whole truth to tell, Foster had no money and I had left most of my own small amount with my lonely little wife at home, so that we were only living as we could afford. The wife of an anti-slavery apostle then, enjoyed no enviable lot.

And this may be the place to repeat of my own wife, that she supposed, and all her friends supposed, and I supposed and all my friends supposed that when she wedded, it was to a Congregational minister who had, even while a theological student remarkable experiences and successes in revivals of religion, and had besides four invitations from parishes in New Hampshire and Massachusetts to preach as a candidate for settlement. But while preaching a year as a hired supply, it became unmistakably certain that I could never do any good, honest, hearty anti-slavery work, such as the nation and the times demanded, and retain my standing in the Congregational pulpit. I found the neighboring ministers were prowling about among the church and people of my congregation whispering surmises that my anti-slavery zeal and my intimacy with the "Infidel Garrison," and the already suspected Rogers were shaking my own orthodoxy too.

And one day a member of our church was sent to remind me that the brethren were fearing I was getting too much in the way of preaching *works* instead of faith as the means of salvation. He brought me several texts, such as : " By grace are ye saved through faith ;" and others of like import, a whole foolscap page of them, the last being : " Not of works lest any man should boast." I pleaded guilty as to the charge of dwelling more on *works*, and gave as reason that I thought we failed less in faith than in works. But he did his errand and went his way. And I went mine, though it soon led a long way from that and every other pulpit. · But more about this hereafter. Possibly a·good deal more. Here it need but be said that it was only after serious, solemn considera- tion that my resolution was formed. That however hardly made the disappointment less, to wife, or her friends, or mine, and, possibly, to myself least of all.

But our breakfast over we returned to the tavern, on which the sun had not yet risen. I greeted the landlord and called for our bill. " Bill," he said good naturedly ; " bill, why, you don't owe anything, do you ?" He knew we could have had no supper, and the tavern breakfast bell had not yet rung. So I explained to him that our last evening meeting held late, and that we had to drive to Epsom for another there to-day at one o'clock. So we had to catch a bite at the grocery across the street, and get on our way, but that we owed him for horse-keeping and our lodging. He poured a good natured glass of satire· on our anti-slavery friends who would treat us so gen- erously, and said we might pay him half a dollar if we had a mind to, for our horse, but for us he should charge nothing. So we were soon off for Epsom. The morning was fine, but the roads were hilly and

rough, so that when we arrived it was time to commence, and a good audience had assembled, some
from several miles away. The days were at the shortest, and we were to hold an evening meeting, so that
there was not much time to be lost. It was quite sun-
set when we closed. A Mr. Sanborn came and said
we had better go home with him to supper, as probably no other family would invite us, and there was no
tavern in the town. He told us he and his family were
anti-slavery, and kept to the old organization, and
would be extremely glad to entertain us, though he
lived two miles away, and up the mountain besides.
And he also said, and much to my joy, that we need
not take our horse out in the evening, as we could be
brought back in the family wagon, "Catamount
hill," as it was and is called, proved to us the " Delectable mountains" of Bunyan's pilgrims. We had two
interesting meetings, but New Organization had
preceded us and captured the church and minister, so
that those who aided us there, as elsewhere, with hospitality, with sympathy, or otherwise, were outside of
the sectarian folds. The experiences of Monday and
Tuesday were a fair average of the experiences of the
week, for we reached Concord on Monday, having
been absent eight days ; and we had held one or two
meetings every day. A snow storm came in the time,
and we were compelled to have our Tunbridge winter
shod in consequence. We had had some success in
disposing of our shares to the debt, but beyond that
our financial operations would not to-day be pronounced a success. On reckoning up we had exactly
thirty-seven cents more than when we set out, and
that was in my hands. I did not smile if Foster did,
when he said : " Well, Parker, I have no wife and
you have ; so this time we will not divide." Nor prob-

ably did my wife smile heartily when I reached home
and disclosed to her the situation.   We made our supper of plain coarse bread and butter.   But next morning, to my wonderment, we had just the same for
breakfast.   In a joking way I complained of her fare,
and said something about a new boarding house unless she set a better table.   The wit was a little too
cool and deposited a dew drop or two in her eye and
down her cheek, as she told me her money was out,
and she did not like to break our resolution, never to
be in debt.   It would have been in order then for my
eye to reflect back her's, but a rainbow in her sky
seemed to me just then the needed return.   It was
true we determined in our little forty dollars a year
rent never to be in debt ; but her health then was not
as robust as mine.   Such a breakfast was soon dis-
patched, and nearly as soon I was on the street to
break our good resolution, if there was strength in my
credit to do it.   Mr. Franklin Evans then (as I believe ever since) kept an excellent general country
store, and readily consented to trust me for whatever
was needed.   When I asked for my first and costliest
article, which was fourteen pounds of good flour, he
advised my taking a half barrel, as more economical.
But I declined his generous proposal, and kept my bill
within three dollars, though some nice butter and sugar
were in my purchase.   Before bed-time three dollars
came from some unexpected source, with which the
debt was paid as promised, and wife and I slept that
night as before from our marriage, "owing no man
anything, but to love one another."   And it is only
truth and justice to say that from that night, the
handful of meal and cruse of oil never wholly failed
    our humble home.

CHAPTER VIII.

ACTS OF THE APOSTLES CONTINUED—LETTER OF CON-
CORD WOMEN—CLERICAL USURPATION—MORE REVE-
LATIONS OF NEW ORGANIZATION—RIOTOUS PROCEED-
INGS AT DOVER—BY THE EDITOR OF THE HERALD OF
FREEDOM.

As we are now back in Concord, we will once more
recur briefly to the South church. Readers doubtless
have seen, if not deplored, some repetition in previous
chapters—only necessary till they become acquainted
with the persons and the principles mostly presented in
these pages for their consideration.

It is now proposed to present a new phase of anti-
slavery action and effort, in which all could bear active part who chose. Concord South Congregational
church had several excellent men and women, who
had made themselves quite offensive to the minister
and some prominent members by their fidelity to the
anti-slavery cause. Some had even withdrawn, both
from communion supper service and Sunday worship.
Some were women who were denied all speech or
prayer, in private as well as public assemblies. They
addressed a formal communication to the church, expressive of their views and determinations, and then
withdrew wholly from such fellowship.

And in presenting that letter here it should be said
that the same course became common, if not general,
·among genuine abolitionists all over the country, until
the sect known as *Come-outers* grew to be numerous,
and odious, too, to all who lacked courage or honesty
to imitate that entirely scriptural course. Great
numbers of these church withdrawal letters are before

me in the bound volumes of anti-slavery papers, some of them of diamond points ; those of Mr. and Mrs. Rogers among them.   New organized and third political party abolitionists displayed most fiery zeal at the ballot box once or twice a year ; would vote for no whig nor democrat to fill the meanest office.   At the baptismal and sacramental altar whig and democrat shrunk into " gnats," and were swallowed in the communion wine, who, on Monday at the polls, swelled into larger " camels" than ever were exhibited at Barnum's menagerie.   Not so the women, nor some of the husbands of the women who addressed the subjoined

Letter to the South Congregational church in Concord, under the pastoral care of Daniel J. Noyes:

DEAR BRETHREN AND SISTERS :—We, the undersigned, members of the South Congregational church in this town, feel bound in duty to God and man to address to you the following communication :

Three millions of our fellow beings are living in our midst under the following circumstances :   The family institution is abolished among them—husbands and wives, parents and children, are torn asunder to gratify the cupidity of their oppressors ; they are punished as felons for any attempt to learn to read the Holy Gospel ; parents are liable to be scourged and punished with death for teaching their children the way of life and salvation by Jesus Christ.   Eight thousand children are annually stolen, labeled as property and converted into merchandize.   One sixth of the population of this nation are driven to incessant and unrequited toil from the dawn of life to its close. Three millions of God's immortal children, our brethren and sisters, are held and used among us as chattels personal, and bought and sold as brute beasts. Parents not unfrequently sell their own children. Thus a cloud of frightful, perpetual night is drawn over millions of souls in this land of Bibles and professed christian ministers and churches.

The American church and clergy constitute a main pillar of support to this system of unutterable crimes and woes. Thousands and tens of thousands are received as christians and christian ministers who are identified with this system as slave-holders and apologists for slavery. These millions of imbruted slaves, our brethren and sisters, are fallen among thieves and robbers by your church door. The church has refused to pour in the oil and the wine. Both pastor and church have acted the part of priest and Levite to these suffering beings. By your silence as a church you are lending the most efficient support to this system. You fellowship man-stealers as christians and christian ministers.

We owe it as a duty to Him who hath loved us and died for us, and to our suffering brethren and sisters in bonds, to refuse all participation in slavery. We feel that we do participate in that sin while we recognize any body of men and women as a christian church that refuses to bear an open, clear and solemn testimony against it.

With such views and feelings we can no longer recognize you as a christian church while as a body you continue in your present position of silence to the wrongs of the slave. * * *

* * * And we furthermore feel bound to protest against the spirit of a church which could prompt to the exclusion of two of its most worthy members, who, that they might keep a conscience void of offense towards God and towards man, have absented themselves for a season from your meetings ; while others far behind them in spiritual attainments, and over whom you have solemnly promised to watch, are guilty of the same offense, and are suffered to remain without advice, warning or expostulation.

May we all be directed by that wisdom which cometh from above, and at last be reunited in the church triumphant.

LOUISA W. WOOD,
ESTHER W. CURRIER,
MARY ANN FRENCH,
SARAH H. PILLSBURY.

CONCORD, N. H., January 16, 1841.

The last signer of this letter supposed, when she married, one year before, that she was the wife of a reputable and very promising young Congregational minister, and a large and highly conservative circle of family connections, one or two of them members of this same South church, and all of them of the best society in Concord, presumed the same. It can readily be supposed that at that time it required no little heroism in a young woman of two or three and twenty, thus to come out from all church, and family, and society relations, and continue her future destiny with an anti-slavery lecturer who had also made himself doubly odious by renouncing church, pulpit, and society and party affiliations and united himself with Garrison, Rogers and the school of "Come-outers," already more odious, if possible, than any other infidelity or heresy of those days. It may be added that most of the relatives of that then young wife, are now no more of earth, but such as do remain, have come, and not recently neither, to hold her in high and well deserved esteem. The other signers of the letter, who survive, are, and ever have been, among the truest and noblest women in the land. And all of them lived to prove to the world that in their whole anti-slavery course, they were guided by the highest, divinest dictates of conscience and humanity.

The next movement of Mr. Foster and myself was into the counties of Rockingham and Strafford. Wherever we went our great difficulty was to reach the ear of the people. The clergy, especially the new organization clergy, seemed most incorrigible, most unscrupulous of all. They appeared, as already intimated, to have conspired together against us. The following extract from one annual report of the Vermont Domestic Missionary society, signed by

Rev. Samuel Delano, corresponding secretary, "in behalf of the directors," gives the sentiment of that numerous and powerful body, embracing the strength of the whole Congregational and Presbyterian church of that state :

The ministers are the heads of the churches—the leaders in the sacramental host of God's elect. No measure can be carried without them, much less in opposition to them. And scarcely any proper measure can fail to succeed, when the ministry put forth their power. In view of this fact, it is asked, with the utmost earnestness, ought they not, and in view of their obligations and of the glorious results sought, will they not come up to this work, and lead on the churches? The churches can be reached in no other way. No man can approach a church when the pastor interposes. He cannot, and he may not if he can. To give Vermont to Christ—this is the peculiar work of the church of Vermont. It is the field given to these ministers and churches to cultivate and keep.

Rev. Dr. Lyman Beecher, at the seventeenth annual meeting of the American Home Missionary Society, in a resolution, presented the necessity "of a stated evangelical ministry, as eminently the power of God for the conversion of the world." In his address, he spoke mainly in behalf of the ' " great west." He supported his resolution with characteristic force as against a transient ministry, pointing, perhaps, to the Methodist policy of rotation or change. Summing up, he said :

A stated ministry unites society by strong bonds. A good pastor is a sort of *central power* in society. He holds the affections of those with whom he dwells, and becomes a patriarch among them * * * * Instances of the effects thus produced might easily be mentioned. I could tell you of a minister who having preached in a place fifty years became the *patriarch* of the village. And once when a lecturer came there whom he thought unsafe, he put on his gown and wig and cocked hat, and walked up one side of the street and told his people they had better not go, and then walked in the same way down the other side, and every soul staid at home ! All that is healthful in society, finds support in the stated ministry.

We found clerical authority like that in full force in many a country town, so that much of our work was actual invasion. "The kingdom of heaven suffering violence and the violent taking it by force." In the town of Northwood, we found the minister, was in every important sense the "village patriarch" after the very heart of Dr. Beecher. He would not give our notice, and no public notice had been given of our meetings, which we intended should continue two evenings. And when Foster called on him and solicited the use of his vestry and his own attendance and coöperation, he quite spiritedly refused having anything to do with him. The vestry, however, was not too holy to be used for whig and democratic caucus and convention, not always conducted in very orderly or decent manner. A mile away from the church we had the use of a school-house two evenings, as at first intended. We spent the cold day in going from house to house, endeavoring to waken an interest in our movement. At the first meeting but few came, and they men and boys only. One glimmering tallow-dip and a small glass lantern made almost a vain attempt to show us to each other. After prayer, with which we then opened our meetings, we introduced a resolution, declaring all not actively engaged in the anti-slavery enterprise, to be by position if not in spirit, slaveholders. Such a charge brought several of the staunchest advocates of slavery and ablest men of the town to their feet. A lawyer and an old academy preceptor defended slavery from the Bible. And both pleaded earnestly the cause of the church and pulpit against our charges as deduced from the resolution presented. The ex-preceptor said he had lived at the South among slaveholders and that our "*Southern brethren,*" emphasizing the words, were "as high minded, hospitable and pious a people as could be found on this globe." And moreover, that no happier class of persons could be found anywhere than the slaves. Indeed, he earnestly declared their very labor was a source of happiness, as he knew from his own experience, never having been so happy in his life as when at work on his father's farm.

Toward the close, the debate ran high, and a member of the Congregational church, not relishing a discussion when the truth was so manifestly against him and his side, tried hard to adjourn us, complacently assuring Foster and myself that "our further labors in the town could be dispensed with." But hoping to get access to a better class of people, we succeeded in an adjournment to next evening, much to our surprise as well as gratification.

The next evening brought a full house, but the enemy overpowered us, and organized and officered to suit themselves. Some would have gladly heard us had they been permitted. We did get an opportunity in the course of the evening to present one more resolution, which we had prepared before hand. It was our custom when we saw that a mob was inevitable, to try to turn it to good account, by making what we did say, as effective and as likely to be remembered as possible. So my second resolution read in substance that no person should be regarded as a christian or christian minister, who was not an earnest, active, outspoken abolitionist. The uproar was renewed at once with augmented violence, the moment the resolution was heard. After a time Foster obtained the floor for a few moments, and reasoned of righteousness, temperance and judgment already come, as few young men of that or any day since ever did. Even our stoutest opponents stood aghast, if, like the Roman Felix, they did not tremble. But our meetings showed no immediate good results. One old gentleman kindly entertained us, and with his family sympathized deeply with us in our seeming disappointment. But we devoutly thanked him and the family, and assured them on parting that we were already accustomed to such repulsions, and were prepared for whatever awaited us.

Deerfield, the next day, proved equally inhospitable to the truths we carried there. The Calvinistic Baptist minister was personally very friendly to us, and an abolitionist, too, but had not heard of our coming, and no notice had been given of our intended meetings ; nor was it convenient for us then to attempt any meetings. We called on the Free Will Baptist minister, and found him a hard-headed, harder-hearted democrat, of the most pronounced pro-slavery type. Doubtless he has long since passed away ; but to his dying day, I dare affirm he remembered the remonstrances and rebukes he, on that occasion, received from the inspired voice of Stephen Foster.

At Nottingham I was invited by the Congregational minister, Mr. Le Bosquet, to preach for him on Sunday, during the day. I had not then, in form, laid down my ministerial prerogative, and accepted when convenient every such proposal. Mr. Le Bosquet was a new organization abolitionist, and so could not wholly agree with me then, though friendly towards me, and even magnanimous. But he finally lapsed

entirely into the political vortex, and never, so far as
I knew, abandoned the Congregational pulpit or denomination, with all its incorrigible pro-slavery character.

Our reception at Lee, home of the Quaker family
of the Cartlands, was not unlike that at Northwood in
so far as the character of audiences was considered,
though they were numerically larger and more voci-
ferous. Northwood had no Cartland family, as had
Lee, and that made a difference in our favor, morally,
of thousands, though our resolutions were voted down
of course, by stamping majorities. A venerable Baptist minister attended on Sunday evening ; even postponed his own regular meeting for it. He not only
opened our exercises with prayer, but bore friendly
testimony to our general course. So on the whole our
few friends in Lee were much pleased with our visit
and labors there.

Exeter, to which we went next, was one of the old,
aristocratic, wealthy, conservative towns, and a county
seat besides, so that really we had little to hope at its
hand or heart. We had not underestimated the moral
and spiritual quality of the people. In the larger,
most popular, denominations clerical authority was
more malignant, more imperious than we had anywhere found it before. The Christian minister was ill,
and we did not call on him, but were assured that he
was decidedly friendly to us and our cause. The Methodist clergyman showed himself indeed on our side,
for he not only permitted us to occupy his meeting-
house, but suspended some special protracted religious services then holding, that we might have not
only his house, but congregation as well. And we
found two or three colored families in the town
who manifested deep and intelligent interest in our

work, so that on the whole, we found a goodly
number of interested sympathizers in our mission,
if not among the opulent and popular, certainly
of that not less worthy, nor by any means less important class, who, eighteen hundred years before, heard
" gladly " a far greater teacher and lecturer.

One morning call on a Congregational minister of
the place was worthy of remembrance and recall, and
that will be all that need be said of our visit to Exeter. We certainly entered his study in a becoming
manner and proper and kindly spirit. We gave our
names and the object of our coming in tone and temper of which none could complain. But in a bluster-
ing, threatening mood and language absolutely
abusive, he positively forbade our speaking on our
subject in his presence. Mr. Foster told him that we
sometimes had to speak to men whether they would
hear or forbear. He snatched up his pen with the utmost violence and commanded us to leave him to his
work. His large size and great agitation, his lip
actually quivering with rage, and the haughty manner
in which he stormed at us, strongly reminded us of
the caution of Him who spake as never man spake :
" Beware of Men !" As we turned to go we told him
we must express our disapprobation of his course, and
in obedience to divine command, shake off the dust of
our feet as our testimony against him. His treatment
of us compelled the belief of many things told us
against him as to his manner of life. At that very
time men were going home drunk and abusing their
families ; one man actually murdered his wife in his
drunken rage, and yet that same minister was baptizing the rum trade and trader, and receiving them to
full church communion and fellowship. It need not
be told that several of his church members had already

withdrawn from his ministrations. And if other facts concerning him, which were given us from eye and ear witnesses, should be here produced, they would almost exceed belief. But his demeanor towards us prepared us to accept whatever of immorality might be spoken against him. Afterwards we said and wrote truly that we had pleaded the cause of the slave in bar-rooms and in grog-shops, in the field, the forge, the factory and the highways, if not in the hedges, but it was for a New England minister, pastor of one of the largest Congregational churches in his state, to positively and peremptorily forbid us to open our mouths for the dumb in his reverend presence.

Should it be objected that he was only one, and represented only himself, it could be answered that he was one of a powerful denomination and influential, too far above the average membership in every council ; and a denomination, too, that made the heresy of rejecting infant baptism at that day an offense of such importance as to refuse ordination for the ministry at home and the missionary abroad.

Readers by this time understand that every individual clergyman or separate church described in these records is only as representative of large numbers, and by no means as exceptions to general rules. One incident, however, is worthy of mention for its originality. Nor do I remember more than one or two like it in all my lecturing mission of almost forty years, and it was in the afternoon of the day we left Exeter.

We drove into Stratham, where we had sent on an appointment for afternoon and evening. Inquiring the way as we rode along, we learned that our meeting would be at two o'clock, in a meeting-house, to which we were easily directed, and which we soon reached. It was a small, pretty little steepled building, situated

almost alone, not a house very near it, and only a few
in sight of it.   Driving our horse under a friendly shed
in the rear, we entered and found everything comfortable and desirable as possible, but not a human soul
nor body present beside ourselves,   The hour had arrived, and so had the speakers, but where was the
audience ?   We sat an hour or more, till the sun was
getting low, and then drove on to a little village prospecting ; but soon found to no purpose.   It was made
very certain that the house would not be lignted nor
warmed for evening, so we drove down to Greenland,
adjoining, which we found, spite of its name, a warmer
clime.

But Foster could not forget Stratham.   We had
met mob after mob ; minister after minister, sometimes
the direct instigator of the mob ; and almost always
we had achieved some sort of honorable success ; if
not triumph.   True, it was "hard to kick against
pricks ;" but to kick against nothing, could not be
borne.   However, it was early spring before he found
it convenient to visit Stratham again.   Then he went
alone.   He had his meeting appointed in a school
house, on a bright April moonlight evening.   When he
entered the house, a dozen or two had gathered.   He
waited a reasonable time, hoping to see more.   But no
more came.   So he commenced his lecture.   I do not
know what he said or did not say.   Probably it would
have made no difference.   For just as he grew a little
animated and earnest in gesture as well as utterance,
his audience rose, probably at a preconcerted signal,
and deliberately and respectfully walked out of the
house, leaving him entirely alone !   So there he stood,
a sentence half uttered, a gesture struck down in its
formation.   Perhaps never before nor afterwards, was
he more completely subdued.

At North Hampton, we had a little clerical experience not unworthy of mention. No meeting had been appointed so we assumed all responsibility, not "mobbing," as Mr. Emerson charged, but taking possession of the town. We fortunately found one good man who went with us to call on the minister to ask for his vestry and his coöperation for an anti-slavery meeting. The minister was a mile away visiting a winter school. Foster sat in the sleigh while our friend with me knocked at the school-house door. The minister appeared in the entry as we desired, but no sooner were my name and business announced than the clerical wrath kindled. He did not, like his stalwart Exeter brother, forbid my speaking in his presence, but in similar spirit declared he would hold no communication. No, said he, "I have heard of you and Stephen Foster, and I want nothing to do with you. You abuse the ministers in your *Herald of Freedom ;* men that I respect. I know what it contains. I read it."

So do most of the ministers, might have been responded to him, but I did not interrupt him. When I did speak I said, you treat us just as do most of the orthodox ministers ; and you need not wonder that we expose them in the name of humanity and for the sake of the down-trodden slave. "O, I see," he said, "what you are after. You want to draw me into argument and then hold me up in your *Herald*, as you have so many other ministers ; but I shall not put myself in your power." I then made some little remark, which stirred his indignation, and he broke forth again and charged me and my companion very vehemently with attacking holy institutions, rending churches, abusing ministers, disturbing the public peace and seeking to undermine all the institutions of society. He forgot what he said a moment before about putting himself in my power and stormed along till all he said would have made a very much longer account than is here given. I did send what made nearly two columns in the *Herald*, and mailed copies of it to most of the leading men of the town, there being then no subscribers, or not more than one there.

It is highly probable that Mr. Foster and myself in the lecture field, with Mr. Rogers at the helm of the *Herald of Freedom*, were justly chargeable with not a little disturbance of the public peace. I wrote a sermon at the time from the text, "Think not that I am come to send peace on earth : I came not to send peace but a sword." It was strictly orthodox in doctrine, so I sometimes preached it in orthodox pulpits ; did so in Concord South church, which was the beginning of its anti-slavery sorrows, for Foster did not go there till more than a year afterwards. Rogers was present, and here are a few things he said of it in the next *Herald*. I had not then wholly abandoned preaching, nor been disowned by the Suffolk association of ministers from whom I received regular license in Boston to preach the Congregational gospel. But I was soon called to account after my presumption in preaching such a sermon to such a body as Foster proved the South church to be in its coming judgment day, some year or two afterwards.

After a few words on ministerial influence and what constitutes it, and who it was who "made himself of no reputation," and had "no weight of influence," Rogers proceeded to say :

Parker Pillsbury is doubtless one of the three intended by the *Christian Panoply*. He has no influence. But the *Panoply* and kindred ministers abound with it. Those who heard brother Pillsbury on Sunday

evening before last, may understand what it is that
gives "influence and weight" to a New Hampshire
minister. The full auditory that heard him that evening, with the attention of life and death, and the
hushed stillness of the churchyard can tell how
necessary "influence and weight" are to constitute a
preacher of the gospel.

The text was the declaration of Christ, that he came
not to send peace, but a sword, on the earth. Then he
spoke of the human character ; the agitating, disturbing influence of truth on that character — he glanced
at the turmoil and confusion into which truth had ever
wrought it, and the bitter hostility the church and
ministry had manifested towards the spirit of reformation, from the days of Him who came to bear witness
unto the truth down through the times of Luther to
our own. He spoke of the necessity, safety and whole-
someness of moral agitation in society and in the church,
and the deadly danger of moral stagnation. He illustrated the one by the tossed ocean, ever pure and whole-
some from its ceaseless inequietude, and the other by
the stagnant, lifeless pool, become putrid by its own
quiescence, breeding only croaking frogs and noisesome,
hurtful reptiles. He declared the duty of the watchman on the walls of Zion was to be ever in the van of
moral agitation. When the tempest was up he should
be prompt to mount the foremost billow and direct the
storm. And in time of dead calm, the watchman of
all men, should wake the moral hurricane.

We can merely touch on this sermon. The breath-
less auditory best attested its power and its palpable
truth. But the *Christian Panoply* says brother Pillsbury has no weight of influence. Of the manner of
the speaker, we can only say he seemed to us to be
mightily *in earnest ;* to believe solemnly what he was
preaching and not at all like one reciting a task.

This testimony from Mr. Rogers is only produced
here to show what really was the disturbing element
among the clergy, and gave such point and significance
to the anti-slavery movement, especially to the labors

of the field lecturers ; and at that time in New Hampshire and Massachusetts much more than anywhere else.   The cause was now eleven years old, but never before had the sin of slavery been so directly laid at the door of the church.   But the time had come when "judgment must begin at the house of God."   Even Judge Birney's "American Churches the Bulwarks of American Slavery" had by no means produced the desired effect. For some reason, it was first published in England, and seems not to have had much circulation in the United States till its second edition revised by the author, in 1842, and published in Garrison's native town, Newburyport, Massachusetts.

While slavery was only an *evil*, the church and even the clergy could be, and many of them were opposed to it.   Professor Stuart, of Andover Theological Seminary, denied even that doctrine, and wrote and published a tract entitled, *"Slavery not a malum in se,"* which had many readers and believers, and produced a marked effect, particularly among the ministry. But Garrison was already in the field, and slavery was branded as a sin against God and a crime against man, always and everywhere ; and the only remedy for it was immediate and unconditional emancipation of every slave.   This demand had many supporters in the church and pulpit, till the application was made directly and forcibly to them, with the more startling declaration that no slave-holder could be a christian. And when at last the uncompromising abolitionists proclaimed their determination to have "no union nor fellowship with slaveholders, in state nor church," and pronouncing the northern apologist and abettor, no less wicked than the slave-holder, because sinning against more light, and with less motive and temptation, then the alarm pealed out so as to reach the

deafest ear, the deadest church. Almost every Congregational and Presbyterian minister in the north
heard it and stood aghast ! Even President Lord, of
Dartmouth college, fled in dismay ; though he, like
Rev. Mr. Curtis had preached and written plainly
against slavery as *sin*, not the "malum in se," of professor Stuart. The most anti-slavery ministers made
haste to find, or base a remedy in new organization.
So especially was it here in New Hampshire, as has
been sufficiently shown. Only three Congregational
ministers, I think, in the state remained to the old
society, and one of them was unordained, and another,
Rev. Benjamin Sargent, was Presbyterian, settled in
that part of Chester now known as Auburn. He and
Thomas P. Beach, who has already appeared in these
pages, and will again, next year (1842) remained true
to their convictions, though at cost of much personal
bitterness and even cruel persecution from their clerical
brethren and other opponents of the anti-slavery cause.
The third was he of "no weight of influence" in
Christian Panoply esteem ; and more especially after
he had preached his sermon on moral and religious
agitation, from the text, "I am not come to send
peace, but a sword."

I pass over several meetings of much interest,
attended by Mr. Foster and myself, one at Great Falls,
which continued two or three days and closed on Sunday afternoon in time for us to ride to Dover for a
meeting there in the evening.

Mr. Rogers had come down in the last of the week
and was with us a part of the time at Great Falls. But
the Dover meeting on Sunday evening proved of
greater interest and more importance than had been
anticipated. And so marked were some of its peculiarities and so prominent was the part borne in it by

Mr. Rogers, that readers will surely be grateful to me
for permitting them to read his description of it, in his
next week's *Herald*. The heading to his editorial
read thus :

VIOLENT BREAKING UP OF A MEETING AT DOVER—
    REV. MR. YOUNG, FRANCIS COGSWELL, ESQ., AND
    COL. ANDREW PIERCE.

We mention the names of these three individuals
here in the same connection with the words above in
which they appeared with the disturbance and breaking
up of an anti-slavery meeting in the place last Sunday
night. We give the public the facts.

Sunday evening, accompanied by our state agents
Pillsbury and Foster, on our way home from the
Somersworth convention, we met a very large and most
respectable assemblage of the people of Dover in the
Orthodox Congregational meeting-house. It was, so
far as we could judge, as intelligent and enlightened
an auditory as that large town could furnish. The exercises began by reading a hymn by Rev. Mr. Young,
minister of that house, singing by the choir, prayer by
Rev. Mr. Haydon, Baptist clergyman, then a hymn
read by Mr. Young and singing again ; when, after
explaining to the audience the mistaken notice that
had been given which might have led to an expectation of a prepared address from us, we offered for the
consideration of the meeting, a resolution of the following purport :

That at this stage of the anti-slavery enterprise, no
intelligent person, not openly and faithfully engaged
in it, ought to be recognized as a christian, or as
possessed of common humanity. After reading the
resolution through distinctly twice to the meeting, we
proceeded to enforce it in the plainest, most faithful
manner we were able to do without any preparation
except the brief prayer we offered to God in secret
that he would enable us to say something to reach the
heart and conscience of the influential and high minded
auditory before us. Owing to severe exhaustion and
indisposition, we had intended to say but few words
at the meeting, and to leave the main service in the

hands of our brethren, the agents ; one of whom took the resolution to the meeting with that understanding. But just before the close of the second singing he handed it to us with the wish expressed that we should lead in the discussion, to which we assented, trusting in God to give us somewhat to say on so embarrassing an occasion. We proceeded to remind our audience of the fact of our country's enslavement of a sixth portion of the people, of the character and objects of the anti-slavery enterprise, of its advancement from the beginning and its present stage, and of the unchristian and *inhuman* position of all in the country who refused to enlist openly and faithfully in it. We talked some forty minutes as near as we could judge, and as plainly and faithfully as we were able. The audience gave us the stillest and most active attention. Considering the pointed character of the remarks we were obliged to make and the auditory we were addressing, proud in talent, influence, wealth and reputation and all that finds human self-respect, we were deeply grateful and somewhat surprised that they gave us such patient and forbearing audience. May God bless it to the anti-slavery repentance of them all.

We were followed by our brother Foster in a strain of the pertinent, eloquent and solemn remark which distinguishes him as an anti-slavery speaker. In the course of his exposition of the character of the community in relation to slavery, he remarked on the support given the slave system by their honoring it in the persons of distinguished slave-holders for whom they had recently voted for high offices in the gift of the people, and by their fellowshiping slave-holders and their apologists as christians and ministers of the gospel. The auditory awarded him throughout the most pointed attention.

When Foster closed, we addressed them to show that their position while out of the anti-slavery enterprise, was the one, and the very one, and the only one which could aid the south in their slave-holding, and which the south desired them, or would consent that they should take. We spoke of their estimation of the free colored man, and of the estimation in which he was held abroad—by subjects of monarchy, by the first talent and character in Great Britain—and of the reception we met with there as abolitionists on our recent visit abroad, compared with the estimation we were held in here at home. The same attention was vouchsafed us while we spoke, as before.

At our closing, brother Foster arose and requested the enlightened audience, if any among them denied or doubted the soundness of our positions or the truth of our facts, or of the resolution before us, they would give the meeting the benefit of their opinions, and set us right. No one rose nor moved from his seat. A considerable time elapsed in perfect silence. Brother Pillsbury privately asked us if it were advisable to offer anything farther. We advised him to consult his feelings and follow his duty.

He arose, and after alluding to the lateness of the time and the probability of his wearying the audience, went on to speak of the effect produced by him on the last fourth of July upon an auditory in that house by an anti-slavery address, when nearly all the people, ministers and all left him at the sound of martial music which struck their ear as it was heralding in the streets a liberty procession in honor of the declaration of man's inalienable birthright to freedom. He then referred to the resolution, and was proceeding to illustrate and enforce with striking power the implied charge of the unchristian and inhuman character of the pro-slavery community, by its fellowshiping and honoring slave-holding in the professor and in the minister of the gospel, when he gave the name of the Reverend Edwin Holt, of Portsmouth, as a highly honored and ardently fellowshiped instance of the slave-holding minister who had, he averred—bought a woman, held her as a slave and sold her again and deeded her away body and soul to the slave purchaser, and had never repented of it nor confessed it, and notwithstanding was held in high estimation by the brotherhood of the ministry. He spoke of the impossibility of putting down slavery while slave-holding was so esteemed—declared Mr. Holt's offence worse

than killing the body — that slavery was rightly estimated by Patrick Henry, when he exclaimed, "give me
liberty or give me death!" He was proceeding to
compare Mr. Holt as a murderer with Ferguson, the
Exeter murderer, and to give his offence the preëmi-
nence, when the Rev. Mr. Young, rudely and with
great excitement and violence of manner, broke in
upon him: "Mr. Pillsbury, Mr. Pillsbury, you must
stop! I must protest solemnly against such slanderous
accusations being thrown out in this house. I cannot
consent to have my brethren in the ministry thus
slandered in my presence when they have not been
impeached by their brethren," and more in like strain
and temper.

Brother Pillsbury calmly asked him: But is not
what I say true? If I have uttered anything slanderous before this audience I wish to be convinced of it
that I may make becoming acknowledgements. Mr.
Young replied, this is not the place to settle that—his
brethren in the ministry were the tribunal to settle
that, and he should not discuss it. Brother Pillsbury
replied that any one had a right to state the truth, and
particularly such truth as that. Whereupon Francis
Cogswell, esq., rose and in vehement voice and manner said, that as a member of that church, he would
not sit there and see that sacred place desecrated by
the slanders that had been thrown out by the speakers
that evening, and that the meeting ought to break up,
etc., whereupon a voice of similar earnestness came
down upon us from the gallery in the same strain,
accusing the speakers of slander, and of profaning
that holy place, (pointing to the foot of the pulpit
where we were standing) with delivering political
addresses on that holy day—and when he had spoken
as long as he wished, proposed that the meeting now
close. The speaker, we were sorry to see, was Colonel
Andrew Pierce. We immediately demanded of him
to state before that audience, a single slanderous word
we had uttered that evening ; stated that we submitted
ourselves to the auditory, and if we had said a single
untrue thing, or anything not demanded of us as an
advocate of the slave in their presence, we would

retract it and make them acknowledgement to their
entire content.   Col. Pierce then confined his accusation to the other speakers, whom he said he did not
know ; and on our asking what they had either of them
said that was slanderous, he replied that they had said
that three-fourths of the professors of the religion in
the country were on the road · to hell—alluding to
brother Pillsbury's remark, that if the resolution were
true, three-fourths of the professed christianity of the
country were in the broad road to death, and that the
church and ministry of the country were the strongholds of slavery.   There had been no argument used,
he said, by the speakers, and he declared there was no
one in the house who was not opposed to slavery.   We
replied by asking him if it was not a truth that the
church and the ministry were the stronghold of
slavery ? when Mr. Cogswell again furiously interfered
and protested against further discussion and hoped
the meeting would break up and go home ; whereupon
we were greeted with a tumultuous rising all at once,
a smart hissing from the vicinity of Messrs. Pierce
and Cogswell, and a violent slamming of seats and
going out of the house ; all of which struck us as
savoring more of desecration of the house than any
" words of truth and soberness " that had been uttered
by the speakers.   One rose out of the auditory about
the middle stage of the disturbance and demanded to
know of those who accused the speakers of slandering
Mr. Holt, whether the accusations against him were
true—he wished for information to know if it were
denied by any man.   It was the first time he had
heard of it, and he wished seriously to be informed if
Mr. Holt had done what was charged, and what was
pronounced slanderous.   The questioner was John
Parkman, Unitarian minister, whose position on the
occasion we really respect too much to attach to his
name the unwarrantable title of Reverend.   His
questions for the moment hushed the tumultuous
tempest, but no one answered him.   We had been
accused three times by three different speakers of
slander in relation to Mr. Holt, and when a denial of
the slanderous charge was called for, no man was pre-

pared to deny it or offer the least word in support of the false and wicked accusation made against us. Our meeting had been rudely and violently broken up, and the auditory thrown into a spasm of mobocratic excitement by Messrs. Young, Cogswell and Pierce and the speakers falsely accused of slander, and when called on even to deny the truth of what was charged as the slander, neither of them had the hardihood to deny its truth. Indeed Rev. Mr. Young shortly after in private conversation at the pulpit foot, admitted the truth of the charge, and said that Mr. Holt knew his sentiments in relation to slavery; that he had proclaimed them before the people there, and that he himself felt that he could not again exchange pulpits with Mr. Holt. Why then, we asked, did you accuse our brethren of slander, when you knew the charge was true? It was not the charge, he said, but the manner, and time, and place! He said Mr. Holt had not been impeached by his brethern. That was the very thing complained of, we responded; it was that our brother Pillsbury was complaining of, when you interrupted him; he was charging that very fact on the ministerial brethren, that they were fellowshiping a slave-holder as a minister of the gospel, and that slave-holding in their estimation, was no ground of impeachment. It was an unhappy state of things he admitted, but here was not the place to discuss it. There was coming up at this moment, a part of the audience who had retired.

About the time the hissing commenced, Mr. Young had quitted his seat in the pew and taken his place on the platform with us and requested the people not to hiss. In justice to Mr. Cogswell we add that we understood by someone that he endeavored to check the hissing which took place while he was speaking and very naturally accompanied the furious tone in which he spoke.

As the meeting was breaking up, brother Foster proposed that the singers retain their places till the noise subsided, that we might close our meeting with singing. The choir were prevented from this, had they been disposed to it, by an immediate extinguish-

ment of the lights, which took place at the call of some
one in behalf of the disturbance. " Put out the lights,"
was the cry in real 1835 style, and we supposed it was
preparatory to a personal onset. After the singing
was prevented, and the lights out in the gallery, and
silence restored, brother Foster called on Rev.
Mr. Young to close the meeting with prayer. He
declined, and brother Mack of the *Morning Star*, was
called on and immediately complied. And his prayer
was most appropriate to the occasion. We told
Mr. Young that the whole violence and outrage were
chargeable to him; and he promptly admitted it.
The lights were quickly extinguished and we were
left at the foot of the pulpit stairs to grope our way
out in utter darkness as best we could. But we left
the house unmolested.   *   *   *   The
people of Dover had their option to admit us to the
meeting house or not—they acted their pleasure as to
coming to hear us; they had opportunity any of them
to reply to anything we had said; they were so
apprised; they were invited to; they were urged to.
They declined, and they knew they could be heard
after brother Pillsbury should close. Were they not
bound then to suffer the meeting to proceed and to
close in quiet? Had Mr. Young, Mr. Cogswell, or
Mr. Pierce, either of them a right to excite the meeting as he did, as they all did, and hazard the disgraceful
and infamous results of a mob, after they had declined
an invitation to say regularly and properly all they
wished to say? Is that their christianity? Is that their
respect for the liberty of speech?

Such was the account of the Dover meeting-house
mob given by the editor of the *Herald of Freedom* in
the same week of its occurrence. If nothing was ex-
tenuated, surely nought was set down in malice. But
it was an act of peculiar aggravation, when the circumstances are put in the record of it. Dover had had
for several years one of the ablest and best Congregational ministers in the state, and certainly one of
the most active in the anti-slavery cause, Rev. David.

Root.   Nor was his church as a body, far behind him.
Nor was he by any means among the first, nor most
active in the clerical conspiracy which led or drove to
the division and new organization.   Had northern
clerical coöperation and church participation in all the
crimes, cruelties and damning guilt of slavery never
been arraigned, Dover had never had a mob in defence of such partnership in the sin.   Had Mr. Root
remained the minister of that church, it is hardly
probable that scenes so disgraceful would have been
witnessed.   But Mr. Root had left Dover and New
Hampshire, and the Rev. Mr. Young was in his stead
straight from the sombre shades of Andover Theological Seminary.   It was a large, rich church and
society that had settled and ordained him, and they
worshipped in one of the largest and finest meeting
houses then in the state.   Some of us who were with
Mr. Young at Andover rather wondered at their selection to succeed such a man as David Root.   But so it
was, though his stay in Dover was short, and he early
abandoned the ministry altogether.

The mob of that dark December night was precipi-
tated by the arraignment of Rev. Edwin Holt, of
Portsmouth, as a slaveholder.   And yet Mr. Young
knew the charge was true.   He admitted it to Mr.
Rogers at the very steps of the altar, before the
tumult had wholly ceased.   His church must have
known it was true.   And Mr. Holt knew that Mr.
Young knew it was true, because Mr. Young told us
that Mr. Holt knew what his opinion of the business
was, and he gave us to understand, doubtless intended
that we should understand, that he had dealt very
faithfully with him, as an offending brother.   Why,
then, did he cry havoc, and let slip the dogs of war
on our meeting for free and friendly discussion ?   A

meeting, as were all the meetings we ever held, free alike to our foes and friends. A meeting in which Mr. Young or Mr. Cogswell, or Mr. Pierce, could have had half of every hour, and more, had he desired, to contradict or disprove any statement of ours, about Mr. Holt, or anybody, or anything else. But the truth was, there was nothing to contradict. We knew whereof we affirmed. That was no new scene to us. On that very night, Foster had on a coat, (a dress coat of the style of that time), one skirt of which was torn square off in a violent mob at Portland, only the week before, and which coat he wore for weeks afterward, as a testimony against Portland christianity, though his friends very soon furnished him another.

No, it is not very likely we could be convicted of false statements in the face of two or three mobs in a week. For we were not courting persecution. We were not ambitious for martyr honors, nor confessors' crowns. But we spoke the truth, and if not the whole truth, certainly nothing but the truth in the love of God and man. And we could not often be successfully contradicted, as most who heard us knew full well.

Mr. Young was not countenanced by all his congregation in his strange and unwarrantable course on that occasion. Indeed, he was quite sharply, though good-naturedly rebuked by one parishioner as we groped our way out in the total darkness. He happened, unfortunately, to tell us what we could not mistake, that it was *very* dark. Then responded his parishioner, who could hear but not see him, "True, Brother Young, but it is about as light as you ever make it for us."

CHAPTER IX.

MEETINGS IN WEST CHESTER—RIOTOUS AND SHAMEFUL
CONDUCT—RIDE TO DERRY, AND WHAT CAME OF IT—
FRANKLIN MOB DESCRIBED IN LETTER BY MR. FOSTER.

That the churches were indeed the bulwarks of
slavery grew every day more and more apparent.
And as Dover, and several other of the larger towns
have testified, it may be proper to report briefly on a
few of the smaller places we visited, such as Auburn,
Chester, and Derry. Auburn was at that time known
as West Chester. Its church was Presbyterian, its
minister, Rev. Benjamin Sargent, already introduced
in these pages, venerable in years and rich in the
graces of the true christian minister and man of that
period.

The Methodists had a strong hold in West Chester,
but at the center of the town, Congregationalism held
undisputed sway and ruled with rigor not often surpassed. No town ever more sternly or successfully
resisted the anti-slavery, or other unpopular reforms.

In conversation with a venerable deacon of the
church on the Indian question, so prominent at the
time of the Seminole war, he declared to me that it
was the duty of the first settlers of the country to ex-
terminate the Indian tribes as completely as did the
Israelites the inhabitants of Canaan and of Midian';
"killing everything that breathed." He said all our
Indian wars ever since were God's judgments, sent as
penalty for neglecting that duty! And, moreover,
that they would be inflicted till that duty was done.

He seemed exactly of the spirit of some Connecticut colonists, who, it was told, seized the territory under two resolutions, unanimously adopted :

I. *Resolved*—That the earth is to be given to the saints as an inheritance forever.   And

II. *Resolved*—That we, being saints, do hereby take possession of that portion of it bounded as follows, etc., etc.

I never heard that the Chester Congregational church, or its deacons, or minister, held ever afterwards any more humane sentiment towards the Indians, or even the slaves, while slavery lasted.

Our first anti-slavery meeting at West Chester was held in the Methodist meeting-house — adjourned there from the school-house, which was too small for half who came, the evening being Sunday.   Most of the time was occupied by Mr. Foster, who paid the Methodists, who were present in large numbers, the compliment of presuming that they wished to know the exact truth as to their connection with slavery, that they might be governed accordingly.   So he opened Judge Birney's tract and proceeded to read exactly the record the denomination had furnished for itself in the past as far back as 1780 ; when it was

Resolved,. That the conference acknowledges slavery contrary to the laws of God, man and nature ; and hurtful to society ; contrary to the dictates of conscience and true religion.

In 1784, when the Methodist church had been fully organized, rules were adopted fixing the time when members who were already slaveholders should emancipate all their slaves, and then followed this solemn injunction :

Every person concerned, who will not comply with these rules, shall have liberty quietly to withdraw

from our society within the twelve months following
the notice being given him as aforesaid. Otherwise, the
assistants shall exclude him from the society. No
person holding slaves shall be admitted into our
society or to the Lord's supper, till he comply with
these rules concerning slavery. And those who buy,
sell or give away slaves, unless on purpose to free
them, shall be immediately expelled.

And then, again, in 1801, the conference declared :

We declare that we are more than ever convinced
of the great evils of African slavery, which still exists in these United States. * * * * * Every
member of the society who sells a slave shall, immediately after full proof, be excluded. * * * * *
Proper committees shall be appointed by the annual
conferences out of the most respectable of our friends,
for the conducting of the business. And the presiding elders, deacons, and traveling preachers shall procure as many proper signatures as possible to the
addresses : and give all the assistance in their power
in every respect to aid the committees and to further
the blessed undertaking. Let this be continued from
year to year, till the desired end be accomplished.

So much, and more of the same character, Mr.
Foster had in hand to read to the Methodists who on
that evening composed a large proportion of our numerous audience. And so much he read to the credit
of early Methodism. But then he had to unfold and
expose the terrible degeneracy and apostasy in a
single generation. And this was his offence, though
his testimony was still as before only what the denomination itself furnished him.

In the year 1836 the general conference was held in
Cincinnati, Ohio, and adopted with only fourteen dissenting voices this resolution :

Resolved, By the delegates of the annual conferences in general conference assembled, that we are
decidedly opposed to modern abolitionism ; and wholly

disclaim any right, wish, or intention to interfere in the civil and political relation between master and slave as it exists in the slave holding states of this Union.

And this resolution, though ample to the purpose of Foster, was a small part of the stunning testimony he presented to show that the northern Methodists were fully as guilty as their southern brethren of all the abominations of slave holding. For instance, he cited the declarations of the most eminent northern ministers and doctors of Methodist divinity. Rev. Dr. Fisk, president of the Wesleyan university of Connecticut, said and published to this effect :

The relation of master and slave may, and does exist in many cases, under such circumstances as free the master from the just charge and guilt of immorality. The text, 1 Cor., 7th chap., 20 to 23d verse, seems mainly to enjoin and sanction the fitting continuance of their present social relations. The free man was to remain free, and the slave, unless emancipation should offer, was to remain a slave. The general rule of Christianity, not only permits, but in supposable cases, enjoins a continuance of the master's authority. The New Testament enjoins obedience upon the slave, as an obligation due to rightful authority.

Only so much from a great deal by Dr. Fiske, in like vein and tone. And this one baptismal seal by Bishop Hedding, then living in Lynn, Massachusetts, as read in the *Christian Advocate and Journal :*

The right to hold a slave is founded on this rule : " Therefore, all things whatsoever ye would that men should do unto you, do ye even so to them, for this is the law and the prophets."

The argument of Mr. Foster enraged as much, as surprised the Methodist portion of the audience. He showed slavery to be wholesale adultery and concubinage, and that all, who upheld it by fellowshiping it

13

as christians, or fit to be regarded with anything less
than abhorrence and execration, were partakers in
those sins and shames. He proved, that Methodist
church members and ministers had held, or still held
hundreds of thousands of slaves, while pretending to
detest slavery and to be seeking its overthrow; holding
them as "goods and chattels," robbing them of marriage, and dooming them to perpetual prostitution, till
the southern Methodist church had made itself a great
house of ill-fame, a vast brothel, into which the Son
of God himself, in the person of his forlorn brethren
and sisters, was continually and hopelessly cast ! He
declared no house of ill-fame in New York was guilty
of such fearful impiety, such frightful abomination.
For there the victim or the guilty could flee out and
escape, while in the churches they were held, were
compelled by both religion and government, to stay
and endure, even though their soul and spirit were
pure as the angels of God !

Mr. Foster was heard an hour or more with comparative order and attention. Suddenly a man rose
in great agitation, much as a drunken man or lunatic
some times did in our meetings, and demanded proof
of what had been said. Nothing needed proving, as
the church and clergy supplied all the argument, and
the inferences were as self-evident as heat from fire,
or light from the heavens. But instead of drunkard
or lunatic, the man proved to be one of the leading
members of that very church, and it required the aid
of some of his brethren to quiet him and restore the
order of the meeting. Foster then opened the Bible
and read the eighteenth chapter of Revelation down
to the thirteenth verse, and sat down, leaving the remaining time to me.

The verse containing the injunction : "Come out of her, my people, that ye be not partakers of her sins, and that ye receive not of her plagues," read in Mr. Foster's deep, earnest, solemn tones, produced a deep impression ; and a man rose with much apparent sincerity and asked : "Would it not be better to remain in the churches and reform them ?" He, too, was a Methodist brother and, we were told, was a reformed inebriate. Had I known that at the time, I should have asked him whether dram-shops and brothels were fit haunts for those who had abandoned them, even to save the still lost ones, when everything and more could be done, and better done, from the outside ? and especially if remaining within, or going within, involved eating of the same loaf and drinking the same cup with the guilty.

But as it was, I asked why Wesley did not remain in the old Episcopal church ? Why not so preach his doctrine as not to create schism and separation ? I asked if Unitarians or Universalists were ever exhorted to remain in their communion and work reform there, instead of coming out and uniting with the more evangelical churches into whose faith they had been converted. On the question of changing their religious preferences or beliefs, by leaving their pro-slavery communions to become abolitionists, I remarked that no such change would be required. I said, do you wish or prefer to be a Methodist ? Then be a Methodist with all your heart ; be such a Methodist as was Wesley who declared slavery *"the sum of all villanies,"* which must brand a slave-holder as the sum of all villains ; such a Methodist as was Dr. Adam Clarke, your own great Bible Commentator, who said and wrote : "If one place in hell is hotter than any other, that place should be appropriated to slave-holders." To the Presbyterian and Congregationalist, my doctrine was substantially the same. To the Baptist, I asked, do you wish to be a Baptist, and be immersed bodily in the beautiful Massabesic, whose waves roll in here almost to our very feet ? no abolitionist shall say you nay. Only carry out your own avowed principles, and inasmuch as you will not drink the sacramental wine with such as have only been sprinkled with clean water in baptism, or with such as will commune with them, they themselves having been immersed, so in relation to slave-holders. Have no religious fellowship with them, nor with any who do commune with them as christians. Exclude the slave-holder and all who will not exclude the slave-holder. Not that I hold to your doctrine of "Close Communion," as it is called : but that is your affair, not mine. Your right of religious freedom is as good as mine, and shall be respected and defended by me as sacredly as my own. Only be consistent in other particulars as well as in that already suggested. And that is, do not make infant baptism a greater heresy, (more *damnable* heresy, the apostle would call it,) than infant stealing; robbing cradles of their priceless contents, and helpless mothers of their innocent babes. Do not exclude from fellowship the infant sprinkler, and then welcome the infant-stealer, the cradle-robber, the trundle-bed-plunderer to pulpit and sacramental supper, as of the same "one lord, one faith, one baptism" with yourselves. That, I said, is all we abolitionists have a right to ask.

The meeting closed at a late hour, in good order, and apparently, in the main, friendly spirit. We appointed meetings for Monday and Tuesday evenings, the latter in the school-house of the village where we then were.

On Monday I met the Methodist minister, and held
with him a long conversation. He assured me he
would gladly attend our meetings and hold discussion
with us, but his engagements rendered it impossible.
He gravely charged Mr. Foster and myself with incul-
cating the most wicked and abominable sentiments ;
accused us of the grossest misrepresentation and
falsehood on the previous evening, and said he should
take a public opportunity *after we were gone* to expose
us. I told him he should have been at our meeting
of last evening and heard for himself ; for it was evident he knew nothing at all about what was said or
done. He insisted that he had full confidence in his
informant, though it was plain that he had talked with
none better than the half-crazed being, who so rudely
and wildly interrupted our proceedings. But I again
invited him in most cordial manner to come to our
meetings, and proposed to go in to one of his, but he
gave me no further attention.

When we went to our meeting on that evening, we
found the school-house door locked against us. This
was done by a prominent member of the Methodist
church, on his own responsibility ; in full assurance
that anti-slavery sinners had no rights that Methodist
saints could be bound to respect. A noble and gener-
ous-hearted man of the world, opened his commodious
dwelling, and there we held our meeting. The Presbyterians were holding their monthly concert of prayer
for the heathen, close by, and at the same hour.
Mr. Foster left me to conduct our meeting, and went
into the Presbyterian's concert of prayer and was permitted to address them a half hour, as afterward
appeared to effective purpose. And whom should he
meet there cheek by jowl with the rest, but my Methodist minister, who in the morning, assured me he

would certainly attend our meeting, "but for positive engagements!" He had passed directly by our meeting, and gone to a Presbyterian concert of prayer ; what he had never in his life done before, and in all probability, never did again.

Mr Foster addressed the concert on the character and conduct of the American Board of Foreign Missions in regard to the heathenism of our slave system at home. He showed how the treasury of the Board was replenished by robbery. Man-stealers, and the buyers and sellers of stolen men, women and children,. not only contributors to, but controllers, with other officers, of the moneys raised—the price of blood, the very blood of Christ himself, in the person of his children and little ones, the price of his blood given in contributions to publish his name to the distant tribes of Africa, and the heathen world! Showing from Judge Birney's American Churches, the Bulwarks of American Slavery, that the Board even had slaves. bequeathed in will to its funds, by pious persons at the south. It was said that in the case cited by Judge Birney, the bequest was not accepted ; but the reason probably was, that to receive it, involved attendance "on the part of all who claimed it" at the Superior Court of Bryan county, in the state of Georgia. None will doubt this when that stupendous body, the American Board of Commissioners for Foreign Missions shall come hereafter into these chronicles for examination. On the next morning, Mr. Foster was told by some who heard him at the concert, that they had withheld their contributions, never before having dreamed that the American Board was sustained by robbery, and controlled in part by man-stealers.

In the course of Tuesday, we learned that attempts. were making to close the school-house against us on that evening also. The plan was frustrated by our friends who secured the key. Then a riot was concerted ; we knew that, because the zealous Methodist, who, on Sunday evening came so near utterly routing us, told us he "had labored hard more than three hours, to prevent a riot this evening." We always knew well what to expect, when ministers and other like good and influential men told us how much they feared a mob, and how hard they were working to prevent it, and how they *hoped* that now there would be no mob.

On this occasion, we had a large attendance, and the best and most respectful attention to the close. But the Methodist minister did not appear. Our zealous Methodist friend, who had labored three hours to prevent a riot, was conspicuously absent. Some others, also, who had been quite demonstrative in defence of the church and clergy, especially the Methodist church and minister of that place, were absent, *in body*, to say the least.

All this absence was easily accounted for when we came out. The evening was dark and rainy. Several had brought lanterns. Our horse and carriage stood outside, with others, but ours had been singularly distinguished. Past experience had taught us that it might be so, especially when *good* men "had labored hard to prevent our being mobbed." Borrowing a friendly lantern, we discovered that all the upholstery of the carriage, (a new comfortable, covered buggy,) cushions, whip, reins and valisses, had been deeply "daubed," not with the untempered Methodist "mortar" of those days, nor the super-fragrant eggs of Sanbornton Bridge, which our readers cannot have forgotten, but with an anointing quite as unsavory and unclean, furnished by some grass-fed and well

fed Chester cow.   The Methodist minister, a Mr.
Quimby, had assured me he would be with us that
evening and take part in our meeting, but for positive
pre-engagement.   He was surely well represented
outside the school-house, and had no need to attend
himself.

Next day but one, all damages were repaired in
time for us to drive over to Derry.   There, again, we
fell into Methodist hands.   Both the Congregational
and Presbyterian pulpits and churches had long before proved themselves impervious to anti-slavery
truth by word or deed.   Accidentally, we encountered
the Methodist minister, Mr. Hazeltine, who seemed to
speak us kindly, and tendered us his meeting-house
for two evenings.   We blessed and thanked him devoutly, and soon had notices posted about the village
accordingly.   Then we drove away two or three miles,
to look up some abolitionists of whom we had heard
but never seen, and to extend, as widely as possible,
notice of our meetings.   At the hour appointed we
were at the meeting-house, but, to our surprise and
disappointment, we found the door locked against us.
Nor was anybody in sight of whom we could ask explanations.   We went into a shoemaker's shop to make
inquiry, and were told "the brethren" had been together, and unanimously vetoed the kindly offer of
their minister.   We demanded of the minister, who
came in, what the strange procedure meant.   He said
that since he had offered us the house he had seen
the West Chester minister, who, it appeared, had
scampered down after us as quick as possible, to
sound an alarm, and that he had given such report of
our meetings in his parish that it was not deemed advisable to have anything to do with us.   For his own

part, he said, he was still in favor of our having the
meeting-house, but the Discipline did not warrant it,
as he had not appointed the meetings.

It somehow got abroad in the village that we were
in the shoemaker's shop, and very soon the room, entry, steps and all, were thronged with a noisy, babbling
rabble that it would wrong the real brutes to call
brutal, all burning with indignation, because, as they
most vociferously declared, we were seeking to tear
down the Church and the Sabbath.   I never met a
more abusive gang in any grog-shop.   We congratulated the minister on the number and quality of his
defenders.   The three most prominent, the actual
leaders, were all members of his own church.   One of
these taunted Foster with wearing spectacles.   This
raised a great laugh.   I asked the man, "Do you
know God could, with one lightning flash, so blind
you that, even with spectacles, you could never see
more?"   Another of them said, "The Chester Methodist minister was here to-day, and told us you called
his church a brothel."   Then one cried out, "O, they
know what a brothel is!" which raised a yell of glee,
with clappings and stampings that shook the whole
building.   "Yes, yes," bawled another, "their looks
show it."   And this, to them, minister and all, seemed
to clinch the argument wholly in their favor.   The
victory was theirs.   We admitted it, and left the town
to celebrate and enjoy it to all hearts' content.   I
never heard that a genuine anti-slavery meeting was
ever held in that town.   There might have been.
Doubtless, New Organization lecturing might have
been called in to take away the reproach and shame
of driving away the earnest and devoted abolitionists,
who had taken their lives in their hands and gone
forth everywhere, proclaiming liberty to the captive,

whether guilty men and ministers would hear, or whether they would forbear.   Both those ministers were New Organizationists of most Pharisaic type. And both declared they preached, themselves, once a year, on slavery, though they always selected Fast or Thanksgiving day for that subject.   And both seemed to think that entitled them to our acceptance and respect as abolitionists.   As we drove slowly out of the village, in the dark evening, and with sad hearts, the crowd of "brethren" and others from the shoe-maker's shop pursued us with their shouting and howling, some of them seizing our carriage wheels and holding back so that our poor little Tunbridge had hard work to pull us out of their power.   What they wanted was to provoke us to resistance.   Then they would have taken sweet revenge by violence on our persons, perhaps to the extent of Lovejoy's mur-derers at the west, a few years before.   We never doubted that our non-resistance principles saved our lives in many a desperate encounter.   And in them and their heroic Author we confidingly reposed our trust.   Nor surely, under the circumstances, could we have pursued a wiser course, whatever might have been our principles.   For we stood almost always nearly alone against the towns, at first.

In the account thus given of our reception in some of the smaller or average New Hampshire towns, the object can hardly be mistaken.   Almost exactly such reports could be extended to length beyond human patience and endurance.   And without going out of New Hampshire, or including any other persons than the three already named, the editor of the *Herald of Freedom*, Mr. Foster and myself.

It must not be supposed, however, that we did not find or make excellent friends and glad co-workers with us in our mighty mission. ' We lived, when abroad, much of the time on the fat of the land ; only metaphorically as to the *fat*, for we entered the field vegetarians, and Foster so continued till age, infirmity and medical men counselled him otherwise, though possibly, neither wisely nor well. I always doubted it. We collected money, and in two years paid off the society-debt and bought press and type and office appointments for the *Herald of Freedom*. We broke down the Democratic party soon after, and did vast damage to many pro-slavery churches and pulpits by exposing them to the light of day and truth. My salary the first year was exactly eighty-three cents a day. The second year I was voted four hundred dollars, all collections above that sum to be paid into the treasury of the society. And Mr. Foster's pay was probably less, but he often insisted on a too liberal division with me, on the ground that I had a wife and he had none.

In West Chester were, besides Rev. Mr. Sargent, whose faithfulness cost him his pulpit, Mr. Benjamin and Mr. Amos Chase, not brothers, only in soul and spirit, whose anti-slavery devotion was too deep and divine for human praise. Sadly as our carriage suffered, they did not permit it nor us to leave the place till all damage was repaired and everything rendered clean and sweet, and new, so far as necessary. Once afterwards Lucy Stone and myself had an engagement there, and no conveyance could be had nearer than two miles and a half. Two or three inches of snow had fallen that day, and the road we had to take was through woods, and not a track had been made. No conveyance possible, I proposed to walk on to Amos Chase's and send him back for my companion, while I would commence the meeting alone. To this

Lucy bravely objected, saying her bloomer dress and calf-skin boots, made like mine, would carry her safely through with me on foot. And they did. She was hardly willing to allow me to carry her bag a part of the way. It was pitch dark some time before we arrived, and the soft, damp snow had wet our feet as though we had walked in water all the way. Mr. Chase insisted that I should wear his boots to the meeting, and socks, as well. The family took Lucy away, and, as she told me next day, put her in a complete change from head to foot, which perspiration, added to the wet snow, had made absolutely necessary. Had West Chester been Derry on that night, our situation must have been deplorable indeed. But we knew into what hands we should fall, and so trudged cheerily, though wearily on, through darkness, forest and snow. Mr. Benjamin Chase still lives, an honor and ornament to the best rural society of the Granite state.

Most of the mob violence yet described, has been rather of the harmless sort, so far as bodily injury is considered, since Mr. Foster and myself together took the field. And Mr. Foster has hardly yet been heard through the *Herald* columns. He shall now have his turn, and readers will soon see to what purpose.

In the same month, (or within four weeks, a part of two months), of our Chester and Derry encounters, we attempted to hold some meetings in Franklin. I told Foster it rather appeared to me that he could give a better account of our experiences there than any one else, and besides, that it was time for him to do part of the reporting, were it only for the sake of variety. Though dreading a pen almost as much as a sword, in his own hand, he reluctantly consented ; and the

following description, every word, every way as truthful as it is graphic, is his own verbatim letter, as in
the *Herald of Freedom*, of November 19th, 1841 :

ANOTHER MOB — THE PULPIT ITS ORIGIN.

*To the Rev. Isaac Knight, pastor of the Congrega-
tional Church in Franklin :*

SIR—Impelled by a sense of duty to you, to your
flock and the public, I sit down to address you relative
to the recent outrage that was perpetrated upon an
anti-slavery meeting in your parish, and by persons
under your immediate supervision. That transaction
has inflicted a blot upon the character of your once
respectable village, which time will not soon efface.
It has degraded it in the eyes of all who respect
either the laws of God or man, by openly setting both
at defiance, trampling under foot the rights of the de-
fenceless and unresisting, and spurning every appeal
to the claims of justice, humanity and pure religion.
That savages and barbarians, whose trade is war, and
whose only law is the dictates of unchastened passion, should occasionally indulge in acts of brutal
violence, is not surprising. But a *mob among christians*, under the very eye of the pulpit, and in defence of that pulpit fills the mind with astonishment-
It is sad proof that the pulpit and mob are identical
in spirit and coincident in their aims !

My object in this communication is to call the attention of all who will take the trouble to read it, to
the origin of those disgraceful proceedings, which
have earned for Franklin the unenviable reputation of
having riotously broken up and dispersed an anti-
slavery meeting ; but more especially to hold up a
mirror in which you will be able to see your own
character and that of your fellow craftsmen. Like
David in the matter of Uriah and Saul of Tarsus in
the martyrdom of Stephen, you are doubtless unconscious of your guilt. But will not posterity and a
coming judgment assign to you the authorship of
that outrage ?

Was it not through your influence, aided by that of
your clerical coadjutors, that your parishioners were
induced to trample upon their own laws, brutally

assault the friends of liberty, and transmute the quiet
and security of their village into uproar and lawless
violence? Such I solemnly believe to be the fact.
Am I mistaken in this opinion? Let a rehearsal of
the scenes of that dismal night, and of your contemptuous treatment of the anti-slavery cause on the
previous Sunday, answer. Notice had been given,
through the *Herald*, that brother Pillsbury and myself would hold anti-slavery meetings in your parish
on Sunday and Monday evenings, in which all parties
would be allowed a hearing, and in the discussions of
which all would be allowed to participate. Your
meeting-house was closed against these meetings, and
you were generally understood to regard them as a
nuisance, and those who were to conduct them as infidels and "dangerous men." You had said that you
"would sooner co-operate with fiends from perdition
than with them." So inveterate was your hostility,
that our friends thought it useless to ask you to read
a notice of the meetings. One was, however, posted
up within the walls of your meeting-house. But it
soon fell a sacrifice to the piety and loyalty of your
parishioners, and shared a kindred fate with the meeting it was designed to notify.

No inconsiderable portion of the people of Franklin
regard you as their spiritual guide. Your opinion on
all moral subjects is their supreme law. Wherever
you lead, they implicitly follow. What you recommend, they cordially support. What you repudiate,
they feel religiously bound to oppose. I knew this,
and that your hostility to anti-slavery would, in all
probability, deter most of them from attending our
meetings. I knew, also, that they were profoundly
ignorant of the character of our enterprise, and of
their own guilt as accomplices and abettors of southern man-stealers, and that they were likely to remain
so. To enlighten, and, if possible, to reclaim them
from the idolatrous worship of a slave-holding religion
to the pure doctrine of the gospel, was my aim and
purpose. For that purpose I attended the meeting
over which you have assumed the authority of a
"Rabbi," which is to say, being interpreted, (a)

Master. In doing this, I was clearly within the rights guaranteed to me in the New Testament. The meeting was public. Everybody was invited to attend, and by the law of God, which you profess to preach, all who were present had an equal right to speak. I chose to avail myself of that right in behalf of the despairing bondsman, who has neither Bible, Sabbath day nor marriage institution. But, no sooner had I commenced speaking than the house was thrown into utmost disorder and confusion through your agency. Your abrupt descent from "the sacred desk," and exit from the house, was the signal for a general retreat. The meeting-house was instantly in uproar. Seeing their "guide" retire, about two-thirds of the vassal audience immediately followed. But they went out at your beck, and not prompted by their own consciences. They were anxious to hear, but were afraid of displeasing their master. But, having satisfied the claims of the pulpit, as they supposed, by leaving the room, most of them remained in the entry, literally choking up the doors, so desirous were they of hearing what I had to say. A few had the courage to return and resume their seats after you had left.

Evening came, and brought together an unusually large number for an anti-slavery meeting, but your seat was vacant. "Here are the sheep," thought I, as the seats of the capacious town hall were rapidly filling up with men and women, some of whom were from a distance of three or four miles, "but, where is the shepherd? He fancies they have broken loose from the fold, and that wolves are among them. Has he left them and fled? Is he indeed a hireling?"

The exercises of the evening elicited a good degree of interest. After some preliminary remarks from brother Pillsbury, I addressed the meeting for nearly two hours, on the slave-holding character of the American church and ministry. The audience was unusually solemn and listened with marked attention and much apparent interest and conviction, while the religious professions of the country were successfully shown to be at war with christianity, and to constitute the main bulwark of slavery. Every sect in the country was shown to be more or less contaminated with the spirit of slave-holding, while in most of them, man-stealing is not a disciplinary offence. Nor is it regarded as a sin, as is apparent from the fact that many of their most popular ministers are man-stealers; and their theological seminaries, such as Andover, Princeton, and Middletown, teach the doctrine that man-stealing if accompanied by mild treatment, is not sinful.

As our remarks on Sunday evening were confined to the church and ministry, I was not a little surprised on entering the meeting on the following evening, to find there a large number of men and boys "of the basest sort," some drunk, some sober, apparently much exasperated at our doctrines, and determined, if possible, to put a stop to their spread. They could not endure to hear their ministers and churches so traduced, and had come to their defence. The leader of this gallant band, a Mr. Hilton, whose intoxication was only zeal for the honor of the church, rather than of new rum, was in shirt sleeves, as the insignia of his office. Several others had appropriate emblems. The room was filled with a dense, fetid smoke, which was exceedingly annoying, and rendered respiration in some parts of it difficult. On examination, it was found that these fumes proceeded from breathing holes of perdition in a remote part of the room, which Satan had contrived to open for our special annoyance, through the lips of some half a dozen of your young parishoners, by means of some ignited tobacco leaves, which he had caused to be rolled into the shape of a pig's tail, and put into their *delicate* little mouths. Brother Pillsbury commenced speaking, but was soon interrupted by the talking and racket of these young gentlemen of the cigar. Finding it difficult to proceed, he remonstrated against such rude behavior, and expressed his regret that youth of so much promise should, in an unguarded hour, suffer themselves to be made a cat's paw by their parents and other superiors in age, to tear in pieces the sacred charter of the liberties for which their ancestors bled; and which it should be their highest honor to inherit and transmit, unimpaired to posterity.

This appeal was not without effect upon most of those for whose particular benefit it was intended. But the speaker had not proceeded far when he was again interrupted by an outburst of holy indignation at his infidelity and irreverence for man-stealers and their abettors from an opposite quarter of the house. This proved a more serious affair. Captain Hilton, accompanied by his tipsy corporal, one Kimball, made a pass at the speaker. Their feelings, it appeared, had been deeply wounded by some of the speaker's remarks, and nothing would appease them short of a total retraction of the obnoxious sentiments. They were no non-resistants. They had embraced the christianity of the Concord church. They wanted satisfaction and they knew how to obtain it. Brother Pillsbury coolly replied to their demands that he had spoken the truth and should make no apology for it. "Damn you," said the captain, "you have slandered and abused all our ministers and churches, and every-thing that's good among us." "Damn you," cried another, "you shall take all that back ;" and imme-diately seized him by the collar. The room at this time exhibited a scene of dreadful confusion and alarm. Observing that the women were preparing to leave the house, I left brother Pillsbury in the hands of his assailants and to the protection of his heavenly Father, and passed to the other side of the room for the purpose of allaying their fears and encouraging them to remain.

As the crowd had by this time become so dense around brother Pillsbury that I could not approach him, I stepped upon the railing and with much strength of lungs, succeeded in raising my voice above the uproar that filled the house. My expostu-lations with the mob on the meanness of disturbing a free meeting, where all enjoyed equal privilege of being heard, succeeded in restoring quiet, when it was found that brother Pillsbury, with an unresisting demeanor, had protected himself from personal in-jury, although for a time entirely in the power of infuriated drunkards ! Order being restored, he resumed his remarks.

14

But the mob were not yet satisfied.   They had not fully vindicated their character nor that of the church and ministry from the slanderous accusations of the anti-slavery agents.   After the lapse of about three-quarters of an hour, most of the rioters retired from the hall.   Joined, as we supposed, by a new recruit from the bar-room, they soon came back and commenced a hideous noise in the entry, which entirely overpowered the speaker's voice, and gave signs of another brutal assault.   Several persons, not abolitionists, attempted to hush the noise, but to little purpose. One of them called upon the constable to take the leaders into custody, but he declined on the ground that he had no precept.   I took occasion to remind this scrupulously conscientious political "minister of God" that when I entered your meeting-house for the purpose of preaching the gospel in an orderly manner, it was not thought necessary to obtain a precept in order to dispose of me ; but that any member of the congregation who chose, the minister himself not excepted, turned constable and thrust me from the house.

Finding it impossible to proceed with our exercises, brother Pillsbury and myself felt it our duty to shake off the dust of our feet and leave the place.   This we did by a short, though solemn testimony, against all those through whose agency the meeting had been broken up.   While recording that testimony, a death-like silence pervaded the room.   Even the infuriated ranks of the besotted rioters that were momentarily threatening to break forth upon us, were overpowered by its fearful import, and they silently retired in dismay at the terrors of the coming judgment, leaving us to return in safety and unmolested to our lodgings.

Such are the prominent facts connected with this disgraceful outrage.   It only remains for me to submit the question whether, in view of them, I am not fully justified in the opinion that you were the guilty author.   What possible interest had Mr. Hilton and his associates in the breaking up of our meeting? The anti-slavery enterprise does not and cannot molest them.   *They* have nothing to fear from the prevalence of free principles.   The mob was on your be-

half.   Its avowed object was to defend your character, and that of the church and ministry generally,
against what it professed to regard as the slanderous
accusations of the abolitionists.

How is it, sir, that the bar-room has disgorged itself to furnish a body-guard for the pulpit ?   Why
are the most vicious of your citizens so jealous of your
reputation ?   Can we suppose that they acted contrary
to your wishes in this matter ?   Men may oppose, but
will rarely defend us by means which we do not sanction and approve.

You declared you "would sooner co-operate with
fiends from perdition than with Rogers and his coadjutors !"

Is not this mob alarming proof that you are co-
operating with fiends from perdition in the *perpetuity*
of slavery, and not with Rogers and his coadjutors in
its overthrow?   Respectfully yours,

STEPHEN S. FOSTER.

Andover, Mass., Nov. 7, 1841.

CHAPTER X.

DARTMOUTH COLLEGE—RIOTOUS BEHAVIOR OF THE
STUDENTS—STRAFFORD COUNTY ANNIVERSARY—EAST
ERN RAILROAD AND ITS JIM CROW CARS—OUT-
RAGES ON COLORED PASSENGERS.

Franklin was but a specimen of New Hampshire,
and Mr. Knight was in immense majority, and Dartmouth college was helping to keep the number of his
kind good, if not increase it. At Franklin, the rioters
were mostly boys, set on or led on by some old enough
to be their fathers and grandfathers, drunk on rum or
rage, spleen and spite, but doing the will and pleasure
of church and minister. Their ribaldry was as offensive as their blasphemy. What we most feared, had
most reason to fear, was that some indiscreet friend
of ours might be impelled to resist their outrages of
word and deed by force. True, the provocation was
very great. But had such resistance been made, even
to a single blow, however slight, it would have filled
the hordes surrounding us with fiendish delight, and
bloody scenes must inevitably have followed. Since
the war of the rebellion, almost every ruffian appears
to be armed with dirk, pistol, or both, ready for use at
any moment. It was not so then and there, but I long
kept in my cabinet stones and other missiles, including heavy bullets, which had been hurled at me and
my brave companion, through windows, or as we
walked or rode along the streets to or from our meetings. We read in New Testament times of a Stephen
stoned *to death* by a mob. I traveled and worked

with another Stephen who would have cheerfully suffered similar fate.   And who shall say it would not have been in an equally holy cause?   And in deep humility and sincerity I can say we together passed through many scenes where it would have been our joy, and true honor, too, to fall as did the ancient Stephen, could our cause have been best subserved thereby.   But it was only in extreme peril that my constitutional cowardice was so far overcome.   Mob violence was ever my aversion and dread, till deep in the midst of it.   Brave old military heroes have often told me that they trembled at the outset, and till after the first few shots had been exchanged.   Then there was no more fear.   I could well understand them. But not so my friend Foster.   He seemed ever cool and serene, before and through the fiercest encounters.   Nor did any one ever see him exultant, in his most brilliant successes.   But to return to our narrative.

The next experiences and their results to be described occurred, soon after at *Dartmouth college,* which introduced me to society and scenes unknown before.

The question has often been asked me, sometimes in letters from distant states, at what college I received my education.   It always sounded strangely in my ears, when remembering that at seven and twenty there was not a harder worked, nor working man, young nor old, in my native state of Massachusetts, nor my involuntarily adopted state of New Hampshire, at four years old.   At twenty-four, I joined the Congregational church, in Henniker.   To me, it was the most sacred, solemn step of my whole life.   There had been none of those dark, despairing convictions, so frequently felt and described, and still less had

there been any of the raptures, the "joy unspeakable
and full of glory," that so many experienced, and
even loudly boasted. I waited for such, long, earnestly, expectantly, and confidently. A doubt that
such were necessary had not entered my mind, though
many around me gave sad evidence in their lives and
conversation after their experience, that even the most
intense anguish of conviction and exttaic joy in the
hour of conversion, were no assurance of regenera-
tion or change of heart. The reasonableness, wisdom
and righteousness of the divine requirements were
made so plain to my understanding, and the observance of them, according to my enlightenment, so
necessary to the highest happiness and welfare of the
human race, that in the very love of them, I accepted
them, irrespective of all questions of perdition as
penalty or paradise as reward. Educated almost
from infancy in the Congregational Sunday-school,
and corresponding religious teaching with scrupulous
care and faithfulness at home, it was easy to *assume*
as true all the doctrines of our denomination, trinity
atonement, total depravity and election, as well as
everlasting rewards and retributions. If away beyond
my comprehension, I remembered how many great
and holy men had embraced and defended them ; how
many godly men and women had died martyrs for
them on torturing racks and in burning flames, and
who in my situation could doubt their truth without
violence to every pulsation of soul and spirit?

And so I entered the church tremblingly, but resolved to the best of all I was, or could become, to
adorn my profession. And whatever duties were
taught me as a christian professor, I endeavored to
perform. Temperance and anti-slavery were among
my first espousals ; the former with the approval of

and encouragement of our pastor, but the latter rather in spite of him. Our first anti-slavery lecture was delivered in the Methodist meeting-house, by Moses A. Cartland, then a most excellent Quaker school-teacher and principal, if not founder, of the once well-known *Clinton Grove school*, in the adjoining town of Weare. It was in the spring of 1835, while I was yet with my father and family on the farm. The lecture was a calm, serene, but truthful and faithful presentation of the wrongs of the slave, the crimes and cruelties, the outrages and abominations inseparable from the slave system; but all delivered with the gentleness and spirit of Lydia Maria Child, from whose writings he frequently and liberally quoted, and several older members of the church than myself were deeply impressed by the important truths we heard. Not so, however, the minister and most of the leading church members and officers. A general town meeting was called at the town house, and speeches were made and resolutions adopted denouncing and condemning the anti-slavery agitation and all who abetted or encouraged it. And similar meetings were held in many towns all over the state, and their proceedings were published in the newspapers. At this time, and for three or four years afterward, the agitation had not jarred the foundations of church or pulpit to such a degree as to produce the winnowings, the separations and rendings that were to ensue in 1839 and 1840, when in very deed judgment had to begin, and did "*begin at the house of God!*" Till then, there were many in the churches, ministers as well as others, who hated slavery and were willing it should be abolished if the peace and sleep of their organizations be not thereby disturbed. But so it could not be. In our church at

Henniker, temperance was held and preached as a cardinal christian virtue. The church covenant required of every member "total abstinence from ardent spirits as a drink," as early as 1835, if not before. Had the ministers espoused and proclaimed the doctrines and duties of anti-slavery as earnestly, most of the church would as cordially have embraced them. My anti-slavery gave some offence, especially when once a slaveholder came and preached in our pulpit, and I absented myself from meeting solely in consequence. But only few held with me, and none had gone so far as to refuse sermon and sacrament from a slaveholder, though several men and women approved my course in such refusal.

It was to the question however, at what college my education was obtained, that I proposed to answer a few words, and directly in continuation of the matter in hand. In prosecuting our mission, Mr. Foster and myself found ourselves at Hanover, and the gates of Dartmouth college, from whence Foster had graduated only three years before, and with more than ordinary college honors. I had never before seen the interior of that, nor of any other college, in my life ; and to academies and high-schools I was scarcely less a stranger.

The annual meeting of the Grafton county society had been already held, but in the south part of the county, a full day's drive from Hanover, and a similar convening seemed desirable in the northern section, and Hanover was the selected place. It was a full week, however, before any house could be found in which to assemble, and the committee were at length, after that delay, compelled to call our meeting at the dancing hall of the principal hotel. Neither church nor college would open to us a door, nor condescend to give us any reason why we were so summarily denied.

At the time appointed, however, the convention assembled in encouraging numbers, was duly organized, opened with prayer, and we proceeded to business. Henry C. Wright, of Philadelphia, formerly a Congregational minister, Mr. Foster, and myself were present as principal speakers, though all persons present were cordially invited, as was our invariable custom, to participate in the discussions. The first resolution presented was to the effect that in any moral conflict, strength and success depended, not so much upon numbers, as on inflexible adherence to principle. An interesting debate ensued, which occupied the remainder of the morning session, when the resolution passed unanimously, and we adjourned till afternoon.

At two o'clock we again assembled, when after prayer the following resolution was offered :

Resolved, That every person in the nation, north or south, who is not an open abolitionist, is by his influence, sustaining and perpetuating slavery, and should be regarded by every friend of humanity as a virtual slave-holder.

This resolution was the order for afternoon. A clerical agent of the new organization came also among us. He moved an amendment diluting the resolution to his taste and temper. And as church, college and village made a large part of the audience after closing all their doors against us, the original resolution was rejected, by small majority. ·In the evening, our resolution read as below :

Resolved, That American slavery is a complication of the foulest crimes ; robbery, adultery, man-stealing, and murder ; and should therefore be immediately and unconditionally abolished.

The college students crowded themselves together
and were very disorderly, both before and after the
exercises began, clapping, hissing, and hooting, in
most indecent and vulgar manner.   Mr. Foster opened
the discussion in an address of wondrous eloquence
and power of argument, showing how slavery was all
the resolution charged and a great deal more, and
that logically, morally, every way, the slave-holder
must be robber, adulterer, man-stealer and murderer.
Then he illustrated what these crimes meant in slavery;
how a man-stealer must be as much greater than a
horse or sheep-stealer, as a man is better and greater
than sheep or horse.   Then he asked : " How much
greater is a man than a sheep ? "   " Who in Dartmouth
college can solve that problem ? Who ? " And yet, he
declared, " those monsters are hourly stealing the very
Christ who died for them, in the person of his little
ones.   For inasmuch as they do it to the poorest,
blackest of his children, they do it unto God !   And
to Christ his Son.   All this, not to speak of the other
capital crimes mentioned in the resolution.   And who
perpetrates these outrages ?   They are ministers,
bishops, elders, doctors of divinity, deacons, and
church members, presidents and professors of colleges
and theological seminaries." And he declared, "those
at the north who fellowshiped such as christians and
christian ministers, are bad as they.   They voluntarily
make themselves man-stealers and robbers, adulterers
and murderers, in position, all of them ; and many of
them in heart.   We do not see them do the deeds,
and so we hold them innocent.   But what would you
say if President Lord, of your own college, should be
seen carrying home at night, a stolen sheep ? or buying one he knew had just been stolen ? "

From that time, the order and quiet of the convention were no more. But the disturbance did not begin then, it was only mightily increased. It commenced before the opening prayer, and did not wholly cease during the evening. There were those, not all boys, who, during some of Mr. Foster's most thrilling appeals, and blood curdling descriptions, would keep up their scraping, whistling, and snickering, as though they were in some cheap circus or minstrel show. Possibly on some battle-field in the Rebellion, they learned their mistake.

For a time we were completely silenced by the uproar. The editor of the *Hanover Amulet*, who happened to enter at that moment, said in his next paper: "Judge of our surprise when we entered the hall where we supposed every heart beat in unison with sympathy for the oppressed, to find general tumult and confusion," which *tumult* continued through the evening with greater or less atrocity to the very last ; and the clerical new organization agent added greatly, and seemed to enjoy greatly, the outrage.

But no explanation which Mr. Foster could make availed anything. For a long time, he had no hearing at all. When he obtained the ear for a few moments, he abjured utterly, any disrespect to President Lord or to the college. He only wished to impress on the minds and hearts of his hearers, the awful wickedness of slavery, and not less of the north, especially the northern church and clergy, in fellowshiping as christians, these monsters of iniquity—that for Dr. Lord he had only profound respect ; and with good reason, he said, for he had ever been as a father to him, both while he was at college and since he graduated ; and that sooner should his tongue cleave to the roof of his mouth than be guilty of uttering one word to his injury ; but all to no purpose. He was constantly hissed and insulted till he closed his remarks, and afterwards, if he attempted to speak, until we closed the meeting.

Henry C. Wright was not much better received, though in most pathetic word and tone, he depicted the condition of the enslaved, completely, hopelessly, and to their last breath, in the power of those who had been proved beyond all possibility of doubt, robbers, and adulterers, man-stealers and murderers ; cruel, remorseless, relentless as death. Mr. Wright was heard, with more or less interruption, nearly half an hour.

The next speaker was the new organization minister. He was from some place in Massachusetts. In rather a sneering, contemptuous manner he asked, not the mob, but us who had called the meeting, if he might speak. He had surely heard the resolution offered, and seen it adopted unanimously, that " all persons present be invited to participate in the deliberations of the convention." In his conventions and meetings, no such resolution was ever offered, speaking and voting being always insolently denied to women, even such women as Abby Kelly, the Grimke sisters, and Lucretia Mott. He, of course, as in the afternoon, strenuously opposed our resolution, and presented a stupidly modified and diluted substitute. The solemn and pathetic address of Mr. Wright had produced a deep and desirable impression on many minds, and the object of the substituted resolution and its mover was to efface it. His low, vulgar wit, the farthest possible remove from the searching description and appeal of Mr. Wright, was loudly cheered and applauded by the uproarious crew for whose benefit it was uttered. Very sapiently, he quo--

ted the law of his state of Massachusetts as to what
constituted murder. He was applauded and approved.
Mr. Foster responded from his seat with the scripture
law, "He that hateth his brother is a murderer," and
was loudly hissed. As the best our opponent could
do with the scripture allusion as a higher law, he began a taunting strain of remark about our being, not
an anti-slavery society, but a non-resistance, no-gov-
ernment association ; and gave as his proof that we
quoted scripture instead of ordinary, legal definitions.
This false and foolish charge, two or three times repeated and boisterously applauded, was all the irrelevant matter thrust upon us in a business way. No
notice was taken of this, except by Mr. Wright, who
very coolly remarked that an anti-slavery convention
was not the place to discuss non-resistance. Our opponent admitted that the resolution was strictly true
in every charge but that of murder. In our argument
we had not alluded to scripture at all on any of the
counts in the resolution. We had judged slavery by
ordinary statute and the natural rights of common
humanity. At this point, we asked our opponent
whether to shoot down, or tear in pieces with trained
blood-hounds, a poor slave who, under cover of night,
was quietly, peacefully fleeing to Canada for freedom,
was not murder ? "No," he said, "not *legal* murder,"
and this answer elicited applause loud and long, making the floor to tremble under our feet. From this
time, if not indeed long before, all sense of honor,
propriety, decency, was disregarded. The women
present had before retired in disgust, and it seemed
probable that we who had called the convention
would no longer be suffered. But Foster determined
to make one more effort at a hearing. Seizing on a
moment of comparative silence, in a loud voice he

proceeded to say that he had a few days before visited
Hanover, to secure a place for this convention, but
was unable to procure any place whatever that was
controlled by the college ; that he then applied for
this tavern hall, and, after some delay and delibera-
tion, he secured it, at the not unreasonable price of
three dollars a day ; that it had been our intention to
continue the convention two days and evenings, but
such had been the confusion and uproar of this evening, and such the manifest intention, if possible, to
hinder the orderly and quiet prosecution of our business, the meetings will be closed to-night ; *and the
responsibility of disturbing and breaking up an open,
free-discussion, anti-slavery convention, may rest on those
to whom it justly belongs.*

These remarks, in good, strong, earnest tone and
spirit, made a deep impression. Many had not before
comprehended the position in which they had placed
themselves and their college. One young man, afterwards a professor in a theological seminary, rose and
attempted what proved a most lame and impotent defence of the rioters. He said it was the custom of
the students to express their approval or disapproval
of whatever passed before them in this way ; that an
attack had been made on Dr. Lord, an honored and
respected officer of the institution, and it was not
strange that those who honored and venerated him
should thus manifest their disapprobation. And besides, the students themselves had been reproached,
and took this method to express their displeasure at
that also. One or two others also spoke to about the
same import ; one adding to other charges, that our
"speeches were wild and windy," and another, that
they "were long and tedious."

Glad at seeing any change for the better in the temper or methods of our opponents, I ventured, for the first time during the evening, to occupy a few minutes, and began by assuring the meeting that it was not strange, since the president and college professors had driven the poor slave to the tavern hall as the only place where, with their approval, his friends could assemble to plead his cause, the students, imitating their spirit, should come here also to drive us from this, the slave's last refuge. I reminded them that this, like all our meetings, was open to free and friendly discussion ; unlike most assemblies, as free to our opponents as our friends. We learned afterwards that the committee of the Congregational meeting-house, which was also refused us, was composed in part of the college faculty, the very chairman of the board being one.   I said further, what surely was always true at that time, that we found the most violent opposition to the anti-slavery cause among the so-called "educated ministry," and that from this time we could not be surprised at it, for here at college, they see the doors of meeting-houses, vestries, lecture rooms, shut against us, and commence their hostilities by driving us even from tavern halls, Here to-night, I said, we see what the candidates for the ministry can do through hatred to our movements. and in imitation of the spirit of those under whose tuition you have placed yourselves ; and everywhere we are seeing and feeling what you may do when you come to be ministers. I said that my own life had been anything rather than a student's life ; that, though I had traveled and lectured extensively throughout New York and New England, singularly enough, I had never, till to-day, seen even the outside of a college (we thought of that, exclaimed one in the crowd) ; and I hoped as to moral character, that what we saw here, was not a fair specimen of our higher institutions of learning ; though I felt compelled to say, that, judging from the spirit and position of the clergy and most of our educated men on the great questions of moral reform, I feared most of our large seminaries of learning had not been much misrepresented by the students of Dartmouth college, here to-night. It did not surprise me that by this time the tumult was renewed by some of the younger portion of the disturbers, nor did I greatly regret it, for I felt that my rebuke was as necessary as it was richly deserved ; and that kind of hostile demonstration only clinched tighter the argument. Many endeavored to hush the confusion and some cried loudly, "Hear him, hear him." But I had closed my remarks, and kept my feet till it was possible to be again heard, and then moved that the convention be now finally adjourned; which was immediately put, and carried unanimously. And with that closed my first and last connection with any college. And now the question is answered ; *at what college I obtained my education?* The answer ; my *collegiate* education, at Dartmouth ; and all in one day. There needed no more. One or two later, fiercer, college mobs added nothing new, nor important to my stock of knowledge in that department.

Still, why blame the students? They had good reason to suppose they were serving the college, and doing the will of its officers. It was no worse for them to mob us out of the hotel hall, than it was for their masters and the church authorities to send us there, by shutting us out of every other place. Our cause was then passing through its most fiery ordeal. The time having come "that judgment must begin at the house of God," church and pulpit, college, university and theological seminary seemed to have made treaty, offensive and defensive, against it. Most of those institutions, as well as the academies and lesser seats of learning, were then, as always, largely under clerical control. The writings of President Lord, of Dartmouth college, on slavery and the abolitionists, were fearful. Some of them lie before me. In the light of the "Golden Rule," of Confucius, and of the Sermon on the Mount, centuries after, they are infamous. Amid the blazing terrors of Fort Wagner and Port Hudson, the torments of Andersonville and Libby prisons, they are truly diabolical. Shall we blame the pupils of such a president for a few hours of rude, indecent and vulgar behavior, and riotously breaking up of a county convention with welcome entrance to what might have been a free, friendly anti-slavery discussion? Verily, no!

Andover Latin Academy and Lane Theological Seminary had driven away large numbers of their bravest, most conscientious and high-minded students by downright pro-slavery intolerance. Canaan, New Hampshire, Academy, had been broken up for the unpardonable sin of admitting a few colored pupils on equal terms with the white, by vote of the people in legal town meeting assembled. A committee was appointed for the business, and, as officially reported in the *N. H. Patriot*, the edifice was lifted from its foundations, and by three hundred men and a hundred yoke of oxen was hauled out of town. The most respectable and wealthy farmers in the place assisted in service like that at the bidding of the slave-power, which then ruled supreme. Well does Senator Wilson, in his History, ask in his account of it, " Could the fanaticism of slavery go farther than

15

that? how demoralized the community which could furnish the actors in such a drama, and applaud it when enacted!"

But "the fanaticism of slavery" could and did go a great deal farther than that, as Senator Wilson and his country learned to their cost, in the coming years.

Miss Prudence Crandall, a benevolent and philanthropic woman of the Society of Friends, had her school in Canterbury, Connecticut, utterly broken up and routed for the same offence as that of the Noyes academy at Canaan. Her's was a school for girls, and the outrages attending the transaction were some of them too shameful to be told. Town meetings were held, resolutions offered and discussed in words harder than bullets; Mrs. Crandall was arrested, thrust into prison, dragged to trial, and, though acquitted by the court, was re-arrested, tried over again, and this time convicted. Her counsel filed a bill of exceptions, and appealed the case. By the highest tribunal in the state the verdict was overruled. Then a ruffian crowd assailed her house, and destroyed it, and the pupils were all sent to their homes, to return no more!

We could easily forgive the rioters at Dartmouth college. And moreover, a clerical new organization agent was present, greatly to encourage them. The churches had already been proved, by their own voluntary testimony, "the bulwarks of American slavery," and nearly all the large literary and theological institutions in the land were buttressed about them. We forgave the students, remembering who it was that said, "It is enough for the disciple that he be as his master, and the servant as his lord."

This chapter will close with a highly descriptive and instructive account of the annual meeting of the

Strafford County Anti-Slavery Society, in 1842, at
Dover, much of it from the pen of Mr. Rogers. It
was largely attended, and continued three whole days
and evenings. Many resolutions were discussed and
adopted with entire unanimity. The most important
are given below. The first was offered by Rev. John
Parkman, then Unitarian minister of Dover :

Resolved, That our devout acknowledgments are
due to that Almighty Power whose arm has sustained
us so graciously in every stage of our enterprise, for
the encouragement furnished to future exertion by
the successes of the past.

The resolution was earnestly supported by the
mover and Mr. Garrison, and unanimously adopted.
The next were as below :

Whereas, According to the recognized interpreta-
tions of the United States Constitution, and the uni-
form practice of the federal government, *the free states
are pledged to the support of slavery ;* and whereas,
southern slaveholders, by their oppression and cruelty,
are doing all in their power to incite their slaves to resistance, at the same time relying upon our aid to deliver them in their hour of peril ; therefore,

Resolved, That we solemnly warn the whole country
that, come what may come, compact or no compact,
Constitution or no Constitution, Union or no Union,
neither duty to God nor allegiance to law would ever
allow us to obey any requisition of government calling us to put down by arms any rising of the slaves.

Resolved, That it be recommended to abolitionists
to call town meetings in their respective towns, to
consider those terms of the federal compact which
have been construed to bind them to the support of
slavery, and whether they would comply, should they
be called upon to do so by the United States Government.

Resolved, That the church that has set and that continues the example of the negro pew, (and which
example has been so eagerly followed by the proprietors and conductors of our steamboats and railway

cars,) is guilty of an attack on the works of the great
Creator which gives convincing assurance that it is
not governed by the spirit of Christ, nor the fear of
that God who is declared to be "no respecter of persons."

Resolved, That the Eastern Railroad corporation, in
compelling its servants to outrage people of color by
invidiously commanding them out of respectable into
inferior cars, and even in dragging them out by force
and violence, is cruelly proscriptive and insulting to
our common humanity.

Resolved, That in the rejection, by the United States
senate, of the nominations of Messrs. Everett, Wilson
and Eastman, upon the alleged ground of opinion in
regard to slavery, we see another proof of the undue
predominance of southern interests in our national
legislature, and we regard the expression of public sentiment recently manifested upon this point as a
sign that the free states are becoming sensible of this,
and of the connection between their own rights and
the assertion of the rights of the slaves.

Resolved, That the omission of the United States
senate to confirm the nominations of Everett and
others, on account of their anti-slavery opinions, just
named, reveals the horrid truth that the South holds
slavery to be the paramount interest of the country;
and that the resentment manifested at this refusal by
the pro-slavery northern press betrays the humiliating
truth that the North regards the rejection of party
nominations as a greater insult to liberty than the enslavement of one-sixth part of the people.

Resolved, That the course of Andover theological
seminary in attempting, through some of its professors, to justify American slavery from the Bible, in
openly opposing the anti-slavery enterprise, and in
giving to the community a ministry that has generally
proved itself the sternest obstacle to the progress of
anti-slavery truth, has been such as should excite the
deepest apprehension and alarm for the cause of humanity and of christianity, and calls loudly for the
severest rebuke of every abolitionist.

Subjoined are the editorial remarks of Mr. Rogers, in the *Herald of Freedom* :

The Dover Meeting.—We had intended• a full account of this great and interesting and most important convention, for this week. It was the more necessary as the report of the officers of the meeting is so condensed and bare. The proceedings lose much of their intrinsic force by the compressed form in which they are presented. Several resolutions, for instance, that were acted on separately, are given in one and as if passed together. We are about starting to accompany Brother Pillsbury to Hancock and Francestown to a series of anti-slavery meetings, and can say now but a hasty word and be more particular hereafter. The meetings were held in the old Court House, a very convenient and comfortable room, and well employed ; and as fit as a meeting house would be, and more free. There was a goodly attendance. The mass of the people did not come in. They were not advised to by their controllers. The ministers did not as they ought to have done, give the people notice and exhort or encourage them to attend. They did not want them to. They wanted them not to. They were there themselves, led by curiosity, or policy, or fear, or all three. The Rev. Mr. Young was there, in nervous but heartless attendance, during the entire meeting. He looked on verily like a priest and a Levite. The Rev. Mr. Horton was in and out, with his sneer and his laugh, looking and acting more like a jolly friar than a christian. He is professionally engaged in reading Church of England service Sundays, and that is the worship of his sect. Nothing would be deemed by him "a greater insult," he asserted to some one during the convention, "than to be called an abolitionist." Nothing, we remark, would be so deep an insult to abolitionism. "I would not be caught shaking hands with Mr. Lloyd Garrison," he said.

We intend to give a full and particular representation of the meeting, and of the part acted by prominent opposers in attendance as well as the abolitionists, if we can get time before we forget it. It was a marvellous meeting, and there were marvellous human developments there which would instruct the times if they could be graphically delineated. Hogarth would be the narrator to give the demeanor of a pro-slavery minister or politician at an anti-slavery meeting.

This is all for which Mr. Rogers had time during the week of the convention. Attending other meetings with Mr. Foster and myself the next week in other counties, to which his presence added great charm and force, prevented but a few more remarks on that at Dover, in the next *Herald*, to this purport;

THE DOVER MEETING is not forgotten, but unavoidably deferred. We have never attended a meeting of any character so splendidly sustained and so orderly, voluntarily and beautifully conducted. It was a self-governed meeting. Our nominal president declined *keeping order;* and when, once or twice, some, who came in to dispute, called for order and bred some little disorder, he threw the meeting on its *self-government*, and all was quietness. Oh, that the people, the laboring people, the toiling people, the livelong-day working men, and the women, whose task is never done, oh, that they had been allowed to be present and hear the truths that would have found response in their unsophisticated hearts! They were not allowed to be there. They were discouraged away by the unprincipalled politician and the Jesuitical priest. How shall anti-slavery get at them? Must it go with Foster into the synagogues on Sunday, and speak to them in the face of the cannon's mouth and bayonet's point? When shall anti-slavery find a chance *to speak to the people!* We were amazed above measure to hear brother Francis Cogswell and Rev. Brother Young eulogizing Garrison. "I have been highly pleased with Mr. Garrison," said brother Young. Brother Young's being pleased or displeased, by the way, was infinitely unimportant. *He* seemed to think it more material than to repent of his mobocratic, pro-slavery spirit, which could outrage the decencies of an anti-slavery meeting, last winter, in his own meeting-house! He declared *solemnly*, the

second evening of the convention, that *he was pleased*
with some of the proceedings of the meetings ! an indirect clerical blow at other of the proceedings—viz.
at the apostolic plainness of Pillsbury, and the Nathan-
like directness of the faithful. Foster.   He would
compliment the *infidel* Garrison himself if he could
do it at the expense of these men.   "If you would
send out such men as Garrison," said friend Cogswell, "your cause would prosper."   "How long have
you been an admirer of Garrison, brother Cogswell?"
said we.   "Oh, I have not liked his writings," said
he.   "He has not written as he speaks, here."   "Always," said we, "only he speaks with more ultraism
and denunciation than he has ever written.   "Impossible!   I find no fault with anything he has said
here," said Brother Cogswell.   "Everybody finds
fault with Garrison," said we, "until they see him and
hear him speak.   If you had read what you have
heard, it would have been *ferocious denunciation.*   But
when you see the man and hear him, it is quite another thing.   And, brother Young," said we to him,
as he stood by, praising Garrison, "brother Young,
we never shall hear anything from you of Garrison's
infidelity hereafter.   Remember that."   *   *   *   *
*   *   *   The Strafford-county anti-slavery society
is auxiliary to the N. H. anti-slavery society.   We
mention the auxiliaryship, for, on that point, our
friends were strenuously assisted by the genius of new
organization under the treacherous form of neuterism.
A few clergymen, afraid to espouse the unpopular
side of old organization, and ashamed of the revealed
infamy of the new, took refuge under the name of
neutrality, or neither one thing nor another.   This anniversary was not of the excrescence which they contrived to form.   Such excrescences have no anniversaries.   They do not live long enough.   They never
live a year unless kept alive by external galvanic influences.   The American Union lived but a day.
The new organization lived longer, but it was by gal-
vanism.   It has undergone a change, now, "in its
mode of existence."   It is a third political party, with
liberty poles up and flags flying, as smart as any of
the "nations round about."

Strafford anti-slavery organisęd itself as an auxiliary to the old movement. And it is its grand anniversary we are noticing. We spoke last week of some of the names in it. * * * We do not eulogize abolitionists as men do the politicians, but we proclaim their excellencies, if at all, in behalf of our despised and down-trodden cause. We claim for that cause the worth of those enlisted in it. We remind the scornful world that "the salt of the earth is with us." And we bid them beware on whom they are trampling. But anti-slavery leans not on the merits, however great, of those who have embarked in it. It is among the chief merits of any man, that he has espoused so glorious a cause as this. But this is delicate ground and we hasten from it. The forenoon of the first day was spent, after getting over the choice of officers, which being matter of constitutional obligation could not be dispensed with, had it been desired, but which was disposed of in the most summary manner possible, by choosing, at one vote, all the last year's officers, *en masse*, in discussing a resolution offered by John Parkman. A resolution touching the influence of the church and clergy on our enterprise had been offered by Brother Lunt, of Somersworth. It went to the very gist of the movement, and touched slavery in the apple of its eye. At Brother Parkman's request, it was deferred by the mover till the consideration of one he desired to introduce, which came very properly as a threshold topic—to wit: acknowledging obligation to God in view of the past successes of the cause, and the grounds of encouragement found in them to future effort. This was beautifully discussed by Brothers Parkman and Garrison.

The afternoon was not, in our opinion, so wisely nor profitably spent. Instead of taking up Brother Lunt's resolution, as should have been done in its order, Brother Henry C. Wright, with a view perhaps to bring out the eminent talent present, on the constitutional question, introduced a series of resolutions involving the relations slavery sustains to that poor old unprincipled compact. The afternoon was wasted in a waste of ability on a heartless theme. There was much good speaking, which in Faneuil hall or any of our meeting houses, on some patriotic occasion, would have been lauded to the stars by the party presses. But no appeals were made to the heart or conscience of a slave-holding people. For one, though, we once labored a good deal to vindicate the old military compact from the reproach of slavery, we care very little about it now, as an anti-slavery question. It will move the hearts of the people neither one way nor the other. While as pro-slavery as they now are, the thunders of the Almighty alone can rouse their attention, or lead them to repentance. The awful truths of the BIBLE, not the constitution, are to be poured on their obdurate hearts. We care nothing for our obligation, one way or the other, under this compact, to interfere in a rising of the southern slaves. Abolitionists, as such cannot fight for the slave, nor need they tell the south they will not fight against him. The south don't expect us to. She thinks, or pretends to think, abolitionists are for inciting the slaves to rise and kill them all. Of course the masters need not be told, nor the north either, that we will not take arms in behalf of slavery. That slavery is unconstitutional, we have no doubt. But the nation does not care for that. They will interpret the constitution as they choose to understand it. Least of all, would they ever alter their habits, or change their social character to suit a mere heartless political compact. They will hold slaves in spite of everything but the *fear of hell*. We would urge on them the horrible iniquity of incurring that awful retribution. They would fear it now but for the ungodly influence of the clergy. That sears their conscience and hardens their heart. The *mind* of the convention was perplexed by an argument on the constitution. No doubt the clergymen present were greatly edified and relieved by it. We put it to the sound judgment of all concerned, whether the subject is worth our *anti-slavery while*. The constitution can't hold slaves when the great national brotherhood of thieves shall have relaxed their grasp upon them. Had the Strafford bar been present, who usually occupied the room, or had the court been sitting, the argu--

ment would have enlightened their heads, if it could not have softened their hearts. But the convention was a body of plain-minded, simple-hearted men and women, whose souls would starve on such *husks* as statutes and constitutions.

The evening meeting was at Rev. Mr. Young's synagogue. He did not break it up *riotously*, as he did the meeting of our state agents last winter, which disorderly and mobocratic proceeding was suffered to pass too lightly. Had poor laborers mobbed the meeting, we should have treated them with much less ceremony. But it was the reverend and elevated Mr. Young, and we treated it, as well as bore it, with very deferential submission. It was really a *ruffian* disturbance. Jeremiah Young broke in upon the decency and order of the meeting with the rudeness and lawlessness of a *ruffian*. He differed from a drunken brawler only in form. He as clearly violated the right, and so did friends Cogswell and Pierce. They declined speaking when invited, and when they had the right. They held back till they were excited by their mobocratic minister, and then they broke out. They must not think to treat anti-slavery quite so contemptuously, and go unreproved. We ought to have reproved them on the spot, as riotous and disorderly men. But the evening meeting at the anniversary was not disturbed. We take occasion, however, to enter our disapproval of its arrangement. It was planned beforehand for the purpose of an intellectual impression. Not exactly so, but in accordance with that sort of policy. The ablest speakers were *selected*, instead of leaving the meeting, these among the rest, to its spontaneous action. Garrison and Phillips spoke, but not like themselves. They were hampered by the arrangements of the meeting. They were not *impelled* to speak. And the fugitive Douglass was mounted away up into the mahogany perch, where the people look up to gaze at Rev. Brother Young, Sundays, as the Israelites did up Mount Sinai after Moses, or after him who abode in the thick clouds about its summit. What a place for a fugitive slave to speak in, and to tell his simple story ! It was incongruous enough to be in the synagogue itself, where a free colored man can't be allowed a pew, as we understand.   But it was the awkwardest of all places, to be mounted up among those astral lamps, as high, almost, as the stars.   The parties all performed as well as men could under the circumstances, but it was no evening for the afternoon that preceded it.   Rev. Brother Young was "delighted" with it.   No mob dog moved a tongue, whereas, had the meeting been spontaneous, Douglass would have moved hearts of stone there, and Garrison and Phillips would have made the house quake through all its *dedicated* recesses.   Brother Young was so pleased with the meeting that he condescended, the next evening, to declare his satisfaction publicly.   He was pleased, he graciously said, with *most* that he had heard ; meaning, of course, the parts of the meetings we have noticed.   Collins said something, at a late hour, of the outrage inflicted on himself and Douglass on board the railroad cars from Boston.   Douglass gave a sketch of his slave experience, and of slavery itself, but somewhat embarrassed by his unnatural position. He told how he learned to read—of his conflict with the alphabet and the *abs* amid the hazards of slavery. He learned to write on board fences, making some of his early capitals with their heads downwards and looking the wrong way.   It was laughable to hear him.   Still, we could not help thinking of humanity driven to such extremity for the rudiments of knowledge, here amid the lights and professions of a *religious* republic.   Here, where learning is as common as the air, the poor slave, trodden down below humanity, has to steal the crumbs of intelligence that lay about almost within reach of the dogs in the street.   Thanks to our missionary, theologizing, Bible-circulating, tract-spreading religion !   It has *slaves* whom it *dooms to death* for learning the letters and syllables of the language they have to speak, and in which they want to read the Bible !

Next morning the meeting opened free and unfettered.   A voluntary prayer was offered, not as an unmeaning ceremony, as is common in *fettered*

assemblies, and Lunt's resolution was called. He made a plain, sensible, spirit-moving speech upon it. Many others spoke, as mentioned in the report of the meeting, and with exceeding power. We hardly ever witnessed a half day like it ; it was an uninterrupted stream of solemn interest throughout, particularly the passage between brothers Coues and Garrison. Brother Coues had rarely attended anti-slavery meetings, and had been rather repelled by apprehensions of anti-slavery harshness and denunciation. He deprecated in his speech, which was very beautiful in manner, but we think, too full of allowance in sentiment to pro-slavery claims, the denial of christian character to all slave-holding ; and claimed for them a sort of indulgence to remain in their unhallowed relation to their fellow-men. Garrison answered him in apostolic style ; and the manner in which brother Coues received his over-powering admonition, was most affecting and delightful. It was uttered with christian fidelity, and received with christian magnanimity. Garrison's appeal was one of the best expositions of christianity we have ever heard. Sundry clergymen heard it, who had doubtless often warned their flock against anti-slavery, on account of "the infidelity of Garrison." They now heard him, and how must the remembrance of their falsehood have blistered their consciences, if hot iron had not seared them !   *   *   *   *
The *Dover Enquirer*, one of the party presses, in the magnificent struggle going on in the country for the loaves and fishes of office, ventured the other day to speak of the meeting, and of our remarks upon it. The editor supposed he had espied out an indefensible sentence or two, and he seized upon them with true pro-slavery veracity, leaving out all that common honesty would have published in connection, to give the reader opportunity to judge of the unwarrantable extracts. Colonel Wadleigh (for most all of these political editors are colonels or majors), is almost ferocious for the sacred honor of the meeting house. The politicians and militia officers nearly all are. They think meeting houses are the sure defense of religion,

as the clergy think the militia is the sure defense of
a state, which the ministers profoundly believe.   They
have little confidence in any other security but military.   " Trust God " they say with Cromwell, but like
him they would emphasize particularly, "keep your
powder dry."   The editor imagines a discrepancy
between our doubting whether we could have had a
meeting house for our discussion meetings, and the
fact that one was opened to evening lectures.   It was
of them of which we spoke, and not of the public lectures or set speeches.   These are not near so sacrilegious as free discussion on resolutions.   We do not
think Brother Young would consent to have his tabernacle exposed to another *discussion* meeting when
Parker Pillsbury and Stephen S. Foster were to be let
loose among the speakers.   The Rev. Brother Horton,
of the elegant piece of gothic that stands in the shoes
of Brother Freeman's old law office, would have hardly
allowed Garrison to profane his solemn sanctuary.
But they were not asked for nor offered.   It was very
convenient, for Dover has so few that are interested
in anti-slavery, that almost any building is big enough
to accommodate its meetings there.   A " hard cider "
meeting, to procure for the poor, bleeding, miserable
country THE RELIEF of a couple of bank vetoes, would
have called for a more spacious apartment.   Friend
Wadleigh would have been out at that, with a log
cabin or musty cider cask about him in the way of
badge, chock full of patriotic excitement.   He spoke
of our hard talk about Dover people.   We have this
to say of them, whether we said it before or not; that
so small an attendance in so populous a village, on a
meeting, that for magnitude of subject and for talent
and ability in the discussion, has never been paralleled
in New Hampshire, betrays a peculiarity of taste not
the most creditable.   A whig hurrah, or a democratic
Van Buren row would have assembled twenty times as
many at least, if not a hundred.   The laborers of the
place would have gladly attended, had they understood the character of our meeting and been permitted
to go.   The rulers and priests dare not have them go.
Any laboring people under heaven, if sober, would

have been delighted with that meeting. Probably
Friend Wadleigh would not. He is a politician. Politicians' tastes could not like it, any more than rum-
burnt, tobacco-steeped palates can like spring water.
O, the miserable lot of a political editor ! We know
none more deplorable, except a rum-selling store
keeper's or taverner's, All his life long, he has to
stand and watch the weathercock, and drop in with its
variations. To conclude with Friend Wadleigh, we
ask him, if he ventures to publish anything more from
our paper, to give enough for a sample, if he have not
space, after giving the *whig* victories, to publish the
whole.

The second evening of the meeting went off far
better than the first. The church and minister resolutions were discussed. The meeting was not quite so
unshackled as it would have been out of a Solomon's
temple. For dedication is a *decayer* of free discussion.
"Sacred architecture," as Daniel Webster calls it, is
not so promotive of free talk or thought as it is to
something more agreeable to the apprehension of car-
dinals and clergy. The resolutions, however, were
pretty profitably discussed. Friend Smith, of Somersworth, made a good speech. Henry C. Wright got
Rev. Brother Young into the sled where anybody but
a divine would have had his legs broke. A divine can
get out of a sled where nobody else could. And if
his legs are broke all up into fragments, he can walk
off on them as though nothing had happened. Or, if
he limp, he is so solemn and sacred nobody will notice it. The auditory were called on to vote. They
could vote as they pleased. They had a right to
speak. So had Rev. Brother Young. But he did not
choose, or dare to. But when the vote was about to
be taken, he got up in true cardinal style to *warn* the
congregation not to vote for the resolves. He offered
no argument. He had none to offer. Nobody could
have any, in truth. So he offered his *ghostly* warnings
and caveats. He whined and looked solemn, and
tried to *clergy-fy* the people out of their free vote. It
was a blockhead effort. He had no right to try to
induce that audience to vote by any other influence

than argument and reason. He did not attempt to
offer any of either. And Rev. Brother Scott, too, of
the Methodist-Episcopal order, who had through the
two days kept his solemn and cunning peace, he rose
up on the eve of the vote to interpose his sacerdotal
authority. Peradventure some poor class-led soul
there, had been delivered enough to follow conscience
a short space, and vote condemnation to a church and
clergy that enslave humanity. He groaned out his
naked opinion with all the impudence of Yankee sect,
and all the importance of the Episcopal high church,.
which characterizes that order of our priesthood.
Why did he not attempt an argument, or else hold his
tongue? What right had he to try to influence responsible immortals by long-faced *authority* merely?
It is supreme arogance, and an insult to all who have
to hear it. Rev. Daniel I. Robinson attempted an argument. He is a Methodist, but he is a man, also,
and although far out of his old and right way, as we
think and see, he does not attempt to lead people after
him, by merely a denominational disfigurement of
face. We detest this holy *puckerism*, and will scout it.
It makes fools of men, and roguery under it is supremely detestable. The resolutions passed, in spite
of the reverend scarecrows and lamentations.

The next morning, our Massachusetts friends
returned to their homes, and the society met by
adjournment to close the unfinished business ; expecting only a short morning session. Reverend Brother
Young, Francis Cogswell, esquire, and some other distinguished persons were promptly in attendance.
Brother Young seemed to feel relieved, by the absence
of the Massachusetts men, of the embarrassment which
had kept him two days silent, and he entered bravely
into debate. A resolution was up, censuring those
churches that still maintain the abomination of a
negro pew. Brother Young took hold of it with
quite an unceremonious hand. He spoke with true
clerical superciliousness, of the rashness and indiscre-
tion of abolitionists, and of the inacuracy of the resolution. The church, he said, was not at all responsible for the negro pew. They did' not own the pews,.

nor build them ; it was the parish, and the church and parish were two things—quite distinct—as distinct as husband and wife, he said. He did not offer any amendment to the resolution, nor take any responsible part in the meeting, but only condescended to show the absurdity and folly of the resolve, and of those who advocated it. Brother Cogswell spoke of "the confusion of ideas" that seemed to prevail there, in mistaking pew-owners for the church, and in supposing that the churches had the real estate in meeting-houses, and the regulation of negro pews. He denied that there were any such pews, and so did Brother Young, and called for proof. In reply it was said, after thanking the gentlemen for condescending to our debate, that there was some "confusion of ideas" in the meeting, but that it still appeared to abolitionists that the allowance of such an infernal exclusion in a house of worship, as negro pews, was the prerogative of the church and clergy who led the worship and accepted the house and the act of parish—that it was not a question of estate, but of unrighteous distinction ; that as to the existence of it, the existence of the colored people in the country, might as well be questioned and as reasonably attempt to be proved. The pertinency of the comparison to "man and wife," by Brother Young, when speaking of church and parish as two distinct things, was remarked on, as not expressive of vast separation, inasmuch as they twain were one flesh, etc., whereupon Brother Young denied that there was any prejudice against colored people, or desire to exclude them—referred to distinction between domestics and employers, by way of showing that there was none between white people and colored. On being routed from that by innumerable instances of negro pews, and the like exclusions all over the country, which were poured in upon him by the meeting, the reverend brother adroitly retreated upon this, that he had not denied the existence of prejudice, but that it was only against the color of the skin. It was against something else, he said ; a matter which nobody had agitated, or cared about ; a poor attempt to get off, not candid, nor true. But these great

meetings should have reporters. That Dover meeting
fully reported, would have been one of the most
entertaining and instructive ever holden. The eloquence poured forth on that occasion, should not be
lost.   *   *   *   A report of it would fill a
volume ; and whoever began it would finish it.

So far the *Herald* report of Mr. Rogers. Surely
but for him, the outside world would have known very
little of one of the most remarkable and important
anti-slavery conventions ever held in the state or the
nation. A note was struck in it which rang out loud
and long over New England and round the land, as
will be seen, if these chronicles get truly and faithfully recorded, even though to but limited extent,
which may be their chief calamity. A few special
explanatory remarks on the resolutions adopted,
may still be in place for the benefit of those
whose fathers and mothers had no active, friendly
hand in the mighty moral upheavals of that period.
And surely they were almost the whole nation then,
whatever may be the boast of to-day.

The first resolution, though wholly devotional, had
in it no unmeaning cant, for our movement was strictly
moral and religious, and probably a large majority of
the convention were devout members of some christian church.

The resolution declaring our determination not to
aid in the rendition of escaped slaves, was at that
moment especially proper, were it only as an agitating
and educating instrumentality. The constitutional
obligation was then beginning to be more strenuously
insisted upon, as anti-slavery sentiment increased.
And the way to Canada was more and more patron-
ized, and many faithful conductors were found for the
underground railroad up to that city of refuge from

our republican, democratic system of whips and
chains, blood-hounds and red-hot branding irons.
And the lore of college and university and the wisdom and piety of the theological seminary had been
called in or voluntarily tendered in support and sanctification of such diabolical doings. And the great
body of the clergy, as well as the rank and file of
both political parties, were ready spaniels, sharp of
scent, fleet of foot, to run and bark, to catch and
hold as bidden. And this explains the reason why we
publicly resolved that we would not obey the fugitive
slave law.

The two long resolutions relating to the nomination of Edward Everett, as minister to Great Britain,
with two other appointments of less significance,
hinted at a good deal more than was true. No such
refusal was meant or intended, nor certainly for any
such reason as was held out. Neither was there really
reason for abolitionists to stoop to pick up such
crumbs of comfort from the circumstances, as some of
us appeared to hope. It was not regard for northern
rights which led to such little resistance as was made.
It was only fear of disturbance in the party ranks,
and dread of loss of party supremacy.

And then as to Mr. Everett's anti-slavery sentiments, the south had no fear of them. He had already given full proof of his subserviency, at sundry
times and in divers manners. The slaveholders frequently chastized their slaves, not for any offence
committed, but only to remind them that they were
still slaves, and must know and keep their place. Mr.
Everett was now called to a new and high dignity,
and it seemed proper to his northern masters, or at
least prudent, to impose a few cracks of the cow-
skin, were it only to quicken his memory, as well as

movement, in their foreign service, to them at that time, nearly as important as any at home. Mr. Everett was a member of congress in 1826, when an amendment was submitted to the federal constitution, which brought up "the vexed question" of slavery. Then came his opportunity to declare what he called his "*confession of faith,*" on the terrible problem. His large learning, gained at Harvard and the institutions of Germany, and especially scripture learning, for it must be remembered, he was *Reverend* Edward Everett, led him to strictly examine and expound to his fellow congressmen the true meaning of the Greek word, *doulos*, as used in the New Testament. His speech on the occasion was printed under his own supervision, and the following is a paragraph :

The great relation of servitude, in some form or other, with greater or less departure from the theoretic equality of man, *is in*-separable to our nature. I know of no way by which the form of this servitude can be fixed, but by political institution. Domestic slavery, though I confess not by that form of servitude which seems to be most beneficial to the master, certainly not that which is most beneficial to the servant, is not, in my judgment to be set down as *an immoral and irreligious relation.* I cannot admit that religion has but one voice to the slave, and that this voice is "rise against your master." No sir ; the New Testament says, "*slaves* obey your masters ;" and though I know full well, that in the benignant operation of christianity which gathered master and slave around the same communion table, this unfortunate institution disappeared in Europe, yet I cannot admit that, while it subsists, its duties are not pre-supposed and sanctioned by religion. It is a condition of life, as well as any other, to be justified by morality, religion and international law.

In another paragraph, Mr. Everett declared :

Sir, I am no soldier ; my habits and education are very unmilitary ; but there is no cause in which I would sooner buckle a knapsack on my back, and put a musket on my shoulder, than that of putting down a servile insurrection at the south !

In 1834, Mr. Everett was elected Governor of Massachusetts. The anti-slavery enterprise then in its fourth year, had already greatly agitated the north and south, and filled the latter with apprehension and alarm. While northern politicians of both parties were clamoring for the suppression of *The Liberator* and other anti-slavery publications, as "*incendiary matter*," Governor McDuffie of South Carolina, in his message to the legislature, pronounced slavery "the corner-stone of the republican edifice." And he moreover declared that the laws should punish such interference with slavery as that of the abolitionists, by death, without benefit of clergy.

And Governor Everett, of Massachusetts, in his message to the legislature, responded on this wise :

Whatever, by direct and necessary operation, is calculated to excite an insurrection among the slaves, has been held by highly respectable legal authority, an offence against the people of the commonwealth, which may be prosecuted as a misdemeanor at common law. The patriotism of all classes must be invoked to abstain from a discussion, which, by exasperating the master, can have no other effect than to render more oppressive, the condition of the slave ; and which, if not abandoned, there is great reason to fear, will prove the rock on which the union will split.

Surely, with such a record as this, unsullied by any anti-slavery blemish except of most indirect character, and above all, never having by word or deed expressed sympathy or approval towards the anti-slavery enterprise, it is hardly possible that the south felt any fear or distrust of Mr. Everett, as ambassador to the court of Great Britain. If we cannot trust him, the slave power might well have asked, whom can we trust? They first whipped him with seeming rejection, that he might not forget who were his masters, and then confirmed his nomination.

The outcry raised against the south, by the northern pro-slavery press, for its apparent distrust of Mr. Everett, is well characterized in the second of the two resolutions at the Dover convention.   It was the rejection merely of *a party nomination* ; not any insult to liberty!

All three of the nominations named in the resolutions, were confirmed ; the other two were New Hampshire men.   Hon. Joel Eastman was appointed to a local position in his own state, and Gen. James Wilson to be surveyor-general of Iowa.

The other resolutions in the report relate to some proscriptive outrages perpetrated on persons of color by the officials of the Eastern railway, then running from Boston eastward through Lynn and Salem.   The church setting the example of a "negro pew," extending often to the sacramental table, as well as to seats in the meeting-houses, the Eastern railroad made haste to follow it in arranging its passenger cars.   A "negro car," always inferior in convenience and comfort, was provided, and all colored people, men, women, children, well-dressed or ill, cultivated and accomplished, or barbaric and rude, were driven into it.   Charles Lenox Remond, an elegant, highly-bred colored man, a perfect gentleman in whatever exalts and ennobles manhood, an intimate friend of Lady Byron, and other of the most distinguished personages in Great Britain ; and Frederick Douglass, now so well and widely known in two hemispheres, intimate while abroad with the like of O'Connell and other eminent men of the two houses of parliament, both of these, on returning from their foreign travels, were subjected to such cruel indignities, and two or three times with added and most aggravating accompaniments.

Senator Wilson, in his "History of the rise and fall of the slave power in America," volume first, page 492, refers to "*the unchristian prejudice*" which induced the regulations adopted by railroads to exclude persons of color from the ordinary passenger cars, and compelling them to ride in cars by themselves, or sometimes, without regard to tastes, character or means, in "second-class cars," bare and comfortless, the enforced receptacle of all who from any cause, could not, or would not take seats in first-class cars. The two corporations in Massachusetts, which were prominent in making and enforcing these odious regulations, were the Eastern and the Boston and New Bedford. * * * * * In the year 1841, David Ruggles, a colored man of New York, who had aided six hundred of his countrymen in escaping from slavery, was ejected from the cars against the earnest protest of Rev. John M. Spear, for the simple offence of taking a seat with white passengers. He brought an action in the New Bedford police court against the employes of the company for an aggravated assault. But Justice Crapo discharged promptly the offenders. On the Eastern railroad, scenes of violence were of frequent occurrence. Colored persons of character and intelligence were, in several instances, violently dragged from the cars occupied by white passengers ; and in some cases their friends, who remonstrated against such brutality, were treated in like manner. Among those forcibly ejected from the cars, was Frederick Douglass. * * * * * The general agent of the Massachusetts anti-slavery society was repeatedly insulted while traveling on that road, for remonstrating against its unjust and inhuman usages. In one instance he received blows and kicks, from the effects of which he did not recover for a number of weeks. Once, a colored man being ejected, Dr. Daniel Mann and several other white passengers remonstrated, when they, also, were seized and dragged violently out and prohibited from pursuing their journey, "unless they behaved themselves!" Dr. Mann brought an action in the Boston police court against the conductor of the train, but could obtain no redress for such high-handed outrages. * * * Charles Lennox Remond was a native of Salem, a colored gentleman of intelligence and worth, and of highly preposessing manners. In England, where he had spent nearly two years, he had vindicated the cause of the oppressed, and had won the confidence and applause of the British abolitionists. He was everywhere hailed as the champion of his race, and treated with most friendly and respectful consideration. He bore from England the warmest sympathies and best wishes of the friends of emancipation. He was commissioned to bear the address of sixty thousand Irishmen to their countrymen in America, headed by the names of O'Connell and Father Mathew. Arriving in Boston, he went to the Eastern railroad station to take passage for his home in Salem. He was not allowed to take his seat with other passengers, put was compelled to occupy what was called the "Jim Crow" car. Several of his white friends, wishing to welcome him on his return, met him at the station and took seats with him. They were, however, ordered by the conductor to leave the "Jim Crow" car, voluntarily, or to be removed by force! Thus was this gentleman of character and culture, fresh from his travels and the hospitalities of the best families of England, rudely and roughly treated on his arrival in his native state.

And Senator Wilson could have named others besides Dr. Mann, who suffered similar indignities and for the same reasons. James N. Buffum had traveled extensively in Britain with Douglass, addressing immense anti-slavery meetings ; but in his own town of Lynn, with him was dragged out of railway cars, making no resistance except to cling to the backs of the seats, which, as they were athletic men, they generally brought out with them, " one in each hand." The railroad authorities at length became so indignant that they refused to allow the trains to stop in Lynn at all. And for several days the rule was enforced. At one time they sent a police-officer with the trains to see that their atrocious mandates on the subject of negro hate were obeyed. One day Mr. Buffum saw a white man riding in the cars with a pet monkey in his lap. He good-naturedly asked the conductor : " How is this, that you drag out ' *the connecting link*,' as you call the colored man, and permit the two extremes, the white man and the monkey, the opposite link on the brute side, to ride unmolested as any white gentlemen ? " The conductor did not reply. He had his orders and must obey them. And the shameful " *Jim Crow* " car continued, with occasional outrages, till public opinion rose indignantly on legislation, and compelled enactments sweeping them out of existence. " The *negro* pew " in churches can still be found, north, east and west, as well as south.

CHAPTER XI.

DISCUSSION ON CHURCH ORGANIZATIONS BY REV. MR.
PUTNAM AND REV. MR. SARGENT — HILLSBOROUGH
COUNTY CONVENTION AT HANCOCK — AND MEETING
AT NASHUA, BY MR. FOSTER, AND WHAT CAME
OF IT.

The Strafford-county anniversary has occupied much
space, but discloses the genius and spirit, philosophy
and methods, of the anti-slavery enterprise ; and could
the addresses and speeches have been reported and
published with the proceedings, the wondrous ability
of at least some of its advocates, would have been no
less apparent. The editor of the *Herald* earned un-
payable thanks for his glowing descriptions which are
as just and truthful as they are brilliant and beautiful.

New organizanion was now asserting itself, and
gave us some inconvenience, chiefly through clerical
influence and action, as the following incident will
reveal :

In the winter of 1841, Rev. Rufus A. Putnam, Congregational minister, of Chichester, proposed an evening discussion with our faithful friend, Rev. Mr.
Sargent, of West Chester, on the question : "Are our
church organizations christian ?" Happening that
week to be at home in Concord, and the moon and
sleighing favoring, I proposed to Mr. Rogers that we
attend and hear the arguments. Knowing that our
new organized clergy, of most of the sects, were then
in arms to defend them, he readily consented, and
just as the sun was setting and the moon rising, we

set out on our ride of seven or eight miles. A mile
short of Mr. Putnam's meeting-house, where the
meeting was held, lived Mr. Benjamin Emery, a true
anti-slavery man, and there we left our horse and
sleigh, and with him walked the remainder of the distance. We arrived in time for the preliminary exercises, which were quite as many and lengthy as at the
ordinary Sunday services of that day, now over forty
years ago. Mr. Putnam read a hymn, which was sung
by the choir. Then the Methodist minister offered
(*performed*, Rogers called it), a long, miscellaneous
prayer. The people were not impressed, nor interested ; and it seemed a waste of valuable time. Some
had come long distances to attend what it was presumed would be an interesting, instructive and profitable discussion, and were impatient, evidently, to get
at the business of the occasion. It might be unchar-
itable to presume that the unexpected arrival from
Concord had something to do with the prolonged devotional exercises. But the editor of the *Herald* had
voice as well as pen, and it would have been uncourt-
eous not to have invited him to a part in the proceedings of the meeting. But undoubtedly the less time
allotted to him, the better it might be for the affirma-
tive side of the question in hand. And so some were
not surprised that prayer and praise were thus prolonged, even though inopportune, for still another
hymn had to be solemnly read and then sung.

There was a good country audience, some, like Mr.
Rogers and myself, having come several miles. Pre-
liminaries being settled at last, Mr. Putnam appeared
behind a huge pile of notes, newspapers, and other
signs of most elaborate preparation, and commenced
a tiresome apology, for ill health, many duties, including attending a funeral, and general want of suitable

preparation and arrangement. He feared he should not be able to speak to acceptance, on account of bodily infirmity, but would do the best he could, and there were others present who would take part in the meeting, which was to be free to all. He continued in this strain till we felt constrained to believe that he had made all possible preparation, and, besides, was not over-desirous that his opponents should have more time than was their right. And so it turned out. He had a manuscript discourse of, apparently, about his usual length, besides piles of newspapers, which he read at intervals, with dry and desultory comments and needless explanations, consuming quite two hours, in spite of "bodily ailments," which, had they been as described, should have kept him at home.

His main subject, instead of being as was expected, the christianity of the churches, was the infidelity and Jacobinism of the old organization. And he tried to prove it by showing that Garrison and others in Massachusetts had betrayed the anti-slavery cause, by sifting into *The Liberator* other subjects than anti-slavery, such as non-resistence and woman's rights, no Sabbath, no ministry, no church of Christ. He did not pretend that these subjects were brought openly into the anti-slavery society, but we were secretly promoting them. He read a part of the phrenological character of Garrison, as given by O. S. Fowler, to prove his secretiveness, and that he did not tell everybody all he thought. And Rogers and Pillsbury and Foster had introduced these subjects into New Hampshire, and Garrison and Rogers had even carried them to England. He read with all the emphasis at his command, something from a print he had brought, advocating the right and propriety of unlimited intercourse of the sexes, and placed it with his other documents, which he had given his audience to understand were publications of old organization abolitionists. That was a little too atrocious for Mr. Rogers. He at once rose and demanded of him "the author of that beastly stuff!" and, moreover, why he read it here. Mr. Putnam admitted that it was not an anti-slavery publication, but then Garrison associated in convention with persons of such sentiments, though he by no means presumed he held them himself. "But why, then, produce them here, and read them as though you believed, and intended your hearers should believe, that he both held and inculcated them?" I had till that moment thought Mr. Putnam honest, but easily influenced by his abler clerical brethren; though I could never have suspected him of any such duplicity, not even as a "pious fraud." Had not some one been there, however, to arraign him, probably many present, and nearly all his own people, would have supposed such "beastly stuff" old organized anti-slavery morality. The purpose was palpable that by such reckless audacity he expected to prove that the abolitionists were promoting the most shameless libertinism, under the guise of anti-slavery. Had he been let alone, he doubtless would have done it, at least to his own satisfaction, and to the great delight of all who implicitly trusted him. And yet we certainly always regarded Mr. Putnam as, on the whole, one of the very best of the new organized ministers. But there he was in a dilemma like that. Self-convicted, too. Mr. Rogers charitably attributed it to ministership. The end he imagined to be right. Of the means there need be no scruple nor hesitation. Mr. Rogers said, and doubtless truly, that had the device of reading that filthy newspaper been perpetrated in a law court, it would have excluded the daring offender from the court, and the rabble that haunt the court-house would have spurned him from their groggy circle.   In his own words, Rogers, in describing the scene in the *Herald*, farther said :   " There is some regard for principle in a desperate game of sharps before a jury ; but not a shadow of any in a church trial.   *   *   *   *   Every man's and every woman's experience, who has had trial of them, can testify that this is true.   *   *   *   *   *   We are not speaking of the clergy as men, aside from their office.   But bring the church into straits ; disturb their denomination ; touch their clerical power, and they will out Herod the evil one himself in their obliquity.   Literally they stick at nothing."

Certainly every word of this was warranted by what we saw that evening.   But at the end of nearly two hours' weary reading and not less tiresome talking, Mr. Putnam sat down.   Once in the time, his opponent in the discussion, Rev. Benjamin Sargent, asked him one simple question.   He was reading a charge against the Methodist church, relating to slavery, made by Stephen Foster in some printed paper. Mr. Sargent asked if the charge were not true.   Mr. Putnam declined to answer.   One of his church members came to his rescue, and in most flippant tones protested against any interruption.   When Mr. Rogers asked why Mr. Pntnam read the "beastly" newspaper he did, the same church member had interposed, and quite officiously, as if in some sense the armor-bearer of his chief.   He said " Mr. Putnam might as well answer forty questions as one."   Of some questions, he could more easily have answered forty thousand, than the single one then asked.

Mr. Sargent, in his brief reply, expressed a just and proper regret that the question proposed, had not yet been even approached. He asked what the opinions of William Lloyd Garrison, on the sabbath question, the non-resistance, or woman's equality questions had to do with "The Christianity of Church Organizations?" to consider which the meeting had been called. He had no objection to stating what were the views of Garrison on all those subjects. As to the Sabbath, he showed and proved that Garrison held exactly with the Quakers, and they with John Calvin, Martin Luther, Archbishops Paley, Whately, and several others whom he named. On non-resistance he cited Jesus, the Christ, in the whole letter and spirit of his memorable sermon on the mount. For woman's equality in the church, he quoted him who said : "there is neither Jew nor Greek; bond nor free; male nor female." He spoke of sectarianism as non-christian, as a denial practically, of the christian name and faith ; that as there was neither Jew nor Greek, male nor female, so there could be neither Congregational nor Presbyterian, Baptist nor Methodist ; and consequently, that our church organizations, whatever else they may be, or may not be, are surely not Christian, nor even *Paulian*. He thought Mr. Putnam admited that sectarianism was unchristian, by his frequent association with his neighbor, the Methodist church. Mr. Putnam denied that his association with Methodism was frequent. Mr. Sargent said he had been told moreover, that a member of Mr. Putnam's church had been excommunicated for attending Methodist meetings. That, too, Mr. Putnam denied. But we were assured on the spot that it was true, and that the person was then present. Mr. Rogers offered the columns of the *Herald* for any authentic statement of the facts, but I think no statement by either side ever came.

Mr. Sargent spoke but briefly, though every word was to the point and the purpose, and on the question mainly for which the meeting had come together. On sitting down he expressed the hope that Mr. Rogers and myself might have a little time, late as it had become, Mr. Putnam having occupied quite two hours. But before either of us could speak, Mr. Putnam had to reply to Mr. Sargent ; though not with success, but quite otherwise, we thought. Next, the church member who had frequently spoken, or interrupted speaking, had to be heard at some length, he too having numerous minutes and documents to assist his memory. Finally, the coast being clear, Mr. Rogers rose, evidently much to the satisfaction of a large part of the audience. He expressed his satisfaction at seeing so goodly a number present to hear for themselves. Anti-slavery he thought had been deprived of a fair hearing before the people, who had been greatly alarmed or hindered by the calumnies of the clergy and church. But he believed if the people could hear candidly and impartially, they would render a just verdict and the slave would have his liberty. He said the drift of Mr. Putnam's reasoning was to convict the old organized abolitionists of wickedly incumbering the anti-slavery cause with extraneous doctrines and demands. He denied the charge wholly and totally ; declared the old organized abolitionists had but one fundamental doctrine and demand, namely : that our slave-holding was a sin and a crime, and should be immediately and unconditionally abandoned. Whereas the new organization had many doctrines, such as sacredness of human governments, and church organizations, and their machinery ; sabbath, ministry, and the like, woman's inferiority, necessity of litigation, and many other things, and he proved all his positions by simply producing and reading the constitutions of both organizations.

Mr. Rogers was asked if he had not changed his opinion respecting anti-slavery political action. He said frankly, he had, but becoming convinced that all legislation was force, and that as anti-slavery, in our opinion, was a strictly moral and religious movement, a work of repentance and reformation, we could not resort to physical force. He contended that without the life-taking power, or the power and right, usurped or assumed right, to enforce its decrees, government would be powerless ; a mere exhortation.   *   * That if slave-holding were forbidden by congress, it must be with penalties and power to enforce them at whatever cost, otherwise all such legislation must be null and void. If the penalty were resisted by force, it must be repelled by force to the extent, if need be, of cutting off the head of every offender by the sword. And so, to enforce a law, would be as the march of an army. Or if the penalty were not death, but only imprisonment, and the culprits refused to enter the dungeon doors, the sword of the marshal must enforce the penalty even at cost of life. Or if fine only be the penalty, it must be collected though at point of bayonet or sword. If law be penal, it is capital ; and if not penal it is no law. "Finally," said Rogers, "legal abolition of slavery would be abolition at the point of the sword, and as decidedly military in spirit, and as far from being *moral* as would be an invasion of the slave plantations by an anti-slavery army." Mr. Rogers told the people no less frankly that as an abolitionist, he felt compelled to denounce the clergy as an anti-christian order, and the sectarian church organizations, as disowned by christianity and forbid-

den of God.   They used their influence, he said, in
the name of christianity, to crush out the anti-slavery
enterprise.   Had they not done that, we, as abolitionists, should have let them alone.   But in doing that,
they proved themselves false to the christian name
and all that it implies, and fidelity to the slave
demanded that we unmask and expose them.   Had
they let the slave and his cause alone, the clergy
might rule the people, and the people might bow to
their authority, as to any other idolatry, and anti-
slavery might never have molested them.   *   *
Mr. Rogers had every ear, and it was a golden opportunity well improved.   It is impossible to convey any
idea of the impression produced at that late hour of a
winter's night, many having come several miles to
attend the meeting.

   My own part in the discussion was of little account,
and almost literally postponed to the *eleventh* hour.
Our church-member opponent, in the plenitude of his
charity, had declared he could even fellowship me as
an abolitionist.   When I rose, at the last moment, there
was only time for me to decline the extended hand, in
the name of, and for the sake of anti-slavery consistency, fidelity and moral integrity.   In the first place,
our friend was an abolitionist, tried and true, as was
supposed.   Then he apostatized into the new organization and liberty party.   Then he back-slid, or down-
slid, into the whig party, and became a champion in
the presidential canvass,

" For Tippecanoe and Tyler too,"

until it was almost as hard to count him as it was the
speckled pig of Uncle Peter.   He said he could
count them all, only that one ; but he jumped and
flew around so, it was impossible to count him.   The
meeting adjourned in excellent humor, though my op-

ponent regretted that there was no time to reply to
my illustration of the pig, which he declared was of
the nature of a libel. And we were afterward informed that he deliberately contemplated a suit at
law, to restore his offended dignity. But no such
calamity ensued.

We footed it briskly back under the bright moon
to Mr. Emery's, the merry sleighbells of the farmers from remote hills and valleys swiftly passing us.
A hasty cup of tea and accompaniments, while the
boys put our Tunbridge in position from her warm
stable, well prepared us for our hour's midnight ride,
and we trotted gaily into our own street and yard just
as the old Baptist church clock told the hour of
twelve.

Such, at that time, was new organized clerical anti-
slavery. And the best of it. It is a sorrowful consideration, that nearly all the parties named in this
narration have gone to the realm of departed spirits.
A good reason why their words and works should be
regarded with all the respect and charity possible.
None doubted Mr. Putnam's hatred of slavery; but,
with his sect generally, especially its ministers, the
church organization and its machinery were more
than the liberty of the enslaved. Strange how priest
and Levite are much the same in all time. And the
"Good Samaritans," though often outlawed by state
and church, are ever foremost in rescuing the robbed
and despoiled, the fallen and oppressed, from even
the thraldom, civil and political as well as ecclesiastical, of the church and clergy themselves.

This work is *Acts of the Anti-Slavery Apostles*, not
history of the anti-slavery enterprise. The present
generation can know little of the labors and experiences of the years between 1831 and 1861 ; nor can

any better lessons be now given than by true descriptions, word pictures, taken on the spot, and by the actors in or witnesses of, the scenes and encounters. The following report of a Hillsborough county, New Hampshire, convention, is also by Mr. Rogers. He aided me immensely in conducting, he shall now aid me no less in reporting it to history and posterity. The world knows far too little of the editor of the *Herald of Freedom*. Part of the account, personal to this writer, is given with deep humility, and only at the earnest solicitation of his few surviving friends and fellow-laborers in the great conflict, whose will and wishes may well be his highest law. It is from the *Herald* of October 21st, 1842 :

THE HANCOCK CONVENTION.—Another grand antislavery meeting has transpired. And truth enough has been told to revolutionize a nation, with either eyes to see or ears to hear, or hearts to understand. Our nation has neither. We can hope for little more than to prevent the coming on of another generation like the present. We may cripple the power of the slaves of the present age to disable the generation that is rising from discerning the truth. If we can, the coming generation *may* have sense and courage enough to perceive that slaveholding is not the quintessence of righteousness.

Six of us went over to the Hancock convention from Concord : Joseph and Mary Ann French, Parker Pillsbury, Stephen Foster and Caroline Farrand, and myself. A half day's ride through a most benighted region, embracing Reverend Moses Kimball's *province* of Hopkinton, whose only remnant of humanity that I know of is their *tasty* jail, the moral aspect of the whole way contrasting mournfully with the glorious upland country and a *yellow* autumn day, brought us to a couple of anti-slavery homes, on the Henniker highlands, George and Daniel Cogswell's. We were welcomed with a heartiness and cheer that fully made up for the utter blank which stretched all the way

from there to Concord. I don't know of a single
habitation in all that distance that would have given
us a *human* reception, had they known us as we were,
the mortal enemies of slavery, and of its patrons, the
priesthood. We left the river road, on the margin of
the Contoocook, and wound our way among the hills
to the southward of the beautiful village of Henniker.
It brought us at length into a valley behind the high
ridge that overlooks the village. We ascended to the
summit, where stand the pleasant and comfortable
dwellings of our two friends. *Brother* dwellings they
are, near by each other as are the families, twin in
affection as in kindred. I could hardly image to myself a more desirable location. Remote, but not lonely,
the two families, alone, affording each other abundant
society. A glorious prospect stretches around them.
Off to the south, beyond the deep, narrow valley, rose
high, wooded hills, their heavy hard-wood growth
touched gorgeously with the frost-pencil of October.
North, the village, shining at their feet, with its
painted dwellings and green fields, deformed only by
a sectarian steeple or two and a kindred rum tavern,
a wide upland country swelling beyond, rising in the
distance and terminating with old Kearsarge, its bare
head among the drifting clouds.

After a most pleasant refreshment, bodily and mental, with our affectionate friends, (who have not *yet*
cast off from their association their pro-slavery church
corporation) we resumed our ride for Hancock, among
some of the boldest inhabited scenery I have ever
seen in New Hampshire. Bold and free as his own
intrepid spirit, we passed the farm on which grew up,
from four years old, our noble coadjutor and veteran
fellow-laborer, Parker Pillsbury. The rugged mountain homestead where he was bred from early childhood—bred to toil ; where he worked through all his
young life, hard and faithfully as his manhood is laboring for the slave, with almost as little acknowledgement or thanks as the world then awarded him, when
he developed obscurely among the rocks. We passed
the solitary school house where he was allowed the
few weeks schooling of his childhood. But thanks

they were so few. He was educating all the better
for humanity's service on that rugged farm. He there
taught himself to be a MAN. A great lesson he had
effectually learned before he came in contact with
seminaries and a priesthood. These proved unequal
on that account, to over-match and cower down his
homespun nobility of soul. They tied their fetters
round his manly limbs, but he snapped them as Samson
did the withes, and went out an abolitionist, carrying
off the very theological gates with him upon his manly
shoulders. He is away from home now ; gone on a
campaign into Rhode Island, and I will have a word
about him. It is due from me, and has long been.

The abolitionists of the country ought to know
Parker Pillsbury better than they do. I know him
for all that is noble in soul, and powerful in talent and
eloquence. The remote district school houses in New
Hampshire and in the granite old county of Essex,
Massachusetts, where he was born, would bear me
witness to all I could say. He is one of the strong
men of our age. I wish he oftener felt his own
strength, if he *ever* feels it and would oftener put it
forth, when he happens among the multitude audiences of the lowlands, where he is too apt to keep
himself in the back ground. And the abolitionists, I
fear, have regarded him too much as he regards himself. He has overlooked himself, and they have overlooked him. He has undervalued his inestimable
services, and the abolitionists have imitated him in it.
He has gone unpaid—not that, it is not the word he
would allow. Paid or unpaid are not the words for
him, but unsustained, unsupported. He has broken
down in two or three years by giant labor, a constitution of adamant, matured and hardened into iron
in the school of his early toil. He has broken it down
and what has he received in requital ? The curses of
the priesthood and their vassal followers, and the forgetfulness of the abolitionists. He has been abroad
in the fields, and they snugly at their homes ; he has
performed the incessant labor of the galley slave, with
little better than slaves' fare, often times, and hardly
better than slaves' wages. He never complains, but

that is no sign that I should not. I have neglected
to complain for him, as other abolitionists have given
cause for the complaint. It is a shame that such a
man as Parker Pillsbury should be unappreciated. I
know the anti-slavery cause is odious in the community ; I know its advocates are detested, but abolitionists should not forget their field laborers. Pillsbury,
and Foster, and Beach have served and suffered in
this cause the last two years as hardly any of its champions have suffered or served ; and their fidelity has
had little other effect upon abolitionists than to cause
them to shake their heads at their daring temerity.
Instead of pouring into the breach made by them in
the wall, abolitionists have, too many of them, halted
and stood gazing to see how it would come out with
them, amid the hosts of the enemy closing around
them, or else absolutely discouraging their gallant advance. So it is, and so it is always to be.

But I must hasten on to Hancock. Hancock, a
revolutionary name—named too for the bold signature
at the head of the brave old Declaration, but the abode
of a population anything but akin in spirit to revolutionary fathers. Contented colonists and vassals,
most of them under the bloated tyranny of Archibald
Burgess, and a subaltern aristocracy. We reached the
dwelling of our friends, the Boutells, at nightfall,
where we were at once at home amid all that is kind
and comforting in anti-slavery hospitality.

We learned that the old Orthodox meeting-house
had been obtained for our meeting, it being so owned
that the Very Reverend Father Burgess could not by
his nod prevent our having it. He had also given
notice of the convention from his pulpit on the Sabbath before, and with all the ghostly importance of a
haughty friar, had warned the church and congregation *not to attend it*. He gave the very sensible and
priestly reason that if they did attend, and the meetings were mobbed, *it would be laid to them !* As honest
and rational remark as commonly falls from a thick-
headed priest. As if a mobbing could be laid to those
who attended the meetings it was breaking up, and
helped to bear the brunt and danger of it. The
course of all others that would prove conclusively to

the abolitionists that they were not countenancing the
mob, so anybody but a *soggy* would perceive.   And
what did he talk about a mob for?   Had he used his
influence to stir one up?   His minions, when spoken
to about our having the house, said "Yes, if the abolitionist will be answerable for any damage done to it."
As much as to say, " If you will pay for what mischief
we may do to it, you may have it."   For who but they or
their children would harm the house, or disturb the
meetings?   The creatures of friend Archibald did stay
away, but they sent their young fry to mob the convention, by ringing the bell, by uncouth pranks and
brute noises, by hurling stones along the aisles and
through the windows.   We picked up two stones
large enough to cause instant death had they struck
any of us on the temple or other dangerous place.
They were preserved and brought away as trophies of
the education of the hopes of the church in Hancock,
and of the godly preaching of the Reverend Archibald Burgess.   He has preached there a good while.
It was his sacerdotal pleasure that his old folks should
stay away from the anti-slavery meeting, and that
their nimbler offspring should go and do what in
them lay to break it up.   And so they did.   The old
ones staid away with commendable self denial.   Many
of them doubtless felt curious to go, but they had to
deny themselves and stay away, and friend Archibald
ought to commend them for it in the pulpit at the
head of the regiment.   Three days the meetings continued, day times and the evenings of two days, in
the midst of a thick settled, populous village, and the
mass of the population had to stay at home; and the
meetings ten fold more interesting and more instructive than any they had ever had among them of any
kind.   They would have thought so themselves if
they could have been *allowed* to be there.   But they
were not. Archibald Burgess, their priest, admonished
them to stay at home, and they did not dare to go.
God admonished them by their consciences to go, but
who was the Lord, that they should obey his voice?
Archibald Burgess was their Divinity, their fat Idol.
They must worship him or he would frown at them

from that *awful* pulpit, on that *holy* day, and, may be, *pray* against them, so that they would not have prospered " in their basket and store."

The godly children of the church, rang that old liberty bell till they made it hoarse, and almost broke their young mobocratic backs with pulling the rope. It annoyed the village more than it did us, who were down under it in the house. We told them to ring on in welcome. It was a free meeting, and every one of them was at liberty to take what part in it he chose. If he had no ability to speak against anti slavery, he might ring the bell, or he might sneeze, or bark, or throw stones. There was one pro-slavery tailor in the entry that had sneezed with great ability. I never heard anybody that had such talent at sneezing. I remembered hearing him sneeze when we were there a year ago. He sneezed out doors then, and he was heard all over the neighborhood. Mr. Burgess himself could not have sneezed like him, I don't believe. He came into the meeting, and when any of the speakers touched on Mr. Burgess' connection with man-stealing, the tailor would sneeze in his defense. Others of his defenders would bark, some whistled, others scraped the floor with their hind feet ; one came in with a great club in his hand and marched up to the altar, and, with mock solemnity, took a seat before it. The young mobocrats " laffed." The abolitionists took no notice of him nor them. He got sick of sitting there and marched out. Then they " laffed " out again. By and by he came in again and marched up into the pulpit. That was a killing manœuvre. They did " laff " " like all possessed." We thought it was the very place for the poor fellow, and that he became it quite as well as their lubberly priest. He began to preach up there. Foster was speaking at the time, but gave way for him. He talked away and could not help saying some good things. One of the young *religious* gentry present interrupted him, for things did not seem to be working just right for the opposition. Pillsbury requested that the speaker be not interrupted, and said he had spoken more important truth, he would be bound to say, than had been spoken in that pulpit in two years. It was so apt a remark, and, with all, so confounded true, that the whole mobocracy cheered it with a peal of applause. They could not help it. They forgot for the instant the errand they were sent on, and gave a volley of spontaneous and hearty cheers. After that they were glad for a while to be still. But Foster roused them again by his terrible invective. He displayed Burgess in such condemning light as one of the great brotherhood of thieves and patrons of robbery and adultery in the slave system, that they could not bear it, and began again to show their religious rage. Several large stones were hurled in at the front door, and went tumbling up the broad aisle to the foot of the pulpit. They were big enough to have broken the legs of anybody who might have stood there. By and by smash went the glass, and in 'at the side windows came the stones, glass rattling and stones bounding against the pew doors. Real clerical argumentation. Truly *religious* weapons of defense for the church and minister.

This was in the evening. The academy students had poured in, in considerable numbers. There are two seminaries close by the meeting-house. A Congregational academy and a Baptist, where Baptist *larnin'* and orthodox *larnin'* are severally taught. *Dipped* arithmetic and grammar at one, and *sprinkled* at the other. With whatever intent the students came in at first, the chief of them, after hearing awhile what was said and done on both sides, manfully moved into the center of the house, away from the mob at and near the doors, so as to separate themselves from it and identify themselves with the meeting. Some of them spoke and protested against the conduct of the mob, and behaved very honorably, and received the commendation of the convention. And I would here add that, if those young men were out from under this priestly control, they would most of them be abolitionists, and make free and noble men. And they will not be such slaves as their fathers. Their young breasts will inhale the reviving and disenthraling atmosphere our reform is generating around them,

and it cannot fail to give them more or less of freedom. Saturday morning there was hesitation about
letting us have the key. It seemed to be feared that
an impression was making in the meetings, dangerous
to the church and the minister, although both staid
away and kept most of the people away. Those
young students would go in, and no knowing what
effect it might have upon them. It was some time
before the house could be got open, and shelter from
a falling rain was obtained in sheds or where else it
might be. No mobbing on Saturday, save ringing
the bell. One young student ventured up into the
pulpit, to show his "gimp." He had not witnessed
the experiment there, probably, of the night before.
The audience were reminded, in his hearing, of their
entire freedom to say and do what they severally
pleased, but on their own responsibilities. If they
wanted to mount up into the pulpit, to play the fool,
or for whatever purpose, it must be on their own account. The convention would not be responsible.
And if any of them wanted to play the buffoon, or
mobocrat, the pulpit was a fit place to perform in as
any other. Every one to his taste. Pro-slavery was
very partial to the pulpit, and the pulpit was open to
it on that occasion, as every other part of the house.
They might whistle, or they might behave quietly
and kindly, as they would be done by. They might
speak, or they might *bark* and play the quadruped, or
they might sneeze, as their champion had done the
night before, or hurl stones through the windows,
only it would all have to be done on their own account, and not on ours. Several of the students did
speak ; some, who seemed to be dieting for the ministry, spoke cant and absurdity. One young man,
Marshall, of Nashua, quite young, spoke very manfully, and with candor and ability. If he follows out
his heart, he will be an abolitionist and make an able
advocate. A young Mr. Chamberlain canted and
cavilled. He was a great friend of religion, and
greatly wounded at our treatment of the *virtuous* and
philanthropic folks, who, as we said, were instigating
what their children had been doing to break up the

meeting, and who had kept the people from attending it.   Mr. Student Bonner was quite loud and vehement in defence of "our church and clergy."   He was not in favor of slavery, but he wanted the blacks sent to Africa if they were liberated.   They did not belong to this country, and had no rights here.   Student Bonner, by the way, belongs to Canada.   He said they did not help carry on the revolution. He denied that liberty would do the slaves any good.   He denied that slave-holding was man-stealing, or criminal.   Foster had declared that it was ; Bonner rose and denied it.   Foster bade the audience beware of that young man ; he would put the community on its guard against him.   He had denied that stealing children and enslaving them was sinful. That young man, he said, was dangerous in community with such notions.   He bade those who had property exposed to beware of him.   He had avowed the principles of a thief : the young fellow had been exceedingly impudent in his remarks upon the abolitionists, saying everything offensive. and abusive, he well could ; specifying nothing, attempting to prove nothing, and well deserved Foster's severity.   Whether there was any peculiar pertinency in the application of the word thief, more than Foster knew of, Bonner's acquaintances can say.   Another young gentleman student was highly scandalized at "the abuse heaped on the clergy and Mr. Burgess."   He was young, but could not refrain, when sacred things were thus attacked.   Foster might speak here, he said, but if he were to go into yonder house, (where Burgess was to speak on Sunday,) he would be among those who would lay hold on him and drag him out.

The students, however, behaved very well in the main ; some of them exceedingly well, considering the pro-slavery influence with which they stood connected.   They did not talk with much good sense ; they spoke like students ; had they been free, unsophisticated youth, uninfected by the schools and the meeting-house, they would have gone *en masse* for the meeting, and borne a generous testimony in its favor.   Pillsbury told them very impressively the obligations they were under to the meeting. It was at the first meeting, he admonished them, where their right of free speech had ever been recognized. They were called and reckoned *boys*, by other meetings of the day, and would not be allowed to speak on equal terms in any of them. Here they were not boys, but men. What would have been their reception, he asked, in an association of ministers, had they ventured to speak as they were free to speak here? He asked them to appreciate it. He told them they were not boys ; they had rights and responsibilities ; and he warned them how they used them. That should be a memorable day to them, he said, when in a convention of men and women, their equal right of free speech was for the first time recognized and asserted for them, even by those to whose objects they were not friendly. Asserted, not for this meeting only, but for all meetings of a public and proper character. He told them they had right to speak everywhere for themselves ; as good right as any number of years could ever confer upon them. He told them of the part they might act for God and humanity, if they would only use their talents and act up to their conscience and their convictions.

Sunday was devoted to the Scriptural evidences of the sacred institutions. The clergy are wielding to overawe and put down the anti-slavery movement, the Sabbath, the clerical order, the dedicated temple and the meeting-house worship, to which anti-slavery as well as every other moral reform, is obliged to give way. All these were freely and faithfully discussed in the light of christianity, and were all shown from abundant scriptural authority and evidence to be unwarranted by the gospel and forbidden by its great Teacher. If the people had been there and dared to hear impartially, enough was said to convince them all. Had the priesthood human ears and common mortal understanding, it would have saved them from their diabolical delusions to have been there and heard, if truth *can* save them. But the people were only few of them there. The clergy would not let them come. The clergy were not there. The two belonging to

that neighborhood were absent. They did not dare
to be there. They would as soon resign their licenses
as meet the abolitionists in presence of the people on
the meeting-house floor.

Now, I appeal to the people if they themselves
ought not to have attended the convention. Subjects
of the utmost importance to them were those to be
discussed, and in a perfectly free meeting. They had
full and equal liberty to speak as well as to hear.
Men and women were to discuss those subjects whom
the community had no reason to doubt were competent to a sensible and profitable examination of them.
They ought to have been there. They would have
been if they had been free. They would have been
had they not been slaves.

And the two clergymen ought to have been there.
Burgess should have given notice of the meeting and
exhorted the people to go and hear for themselves.
If the meeting was free and open to reply as well as
to abolitionist, and he knew it would be, he surely
should have been there himself, and advised others to
be there. If we were propagating errors, he knew the
place to put us down was in our own meetings. If
we were wrong he was the man learned and faithful
enough to put us all right. He would put us right
for our sakes as well as for other people. Why not?
Suppose we did not reverence him. We complain of
him that he wants reverence. Will he prove it by
refraining to meet us because we won't render it to
him? He pretends to regard us as wolves, while he
professes to be a shepherd. What is the duty of a
shepherd when the wolf cometh? To flee and hide
himself? " The hireling fleeth because," etc., but the
true shepherd never. If we were wolves, Shepherd
Burgess was afraid of us. If he is a wolf in sheep's
clothing, he had good reason to fear us.

But the clergy can't always keep us from the people. By the blessing of God, anti-slavery will yet
deliver the people of this clergy. They may as well
let us have a hearing first as last. They may as well
meet us. They must meet us before the people, or
the people shall at length know the reason why they

do not meet us. This skirmishing and dodging will not always avail them. A hand-to-hand conflict must by and by come, and under circumstances most unauspicious to the clergy. They will utterly dishonor and discredit themselves before the world by their behavior in avoiding the contest. We are right, and they shall meet us, or we will fall upon them at their very altars, and take hold of their horns as Benaiah did upon Joab. Foster and Beach, Brown and Allen, are already scaling the walls of their sanctuaries. Others will follow. The pulpit is "coward's castle," but it is being stormed and it will be taken. If the clergy will hide there and by spells and sorcery prevent the people from hearing the cry of outraged humanity, its advocates will point their cannon at the sacred order, and never cease battering till it tumbles to the ground.

Our convention terminated on, Sunday afternoon, near night. There was throughout a goodly, but not full attendance. All the humanity of the place was there. There was a lack of attendance on the part of abolitionists from the surrounding region. Why are they not awake? When liberty lies bound, lacerated and bleeding on southern plantations, and her advocates here in New England are imprisoned for pleading her deliverance, is it time to stay at home for ordinary cause? Would they stay at home if a brother or sister or a wife were a slave, or if a husband were shut up in a loathsome cell at Newburyport, only for liberty of speech?

I must not forget in this hurried sketch, Foster's preaching at the threshold of Burgess' synagogue, on Sunday noon. He entered it in the forenoon, not to speak, but to appal, as I suppose, that haughty hireling by his presence. And it made him turn pale with coward apprehension. He feared Foster would open his mouth to speak. He knew he could oppose nothing to his powerful word but brute, ruffian, *ragamuffin* force. He trembled to be driven to it before his parish. Wicked man! Why does he not give liberty of speech? Can he not defend himself? Foster is an able man, but I am not afraid of him where he is wrong. Why should the *Reverend* Mr. Burgess be? Has he no tongue to defend himself, and in the midst of his own people?

Foster spoke over half an hour, out on the common before the synagogue, at intermission, and with great power. The people heard him. Burgess was within, like Putnam's wolf, but did not dare to come out. He must have heard Foster's voice, and probably ordered the few that were with him to set up a tune, for they did, the cowards! They did not dare to listen to the truth, so they sang a psalm. They were "*not merry*," and so they sang psalms. They were scared at the truth, and so they sang to drown it. Some of the leading subalterns of the priest at length returned from their home to the meeting. They were filled with rage when they came within sound of Foster's voice. They howled like very fiends. One of them, mighty well dressed and respectable looking, said : "The damned creatnre is crazy; what is he here for? "If he is crazy," cried another, "he ought to be kicked off the ground." "Take away your minister," said one of the select men to our friend, David Wood, "or I will have a constable here to take care of him." But Foster was on the common, and it was intermission time, to boot. "I do not keep a minister," replied our friend Wood. "Foster is his own minister, not mine."

We had no officers in our convention, no president, no secretary, no business committee, no resolves passed. The question of president was fully discussed, and officers dispensed with unanimously. There was no vote of invitation to all persons present to participate. We were an open *human* meeting. We were met to promote humanity. And we declared everybody had, of course, a right to speak and act in our meeting, for it was everybody's meeting. Our harmony was perfect. Even the mobocracy was subdued and brought to order by the overpowering influence of liberty.

The foregoing may seem to young readers a narrative too long drawn out. But it conveys only a faint idea of the scenes witnessed and encountered there.

And not only there, but in hundreds of towns besides. And the mob spirit there manifested was mildness itself compared with many other places east and west. When the clerical or political party leaders saw that we were determined the cause of the slave should be presented to the people, they felt safe in setting the mob on us at any time, knowing that we were non-resistants in every encounter. At Hancock, when the volley of stones came crashing in at the windows among the people, the women kept quiet, but a man cried out, " Let's adjourn ; let's adjourn." Happening to be speaking at the moment, I raised my voice so as to be heard in the confusion and asked ; *Did your fathers adjourn at Bunker Hill when fired upon by the enemies of freedom ?* The effect was as sudden as satisfactory, and the silence and order continued to the close of the session. The poor fellow with the *shilalah* in the pulpit had been drinking, but he rose and made a few very sensible remarks, rebuking severely the disturbers, which we applauded, and that rather won him to our side. I had often by strategy captured the champion of rioters whom they had crazed with liquor and put forward to annoy me so as to break up the meeting if possible. Sometimes I would invite him to a friendly discussion and take him to the platform and propose that I would speak half an hour and he take notes and reply as he saw might be needed. I would furnish paper and pencil and proceed. The plan would not always succeed ; neither did it always fail of the desired result. I well recollect such an occurrence one terrible night in Vermont. The moon was bright as silver, but the mercury was much below zero. I should have held my man and the audience had not the rioters began pelting their champion at the table with paper pellets, tobacco quids and similar arguments, doubtless the best they had to offer.   He soon kindled into rage against them, and I think would have died then in my defense had it been necessary.   I was able to continue speaking in the confusion till the disturbing element was shamed into comparative silence, and then closed the meeting. This was unexpected, and some of the most violent begged me to proceed, promising the best of order and behavior to the end.   But I declined, telling them I had captured their champion and proved him the most decent man of them all, and now they might have the responsibility of breaking up a free meeting where they would have been welcome to half the time.

The Hancock convention had no presiding nor other officers, and so was a gathering after Mr. Rogers's own heart, as his graphic but eminently just and truthful description shows.

While on Hillsborough county it may be opportune to report one more meeting held or attempted by Mr. Foster alone.   It was in the town of Nashua, where anti-slavery never had rapid nor healthy growth. The people not coming to Mr. Foster he felt called on to go to them.   It need not be told again that he differed at that time from most of his fellow christians in modes of worship.   He believed devoutly that in all christian assemblies there should be freedom of utterance, whether by prayer, speaking, or song, as was both preached and practiced by Christ and the early apostles.   But into whatever religious assembly he entered, his manner was always decent and respectful, and whether he spoke or prayed, his tones of voice were remarkably solemn and impressive.   But I am sure he never once interrupted any religious services, except in places where political leaders and religious

17

teachers had used all their influence and authority to
keep the people from attending his meetings, which
were always supereminently free.

Mr. Foster's own account of the affair will best
describe it, and as it was written in a prison into
which his faithfulness brought him, it will be all the
.more interesting. A part only of his letter will here
be given. It was dated,

AMHERST JAIL, May 7, 1842.

MY DEAR BROTHER ROGERS—Under the superin-
tending providence of Him by whose permission,
Joseph was cast into prison in Egypt, and the prophet
Jeremiah was incarcerated in a loathsome dungeon,
and Jesus Christ scourged, spit upon, and nailed to
the cross, I have been given up into the power of my
enemies, arrested and confined within the walls of a
loathsome cell. But though captured, I am not conquered ; nay, I am a conquerer. My body is indeed
incased in granite and iron, but I was never more free
than at this moment ; I have at length triumphed
over every foe ; I have achieved this victory by con-
quering my own servile slavish fear of man, and all
the instruments of torture and death, which his mali-
cious passions have invented.   *   *   *   I
was a slave. I am a slave no longer. My lips have
been sealed by man. They will never be again, till
sealed in death. My body is freely yielded to the
persecutors to torture at pleasure. But my spirit must
and shall be free. Equal, unrestricted liberty of
speech at all times, and in all places, is my birthright.
It is the gift of God to every member of the family of
man, and I will defend it in the face of prison and of
death.   *   *   *   You, brother Rogers, and
the rest of my anti-slavery coadjutors may turn your
backs upon our synagogues, or sit silent spectators of
their hypocritical worship, while the dying wail of
millions of your countrymen is borne to your ears on
every southern breeze—if you can. I cannot. I will

not.   So long as the soil of America is polluted by the footprints of slavery, I will speak in behalf of the victim, wherever I can reach a human ear.   *

*   *   *   My countrymen are *pirates*.   They legalize the sale and enslavement of their own "free and equal" brethren.   They authorize their transportation to distant ports to be sold into perpetual slavery. I scorn the friendship of such a people ; it is enmity against God.   *   *   *   My enemies never made greater blunder than when they sent me to this gloomy prison.   It is an honor I did not expect ; one I feared I might never merit.

As your readers may wish to know the circumstances under which I came to this place, I will relate them, with such accuracy as can be done from memory, though there is not time for detail.

Last Saturday I visited Nashua, with the intention of giving a course of anti-slavery lectures, similar to those I have recently given at Dover, Exeter, and Somersworth.   On my arrival, application was made for a house suitable to my purpose, but no such place could be obtained.   The meeting-houses were refused, for no valid reason, except the Universalist, which was engaged for a course of scientific lectures.   I called on Rev. D. D. Pratt, pastor of the Baptist church, and requested permission to address his congregation on the subject of slavery, the next day. Mr. Pratt refused my request, and remarked that he felt himself compelled to decide what was best for his people, and that he would send for me when he wanted my help.   I then called on the Congregationalist ministers, Mr. Richards and Mr. McGee, for similar purpose, but with no better success.

On Saturday evening, I attended a meeting at Mr. Richards' vestry, and spoke twenty minutes or more to an attentive audience, most of whom I presumed were members of the church.   On Sunday morning, after mature reflection and fervent prayer to God for divine guidance, I visited the Baptist meeting-house for the purpose of occupying some portion of the day in advocating the claims of that part of our countrymen who are held in slavery by the minis-

ters and members of the Baptist church.   In doing
so, I acted in good faith to the assembly I met.
They said that place was the house of God, and I
took them at their word and claimed in it the rights
and privileges of a child of God.   They said their assembly was a christian meeting, and I knew if it was,
it would recognize and respect the equal right of all
to speak, or "*to prophesy one by one.*"   They said
Christ was their Lord and Master, and I knew if they
were followers of his, I should be in no danger of being thrust from their house.   For when was it ever
told of "the Prince of Peace" that he was seen running out ot the synagogue with a Pharisee on his
back?   Or when did he privately instruct Deacon Andrew or Rev. Simon Peter to drag out the spies that
he foreknew would come into the temple "to entangle
him in his talk," feigning themselves just men?   They
said they were the sheep of Christ's flock, sent forth
by their divine shepherd into the midst of wolves, of
which I was one, and I knew if such were the fact,
I was in no danger of being devoured by them, or
dragged from their fold ; for when was it ever heard
of sheep that they had devoured a wolf, or ferociously
seized upon him and hurled him from their pen?
They said Jesus had commanded them to "be wise as
serpents and *harmless* as doves," and I knew if they
followed such directions, they would look to God
for protection, and not to a wicked Universalist ; and
would seek to conquer their enemies by the power of
love, and not by the terrors of the avenging sword.
They claimed to be christians, and I knew that among
such, it would be perfectly safe for me to give utterance to my sympathies for God's perishing poor.

I rose for that purpose, but was immediately interrupted by Mr. Pratt, who said he wished to commence
the regular exercises.   I did not notice this interruption, and was proceeding with my remarks, when sud-
denly Deacon Chase pounced upon my back and held
me fast in his talons.   We did not have a regular fight,
like some which have recently disgraced the halls of
congress, for the one only reason, that I declined a
combat with the reverend ambassador of Christ and

his devout deacon.   I would not assert that Rev. Mr.
Pratt would have fought in person, had I stood upon
my rights.   He might have thought that too undig-
nified.   He would doubtless have contented himself with aiding and abetting the affray, by giving
it his countenance and approval, as he did my subsequent ejection from the house.   After being dragged
from the platform by the deacon, I was carried into
the street by three or four men, whose names were not
given.   I inquired of the deacon, who still had me in
his talons, if I was his prisoner.   He replied that I
was not, and let go his grasp.   I then turned to go
into the house, but was arrested by the deacon and
his associates.   A messenger was immediately dis-
patched to the Universalist meeting-house, in search
of one of those "ministers of God, who bear not the
sword in vain."   The messenger soon returned, accompanied by Constable Gillis, by whom, with the assistance of Deacon Chase, I was pulled by the arms
and collar a distance of fifteen rods or more, to a rum
tavern, and thrown on the bar-room floor.   Soon
after, I was seized and dragged up two flights of stairs
and thrown upon the floor of a small upper chamber,
and subsequently delivered into the custody of two
keepers.

Having secured me in this temporary prison, the
deacon returned to his meeting, to tender to the
church the emblems of the body and blood of "the
Prince of Peace."   I was arrested, as the constable
informed me, on complaint of Deacon Edwin Chase,
Deacon David Philbrook, Norman Fuller, and another
member of the church, whose name I have lost.

During the afternoon, Brother Preble, a Free-will
Baptist minister, came into my prison and asked the
constable, who was then present, to accompany me to
Thayer's hall, at five o'clock, to fulfill an appointment
made for me at that place.   This he declined doing,
but said he would release me for that purpose, on condition that Brother Preble and certain others would
be responsible for my return, provided he could obtain consent of the complainants.   Their consent to
this was asked, *but denied!*   During the evening, one

of my keepers left. The other remained through the night, and slept with his clothes on, the door locked and the lamp burning. Indeed, I was as strictly guarded as though I had been a felon, waiting only an opportunity to escape.

At ten o'clock, on Monday morning, I was put on trial before Israel Hunt. The complaint set forth that I had entered the Baptist meeting-house, "with force and arms," and disturbed the meeting by making a noise, by rude and indecent behavior, etc., etc. The principal witnesses against me were Rev. Dura D. Pratt, and Deacon Edwin Chase. As a precaution, Mr. Hunt required them to swear by the living God, that they would tell the truth, the whole truth and nothing but the truth, relative to the case under trial. But instead of so doing, both of them kept back a part of it, as did Annanias and Sapphira a part of their possessions, and, what was quite as unchristian, testified to what was palpably false, and what I think they must have known was false. None present could fail to remark that their memory was all on one side. Mr. Pratt testified that I treated him "ungentlemanly." On being asked what I said or did that was ungentlemanly, he could not recollect, he said, then, but he was certain, very, that I treated him ungentlemanly. His answers to my questions on the point reminded me of the lines I have seen, but cannot now recall where :

> " I do not like thee, Dr. Fell ;
> The reason why I cannot tell ;
> But this I do know, very well,
> I do not like thee, Dr. Fell."

So with the reverend gentleman. He knew full well that I treated him "ungentlemanly," but wherein he *could not tell*. But finally, being pressed on that point, he testified that I told him I would preach to his people whether he was willing or not. This, in his opinion, was ungentlemanly. Well, admitting that it would have been, it so happened that I did not say it, as brother Preble, who was present, will testify. But I did say to Mr. Pratt that I had come to Nashua to obtain a hearing in behalf of my enslaved countrymen, and that, if access to the public ear through the ordinary channels was denied me, I should seek a channel of my own.

As I do not acknowledge allegiance to any human power, I made no defence. I asked the witnesses some questions, and said a few words, but they were designed to influence the audience present, rather than the decision of Mr. Hunt. In that, I felt no interest. My only object was to expose the wickedness and hypocrisy of Dura D. Pratt and the majority of his church, that they might no longer ensnare the ignorant and unwary.

Mr. Hunt's sentence was, that I pay a fine of three dollars and costs of prosecution ; at the same time intimating that a repetition of the offence would be followed by a much heavier penalty. I assured him I had done my duty in attempting to preach the gospel to the Baptists, and it was contrary to my sense of propriety to pay a fine for it. And I should, therefore, refuse to do it. And, as to threat of augmented penalty for similar fidelity in future, I should not be at all intimidated by it. And so long as any portion of my countrymen were held in slavery, my voice would never be silent, till silent in death.

Mr. Hunt then ordered me to be imprisoned till the fine was paid.

At ten o'clock the next day this order was carried into effect, by my incarceration in this loathsome prison, where duty to God and my countrymen requires me to remain at present. Relief is kindly offered me from several sources, whenever I shall think proper to accept it. But I feel that the object is not yet accomplished that my heavenly Father had in view, in sending me to this dismal abode. And till that is done, I have no wish to be relieved. To one as restless as I am, imprisonment is oppressive. But I can endure it patiently for His sake who died for me. I can now surely "remember them that are in bonds, as bound with them."   *   *   *   *
Bid my friends, one and all, be of good cheer. We shall triumph soon. My eye is already on the victory. You and I may be called to yield up our lives in the

final struggle. Be it so. I am ready. I have already passed the bitterness of death. My enemies have done their worst. I fear them no longer. Do not think me *insane*, that I write thus. I know in whom I have believed, and that a happier state awaits me when the toils of life are done.

Your friend and brother,

STEPHEN S. FOSTER.

Brave hero! But many did call him *insane*, even some of his best, truest friends. I remember once, in Faneuil Hall, at an anniversary, we had a discussion lasting all an afternoon and evening. Garrison, Rogers, Wendell Phillips, Charles Burleigh and Foster were, of course, all on one side. Rev. John Pierpont, Theodore Parker, Thomas Earle, of Philadelphia, David Lee Child, the gifted husband of the more gifted Lydia Maria Child, and probably others, were on the opposing side. The house was crowded in every part. Mr. Pierpont was speaking, and with quite his usual eloquence and power. I was sitting with Foster, down in the body of the hall. Every ear seemed to be opened, every eye fixed on the speaker. Suddenly, Foster detected what proved a fatal moral flaw in the logic. Quietly he rose and addressed the chair: "Mr. President." Mr. Pierpont, always the perfect gentleman in every grace the word implies, and never more so than when in debate, ceased speaking and listened. Everybody listened. Foster resumed: "Mr. President, will our friend, Mr. Pierpont, allow me to ask him a question just here?" "Certainly," was the ready response from the speaker, gracefully drawing back from the front of the platform. Foster then proposed his question. I do not remember it, but I well recollect that it lighted up the whole dark, deep chasm between moral rectitude and political expediency, showing Mr. Pierpont far

over on the wrong side. All saw it, but none applauded, though, in that vast throng, thousands must
have approved. The stillness was almost overpowering. Mr. Pierpont broke it in a manner that at once
engraved him on the tablets of my memory, and em-
balmed him in my heart's affection forevermore. He
spoke only this : "Mr. President, some folks say our
friend Foster is *crazy*. But I wonder what this audience think about it?" Only this, when a storm of
applause burst forth almost rocking the old "Cradle
of Liberty" to its foundations. Mr. Foster's triumph
was complete ; but the graceful magnanimity of Mr.
Pierpont I am sure entitled him to a kingly share in
all the honors of that memorable scene.

Mr. Foster, not without reason and propriety, closed
his pathetic prison epistle with the appeal : "Think
me not *insane* because I thus write."

Insane ! Had a like insanity pervaded a small part
of the American church, pulpit and people, southern
slavery would never have attained such proportions in
the name of republican liberty and protestant christian religion, as to demand the blood of half a million
young men, brave and beautiful, to wash its guilt
away.

Insane ! Rogers did not deem him insane. Blazing down two solid columns of the same page of the
Herald of Freedom with the letter, went his editorial
comments, every word of which should be here reproduced, in justice to martyr memory and the facts of
history. On the jail itself he wrote : "It is providential in Foster's behalf that Amherst jail stands so
near Chestnut hills and anti-slavery Milford, so that
the friends of humanity in those favored places can
come to his relief and comfort in his otherwise solitary confinement. Those two localities abound in

ministering spirits to the faithful prisoner. They have seen to the cleansing and purification, to some extent, of this loathsome receptacle of the victims of clerical and deaconish vengeance. They have expurgated Foster's department, I understand, of its vermin. The character of a people may be judged somewhat by its prisons, as well as its deacons and clergy. A savage people will support bloody minded incarcerating deacons and dragging-out clergy, and filthy, noisome, verminous cells, in which to shut up those whom it hates and fears."

Referring to the justice who tried the cause and pronounced the sentence, he said : " The humane magistrate who played the part of Pilate in the matter, albeit he did not wash his hands as the profligate Roman did, fined Foster low, yet so high (three dollars) that he thought in his majestic soul that it would deter him from " speaking again in the synagogue, in this name." He expressed his trust, I understand, to that effect, when pronouncing his solemn sentence. I should love to have witnessed the *look* with which Stephen replied to that magnificent suggestion. Poor depository of a little brief authority ! He little apprehended the character or the calling of the man he was dealing with. He might naturally enough suppose that one who had abandoned all the prospects of young ambition, a pulpit, a chance few young men of the time have had before them, (but for his christian integrity) a reputation, which had he pursued it, would, ere this time, have crowned him thick with literary and ecclesiastical honors ; who had abandoned all and made himself " of no reputation," would now be driven back from the high and solemn duties for the sake of which he had done it all, *by a three dollar fine !* It was an apprehension worthy the official dignitary who could mistake christian participation in a religious meeting for a legal disturbance of that meeting !"

Mr. Rogers had some time before given his opinion of Mr. Foster's right to enter professedly christian assemblies, to plead the cause of the oppressed, in language to this effect :   " Mr. Foster is the agent of the State Anti-Slavery Society, but takes his own way of performing the duties of his agency.   How far the society would approve this new measure we cannot say.   For ourselves, we cannot deny the christianity of it, and we see not how the meetings he enters can, or how they can object to it consistently with their christian profession.   They assume to be christian assemblies, and to be governed by apostolic rules and usages.   They would be scandalized to be designated as any other than christian meetings.   By those rules and usages, Foster has undoubted right to enter, uninvited, unpermitted, and be heard.   They are congregational meetings to be sure, but they claim that Congregationalism is christianity, in its most approved form, and has no other than New Testament organization, principles and usages.   As *political* assemblies, they may deny Foster's right.   As *worldly* meetings, they may charge him with intrusion.   As *heathen* meetings, they may complain and cannot be estopped by the plea that Foster comes in as a christian, claiming under the usages of a christian assembly.   The reply that they are a heathen and not a christian assembly would put him on a different defense.   Whether it would be a defense in that case for him to say that, as a man he has a right, and is in duty bound to enter any human assembly and cry aloud in the *paramount* behalf of perishing humanity, whatever business might be going on there, is another question and need not be decided, so long as these meetings do not claim to be heathen."

This, and much more, was written for and published in the *Herald of Freedom* of the first of October, 1841, in connection with an account of the Hancock meeting of that year.

Whether Mr. Foster was right or wrong in his course, was never considered by the clergy at all. They assumed that he was wrong, and with equal audacity, they assumed always that they were right in ordering him dragged out and sent to prison, or fined, or both, at the discretion of a civil magistrate. Thus they voluntarily placed themselves, as christian ministers, under the protection of the sword of human, worldly authority, while claiming to be, while professing to be, servants and disciples of the prophesied "Prince of Peace." Of him who said : "My kingdom is not of this world. If my kingdom were of this world, then would my servants fight. * * * But now is my kingdom not from hence."

Nor should readers of these chronicles forget who was Mr. Foster, and what was his object in thus seeking the ear, the heart and conscience of the American churches and people, "whether they would hear or whether they would forbear." He was a christian teacher and minister, not then *ordained*, though he had thoroughly educated and qualified himself to occupy any pulpit or professor's chair, in college or theological seminary. He knew profoundly the history of the church and its ministry, from the calling of Moses and the Levites to Samuel, the earliest prophet ; to Isaiah and Ezekiel, and onward to John the Baptist and Jesus Christ and his chosen and ordained apostles. And when or where in all the Jew-

ish or christian scriptures was it ever read or known
that the priests, prophets, or apostles, were to ask
leave of the ungodly to preach unto them the doctrines of repentance, reformation and righteousness?
Or when, or where, was it ever read or heard that such
right, or even duty, was ever forbidden by any "rules
or usages," still less, laws of divine appointment or
approval, in any assembly, Jewish or christian?

Mr. Foster, like Mr. Garrison and Mr. Rogers, was
a christian and christian minister and teacher, in all
that those words of hallowed memory could ever be
rightly made to mean.   And to whom was he sent?
Or, if not sent, to whom did he come?   To a nation
of oppressors, the like of whom, under all the circumstances, no age had ever seen, from the bondage of
Israel in Egypt to the enslavement of Anglo Saxons
by Norman invaders, whose deeds of manumission
were sometimes recorded on the blank leaves of the
parish Bible, kept in the church, secure from all invasion or violation as though sanctioned by a "thus
saith the Lord," with the volume itself.   Foster was
himself part of a nation, (no *unimportant* part, as became apparent), that in the name of republicanism
and christianity, enslaved down to lowest brute-beast
level, one-sixth part of its entire people.   He found
in his own nation, millions of human, immortal beings,
without one marriage sanctioned by law, or sanctified
by religion, among them all !   One-sixth part of the
habitations of the people, houses of open, known
prostitution, the holy rights, responsibilities and delights of parentage as utterly unknown, unrecognized,
as among the beasts of the stable or the stall.   Millions of immortal, accountable human beings, and not
one of them permitted to learn to read the name of
the great creator, under pains and penalties, severe,

sometimes almost, as for murder itself! Millions of men, women and children, held accountable to human law, as well as divine, of whom a commission of the synods of South Carolina and Georgia, in the year of christian grace, 1833, declared, as with astonishment: "Who would credit it, that in these years of religious revival and benevolent effort, in this christian republic, there are over two millions of human beings in the condition of heathen, and, in some respects, in worse condition! From long-continued and close observation, we believe that their moral and religious condition is such that they may justly be considered *the heathen of this christian country*, and will bear comparison with heathen in any country in the world!"

Another writer in that same South Carolina synod, ou his own account, calls loudly for missionaries to those heathens, saying; "I hazard the assertion that throughout the bounds of our synod, there are at least one hundred thousand slaves, speaking the same language with ourselves, who never heard of the plan of salvation by a redeemer!"

To such a people and nation did Stephen Foster come with his terrible words of warning, expostulation and rebuke. Saw Moses and Aaron any such abomination and outrage in Egypt? But they asked no leave to enter the house of Pharaoh and confront the tyrant to his face; demand immediate and unconditional emancipation of every bondman in the land, and all his house hold; and flocks and herds, as well. Isaiah asked no leave nor license to go to the house of Israel and Jacob, and show them their sins, and rebuke them for their vain fastings and solemn, religious mockeries, while refusing to "loose the bands of wickedness, to undo the heavy burdens and let the captive go free," and break every yoke of oppression and cruelty. His commission was, "Cry aloud, and spare not ; lift up thy voice like a trumpet!" And he obeyed ; and so did Jeremiah ; so did Eze- kiel.   To be sure, they were persecuted ; were impris- oned ; some suffered death.   But what then ? They were obeying what to them, was a divine command. "Go thou and speak my words unto them ; whether they will hear, or whether they will forbear ; for they are a rebellious house."   *   *   "They will not hearken unto thee, for they will not hearken unto me ; for all the house of Israel are impudent and hard-hearted."

But can it be shown from any history, sacred or secular, that Hebrew prophet ever saw such oppression and cruelty as our slave-holders created and unblush- ingly confessed !   Or even *paganism* more dreadful than that which southern synods owned covered all their slaveland as with a funeral pall ?

But the no less faithful prophet, Stephen Foster, saw it.   He felt it.   He felt that he was a part of it, till so far as it was possible, he had come out from it, sep- arated himself from it, religiously and politically, and consecrated himself and all that he had, all that he was, all that he could acquire, all that he could become, to the work of redeeming the slave, and rescuing his nation from the righteous wrath of that God before whom Jefferson declared he trembled when he remem- bered that He was just, and that His justice could not sleep forever !

Had not James G. Birney proved by his tract, of stunning power of argument, that "the American churches were the bulwarks of American slavery ;" and every witness furnished by the church and pulpit themselves ; and Judge Birney himself a ruling elder in the most powerful and popular denomination in

all the south ? and so soon as he had washed his hands
clean from all blood guiltiness in slave-holding, a man
of most unblemished moral and social, as well as intellectual character, in this or any natlon. And had not
Foster demonstrated to the whole christian world, and
out of their own mouths, too, that the American
church and clergy were a great brotherhood of
thieves? A great brotherhood of thieves, taking
them at their own word ; not producing a single witness of his own, nor cross-questioning one of theirs ?

Why should he not then enter the synagogues on
the sabbath day, with greater boldness than ever did
Jesus the synagogues of Judea, or the temple at Jerusalem ? enter them, though every New Hampshire hill
had been a Calvary, and every tree a cross ! Who
was Mr. Justice Hunt of Nashua, with his stupendous
three dollar fine, or the deacons of Reverend Dura D.
Pratt, or his reverence himself, with Amherst jail and
a constable drafted from Nashua Universalist church
to drag him away to it, who, or what were all these to
the soul and spirit of one who had heard and heeded
the voice of Him who said ; " I do send thee to a
people impudent and hard-hearted, who will not
hearken unto thee, for they will not hearken unto me.
Nevertheless, go and speak my word unto them, and
it shall be known that there hath been a prophet
among them, whether they will hear, or whether they
will forbear ! "

But this account may be extended too far. In closing it, probably it may be as a *leave taking* from my ever
to be revered friend and companion in arms in our
moral but fearful conflict for the rights of humanity.
Incidentally his name may appear again in these pages,
but that will be all their limits allow. The close shall
also be in his own words, appropriate climax to his letter

from the jail. Under date of Canterbury, January
15, 1842, he wrote to the *Herald of Freedom* a letter
from which the following are extracts. It will be observed that he had almost twenty years yet before him
of fearful encounter, with the no less faithful com-
panionship, who with him endured to the end of the
anti-slavery strife :

DEAR ROGERS—I designed to be with you in Concord to-day, to commence a course of anti-slavery
lectures, but, as you see, I am not there, and for the
very *worst* of reasons. I am disarmed if not conquered by the enemy. My voice for all practicable
purposes is gone. Since the wet weather came on,
the inflammation on my lungs has returned with other
symptoms of unfavorable character than those of the
original attack. * * * I am now laid on the shelf
for the present, perhaps for the winter. Possibly for
even a longer period. Indeed, when I dare look
on my shattered form, I sometimes think prisons will
be needed for me but little longer. * * Within
the last fifteen months four times have they opened
their dismal cells for my reception. Twenty-four
times have my countrymen dragged me from their
temples of worship, and twice have they thrown me
with great violence from the second story of their
buildings, careless of consequences. Once in a Baptist meeting-house they gave me an evangelical kick
in the side, which left me for weeks an invalid. Times
out of memory have they broken up my meetings with
violence, and hunted me with brick-bats and bad eggs.
Once they indicted me for assault and battery ; I
think it was on that notorious band of kidnappers, the
Boston police and their abettors, the judges of the
supreme court. Once in the name of outraged law
and justice have they attempted to put me in irons.

18

Twice have they punished me with fine for preaching the gospel ; and once in a mob of two thousand people have they deliberately attempted to murder me, and were only foiled in their designs after inflicting some twenty blows on my head, face and neck, by the heroism of a brave and noble woman. To name her in this besotted age would be to cast pearls before swine ; but her name shall be known in other worlds. * * Still I will not complain, though death should be found close on my track. My lot is easy compared with that of those for whom I labor. I can endure the *prison*, but save me from the *plantation !*"

Space permits no more. This whole letter is worthy a place by the side of the most pathetic strains in the epistles of the great apostle to the Gentiles.

CHAPTER XII.

THE MARTYR PERIOD — IMPRISONMENT OF ALLEN, BROWN, BEACH, HARRIMAN AND FOSTER.

Two British women wrote each a work on American slavery, of similar character. One was entitled " The Martyr Age," by Harriet Martineau ; the other, by Eliza Wigham, was " The Anti-slavery Cause in America, and its Martyrs." Both were highly interesting and valuable but neither could treat of the later persecutions and imprisonment of Foster and others, for their heroic determination to bring the cause of the enslaved to the doors and altars of the sanctuary. A dozen years before, Garrison had appealed to the pulpit, beginning with his own minister, Dr. Lyman Beecher, then of Boston. But his appeal was worse than in vain. " I have already too many irons in the fire," responded the reverend doctor. But Garrison said, seriously : " You had better let all your irons burn up, than neglect your duty to the slave." " I am a colonizationist," said the doctor ; " your zeal is commendable, but misguided. Give up your fanatical notions about *immediate* emancipation, and be guided by us (meaning the clergy), and we will make you the Wilberforce of America." And so said nearly all the leading clergy of the north ; Congregational, Presbyterian, Baptist, Methodist, Episcopal, Unitarian, all alike. The exceptions, such as were worthy the distinction, were soon proscribed as " Garrisonians," name then below every name. And there seemed a settled determination that the people should not hear the abolitionists, nor know of their doctrines, nor of their own duties and obligations to the slaves. Many proofs of this have already been adduced ; but many more are soon to appear. Another "Martyr Age" was demanded to expose and overturn the power and reign of a pulpit thus given over to work iniquity and practice such oppression and cruelty, in the very name of him who came preaching "deliverance to the captives, and the opening of the prison doors to them that were bound." New Hampshire and Massachusetts were not worse than other states, but in them were many of the fiercest encounters; in them was this spiritual wickedness in high places most fearfully revealed to the gaze and astonishment of mankind.

Take the following excerpts from one *Pastoral Circular*, issued by the Portsmouth, New Hampshire, Baptist association, headed, "To the churches composing the Portsmouth association—grace, mercy and peace from God the Father, and Christ Jesus, our Lord : "

"There are indications that we are on the eve of a moral and religious revolution." This was in the autumn of 1842, and the dreaded "revolution" was indeed upon them, in the new and increased faithfulness of some, at least, of the anti-slavery apostles in breaking down the barriers a wicked and cruel clergy had raised between them and the people, as well without as within the churches. With subtle cunning and real jesuitry they concealed in their *Circular* (wishing "grace, mercy and peace"), the names, not only of persons, but of principles and objects they meant to oppose, and talked about important schemes of moral and philanthropic name under direction of those who have little or no sympathy for pure christianity ; in one breath denouncing the ministry, and in the next calling for its influence to be manifested in support of their favorite measures for doing good.   *   *   * *   *   " Making it difficult to counteract their influence in many cases, because of the goodness of the cause in which they profess to be engaged."

With verbiage vague as this, the *Circular* proceeded at much length to caricature the faithful laborers in the lecturing field, as well as editors and others, and warning their disciples against presuming on the dignity and authority of those who claim to be set over them in the Lord, in strain like this :

Let the churches, directly or indirectly, rule the ministers, let them lose confidence in their religious teachers, as men who merely consult their own personal views and ends, without inquiring what truth and faithfulness to the souls of the people demand at their hands ; let the ministry, by any effort of the church, or of the enemies of God, become despised in the eyes of the world, and the chief instrumentality of heaven's appointment for rearing up the kingdom of Christ on earth is gone.

But the following single paragraph is quite sufficient for all present purposes :

We are also aware that the ministry itself is chargeable, to no little degree, with bringing about such a state of things as we herein deplore. May be they have thought, by placing themselves more on a seeming level with their fellow-citizens, by mingling in their debating clubs, and joining with them in their efforts to bring about certain moral improvements, that in this way they would get a nearer access to them with the gospel ; but we think that by pursuing such a policy, they have *unavoidably lost that reverence which the people must have for their ministers, over that which they cherish for other men,* and lost also the end which they thought to gain, by taking such steps. Nor is this all. Ministers have not been sufficiently respectful and decent in their intercourse toward each other, and the world and the church have seen it, and taken undue liberties from it. Hence, the ministry has plunged a dagger at its own vitals ; and now, as long as they continue to disrespect and accuse each other, they must not be surprised if they are disesteemed by others. Let them begin the work of reformation among themselves, and let them so demean themselves that *the robes of their office* shall be held in future by all, as sacred and inviolable.

Abolitionists soon learned what that "seeming level," and "mingling in debating clubs," meant, without being told by the clergy themselves. In this case they were super-ingenuous.

But Connecticut and Massachusetts were even more definite and authoritative, speaking through Congregational associations in state councils assembled ; and enacted what doubtless to this day is the law of the whole Congregational and Presbyterian church, not only of those states, but of the whole land :

Resolved, That the operations of itinerant agents and lecturers, attempting to enlighten the churches in respect to particular points of christian doctrine and christian morals, and to control the religious sentiment of the community on topics which fall most appropriately within the sphere of pastoral instruction and pastoral discretion as to time and manner, *without the advice and consent of the pastors and regular ecclesiastical bodies*, are an unauthorised interference with the RIGHTS, *duties* and discretion of the stated ministry—dangerous to the influence of the pastoral office, and fatal to the peace and good order of the churches.

The pastoral letter of the Congregational association of Massachusetts, at the same time, contained mandates like these :

We would call your attention to the importance of maintaining that respect and deference to the pastoral office, which is enjoined in scripture, and which is essential to the best influence of the ministry on you and your children.

One way in which this respect has been in some cases violated, is in encouraging lecturers or preachers on certain topics of reform to present their subjects within the parochial limits of settled pastors without their consent. (!)

Your minister is ordained of God to be your teacher, and is commanded to feed that flock over which the Holy Ghost hath made him overseer. If there are certain topics upon which he does not preach with the frequency or in the manner that would please you, it is a violation of sacred and important rights to encourage a stranger to present them. Deference and subordination are essential to the happiness of society, and peculiarly so in the relation of a people to their pastor. Let them despise or slight him and he ceases to do them good, and they cease to respect those things of which he is at once the minister and the symbol. There is great solemnity in these words : "Obey them that have the rule over you and submit yourselves."

And Vermont Congregationalism through its State Domestic Missionary Society, in 1841, spoke officially to this effect :

The ministers are the heads of the churches; the leaders in the sacramental host of God's elect. No measure can be carried without them, and much less in opposition to them. And scarcely any proper measure can fail to succeed when the ministry put forth their power. In view of this fact it is asked with utmost earnestness, ought they not, and in view of their obligations, and of the glorious results sought, will they not come up to this work and lead on the churches? The churches can be reached in no other way. No man can approach a church when the pastor interposes. He cannot, and he may not if he can. To give Vermont to Christ, this is the peculiar work of the church of Vermont.

And as spoke Vermont in these few utterances, so
spoke, practically, the entire church of New England
and of the north, of every denomination, not even the
Quakers excepted.

What now was the duty of every faithful anti-slavery
man and woman ?

The ministers were the heads of the churches ; the
leaders of the sacramental host. No measure could
be carried without them, No measure could fail to
succeed when they put forth their power. No man
could approach a church when the pastor interposed.
" He cannot, and he may not if he can," was the dread
declaration. Here now was the situation. The Portsmouth association had issued their Encyclical for the
double purpose of blasting the name and reputation
of the abolitionists to save not only themselves personally, in their pro-slavery infamy, but the clerical
order, which they dishonored by their character and
conduct.

Massachusetts and Connecticut had spoken a little
before Vermont, but substantially to the same fearful
effect. And New Hampshire had already begun the
execution of the same spiritual decrees, and found the
state ready, willing and waiting with its courts, con-
stables, county houses and jails, to open up the new
Spanish inquisition with all its terrors and tortures.

And the new organization, led largely, almost
wholly, by ministers, endangered the good name of
anti-slavery, though happily only for a short time, for
soon most of the new organized type of anti-slavery
sunk to a political party, pledged to support slavery
in the states as then existing, including the right to
recapture fugitive slaves, only resisting its extension
by congress into new territory. That, and to traduce
and villify faithful, uncompromising abolitionists, and

to apologize for slave-holders, and to defend their
right not only to the christian name at home, but to
recognition and fellowship as christians and christian
ministers at the north, was an important part of the
work of most of the leading clergy, bishops and doctors of divinity included, in every evangelical demom-
ination in the country, whether holding slavery as
sacred or professing anti-slavery. Religious newspapers in all the evangelical sects furnished the evidence of this every month if not every week in the
year. Reports and resolutions of the proceedings of
all the national missionary, Bible and tract societies
often abounded with such evidence. General assemblies, Presbyterian ; general conferences, Methodist ;
association and consociation of the Congregational
churches all testified to the same terrible truth ; and
though the Methodist general conference was rent in
twain by the angry agitation, there never was an hour
while slavery lasted when the northern conference did
not hold in its communion thousands of slave-holders,
with their tens of thousands of slaves ! Their annual
conferences extended clear down to Arkansas, Texas
and New Mexico, according to their own *Book of Discipline*, published so late as the year 1860, and now
lying on my table. Not that there were not many
good anti-slavery men and women in the churches,
but how could they be reached? Stephen Foster
found a way. I had spent most of the summer of 1841
in my native Massachusetts, but when about to return
to New Hampshire I addressed Foster a letter as to
our future course of action, containing these few
periods :

DEAR STEPHEN FOSTER—Perhaps my duty has been
neglected in not writing to you in my absence from
our field of labor. I will now endeavor to make some

amends, though I have not much to communicate. To soldiers like you and me, recitals of sieges, sorties, or battles are not interesting, unless rich in strange incident, fearful encounter, terrible suffering, hair-breadth escape, or wondrous victories. So I do not think much need be said of my work in the old Bay state, beyond what you may have read in the newspapers.

Still, what I have witnessed and experienced in Essex, Plymouth and Bristol counties makes me reluctant to leave the state just now, but I must come to New Hampshire. Brother Stephen, the granite rocks must echo us there in the coming months, and the hills reply as we sound through the state the doctrines of universal freedom to the whole brotherhood of man. They call you and me "dangerous men." We must show ourselves such.

Devise some plan, if you can, by which we may greatly improve on the operations of the past.

If we scourged a pro-slavery clergy and church with whips last year, let us this year lay on with scorpions. Let us make every hold of spiritual tyranny send up its death shriek as we flash down into it the lightning of eternal truth, and roll its thunders among its darkest, deepest caverns. Let us write *Tekel* over every pro-slavery pulpit in characters of flaming fire, until the knees of every reverend Belshazzar who sits enthroned on it shall smite together.

Armed with the truth we shall be omnipotent ; and the hour has come. The groans of our three million bondmen have pierced the heavens, and the arm of the Almighty is made bare as of old, for deliverance. With faith we may be as Moses and Joshua, in hastening its coming, and God helping us we will be. We are prepared to be scandalized as infidels, and reviled as the enemies of man and God. To the popular, prevailing religion we are infidels, and mean to be. Woe to such as are not! The pulpit of our land saith in its heart, "There is no God." It is corrupt. It has done abominable wickedness; and so has the church, which is its own handiwork.   *   *

*   *   Our religious institutions have made themselves the body guard of slavery. We cannot come at the monster but through them. Let us not mistake; a pro-slavery religion must be hunted out of the land; too long has it cursed the earth. It has delighted in blood and tears; it has fattened on human misery. It has extorted groans and wailings from countless victims, but its own hour has come!"

This letter accomplished mightier results than could have been anticipated. In exactly one month from the day of writing it, the answer to the desire that he should devise some new method by which we could greatly improve on our past, was more than fore-shadowed in his heroic and masterly entrance into the Concord North Church, and rising with all the dignity and devotion of an inspired and commissioned prophet of God, demanded to be heard at the hour of sermon, in behalf of the millions in our republican and christian nation who were grinding in the prison-house of cheerless, hopeless and interminable bondage. Of course he was denied, and violently, savagely thrust out of the synagogue.

But the end was not then nor there; the beneficent results of the brave act shall never end. In that hour, Foster might have beheld clerical usurpation and domination, so lately, so audaciously asserted in New Hampshire, Vermont, Massachusetts and Connecticut, and exercised in other states, falling like "Lucifer, son of the morning," from heaven ! falling to rise no more !

For his sublime example soon began to be imitated elsewhere, and a martyr period, all unexpected, burst upon us. Satan seemed to come down in great wrath, as if seeing that his time was short. This generation knows little of the trials experienced by the faithful abolitionists in those times that tried men's souls, and the souls of women as well. Indeed, this generation seems to know little of what slavery was, any more than what was genuine, uncompromising anti-slavery.

The first to follow in the steps of Mr. Foster in his new movement, were two plain, honest, but earnest working men, mechanics in Littleton, by the White Mountains. Their names were Nathaniel Allen and Erastus Brown. Both were heard, but subsequently arrested, tried and consigned as felons, to Haverhill jail. Readers of these pages have heard of that grim bastile before ; and of Nat. Allen and his gift of a new harness to the anti-slavery cause. The principal village lawyer, Mr. Carlton, volunteered his services in their behalf ; the sympathies of the community were greatly enlisted in their favor. Both men were universally respected and esteemed ; they were radical temperance men, and non-resistants ; had no foes outside the church, and were both model husbands and fathers, as well as kind neighbors and faithful friends.

But they endeavored to "remember them that were in bonds, as bound with them," and the church and ministry waxed exceeding wroth against them. They sought to do unto others, especially their enslaved fellow beings, as they would have others do unto them, and the church and pastor haled them to prison; their wives and children weeping aloud as they left their

homes.   Perhaps the church and pastor thought, verily, that they were doing God service; at any rate,
away many miles, to prison, they sent them.

And while in confinement, they wrote me letters,
worthy the persecuted saints of other times; by
Nero, Torquemada and the Inquisition.   These pages
are hardly worthy a few brief excerpts of their contents.   Allen wrote: " We were brought here at the
instigation of the church and minister, Mr. Worcester,
who, as you will recollect, publicly admonished his
people that "*this speaking must be stopped.*"   But I
complain not; I am better off than those for whom I
plead.   I am happy here, and think I may be, in
whatever situation my enemies may place me.   We
were arrested on the sixteenth of August; our trial
was quite interesting; some of our citizens spoke very
feelingly in our behalf.   The people of Littleton outside the church, and a portion of the aristocracy, think
it was the most disgraceful prosecution that was ever
enacted in the town.   My wife and children feel badly
to have me here, but I suppose the church thought it
would be for the glory of God.   *   *   I trust
it will result in good; and I forgive and pray God to
forgive the church and all who sent us here."

In another letter he writes: " If we had but some
clean straw and a block of wood for our heads, it
would add very much to our comfort.   But I will find
no fault.   I was never more happy in mind than at
present.   Tell our friends, especially those whom our
absence most affects, that our situation is rather
pleasant than otherwise."

To Mrs. Allen he wrote: " True, our situation,
filthy and over-run with vermin though it be, is more
tolerable than I expected, so give yourself no unnecessary anxiety on my account.   I am comfortable

and contented.   More than that, I am unusually
happy, and believe I shall continue so, however long
I may remain here."

Mr. Brown wrote under date,

HAVERHILL JAIL, August 30, 1842.

BROTHER PILLSBURY — I greet you through the
bolted doors and grated windows of Grafton county
jail.   *   *   Brother Allen and myself are confined here for the *crime* of opening our mouths for
the dumb and suffering of our common humanity, unbidden by any except our Savior.   I am filled with
strange emotions when finding myself, for the first
time in my life, incarcerated within prison walls.   A
favored opportunity for remembering them that are in
bonds.   *   *   I cast my eyes around, and contrast the dismal aspect of my half-lighted, barred and
bolted cell (where, as I am assured, deeds of darkness
have been indeed done, for two men were murdered,
we are told, in this room, by a third named Burnham,.
all three confined only for debt,) with the inimitable
beauties spread out in the vast expanse between us.
and the setting sun, now darting his last rays far up
a cloudless sky ; though I do not feel like saying much
about myself nor of my situation when I think of the
poor, wretched victims of hate or jealousy who have
suffered, or are now suffering, within these filthy dungeons, treatment which should mantle with the blush.
of shame any human face that witnesses it inflicted
even on a brute beast.   *   *   We are in a cell
with a young man who tells us he has been confined
more than a year on charge of theft, of which he declares he is innocent, and I believe he is.   He has
been in this cell four months, and says it is a heaven
compared with the loathsome den underneath where
he lingered eight months !   He was only removed
from it on account of declining health.   It is sad to
hear the low, murmuring sound of human voices from
distant cells, as they occasionally come up to our
room-mate through a small hole in the huge barred
and bolted door or grated window, through which the
scarcely audible voices can be heard as if in supplica-

tion from the lower world ! * * I regret our
confinement, not so much for ourselves as on account
of the inconvenience, anxiety and privation it causes
our families, who need our presence and assistance,
and the remorse it must yet cause our accusers and
those who stood by them when they sent us here.
Walking my cell in silence, and contemplating the
various pains and penalties which professed christians
have inflicted on their fellow beings, (*for the glory of
God,* we must suppose,) and the cruel privations and
sufferings endured by the body *for the good of the soul,*
I am led to exclaim : " Is this, then, the religion of
Jesus Christ ? Is this the doctrine of Him who came
to teach forgiveness of injuries—the love of enemies?
Is this what He meant by undoing heavy burdens,
and opening the prison doors of them who were
bound ? and when He said, ' If ye forgive not men
their trespasses, neither will your heavenly Father forgive yours ?'" Each morning I rise from my pallet
of straw, or rather of chaff and vermin, with the very
kindest feelings toward my persecutors, and unabated
zeal in behalf of the slaves ; and I remain your friend,
as ever,   ERASTUS BROWN.

These few periods, from letters of Allen and Brown,
show what manner of spirit they were of, and what
was their condition while in prison as to body and
spirit. It is most remarkably true that persons sent
innocently to prison, as were these two brave men,
always become deeply interested in their fellow-pris-
oners, whether guilty of crime or otherwise. It is not
strange, then, that my friend Brown, one of the truest,
bravest, most humane men who ever lived, should
deeply sympathize with the young man, whether innocent or otherwise, who had already suffered the pains
and pangs of a dozen ordinary deaths, before guilt
had been proved or innocence admitted. And many
called Brown *insane.* Some of his accusers deemed it
charitable to think or say that he was not in his right
mind when he persisted in opening his mouth for the

dumb, and for him who had no friend nor defense in the Sunday assemblies of his oppressors and enslavers. Doubtless, many said, "He hath a devil, and is mad," and so they shut him in jail, knowing well the kind of cells they kept for the *heinous crime of insanity!* I felt at the time that Allen and Brown were the sanest men in Littleton, unless their counsel, Mr. Carlton, was an exception. Both men have been dead many years, but they saw the death-blow given to slavery, and departed universally respected and deeply lamented by their families and friends. Their confinement lasted but sixteen days; though their release, like that of Jeremiah, the Hebrew prophet, was by the civil, not the ecclesiastical, authority.

But the powers that ruled in the church, mistook entirely the character of the abolitionists. Had they shown themselves and their discipleship to be followers of him who came "preaching deliverence to the captive, undoing the heavy burdens and letting the oppressed go free," and breaking yokes, instead of laying them mercilessly on the shoulders of men and of women, and on their children after them, in successive generations, there need have been no other abolitionists, no other emancipation. In one word, had the church and ministry been, in any true sense, an *anti-slavery*, a *temperance*, and a *peace* society, there never would have been any other, nor need of any other, nor room for any other.

But the church was neither of these, and so those associations had to appear, to save even the church and pulpit themselves from the guilt of all these evils. And the first and sternest work of the abolitionists was to loose the bands of wickedness in the church, especially such as prevented approach to the people with the claims of the enslaved millions in our own

boasted republican and christian land.   That one
fact proved the truth and justice of Judge Birney's
tract, "The American Churches the Bulwarks of
American Slavery."

The government had decreed slavery, including the
right of the slaveholder to call on the whole north to
defend him against slave insurrection, and to aid him
in recapturing his fugitive slaves, who might take
shelter under any friendly roof ; with heavy pains and
penalties for attempting to shield them. from their
tyrant pursuers.   The supreme court had declared all
this to be the exact meaning of the words of the constitution.

Then the church, everywhere in the country, had
pronounced the same system of all unutterable cruelties, abominations and wickedness to be in exact accordance with the will of God, as revealed in the
scriptures of both Old and New Testament.

And the church, or rather the clergy, presumed on
one step farther.   The federal constitution has something to say about the right of the people "peaceably
to assemble" for any proper purpose.   The pulpit,
far and wide, proclaimed to the extent of its spiritual
jurisdiction and influence, that abolitionists had no
such rights, and for a time the government sanctioned
such a ruling, and, as has just been shown, loaned its
prisons for enforcing it.

For it should be kept in memory that Mr. Foster
never invaded a religious assembly against its own
usages, till the proclamation had gone forth that lecturers had no right to enter *a parish*, not a meeting-
house, without the pastoral consent and approval.
Not till long after that audacious decree had had its
dire result in keeping the people, especially the church
membership, from entering the anti-slavery meetings,

19

free as they almost invariably were of entrance, and
of speech, as well.   And it required many a prosecution, fine, imprisonment and other gross outrages, to
break down that formidable "bulwark" and give the
proclamation of liberty free course to run and be
glorified.

But the strength of the anointed ones became equal
to their day and its duties, and their courage and faith
to its dangers and endurances.

The imprisonment of Brown and Allen awakened a
similar zeal in many others, both in New Hampshire
and Massachusetts.   Perhaps it is true to say that in
those two states, the hardest battle with the ecclesiastical power, and so the severest of the whole conflict,
was fought.

The jails of Newburyport and Salem, Massachusetts, were several times honored by the entrance and
detention for longer or shorter periods, of the victims
of pro-slavery spleen and spite.   I think in every instance church members not only instigating, but actually prosecuting the suits.   Even the county house
of Essex county was put in requisition for the same
unrighteous purpose.   The offender in that instance
was a woman, Mrs. Almira Swett, of Georgetown.   In
a somewhat voluminous history of Essex county, published in 1878, mention is made of the anti-slavery
operations in Georgetown, and the following is ex-
tracted from the account :

No movement in Georgetown was ever of a more
stirring or important character than that of the early
agitation of the question of anti-slavery.   In it were
enlisted many men and women whose hearts were fully
committed to the agitation.   Among the leaders in
the reform were Theodore G. Elliot, Moses Wright,
James H., Asa W. and Almira Swett, and others. The
speakers frequently heard were William Lloyd Garri-

son, Frederick Douglass, Wendell Phillips, Parker Pillsbury, and the long line of the advocates of that cause. They carried the discussion to the doors of the churches, which were then committed to silence. Rev. Mr. Braman was unfriendly to the agitation, which added warmth and interest to the debates. These speakers were bold and incisive in their utterances, which made the conflict between them and the conservatives, as they were called, warm. Mrs. Swett was one of the boldest of the female supporters of the cause, and when she attended church she was accustomed to take her knitting work with her, which led her to be arrested for contempt of worship. For this and for the defense of her brother, who was before the church for waywardness on this subject, she was arrested and tried, being charged in the forms of law with "assault and battery." She was convicted and sent to Ipswich. When arrested, she told the officers she "could not leave home at that time ; that her family needed her attention." She offered no resistance, simply declining to comply with the request of the officer. Assistance was procured, and Mrs. Swett was lifted into the sleigh and carried into the court room in the same way. After trial and conviction she was borne back to the sleigh and carried to Ipswich, but the keeper of the "House of Correction" declined to receive her, declaring that those who had brought her there deserved more than she to be retained. The meetings of the Come-outers were held on the steps of churches, in groves, and in barns. Thomas P. Beach was once rotten-egged while speaking from the steps of a church. To avoid this indignity in barns, the women were seated and the speaker stationed before them, when the doors were opened to accommodate the listening crowd without.

It has been intimated in early parts of this work that the course of Mr. Foster and others in entering the meeting houses during Sunday services and asking or claiming the right to be heard on the subject of slavery, did not meet the approval of Mr. Garrison nor many of the most prominent abolitionists. But the

sin, if it were sin, was like some of the psalms ; one of
"degrees." All anti-slavery meetings would have
been prevented if possible, at the north, as they were
actually at the south. The northern pulpits forbade
them just as far as they had the power. Edward
Everett, a clergyman, when made governor of Massachusetts, said in his message to the legislature, referring to anti-slavery meetings and measures : "Whatever by direct and necessary operation is calculated
to excite insurrection among the slaves, has been held
by highly respectable legal authority, *an offense against
the people of the commonwealth*, which may be prosecuted as *misdemeanor*, at common law. The patriotism
of all classes must be invoked to abstain from discussion, which by exasperating the master, can have no
other effect than to render more oppressive the condition of the slave."

But no abolitionist worthy the name, held, or
attended one meeting the less for any threats of gov-
ernors, ministers or mobs. And what wonder that
some went so far, in the name and spirit of New
Testament christian liberty, as to believe it their solemn duty as well as natural right to enter any *christian* assembly to plead the cause of down-trodden and
bestialized humanity ?

And women not unfrequently carried their knitting
work, as men did their novel or newspaper into the
cars, and entertained themselves as best they might
while they rode along. Women did the same at conventions, and do still ; and more than Georgetown
women did the same thing at the Sunday meetings as
their testimony and rebuke against the solemn mockery of a worship that in long sermons apologized for
slave-holders and proved their right to hold slaves,
both by patriarchal example and the divine approval

in Old and New Testament precept and permission.
And they had other motives, the same as were preached,
and practiced too, by Martin Luther, when he wrote
to his converts ; " If any set up sabbath observance
on a Jewish foundation, or for the mere day's sake,
then I order you to work on it, to ride on it, to dance
on it, or to do anything on it that shall reprove this
encroachment on the christian spirit and liberty."
Calvin and the Fathers of the reformation did the
same.   The taste of such things may be questionable,
especially judged by modern standards.   But the
right is another affair.   Daniel Webster somewhere
said he might have rights concerning which, ordinarily,
he should feel little interest ; but let one of the least
of those rights be invaded or threatened, and he
declared he would plant himself on its extremest verge
and contend for it to the death ; as who would not ?
Mrs. Swett testified against the mockery of a worship
that would not plead for the slave, nor permit others
to do it, by quietly sitting down with her knitting
work in front and full view of the minister.   Her
brother rose in his place and bore testimony in the
same behalf by word of mouth ; and both acted from
religious sense of duty ; and doubtless, with as lofty
spirit of devotion as ever actuated the heart of John
Calvin or Martin Luther, or the most saintly of their
disciples.

When Boston was sending back fugitive slaves,
armed citizen soldiers were brought from distant
towns in Massachusetts, and Faneuil hall was turned
into barracks for their accommodation, to protect the
slave-hunters and their accomplices while they seized
their prey, proved property and triumphantly bore it
away.   It might have been in questionable taste, but
it certainly was a testimony of stunning force, when,

at a great grove anti-slavery gathering on a Fourth of July, Mr. Garrison, holding a copy of the constitution of the United States in his hand, literally and deliberately set it on fire and consumed it, to the delight, as well as with the approval of thousands who sat or stood around him.

That constitution was the pledge and solemn guaranty from the north to the south that any attempt on the part of the slave to escape from his bondage, by fighting or by flight, should be resisted by the north, at whatever cost of treasure or blood. What better did such a constitution deserve than to be branded as "a covenant with death, and an agreement with hell," and to be burned with fire before all the people? And what day so appropriate for such *auto da fé*, as the Fourth of July? And who so worthy to officiate at the altar of sacrifice as William Lloyd Garrison?

And thus did earnest, brave men and women of varied description as to culture, calling and sense of propriety, seek to subserve the interests of their common humanity by such methods and measures as seemed right in their sight.

Arrests and imprisonments were frequent, sometimes for actual offense, sometimes for being present and approving the act. The names of several are before me; most of them now numbered with the departed. Prominent among them, as to order of arrest, or length of imprisonment, were Jesse P. Harriman, of Danvers, Massachusetts, and Thomas Parnell Beach, a native of Vermont, but Congregational minister in New Hampshire, for several years, or till he, as heretofore described, identified himself with the anti-slavery cause. His great labors and severe sufferings, by imprisonments and otherwise, chiefly in New Hampshire and Massachusetts, early broke him

down, and compelled him to retire from the conflict.
Having relatives in Ohio, he removed with his family
to that state, and when able, was successfully employed as a teacher.   But in the year 1846, he was
released to his well-earned rest and reward, when only
thirty-eight years of age.   His longest and severest
confinement was in Newburyport jail, where he was
kept three months, in the winter of the years 1841 and
1842.   He was arrested for attempting to speak in
two Sunday meetings, one in Danvers, the other at
Lynn.   For the double purpose of showing the spirit
and temper of the accused, and the nature of their
offenses, I will first permit one of them to speak for
himself, through his prison bars.   While in confinement, Harriman wrote a number of letters to the *Herald of Freedom*, and the following are excerpts from
two of them, dated :

SALEM JAIL, Sept. 24 and 27, 1842.

DEAR BROTHER ROGERS—I write from within the
granite walls of a loathsome prison.   A rather singular place to put non-resistants, but so it is, and I submit with meekness.   Oh, God, enable me to forgive
my enemies !   This is what I want to feel.   I can assure them I will never be the means of sending *them*
here, or to any similar place.

But the question may be asked, how came you imprisoned ?   I answer, through the instigation of the
church, either directly or indirectly.   Let us see if it
be not so:

On the Fourth of July, it was Sunday, Thomas P.
Beach felt it his duty to go into the Baptist meeting-
house, at Danvers, New Mills, and speak in behalf of
the down-trodden slaves, our three millions of christian
heathen !   He went, and when there was an interval
in their wicked worship, (I think it wicked), he rose
and began to speak.   The committee, Black and Cald-
well, fell upon him and dragged him from the house
with great violence.   He was then prosecuted for go-

ing into the house.   The officer came to my house on Sunday and arrested him.   He commanded me in the name of the commonwealth to help him.   I utterly refused.   My answer was, in the name of God, I refuse.   So I am here for not helping to drag Brother Beach from my own dwelling.   And I now say to the world, I will never commit such a sin, though, as a result, bonds and imprisonments should ever await me.

But how has the church been the instigator of my imprisonment ?   They have sanctioned all the doings of those who put me here.   How did Saul assist when Stephen was stoned to death?   He did not cast one stone at him.   But he kept the raiment of those who did.   To this hour, not one of the New Mills church has visited me, except my wife and Mrs. Porter, who lives in our house.   One of the old members took friend Black by the hand, after he had dragged Beach from the meeting-house, and said : "Major Black, you have my hearty thanks for what you have done." Black testified to this under oath, before John W. Proctor.   That church has never shown to the world that they were opposed to the proceedings in the case of Brother Beach or myself.   On the other hand, they have shown to all around them that they are in full fellowship with our being in jail.   *   *   The scripture saith : "The name of the Lord is a strong tower : the righteous runneth into it and is safe." But the church goes to the state for protection.   * *   Will the church of the blessed Savior cast into prison, or uphold slavery and war?   Never ! Christ said, " My kingdom is not of this world."   *   * Thomas P. Beach is now in Newburyport jail, on two indictments.   One by the Baptist church and society in Danvers, William Black acting as their tool.   After he had caused a writ to be issued against Brother Beach, and the officers had come to my house and taken him, he seemed to repent.   At any rate, he sent and withdrew the complaint, and Beach was set at liberty.   I saw Black the same day, and he said, in front of my house, "I am sorry I had anything to do with this.   I should not, only that I was excited.   I would rather have given ten dollars than made the complaint." To another person he said : "I went to the Baptist meeting to see the fun." Then, when the complaint was renewed, he went before (Justice) Proctor, and stated, under oath, that he made the complaint as one of the selectmen of the town. And when Mr. Proctor commented on his testimony he said, "Mr. Black is one of the fathers of the town, and his testimony, on that account, is entitled to more weight," or words to that effect. What, friend Rogers, do you think the children of such a town must be, from such a father?"

The other indictment against Beach is from the Quaker society at Lynn. I saw the whole transaction—heard Beach speak, heard the uproar, and saw, with astonishment, those worshiping Quakers thrown into whirlwinds of passion. The spirit seemed to move them with great violence. How James P. Boyce and other professed abolitionists can remain in that wicked body, I do not know. This *thee* and *thou* religion seems to me not worth having. Boyce sat looking, at the time of the outrage on Beach, with a complacency to me unaccountable. Had it been in any other than a Quaker meeting-house, he would have cried " Sectarianism ! Priestcraft !" at the top of his voice. I would, in all kindness, advise him and James N. Buffum to begin a little reform in their own society before crying " Priestcraft " so much abroad.   *   *
Thomas Parnell Beach now lies in Newburyport jail, for speaking in the Quaker meeting-house, at Lynn, in behalf of our millions of oppressed and bleeding slaves. And what good does it do the cause of God to go to that house on the first day of the week, and sit there mute as dumb dogs? Why are not Boyce and Buffum mute in meetings out of town? How happens that the spirit moves them to speak in all other places but that Quaker bastile?   *   *   I feel, and the slaves must feel, that it is high time that Quaker nest were stirred up.   *   *   I write this rough letter in Salem jail, on Sunday night, between seven and eight o'clock, with my Bible one side of me, and your *Herald of Freedom*, on the other,

and why may I not speak out ? I write amid granite walls and iron bolts and bars. I am a slave, shut in here ; so bear with me a little longer as your brother in bonds,   JESSE P. HARRIMAN.

Such was the faithfulness with which abolitionists were in those perilous days accustomed to deal with one another, no matter how dear to each other, nor how prominent in position or influence. But it so turned out that our true-hearted friend Harriman received in the same paper with his faithful reproofs of Boyce and Buffum, an announcement which must have cheered and encouraged him greatly in his lonely cell. Beach, too, heard the same glad tidings down in his Newburyport confinement, showing him that his work among the Quakers of Lynn had already borne glorious fruit among the most noble and intelligent young men and women in the society ; for on the next page of the *Herald* containing his letter, Mr. Harriman read the following incidental notice of James Buffum, by Mr. Rogers, giving account of a five days' Strafford county anti-slavery meeting held at Great Falls :

Our gallant friend, James N. Buffum, of Lynn, was at our Great Falls meeting and afforded the usual aid and interest derived from his originality, good sense, and excellent simplicity of heart. Friend Buffum is not a lecturer ; he is better ; he is a talker ; though his talk very often rises into the most effectual eloquence of speech. Give us enough such talkers and we will talk the infernal slave system out of the sympathy of everybody who has humanity enough left to pass muster among mankind. Our imprisoned brother Harriman calls on friend Buffum to deal impartially with Quakerism at home in Lynn, as he does with sect abroad. I can gladden friend Harriman's heart by the fact that James Buffum has already, or is about doing it, renounced that broad-hatted type of sectarianism and given it over to Satan, with the faithful intrepidity of a *Come-outer.*

Before returning to the Harriman and Beach arrest and imprisonment, it will be pertinent and profitable to introduce a brief extract from the history of Lynn, as found in the late, large, and generally valuable history of the county of Essex, Massachusetts. The reasons for it will be apparent in subsequent pages. The extract is as follows :

The year 1841 is to be remembered in Lynn as the time of a fresh efflux of free thought exhibited by what became widely known as the *"come-outers."* These people were primarily Garrisonian abolitionists, starting with the unimpeachable doctrine of human equality before the law. But not finding the cause of the slave well espoused by most of the religious bodies of that day, they unwisely pronounced all the churches, in league with Slavery, and called for good men and women to come out and testify against them. Hence the name, come-outers. They were not confined to Lynn, but they had a strong position here, being upheld by such men as Christopher Robinson, Jonathan Buffum and others, men of private and public excellence apart from the delusion here sustained. The real mischief was from without, as will appear. On a Sunday in 1841, they rallied here in force, determined to try a bold, though foolish movement. The people in general knew nothing of it ; but there were in town, Stephen S. Foster, Nathaniel P. Rogers, Parker Pillsbury, Thomas P. Beach, Henry Clapp, Jr., and many others, full of bitter words and martyr spirit. Dividing into parties, they repaired to several of the churches of the largest congregations, entered without ceremony, and interrupted the services with excited harangues. Foster led off at the first church ; Dr. Cook commanded him to "sit down ;" but as he paid no heed, half a dozen men quietly seized him and carried him out, passive as a log, and set him on the side-walk, his mates following. Pillsbury at the same time, headed an attack on the Baptists ; and proving more troublesome, was shut up in a closet and detained till the end of service. Afternoon, nothing daunted, Beach entered the First Methodist church alone, leaped the altar-rail during the last prayer, and began to talk. No questions were asked, for the thing was well noised about and Methodist blood is not given to hesitation; in a minute, Beach was going "neck and heels," and struggling smartly, down the aisle and steps, more being willing to help than could get a chance. He claimed that his thumb was broken in the affray, but it was not credited. Some of the others had visited the Quaker meeting in the morning, and finding opportunity, without interrupting others, had spoken and been sharply rebuked in turn; but no conflict happened there. About six o'clock in the afternoon, Lyceum Hall was opened, and they made a demonstration of their own, where probably more harshness, more invective, more unreason, were poured out within an hour, than most ever hear in a lifetime. But there was no more disturbance; Foster ranted to small crowds about the streets for a few days, not much noticed, and then disappeared. Others made some trouble for themselves, elsewhere, and their printed effusions were abundant in Lynn; but their strength was all gone in that one effort.

The foregoing has at least the virtue of brevity. But for truthfulness, if this be a sample of his whole work, it certainly is fortunate for Lynn that Mr. Cyrus M. Tracy is not her only historian. His first mistake is as to time; He should have made it 1842. The second relates to number of speakers who "rallied in force." Only four came, and but two of them spoke in any of the churches, or attempted to speak; the other two believed in the right of their companions to speak, under the circumstances, in any *christian* assembly, only observing the apostolic rules of decency and order; and as Beach and Foster felt it their religious *duty* more than right, to do as they did, Mr. Rogers and I accompanied them in part of their attempts to be heard on that memorable occasion. We were all present at the Congregational meeting-house, and saw Mr. Foster dragged out as a wolf might have been from a fold, though hardly by the sheep and lambs themselves. But we did not go to the Baptist house at all till we saw him, from the other side of the common, dragged by a furious crowd down the steps, and thrown violently to the ground, and, as afterwards appeared, quite severely hurt.

It should be remembered that these methods were not adopted at all till every possible means had been used, from fairest to foulest, to prevent our access to the people, and more especially to the churches. Nor was Lynn, by a great way, the first attempt. Nor was there anything peculiar about the movements there, except in their greater number on one day, and in one place.

On Saturday, the 25th of June, 1842, Mr. Rogers and I went to Lynn and called at the very hospitable home of Jonathan and Hannah Buffum, intending to remain over Sunday. I do not recollect, and can now never ascertain, whether we expected to meet Foster or Beach, but certainly no meeting was appointed, till on Saturday evening, Mr. Christopher Robinson called with Foster and Beach at Mr. Buffum's, with proposals that something be done for anti-slavery work on the morrow. It was concluded that he and Foster would call on Rev. Mr. Cook, of the Congregational meeting-house, to procure, if possible, a hearing for him there, and that Mr. Beach and I should call on Overseer Nathan Breed, and ask for the Friend's meeting-house, for similar purpose. But we were denied in both instances. Foster first asked Mr. Cook if he would be willing to allow him to preach for him a part of the day. The *no* was emphatic. Then would you permit us the use of the house at five o'clock, afternoon, or some unoccupied hour? That was also refused, and with threats that if he ever came into the house to speak at all, he "would be taken care of." Foster had said no word about going in, but did say, calmly, that it was uncertain where he should speak next day, but probably somewhere in Lynn. Friend Breed was told, when he denied us the Friends' house, that he must not be surprised if he should hear some of us speaking in his meeting, to which he replied, "You will find us a peaceable people." The next morning, Rogers went by himself to the Congregational house, having understood that Foster would be there, and probably would attempt to address the people. I accompanied Beach and Foster. Foster went forward and sat down in a side slip, opposite the pulpit. It was as perfect a June Sunday as ever shone, but the large house and not less large minister, avoirdupois, had but scattered audience.

At the close of the long prayer, which at that period was offered with the congregation standing, Foster, instead of sitting down, commenced speaking, in very solemn and subdued tone of voice. As soon as Mr. Cook heard him, he turned towards him, and in most military tone, as became a commander in the " church *militant*," ordered him to "sit down." Foster did not obey. "Sit down, sir!" was then uttered with force and gesture. But Foster seemed only to hear a higher command, saying, "Cry aloud ; spare not ; lift up thy voice like a trumpet and show my people their transgressions, and the house of Jacob their sins." At which Cook thundered out, in a tone strangely unlike the solemn voice of Foster, "I command you in the name of the commonwealth to sit down!" By that time, the sexton and two others came to the rescue, and seizing Foster, (whose non-resistance principles on such occasions always put him into a perfectly passive state), two of them by his shoulders, his face downward, and the other, a most conveniently short man, as though gotten up for just that use, catching hold of him by the ankles, as he might a wheelbarrow by the handles, they bore him down the aisle through the porch, and down the steps to the sidewalk, in the most grotesque and ludicrous manner imaginable. Rogers and Beach followed, as did I and several others, who were of the audience, though to us strangers. Foster rose to his feet at once, and, looking at his *bearers*, said, pleasantly, " This, then, is your christianity, is it?" He continued speaking, to attentive listeners, too, till the sexton, seeing the attention given, told the people to go back into the house. "No breaking in upon worship, friend sexton," said Rogers. "We shall have to drag you out if you do. Don't drive folks in, if you do drag them out." The sexton laughed. We all laughed. Rogers advised the good-natured sexton to resign and not do such dirty work for such a minister and church. After speaking some time to excellent purpose, Foster walked directly across the common, not many rods, entered the Baptist meeting-house and sat down till the services were closed and the benediction pronounced. Then, as the people were moving out, he began speaking again. The sexton at the other house had asked Foster, in a kindly way, why he didn't wait till the exercises closed, and then he would not have been molested. But Foster assured him "that would have made no difference. You would have dragged me out then as you have now." As those Baptists verily did. They fell on him the moment they heard his voice, like blood-hounds. They hurried him down the aisle and door-steps to the ground, with such

violence as did him and his clothing serious injury,
as there was good reason to think they intended.   He,
however, rose up and addressed them a few gentle
words and walked away to his lodgings, at Friend
William Bassett's, at that time a most welcome, hospitable and desirable anti-slavery home.   Rogers stood
thoughtfully surveying the scene, when some younger
brethren of "the Baptism of John," assailed him a
little in the style of the high priest's palace, in Jerusalem, eighteen centuries ago.   "This is one of them,"
said a beardless youth, with a leer of contempt.
Rogers did not deny.   "You ought to be tarred and
feathered," sneered out another, spitefully.   "Yes,"
said the first, "and carried to the county jail."   "And
cowhided," said another, "for disturbing meetings on
the Sabbath in such a way."

"Ah," responded Rogers, "is that, then, the spirit
of your worship?   Does your gospel run like that,
my friends?   Is it *tar* your enemies; feather them
that hate you; cowhide them that despitefully use
you?   Why, friends, is that your way?"   Some of the
world's people were rather pleased, and laughed;
whereat, the knights of the tar-bucket ran away.

At noon, we decided to hold a meeting in Lyceum
hall, at six o'clock, and issued notices to that effect.
Mr. Rogers, never having seen a Friends' meeting, in
the afternoon attended their regular service, at three
o'clock.   He found there both Beach and Foster.   I
did not go near.   All was still for a considerable
time.   Beach was first to break the silence.   He said
he had a testimony to bear, and proceeded in his
usual serious and moderate manner, ten or fifteen
minutes, and gradually drew into the then inactive
and very indifferent course of the Friends' societies
towards the anti-slavery enterprise in particular; but

also on the great evils of war, intemperance, and their
like, when a high-seat Friend rose and said to him :
"Thy speaking is an interruption of our worship."
Beach responded that he thought speech was free in
Friends' meetings, and proceeded. Then another
voice came down from the high seat, desiring the
friend to be quiet. But Beach kept on, till a third
elder rose, and asked to be heard. Beach then said,
"If anything is revealed to thee, I will hold my peace."
"I have," said the high-seat voice, and Beach sat
down. Then the "revealed" word was uttered, thus :
"We request thee not to disturb our meeting any
longer by thy speaking." Beach then resumed ; upon
which high-seat members began shaking hands, the
sign for closing the meeting. As the elders and some
others passed down the aisles, William Bassett, then
an esteemed and much respected young member,
called out to them to remain and hear the truth, and
not run away from it. Just then, his mother, a venerable and highly honored member of the society,
rushed forward, and in great apparent grief besought
him, in piteous and pleading tones, to desist and be
quiet. But he answered her tenderly and affectionately, though firmly, "Mother, I am about my
heavenly Father's business, and cannot hear thee
now." He then proceeded at some length, most of
the elderly men having gone out. When Mr. Bassett
had closed his testimony, which he confessed he had
too long neglected, Foster arose, most of the women
and young men remaining, and some of the elders returning, and stepping on a seat overlooking the crowd,
he called attention to "that afflicted mother," as he
designated Mrs. Bassett. "Mark her distress and anguish of spirit. It would be no wonder, nothing
strange or new, should her reason be dethroned by

such shock upon it! And who but you ministers of those 'high seats' would be the guilty cause of her calamity?" He was proceeding in such fervid strain, when the older members, near the door, dashed forward, and seizing him with great violence, pulled him down from the seat and started with him for the door. Friend Nathan Breed had told Mr. Beach and me the evening before, that we would find them "a peaceable people," should we wish to speak. And here and thus they were. But before Foster had been dragged half way to the door, a brave young friend had reached him, and called out to the furious crowd, "Hold! you shan't drag this man out." He was followed by several others, and Foster was rescued and resumed his speaking. Of course the excitement was very great, but Foster now had full opportunity. He cited George Fox and Edward Burroughs, the highest Quaker authorities for entering any religious assembly, and demanding right to be heard. He called for the history of their example, and William Bassett immediately produced and read it to them all, undoubtedly to the astonishment of most of them. The fact was, Beach and Foster had done exactly what the early Friends both did, and defended and taught, if they did not command, and their cause prospered greatly through their bravery and fidelity, as did ours that day at Lynn, as has been already seen.

When, at a late hour in the afternoon, the crowd at the Friends' meeting-house dispersed, Foster and Beach took some notices of our Lyceum hall meeting and walked down, Beach to the First Methodist, and Foster to the Baptist house, from which he had been dragged, a few hours before, intending to read them at the close of their third services. But both were dragged out with savage fury, though both meet-

ings were nearly done when they entered the houses.
Both were non-resistants, and so accepted quietly such
usage as was tendered. Beach had a thumb dislocated by Methodist madness, which cost him severe
suffering, as well as for a long time the use of his
hand. Foster suffered the loss of a part of his coat
collar, through Quaker quiet, and a sleeve cuff by Baptist hands. But that was not all. Though their services were through, he was caught up and carried
down to the porch and thrust into a dark closet under
the stairs, where the sexton kept the lamps, oil-cans,
and other similar sanctuary utensils, and stored him
there "some fifteen or twenty minutes." When they
finally released him, he made them a short and kindly
address, and holding up his damaged raiment, he said,
"This torn collar illustrates Quaker christianity, and
this absent cuff is an emblem of your Baptist
religion."

It need not be said that by this time the town was
quite awake. We hardly dared think that our Lyceum
hall meeting would be tolerated. But it was, and
crowded, too, and continued with unabated interest
three hours, and the order and quiet were all that
could be desired. All four of us from New Hampshire were heard with attention and respect ; and
though we spoke our extremest thought on the rights
of speech and of worship, and of the importance of
a true understanding of them for the success of the
anti-slavery enterprise, beset by foes on every hand,
and of every description, the pro-slavery church and
clergy, of course the most deadly and dangerous, the
very "bulwarks of slavery," not one whisper of doubt
or dissent was manifested by word or deed. Foster
not only invited, but urged discussion on any of our
positions, then and there, by clergy or laity, or any

who might differ with us. We had heard that some of us were to be arrested on Monday, but we voluntarily put ourselves on trial, and were now ready, he said, to meet our accusers. But no one appeared. then nor on Monday. Prosecutions had been threatened, but none came. So on Tuesday, Rogers and I returned to New Hampshire, leaving Foster and Beach to pursue the work in their own way, which they did, and with mighty power, and signal success, too, notwithstanding the complacent conclusion of Mr. Tracy, the Lynn historian, that "their strength was all gone in that one effort" in Lynn, as we shall see.

Foster extended his field with Beach to Boston, and then alone to New Bedford and Nantucket. There the people became so stirred, Quaker population though it largely was, as to break up his course of lectures with one of the fiercest mobs of the whole conflict, and he was solemnly advised to leave the island, "to prevent the shedding of human blood," which he accordingly did. But he soon after more than completed his course of lectures, for at the request of leading citizens of Nantucket, he wrote and published "The Brotherhood of Thieves ; or a True Picture of the American Church and Clergy." The world some day may wish to see it. It ran through ten editions, of two thousand copies each, and produced most millennial results, both east and west. For stunning as the title page sounded, the seventy-two subsequent pages proved beyond doubt or question, that it was true and just.

But Beach and Foster did not hasten their departure from Essex county. Soon they were in South Danvers and Danvers New Mills. Were both dragged out of meeting-houses there as at Lynn, and for the same offense. Their experiences there were varied, sometimes adverse, then more prosperous, as they happened to fall into the civil or ecclesiastical grasp. They could at least be heard in court, as never in the church. And they were even permitted to decline testifying at the civil tribunal, if for conscience sake they declined, as Foster did on one occasion, if no more.

Beach would have been a *dipped* Baptist, at New Mills, whether he would or no, but for the good-natured roguishness of a boy in emptying the water trough; and Foster might have seen one of his South Danvers persecutors severely punished had he been willing to appear against him in court.

The *Herald of Freedom* of the 22d of July, 1842, has this brief notice of the scenes, headed " Beach and Foster Imprisoned by the Church." " Thomas P. Beach, our anti-slavery lecturer, rose to speak in a professed christian meeting at Danvers New Mills Sunday before last, and the professors flew into a rage and fell upon him and dragged him out of the meeting and went to plunge him into a large water trough, they had filled for the purpose, but they found the trough dry. A little boy hearing of their *sectarian* purpose had pulled out the plug and hid it. It is unnecessary to say that they were *Baptists*. The same day Stephen S. Foster, as I learn, at another professed christian meeting at South Danvers, being kicked out by one of the worshippers, and the man kicking him, prosecuted for it by another of the worshippers, (because, as I suppose, he had kicked beyond *worship* measure) and Foster being ordered to testify against him, and declining doing so, on the ground that that was not his way of forgiving an injury, the church fined him. He declined paying the fine, and they thrust him into Salem jail. The New Mills Baptists prosecuted Beach, and sent him also to Salem jail, and placed several Danvers citizens under bonds for declining to assist in carrying the prisoner to jail."

Imprisonments at that period were frequent of abolitionists, some of whom being non-resistants, were committed for refusing to take lessons in the art of human slaughter, under the milder name of " military duty." Most of the victims from our ranks were for the crime of a too liberal interpretation and exercise of the rights of speech and worship, in a country whose government and religion were incorrigibly committed to breeding, trafficking in and holding slaves.

The imprisonment of Thomas Parnell Beach at Newburyport, foreshadowed by the letter of Mr. Harriman from Salem jail, already given, came a few weeks later. He was kept in close confinement three months, on indictments by the Lynn Quakers and Danvers Baptists. His own account written in the jail reads to this purport :

" I was indicted on the Danvers and the Lynn Quaker affair. Those quiet, meek, peaceable, persecuting followers of Jesus have marched up and bowed their joints at the door of the court house and begged the state to stretch out the bayonets, load up the big guns and rifles, and drive this blood-thirsty Beach to prison *sine die*, or till he pay a fine of a hundred dollars, which he has no means of paying, and could not pay conscientiously if he had. For every dollar so paid helps the church to persecute Christ, making the state her more willing tool. I am not astonished that Danvers' Baptist majors and captains should fly to the courts and the forts, but that meek, loving, forgiving Quakers, who cannot *bear arms*, which are the only possible support of human governments, can step forward and say to the state, ' Please imprison Thomas

Beach because *we* shook hands and broke up our meeting! Spirits of George Fox and Edward Burroughs, awake! awake!'"

Most, perhaps all, who were active in this persecution of an innocent but brave, noble, peaceful and conscientious man, have long since passed with him to their final account, so I would tread softly on their ashes, and speak of them only in tones of tenderness and charity. I will let their victim be mainly his own chronicler. He forgave them here; he will forgive them there, or wherever they have gone, and help them to forgive themselves. His friends, while he was confined, brought his family to Newburyport, and kindly and tenderly cared for them. His little boy, three or four years old, shared his cell with him much of the time; and through his prison bars he spoke to larger audiences and to better purpose than ever before; though always one of the most impressive, persuasive, effective pleaders for the deliverance of the enslaved who ever entered the field.

While a prisoner, he not only wrote some powerful articles for the Newburyport *Herald*, some of which are now before me; but the friends of Freedom, not knowing whether he would ever be discharged, established a paper expressly for him, called *A Voice from the Jail*. It ran during his confinement, and was conducted with remarkable ability. Some of its pages flashed as with heavenly fire; every word of them would be worth reprinting, were it only to reveal the power, intellectual and spiritual, of some of the bravest champions in reform, whose word and work ever enlightened and blessed mankind.

With a very few extracts of articles written by Mr. Beach while a prisoner, this account, already too extended, will close.

On the *right* to speak anywhere in behalf of enslaved millions, ground down into the dust as human being never was before ; and when every voice, every press, every pulpit, was bidden to silence, as widely and effectively as possible, he wrote thus :

I will not stop to argue nor question the right. Every instinct of my humanity, or anybody's, will sharply rebuke the cowardly, quivering spirit that should moot this query and respond to it ; is it right to speak for enslaved, crushed humanity any where ? Right to speak in God's house for three hundred new-born babes daily sacrificed to the Moloch of slavery ! Right to echo the prayer of three hundred and fifty thousand women, members of nominal churches, that they may be delivered from the lust, violence, and degradation to which a man-stealing church and clergy have reduced them ! Right to stand on the threshold of the sanctuary, and cry in the ear of the dozing priest and deacon, thus guilty in fellowshipping hell itself as a christian institution ; to beseech them to lift their heel from the neck of my wife, brother, sister, mother ! Right to cry robber, adulterer, murderer, in the ear of a church that buys, sells and enslaves God's own image ; that sells Jesus Christ at auction, and then declare they " *have not violated the christian faith !*" O shame, where is thy blush ? O spirit of 1835 and '37, where art thou ? Does fear wither thy courage ? or startle thee from thy high purpose to deliver the slave, *at all hazards ?* has love, or desire of applause ennervated thy power, or scattered those rays that once came flashing, burning from thine eyes ?　　*　　*　　*　　*

　　*　　* 　　Oh, if the state could have enough of this work to do, it would soon be sick of supporting the victims of church malice and sectarian hate !　　*

*　　* 　I want company here ; I wish every jail in Massachusetts and New Hampshire filled with those who have boldness enough to go and charge upon these God-dishonoring corporations, not only all the guilt, for the tears, stripes, groans and degradation of the slave, but also for the bolting and barring of every

prison door, the beheading and strangling of every
criminal and culprit in the land, together with all the
blood shed, from Abel down to the present hour.
Oh my God, when will thy children be willing to suffer with Jesus, for a perishing world? when renounce
home, money, lands, pride, selfishness, lust, for the
cross of Christ and the crown of glory?   *   *
* * * I am in this prison for attempting to exercise speech freely as a man. I felt called on to open
my mouth for the slave, in places where professing
christians meet to worship. Should I not obey that
call? Am I a man, and may I not speak when I
think and feel that I ought to speak? Why am I made
with these organs of utterance and capacities for
thought and conviction if all may be controlled by the
power of others? Why have I sympathies for my suffering kind if I may not let them flow out? What did
God mean in my formation? Has He made me in
mockery? Is He deluding me? Is He trifling with
His intelligent creation? He, who never trifles with
brutes nor inanimate nature? I spoke for the slave on
my humanity's motion, and at the bidding of God, and
I am here for it. Well, I will bear it as becomes a
man. But let me tell my incarcerators, they commit
a mighty mistake when they imprison a nature that
knows how to endure privation like this.   *   *
I am a prisoner, but no matter, it is *experience*—an invaluable teacher. I am an abolitionist now, and can
remember them that are in bonds as bound with them.
*   *   Oh, the crime of making slaves of human
beings ! Of keeping them slaves ! Oh, the responsibility which lies on this christendom ! Oh, the crime
of professing *godliness*, and keeping humanity in
slavery ! This is the crime of the churches. Oh, the
awful crime against God and man of assuming a priesthood, pretending it to be christian, and using its
mighty influence to perpetuate human enslavement
and hinder a peaceful movement for its overthrow !

Speech, glorious organ of reform among men, will
it ever be free ! Free, it would work wonders. Free,
men and women would then speak like God. Now
speech is enchained. Men speak as they would walk

in fetters, and they look as they speak. The human look is cowered and brought down, and all human action seems constrained and servile.

The list of the imprisoned could be extended, but the instances given already must suffice. They show what manner of spirit actuated both the persecutors and their victims Many more were roughly removed from meetings where they attempted to speak in most decent and proper manner for the enslaved, some of them women of spotless purity of heart and life. The churches lost many of their choicest members and the *Come-outer* connection greatly increased, especially in Massachusetts and New Hampshire. Hayward's "Book of Religions" contains an excellent descriptive account of them, written by William Bassett, whose name has already graced honorably these pages. Many meetings of them were established, and the present Free religious societies, now so widely known, may be truly said to have had their beginnings then and there. Lynn furnished memorable instances Two months after the Sunday demonstration there by Beach and Foster, already described at so great length, Mr. Rogers was again there and attended the regular "Come-outer" meeting. He wrote: "Though the clergy taunt them for their homely name, they must have trembled yesterday when they saw the people throng to their meeting in such numbers." Among the speakers on that day was Frederick Douglass, then comparatively new on the anti-slavery platform. He spoke on the subject of prayer, and illustrated it by his own experience while a slave. He said he prayed long and earnestly for freedom in words as he had been taught but nothing came of it. At length he

addressed his legs :   " O legs, give me freedom !   O
legs, bring me to freedom !   And as you see," he said,
"they did it.   They answered my prayer."

And Douglass might have added, perhaps he did
add, *you " Come-outers" are but fugitive slaves escaped
from your spiritual and ecclesiastical plantations.*

CHAPTER XIII.

Here may be the place to go back a year and give
account of two conventions, memorable in anti-slavery
history, held in New Bedford and Nantucket, in August, 1841. All our meetings, of that and the following
year, as has been seen, especially in New Hampshire
and Massachusetts, were of intense interest, and peril,
too, on account of the new and stern tests demanded
of abolitionists, both in their political and ecclesiastical relations. Both the whig and democratic parties
and all the great popular religious denominations, as
the Baptist, Congregationalist, Episcopalian, Methodist and Presbyterian (new school and old), were all
committed to the power and policy of the southern
slaveholders.

And so the text of the true anti-slavery apostles and
prophets was : "Come out of them, my people, that ye
be not partakers in their sins, and receive not of their
plagues ! "

Prominent among the speakers at that meeting in
New Bedford, were Garrison, Edmund Quincy, and
George Bradburn, then a talented and popular Universalist minister and radical abolitionist ; though
with the other two named, now no more. We closed
late on Sunday, and adjourned to meet at the same
place on Monday morning at half-past seven o'clock.

This early hour was necessary to complete our business and be ready for the Nantucket steamer, at half-past ten, as we were to commence another convention on that island the next day.

The "Report of Proceedings at New Bedford" is not now before me ; but the following resolution, adopted at Taunton, by a unanimous vote, the next week, on my return, after long discussion, is probably a fair specimen, as relates to the church ; and our position was not different towards the political parties :—

Resolved, That American slavery is wholesale robbery, adultery, man-stealing and murder, and is the sin of the whole nation, but preëminently of the north ; and is sustained by both the republicanism and religion of the country, but preëminently by the religion ;   *   *   *   and hence no enlightened person should be recognized as a christian who is not an active, outspoken abolitionist.

Several of our speakers were colored, of whom New Bedford at that time had many.   I think there were two religious societies of colored people there, each with meeting-house and minister.   Many of them, however, fled—men and women—to Canada, in 1850, on the enactment of the new fugitive-slave law, swifter than the exodus of Israel out of Egypt.

One of them spoke so effectively at our meetings that he was invited to go with us to Nantucket, with promise of expenses paid.   Not much was required for fare, for he and his wife were allowed only the forward deck, where they suffered from both sun and rain, especially on our return, by rain.   Our company, of course, protested, but the rule was imperious.

The Nantucket meeting continued two or three days and evenings, most ably sustained, and with increasing interest to the very last.   Till then I had never heard a fugitive slave speak, nor any distinguished colored man. But as Emerson used to say, " eloquence at anti-slavery conventions, is dog cheap."

A young New Bedford barber, slightly colored, named Sanderson, never a slave, tall, handsome, made one of the finest addresses I had then heard on the subject of slavery, Edmund Quincy, who sat by me, remarked, and truly, as the young man sat down, " There was not an error of grammar in that whole speech." And it was more than half an hour in delivery.

Later in the evening, our invited friend from New Bedford, the fugitive slave, came to the platform. The house was crowded in every part, and he evidently began to speak under much embarrassment. To that time the meetings had advanced with increasing fervor, and, as this was the last session, I began to fear a decline for the close. But the young man soon gained self-possession, and gradually rose to the importance of the occasion and the dignity of his theme. In the course of his remarks, he gave a most side-splitting specimen of a slave-holding minister's sermon, both as to delivery and doctrine, the text being: "Servants, obey in all things your masters." I can vouch for the correctness of its doctrine, from a volume of published sermons, preached to masters and slaves, (now on my desk) by the then Bishop Meade, of the Virginia Episcopal church. There was a parody, too, on a hymn then much sung at the south, entitled, "Christian Union." The following verses are part of it:

> Come, saints and sinners, hear me tell
> How pious priests whip Jack and Nell,
> And women buy and children sell,
> Then preach all sinners down to hell,
> And sing of heavenly union.

They'll talk of heaven and Christ's reward,
And bind his image with a cord,
And scold and swing the lash abhorred,
And sell their brother in the Lord
To handcuffed heavenly union.

They'll church you if you sip a dram,
And damn you if you steal a lamb,
Yet rob old Tony, Doll and Sam
Of human rights and bread and ham,
Kidnapper's heavenly union !

They'll raise tobacco, corn and rye,
And drive and thieve and cheat and lie,
And lay up treasures in the sky,
By making whip and cowskin fly,
In hope of heavenly union.

They'll crack old Tony on the skull,
And preach and roar like Bashan bull,
Or braying ass, of mischief full,
Then seize old Jacob by the wool
And pull for heavenly union.

I do not distinctly remember that this parody was given in that sermon, but as we so often heard it, and sometimes *sung* with most exquisite drollery and grace, it is hardly probable that it was omitted there.

When the young man closed, late in the evening, though none seemed to know nor to care for the hour, Mr. Garrison rose to make the concluding address. I think he never before nor afterwards felt more profoundly the sacredness of his mission nor the importance of a crisis moment to his success. I surely never saw him when he seemed more divinely inspired. The crowded congregation had been wrought up almost to enchantment during the long evening, particularly by some of the utterances of the last speaker, as he turned over the terrible Apocalypse of his experiences in slavery.

But Mr. Garrison was singularly serene and calm. It was well that he was so. He only asked a few simple, direct questions. I can recall but few of them, though I do remember the first and the last. The

first was : " Have we been listening to a thing, a
piece of property, or to a man ?" " A man ! A man !"
shouted fully five hundred voices of women and men.
" And should such a man be held a slave in a republican and christian land ?" was another question. " No,
no ! Never, never !" again swelled up from the same
voices, like the billows of the deep. But the last was
this : " Shall such a man ever be sent back to slavery
from the soil of old Massachusetts ?" this time uttered
with all the power of voice of which Garrison was
capable, now more than forty years ago. Almost the
whole assembly sprang with one accord to their feet
and the walls and the roof of the Athenæum seemed
to shudder with the " No, no !" loud and long continued in the wild enthusiasm of the scene. As soon
as Garrison could be heard, he caught up the acclaim,
and superadded : " No !—a thousand times no !
Sooner the lightnings of heaven blast Bunker Hill
monument till not one stone shall be left standing on
another !"

The whole can better be imagined than described
by pen of mine. I could rehearse as well the raptures
of cherubim and seraphim around the throne over the
rescue of a thousand souls from the slavery of Satan
and of sin.

Before us stood one trophy, self-delivered, self-re-
deemed from our chattel slave system, then seething
with all the terrors of the second death. And why
should not we have rejoiced then and there ? For
that proved none other than the baptismal, the conse-
crating service of Frederick Douglass into the life-
work and ministry which he has since so wondrously
fulfilled.

Not long before Mr. Garrison's death, I wrote him
a letter, congratulatory, as was his due, on the singu-

larly successful completion of his life-mission and
work, and expressing the hope that thus "seeing the
travail of his soul" was his supreme satisfaction, as it
might well be. In my letter, I recalled to him the
Nantucket scene, as given above.

DEAR FRIEND PILLSBURY—I did not mean that a
fortnight should elapse before answering your letter,
the receipt of which gave me much pleasure, not only
because of the stirring memories of "Auld Lang Syne"
awakened by it, but also for its very kind and fraternal spirit.

But this delay happily enables me to date my answer on New Year's day, and consequently to offer you
the heartfelt congratulations of the season, and my
best wishes that this may prove the happiest year you
have yet experienced.

However, let it bring forth what it may or must,
whether of prosperity or adversity, joy or sorrow,
health or sickness, even unto death, I have no doubt
you will bear with courage and fortitude what ever
comes, remembering that our earthly existence is con-
ditioned upon ever shifting vicissitudes and final decay.
You will be prepared to say :

> " I'll raise a tax on my calamity,
> And reap rich compensation for my pain ;
> I'll range the plenteous intellectual field
> And gather every thought of sovereign power
> To chase the moral maladies of man—
> Thoughts which may bear transplanting to the skies,
> Though natives of this coarse, penurious soil."

Your anti-slavery reminiscenses seemed almost literally to turn back the wheel of time and make me fancy
that I was still residing in Seaver Place, where our personal acquaintance and friendship began. Since then I
have doubled my age, having completed my seventieth
year on the twelfth of last month. You are several years
my junior, and so at that period were comparatively
a young man, but stout in heart and consecrated in
purpose to the work of breaking every yoke and letting the oppressed go free.

21

Your coming into the field of conflict was specially timely, and displayed on your part rare moral courage and a martyr readiness to meet whatever of religious obloquy, popular derision, social outlawry, mobocratic violence or deadly peril might confront you as the outspoken and uncompromising advocate of immediate and unconditional emancipation.

For then the aspect of things was peculiarly disheartening, a formidable schism existing in the anti-slavery ranks, and the pro-slavery elements of the country in furious commotion. But you stood at your post with the faithfulness of an Abdiel, and whether men would hear or forbear, you did not at any time to the end of the struggle fail to speak in thunder tones in the ear of the nation, exposing its blood-guiltiness, warning it of the wrath to come, and setting forth the duty of thorough repentance and restitution.

If you resorted to a ram's horn instead of using a silver trumpet, it was because thus only could the walls of our slave-holding Jericho be shaken to their overthrow.

I need not remind you of what you were called to confront in the anti-slavery lecturing field, for more than a score of years. Atrocious misrepresentation and defamation on the one hand, and sharp privations and perilous liabilities on the other.

And so in regard to Stephen S. and Abby Kelley Foster and other faithful and self-sacrificing laborers in the same manner. No heavier burdens were borne by any in the abolition ranks, nor borne with greater cheerfulness.

The agitation thus produced, the light thus disseminated were essential to the overthrow of the slave system.

You, too, have seen the travail of *your* soul, and may well be satisfied. *Laus Deo !*

Truly yours,

Wm. Lloyd Garrison.

So much was said in the last chapter about my native county of Essex, that a brief account of my own experiences there may here not be out of place.

A visit I made to Salem in the spring preceding the operations of Beach and Foster in the adjoining towns of Danvers and Lynn, disclosed more vividly the type and temper of " new organization" than anything yet given, not excepting even the Chichester discussion not very long before. It has been clearly shown that the secession of 1840 left the American anti-slavery society bereft of nearly all the evangelical clergy and church members who then belonged to it. Salem had a few excellent abolitionists, including Charles Lenox Remond, and the several members of the family, of whom he was eldest son. It was a cold dismal day when I arrived ; alternate snow and rain rendering it quite as unpleasant under foot as over head. After two hours of weary walking and calling and denials, I obtained the use of a small meeting-house, belonging to the colored people, quite in the south part of the town. Then I set about posting up notices, such as agents then carried, which unruly boys following me tore down almost as fast as nailed up. But the news went round, and the dark evening brought together the few abolitionists of the place and enough colored people to make a fair audience. Salem at that time was almost fatally infected with prejudice against the African color. "Colorphobia" was the name we abolitionists gave the disease, and a more frothing, foaming madness was never visited on the human family. It raged so fearfully that respectable, intelligent, well-dressed, well-behaved colored people, ministers, church members, school teachers, women as well as men, were frequently insulted and outraged, not only on railroads, but wherever they were, if they presumed to exercise the plainest, most simple of the inalienable rights of humanity. In some towns, I am quite certain that Salem was one of them, lyceums refused to sell tickets to the best of colored men and women. Even as late as 1845, if not later, Senator Sumner and Mr. Emerson refused to lecture for bodies so bigoted and proscriptive, and their reasons for so declining were in the newspapers. At my first meeting in Salem, prejudice against color was the theme of remark. The town had furnished sufficient reasons only a short time before for such a course. On the following evening we held our meeting in a commodious lecture room under Mechanics' hall, then occupied on Sundays by a religious society. But for some reason our numbers were not much increased. There was at that time a general determination on the part of leaders in state and church, especially the latter, to keep the people from coming to a knowledge of the truth. Reason enough surely, for the course so soon to be adopted by Foster, Beach and others, of going where the people were.

At my second meeting, I threw down the gauntlet to new organization, by a direct attack on the hypocritical pretensions of its anti-slavery. The Howard-street Congregational church had had for its ministers, Rev. Geo. B. Cheever, an imprisoned martyr, a few years before, for bold and daring faithfulness in the temperance cause ; and Rev. Charles T. Torrey, who had left it a few years before, that he might better serve the anti-slavery enterprise, and who perished subsequently in a Baltimore prison, for the offense, as was alleged, of going into the south to incite slaves to run away from the plantations to Canada or the northern states. With such a previous record, the Howard-street church had set itself forth as a model new organization anti-slavery church, and I proposed on the third evening, to examine its claims, not only to an anti-slavery character at all, but as any kind of anti-slavery instrumentality worthy the respect of the slave or his friends, or the dread or fear of tyrants and oppressors.

The next evening brought together many more than could find admission, and the defenders of the church appeared in force. Some were communicants, though many more were not ; but all seemed inspired, or impelled, or influenced by the same spirit, and of what manner of spirit, the evening was to disclose.

It was claimed for the church that six or seven years before it had passed and registered a resolution of refusal to hold christian communion and fellowship with slave-holders. It was, however, shown that the member of the church who presented the resolutions, had since lived a considerable time in Tennessee ; was in business among slave-holders there, and lived unmolested ; while Birney, Dresser, Crandall and others, not to speak of the murdered Lovejoy, had not only suffered every indignity, almost, short of death, but had finally been driven away from the slave states altogether.

My direct charges against the church, notwithstanding its anti-slavery resolutions and professions, were,

1. That its minister exchanged pulpits with the other Congregational ministers of Salem and vicinity, many of whom were notoriously pro-slavery, and violently opposed the whole anti-slavery movement.

2. When the church celebrated the sacramental supper, invitation was given to "all members of sister churches in regular standing," to sit down at the table.

3. That Howard-street church was part and parcel of the Essex county and Massachusetts associations

of Congregational ministers and churches; all or nearly all of them being in full church fellowship with slave-holders.

4. That it contributed its money to the support of Bible, missionary and tract societies, that were in part managed as well as supported by slave-holders, whose money was the price of slaves bought and sold in the market, or of their unpaid and unpitied toil under the lash of cruel task-masters.

5. That both its meeting-house and vestry were peremptorily refused us for anti-slavery meetings, where all persons present were to have equal right of speech and discussion.

Such were my allegations, and not one of them had to be proved, for every one was admitted, and some of them with unblushing boasts! It was even declared, by one influential member of the congregation, that in his opinion, if a colored family should purchase a pew in the central part of the meeting-house, a dozen families would immediately leave the society. It was doubtless so. Such was the anti-slavery of the Howard-street church, on its own admissions and confessions. And that church was every way as good as the average churches of Massachusetts and of New England, of every evangelical denomination. Instead of meeting my charges, the defenders of the church openly accused me with deliberately meditating the destruction of the christian church, ministry, sabbath and all religious institutions; declared the Garrisonians were doing no good; were arraigning the churches before tribunals of ungodly men; were inducing good men and women to leave their churches, to renounce their Bibles, to disregard their ministers, and closed his harangue, which had wrought him into

a high state of excitement, with expressing a hope
that the audience would not be influenced by any
thing I should say during the meetings.

Others spoke on the same side and to similar purport. Late in the evening, Mr. Remond rose to reply, amid much tumult, but gave way for an adjournment to the next evening, in the same hall. That night
came the crowd, many evidently on mischief intent.
The exercises were opened with prayer and reading
part of the twenty-third chapter of Matthew. I then
made a few remarks on the anti-slavery character of
the Howard-street church, and its strange defense and
defenders of the previous evening, and gave way for
Mr. Remond. His reply to the charges against the
abolitionists and his eulogy of Mr. Garrison, as the
hero and champion of the anti-slavery enterprise and
faithful friend of the colored race everywhere, north,
as well as south, was one of the most earnest, eloquent
and impressive utterances I had then ever heard from
human lips, no matter of what color or race.

But it only roused the rage of our opponents. The
principal defender of the church generally, and of the
Howard church in special, took possession of the floor
and he and his troop held it for the remainder of the
evening. On announcing my appointment for the
next night, I was interrupted by a very ruffianly fellow mounting a seat and declaiming loudly, "You can
hold another meeting in this hall, only on condition
that you say nothing about Howard-street church nor
any other. Our excellent and brave friend, Mr.
Josiah Hayward, who had attended all our meetings,
inquired if that was said in earnest and in good faith,
and was answered that it was, and was *peremptory*.
By this time the tumult became general; but I succeeded in obtaining a momentary hearing, and pro-

tested against occupying any house or hall unless the most untrammelled free speech was permitted, both sides and all sides having hearing on the subject in hand, and insisted that any church, pulpit, or institution that could not bear the light and the lightning of such investigation and examination, was a dangerous element, that should not be tolerated in any government.   Probably not half I said was heard by the now maddened crowd that thronged every possible point of available space.   In less than three minutes every slip on the side of the hall occupied by the men from porch to platform was not only stove down, but pulverized almost to kindling wood ; and most of the lamps were extinguished and their shades and reflectors, if not the lamps themselves, mingled in the general crash and destruction.   Then the other side, as the women rushed forward towards the platform, shared similar fate; the doors and entrance were so thronged as to make escape impossible.   It was most fortunate that we were on the lower floor, so that many of the women, greatly terrified, escaped through the windows.   One fainted quite away and was, with much difficulty restored to consciousness.   We had almost been broken up an hour before, by a false cry of *fire* raised in the vestibule, but the full chorus of confusion and uproar was reserved till now.   I learned next day that my friends kept watch and ward over me, having reasons to fear for my personal safety.   The threatened violence was not offered, however, nor had it once occurred to me that I was in the least peril ; in all those days of darkness and danger, my implicit trust was in non-resistance, and in the infinite wisdom and power from whence, as I then fully believed, proceeded that sublime inspiration.

But we and our meeting were not all that suffered in that visitation of mob violence. While all the proud and popular sectarian meeting-houses of Salem were closed to the cry of the enslaved, and to us who had espoused their cause, Rev. Mr. Comings threw open the doors of the hired hall of his free church and society, and cordially invited us in, charging no rent beyond cost of warming and light ; but seeing the general storm of opposition raised against us, the board of directors of the Mechanic Hall immediately passed the following order :

Voted unanimously : That the Salem Free church be requested to vacate the room occupied by them in Mechanic Hall *forthwith*, and that the Secretary be ordered to notify them by sending a copy of this vote.

Pursuant to the above, I hereby notify you that I shall take possession of the room *immediately*, and request that you will cease to occupy it from and after this day.   Yours respectfully,

HENRY B. GRAVES.

Some little delay was, of course necessary, to procure means of moving, and place where to move ; but the next the society knew, their little library and whatever else they possessed there, were thrown into the street. Their rent was ever paid punctually on the day it was due, and the conditions of contract entitled the society, as we were assured, to three months' notice before they should be required to vacate the premises. So here was exemplified, what really was new organized, church anti-slavery ; and the best of it, too. Shut out of its meeting-houses, vestries, chapels and every place they controlled, as remorselessly as from any others, we found a platform in a basement hall, secular in itself, though rented by a religious society for its Sunday service, and there we hoped for at least two or three evenings, we might enjoy the right and perform the duty, undisturbed, of pleading the cause of the down-trodden, despised and oppressed slaves.   And with such results as are here only faintly and partially, but truthfully described. Thus desperately determined were the leaders and chiefs of both church and state, to prevent, as far as possible, the spread of genuine, uncompromising anti-slavery truth.

I held one more meeting, but had to return to the *colored people's Bethel* where the series began ; and it should be said to the credit of that little despised church and society, that their conduct throughout the whole scene, was noble, manly, womanly, brave and heroic to the last degree, though subjected at times to insult and outrage almost too shameful for human nature to endure.   The last meeting was as riotous as either of the others, though the noise was mostly in the porch and outside, though not all.   One old deacon, who need not be named, as he must have been dead many years, abused the colored people grossly in his talk.   But he was let off as he deserved, as he doubtless felt most, with a silent contempt.   I was told that he was frequently guilty of similar behavior towards the people of color, though many, if not most of them in the town, were in every way his superiors.

One woman, compelled by sickness to leave the meeting, was roughly assaulted in the porch, her cap and bonnet were torn off, and her dress otherwise badly damaged.   An inoffending colored young man was also attacked in the porch, knocked down and then pitched headlong into the street ; he gathered himself up and ran, but was chased.   In the dark, he threw a stone at his pursuers, which, if it hit, did not hurt so badly as to prevent the ruffian from prosecuting him and bringing him, next morning into court.

The case was brought before Hon. J. G. Waters. I attended, determined if possible to see justice done. To my surprise and satisfaction, Judge Waters, after patient hearing of the .parties, dismissed the case, severely reprimanding the complainant, and telling him he was the offender, and more deserved punishment than the young man he had arrested.

Thus terminated my first anti-slavery visit to that ancient town. I had good reasons to believe my humble services were not lost upon it ; Essex county became famous in the cause of true and unfaltering anti-slavery, and even its political abolitionists, some of them, were of the very bravest and best. Its Evangelical pulpits were always conservative, some of them even bitterly so ; the Unitarians and Universalists furnished some eminent exceptions ; and the names of Thomas T. Stone, Samuel Johnson, John L. Russell and Willard Spalding will always be had in honor as the unfaltering friends of radical, uncompromising anti-slavery.

But returning to the narrative, it should be borne in mind by readers that the incidents related here, though numerous, are only representative of thousands which will never be recorded ; or, as is hyperbolically declared in the new Testament of the works of another, "the world itself might not contain the books which should be written ;" for our conflict extended over thirty years.

A day's work and its incidents, in which I had a partner, a quiet young beginner in the service, will not be inappropriate, as following the scenes and experiences of Salem.

In the early spring of 1852, I made a little tour in the state of Maine, in which I was joined by Alonzo J. Grover, now an eminent lawyer at the west. He was then in the course of his studies, but well up in anti-slavery knowledge, interest and earnestness. On a snowy, sleety, windy morning, we arrived in Brunswick, perfect strangers to every human inhabitant. Dropping our not capacious valises at a corner grocery, we ventured out to reconnoitre, with a view to an evening meeting. The low, level land was covered with the melting and melted snow and mud, making walking disagreeable, indeed. And we were not sorry that no suitable place within our means, could be had for our lectures, as it would be nearly impossible, under such circumstances, to secure attendance and a collection that would pay the expenses of the hall. So after an hour or two of prospecting, under much difficulty and discouragement, we concluded to abandon Brunswick, with its college and churches, and try what Freeport, the next, and much smaller place, might do for us.

The skies were still scowling, and some large snowflakes continued to fall, melting, mostly, as they reached the ground. It was ten o'clock, or after, when we picked up our satchels and set out for Freeport, seven or eight miles off. The walking was bad, of course ; but my companion was young and valliant, and I had not then grown old. By two o'clock we reached our destination, having been on our feet nearly five and a half hours, the ground cold and wet and snow falling most of the time. And the Brunswick heart and hospitality were colder and more repelling than the weather. Our first inquiry on reaching Freeport, was for a hall. We soon found one of unattractive appearance, over a store, entered by a flight of outside stairs. It had no seats, only round the sides, being used mainly, probably, for dancing.

We could have it in the evening, seating, warming and lighting it ourselves, for some small sum, probably not more than one dollar.

Our next business was to give notice. For that purpose, after posting a written bill or two at the post-office, and another store, we entered the street, beginning at one end, one of us on one side and the other on the opposite, and walked its entire length, calling and leaving word at every house. That occupied an hour or more, bringing us to the middle of the afternoon. We did not forget that we had not dined, but till our hall was secured and the people notified of our meeting, dinner had to wait. We dined for a few cents, on such crackers and cheese or herrings as the grocery afforded, no unusual occurrence with us in those days, and then proceeded with our evening preparations. There being no tavern in the town, we first looked up lodgings for the night. A woman who kept a few boarders consented to entertain us, though we told her that having just dined, we should need no supper, and might not call on her till after the meeting.

Returning to our hired hall, we called at a house where there was plenty of dry wood, and paid the owner a four-pence-ha'-penny for as much as we could carry in our arms, and that furnished our evening fire. Then for seats, we borrowed some soap or candle boxes of the store-keeper, who seemed much to admire our thrift, and with a few boards laid on them, that need was met. It now only remained to procure the light. For that, we bought a pound of tallow candles, ten to the pound, and the good-natured store-keeper, I am sorry to have forgotten his name, threw us in five good-sized potatoes, out of a barrel, which, slashed in halves and bored, made ten, not the apocalyptic "golden," but good and sufficient candle-sticks. This was nothing new with us. I often lighted halls in that way. Once, I well remember, in Cleveland, Ohio, only with this difference, that round turnips were used instead of potatoes.

It was almost dark when our preparations were completed, so we kindled the fire, lighted a candle, and, contentedly enough, sat down for a little rest, before the meeting should commence

It was more than thirty years ago, in a small coun-try village, the day had been stormy or cloudy, dark-ness came on early, and so did our audience. It was composed wholly of men and boys. That was neither new nor strange. No anti-slavery meeting had ever been held or attempted there before, so far as we could learn. Others might be held possibly to excel-lent purpose. We were respectfully heard, so soon as we could get understood. As no women were pres-ent, some did not hasten to put away their cigars when we commenced speaking. "Chewing the cud" seemed almost as common as among the cattle in the stall. Neither was that any surprise ; seeing it as we had from our boyhood, in even the meeting-houses on Sunday, as well as in the pulpits and pews. Generally if we asked for a collection something would be raised, at least sufficient to pay for the hall. In this instance, as we traveled into and out of town on foot, and paid but sixteen and a quarter cents for fire and lights, and a very small fee for the room, I have for-gotten how little, we surely were not, so far, much out of pocket. What our boarding-house charges would be, we had not then ascertained. But we did learn, a few minutes later, when we put out our can-dles, and, valises in hand, presented ourselves at the door. We were permitted to enter and sit down.

Then our prudent hostess told us that had she known what was the object of our "going about," and what sort of lectures we gave, she should not have consented to take us into her house. Her family, she said, were bitterly opposed to us and our work ; and a good deal more in similar tone and spirit. But as there was no other place where we could get in, she would keep us over night, though we must. leave as soon as we were up in the morning. We staid.

Supperless to bed and breakfastless on the road next morning, baggage in hand, and almost before the villagers were any of them abroad, was pretty rugged discipline for my new comrade, but he bore it well ; and, doubtless, should he write a sketch of that day and night adventure he would enliven it with many incidents which have escaped my recollection, or which, for sake of brevity, I have omitted, and yet it was in no important sense peculiar or unusual. Every earnest, faithful, anti-slavery lecturer in those dark and often perilous days, encountered the same or much more disagreeable every week, all the year through, especially when, as we were then, breaking in to new and unexplored fields.

But older and more cultivated grounds did not always greet the coming of the apostle with anything like the Hebrew strain : " How beautiful upon the mountains are the feet of him who bringeth good tidings," as the following account of a Portland meeting proves :

The autumn of 1842 was memorable for the vigor, earnestness and success, too, of the anti-slavery movement in eastern Massachusetts and eastern New Hampshire.   Extensive accounts of meetings and movements in Lynn, Salem, Danvers, Georgetown and

Newburyport, Massachusetts, and of Exeter, Dover and Great Falls, in New Hampshire, have been already given.

But Portland, Maine, shared in the great and good work. It made itself more conspicuous, too, by its violent opposition to our word and work, than any place we visited in any state named. It did not, like some other towns, arrest, fine and imprison, but its mob-malice and rage did contemplate actual murder, and the wonder is how its myrmidons were restrained from their fell purpose. This report will be condensed mainly from the Portland newspapers themselves. Papers not identified with the Garrisonian enterprise. In September of the year mentioned, Stephen S. Foster and Rev. John Murray Spear held a series of meetings and discussions on slavery in the city hall, Mr. Foster the principal speaker. Mr. Spear had been for some dozen or fifteen years a Universalist minister in different Massachusetts towns, New Bedford, Hyannis and Weymouth chiefly, when the tidal wave of anti-slavery reached his pulpit and swept him onward into the foremost billows of that then tempestuous movement. For some thirteen years he did faithful service in the cause of the enslaved, suffering severe persecution in their behalf, even before he abandoned the pulpit, which he did not do till he had labored long and earnestly to bring his denomination up to an uncompromising and inflexible position of hostility to slavery, but, like many other ministers in more evangelical denominations, labored in vain. A slave-holder bringing a slave girl to New Bedford while he was minister there, he brought her case before Judge Shaw, of the supreme court, who declared her freedom, she being no longer in a slave state. She availed herself of the opportunity. Then Mr. Spear was arrested as a *slave-stealer*, the mob howling after him as he walked the street, " Nigger stealer !   Nigger stealer !"   For some time the peace of the town was disturbed ; threatening and horrible images were hung in the night before his door, and his life was deemed in peril while the agitation lasted.   His interest in the temperance and other reforms was no less than in anti-slavery, and he subsequently became, in connection with his brother, Rev. Charles Spear, pioneer in a grand movement in the interest of prisoners and of discharged convicts ; and originated, and for years edited and published a journal, entitled the *Prisoner's Friend*, which had a wide circulation, and was productive of great good.   In later years Mr. Spear has been closely associated with spiritualism, traveling extensively in both hemispheres, including a tour to the Pacific coast, to promote its interests.

In the Portland tumult, so far as appeared by the newspaper accounts, Mr. Spear does not seem to have given any offense, but being found in bad company he was made to suffer accordingly.   On the way to his lodgings he was violently asaailed and barely escaped with his life.   But in the heavenly home hospitality and care of Oliver and Lydia Dennett, surrounded with other ministering spirits of the city, who watched around him, he was, after seven weeks, restored, though I am assured his attendants once gathered at his bedside expecting to witness the closing scene of his earthly existence.

At the last meeting of the series, in which Mr. Foster was to speak, as previously announced, on " The Influence of Southern Slavery in the Northern States," was witnessed, the Portland *American* declared : " One of the most disgraceful riots ever seen in Portland.   Mr. Foster commenced his remarks in a very

21

mild and conciliatory manner,explaining the reasons for
his peculiar mode of address, and saying that he was
a friend to the laboring classes, and was a working-
man himself. During his introduction he was constantly interrupted by singing, hissing, hooting, by
insulting remarks and throwing of rotten eggs. The
patience with which the audience bore the insolence
of these reckless scoundrels induced them to proceed
farther. The benches were broken, a general fight
commenced, and a rush was made for the speaker.
Our citizens, however, formed a solid phalanx around
the desk, rendering it unapproachable. The mob
pressed on like blood hounds for their victim. Shouts
were heard, 'Hand him over ! Hand him over ! We
want the blood of the d—m—d scoundrel. Murder
the d—m—d abolitionist,' and other expressions
equally characteristic of the temper and intentions of
the miscreants. The mayor was present and ordered
them to leave the hall. After a great deal of effort
he succeeded in clearing the place. A false alarm of
fire was raised, calling off a few, but the mob remained
in a solid body, watching at each flight of steps and
around the windows for the lecturer.

At length, when it was supposed that they had dispersed somewhat, he was taken out under protection
of the mayor and several brave ladies, to the house of
a friend, followed by some five hundred persons. He
was several times struck on the face and back of his
head and seriously injured. We regret to add that
there were some men of respectable appearance whom
we saw and heard encouraging the mob by their voices.
*   *   One old man in broadcloth we mean especially ; whose gray hairs should warn him that it is
time he were thinking of other things than depriving
a freeman of liberty of speech.   *   *   One

man, while the rioters were already worked up to the fury of madmen, shouted at the top of his lungs, ' Turn him out ; bring a pot of lampblack,' and then grossly and vilely insulted the stranger in language too foul for our columns.   *   *   Since the above was in type, the captain, of whom we spoke in our description of the mob, called and discontinued his paper, but admitted all we charged upon him except the shouting at the top of his lungs."

Another article from the same paper, commenting on the Portland *Advertiser's* notice of the affair, says : " The *Advertiser's* notice of the riot was one of the most cold-blooded things we have seen.   Hear it : ' Last evening our city was *threatened* with a mob. The noted S. S. Foster has given two or three lectures on such topics as he sees fit to connect with abolition, and the city hall was thronged last night with a mixed multitude, including some females, mostly composed, as we judge, of those who were inclined to stop his excitable harangue. Some of the friends of the lecturer took such measures to check the disturbances that the crowd proceeded to acts of violence, which broke up the meeting.   A good many blows were aimed on both sides.   As we believe no one was seriously hurt, we do not go into the disagreeable details.'   So much for the *Advertiser*."

To which the *American* responds :   " Monstrous ! Our peaceful city was only ' *threatened* with a mob !' There was no mob.   Oh no !   Those who rushed towards the desk and demanded the life, aye, the life, for we heard and saw the whole, the life of the speaker, who broke settees, threw rotten eggs, knocked Mr. Foster down in the street, struck him some twenty times, and who surrounded the house where he staid, threatening destruction to its inmates, these miscreants

did not, in view of the *Advertiser*, constitute a mob !
* * The charge that 'the friends of the lecturer
took such measures to check the disturbance that the
crowd proceeded to acts of violence,' is false. After
the crowd had commenced throwing missiles at the
speaker ; after the riot had commenced ; after the
rioters had been repeatedly urged to be quiet, a young
gentleman rose and moved that they be expelled from
the house. They went there with the previously expressed determination to break up the meeting, and
to do the lecturer bodily injury."

Such accounts did the Portland papers give, and
such were received as substantially correct. Mr. Foster had his story to tell, and so had Mr. Spear, and
so had their anti-slavery friends. To-day, after a
lapse of more than forty years, little idea is likely to
be formed of such scenes as were then and there, and
often elsewhere, enacted. Foster had offended most,
and so was most hated and hunted. Spear, though
not less faithful when he did speak, had given less
offense, and so was not deemed in such danger, and
was less vigilantly shielded, and thus came nearest to
losing his life. Foster suffered in person and apparel,
though his friends, brave women as well as men, hov-
ered all about him, taking off his spectacles, changing
his hat, and in other ways disguising him. He wore
at the time a dress instead of frock coat, the skirts a
little elongated, as was the style. A ruffian contrived
to get hold of one skirt and tore it squarely off, leaving the other dangling alone, looking grotesquely
enough. But that he turned to excellent account, for
he wore it weeks afterwards wherever he went to tell
its own tale. And surely, " thereby hung a tale " of
sublime import. The coat was kept in the family for
years as a significant trophy of honorable war. But

he suffered severely in person. Mr. Rogers, James N. Buffum, myself, and others were holding a five days' convention at Great Falls, New Hampshire, forty miles from Portland, and Foster was expected to be with us a part of the time, but detained longer at Portland than was expected, he was late in reaching us. When at length he came, his appearance on entering, with ragged raiment, with sickly, worn and weary cast of countenance, stirred every heart and moved many to tears. Mr. Rogers, in his account of the Great Falls convention in the *Herald of Freedom*, thus spoke of it :

" On Thursday, in the midst of our discussions, the meeting was deeply st:rred by the entrance of Foster from Portland. His countenance pale and distressed but not cast down, and his garments torn off of him, fresh from the hands of a terrible mob. I can here only say he was greeted with most affectionate interest by the meeting, and listened to in the account he gave, at the request of the assembly, of the scenes he had just passed through, with solemn attention."

But there were encounters sometimes more trying to flesh and blood than mobs. Just as the last word was written on the scenes at Portland, chance threw before me the *Liberator*, of April 16, 1852, containing the following letter, which the editor headed truly enough, " One Week's Experience of a 'Field Hand.' "

DEAR FRIEND GARRISON—I will write you the experience of the past week. You need not publish it, unless you choose. Sometimes we have such weeks in the field service, in spite of all forecasts and provisions to prevent them.

I left Lawrence on Monday morning on a tour eastward. In the evening of that day I lectured to a respectable audience in Rochester, N. H. Tuesday

morning we were whirling in the midst of one of the
most violent snow storms of the whole winter. At
three in the afternoon I took the cars for Great Falls,
where were to be meetings in the evening, and the
evening following. On account of an accident the
train consisted only of freight cars, into one of which
we were all stowed, men, women and children, as *live
stock* goes to Brighton.

Arrived at the Falls, I wallowed about in the snow
and slush, the storm still continuing, in search of some
one who could give me tidings of the meetings. But
it came out that none had been appointed, nor any
arrangements made. Mr. Grover was to have been
with me, but the snow storms and drifts hindered the
cars, so I took the business into my own hands alone.
By floundering through the deep snow and water for
a time, I learned that the only place we could possibly obtain was Central hall. I found the proprietor,
and he told me it could be had at six dollars an evening, though he afterwards said he did let it for five
dollars sometimes. Before I had time to put in my
plea of poverty, he told me it was to be occupied so
many evenings, that my own prëengagements were
such as to end the whole matter. Thus terminated
the mission at Great Falls.

Having had no appointment made for Thursday
evening, I was induced, by my friends in Rochester,
to return and hold one more meeting there. The
failure at the Falls gave me Wednesday evening also,
and so, on short notice, I called a meeting for that
evening too. By this time Friend Grover had arrived,
and spoke the whole of Wednesday evening, to a
small but attentive audience. He left next morning
to go on to Portland. At the appointed hour on
Thursday. I went to the hall. Not a soul was there,

nor *body* even—for they do not always come together.
Nearly an hour afterwards my audience had not increased in the least. It was *Fast Day* and the
people were keeping such fast as — *they had chosen.*
Such was the termination at Rochester.

On Friday morning, I set off for Kennebunk, the
place of my appointment. At the Kennebunk depot,
I inquired for the persons to whom we had written,
and found they lived five miles distant. I also learned
that nobody lived nearer to whom I could apply, and
that no place could be had in town, unless it were a
small, remote school-house, for even a fugitive slave
to hold a meeting.

Finally, I engaged a poor man, who had lost both
hands and arms, by the premature discharge of a cannon, and who drove his horse by means of hooks attached to the stumps, to carry me the five miles to
where our friends lived. The day was dismal, and
the riding as much so. But we arrived at last, and I
was set down in the center of a *clearing* of a few hundred acres, surrounded almost completely by a low,
thick growth of pine woods. I took out my luggage,
paid my fare, and made up to the house.

My repeated knocking brought no one to open. I
tried the door and found it fast. The other door was
faster yet. Then I went over the way, and inquired.
The young woman thought the family were gone only
a mile. The old lady said they were gone away to a
funeral, several miles, and had been gone all day.

Here, then, I was, five miles from Kennebunk depot,
still farther from Saco, the next nearest, and three or
four miles, at least, from everywhere else—all alone,
with my luggage, the skies scowling with threatening
clouds, the distant forests fencing and surrounding
me with their gloomiest curtains, and the almost im-

passable roads making their worst faces at me, and
elongating their fearful miles to immeasurable extent.
The good old lady, however, insisted on my eating
dinner, from which she and her daughter had just
risen.   Then, with both hands full of bags and bun-
dles, I set off, on foot, for Saco, five or six miles.

I never in my life saw such intolerable walking in
New England.   The soil, much of the way, was clay,
and the frost just coming out of it, and then a mingling of snow, it made a complete compound of Bunyan's "Slough of Despond," "Enchanted Ground,"
"Hill of Difficulty," and all his dragons.   The cold
north-east wind, too, blew full in my face, and every
sign denoted immediate storm.   I plunged along as
fast as possible, to escape that additional woe, and
reached Saco and Biddeford late in the afternoon,
possibly somewhat fatigued, and perfectly parboiled in
perspiration.   It was a pilgrimage not to be forgotten.

The week has gone—and it has been one of most
uncommon labor, disappointment, vexation and suffering.   I have lectured to everybody who came near
me, but my labors in that line were confined to Rochester, and two meetings.   My traveling expenses have
been three dollars and seventy-five cents, to say nothing of my walking, which was worth twice as much ;
my receipts have been *one dollar and five cents*, and I
have not procured one single subscriber to *the Liberator* nor to any of our papers.   Such is the experience
of one week.   Who would not be a soldier in such a
warfare ?

Yours, still full of hope and trust,

PARKER PILLSBURY.

Portland, April 12, 1852.

A. J. Grover rejoined me in Portland, and our next campaign included Brunswick and Freeport, of which report has been already given.

One more riotous demonstration should have place in these chronicles, but space and time must make it both brief and the last. It occurred in Harwich, Mass,. on Sunday, the fourth and last day of a grand anti-slavery convention, held in a beautiful grove, in September of the year 1848. No building on the Cape could have held half the attendance. Cape Cod at that time was the birth-place and nursery of more sea-captains than any other portion, of equal extent, on the whole Atlantic coast. And many of the most eminent of them were early able and faithful friends and supporters of the anti-slavery enterprise.

But sea-captains were not all abolitionists, else the Harwich Sunday tumult, in defense of the church as "the bulwark of slavery," would not have transpired. The constitution of the country, the courts, the political parties, the commerce and trade, had all been shown to be conducted in the interest of slavery, and no riotous demonstration appeared. But not so on Sunday, when the churches and clergy were arraigned as the bulwark and forlorn hope of the accursed institution. The mob at Harwich was the result of an exposure of a diabolical deed by the captain of a coaster, sailing between Norfolk and New York, and other northern ports. I am glad to have forgotten his name, and do not care ever to hear it spoken again.

But while in Norfolk, not long before our convention, a slave came on board and asked this captain what he would charge to carry him and another to New York or Boston. A contract was made for one hundred dollars—paid in advance. The captain pocketed the cash, then went on shore, betrayed the poor slave, had him arrested, imprisoned and advertised, and then sailed north, bringing the hundred dollars.

We who knew the slave system, could imagine the fate of the imprisoned victim, though we never heard what it was. The cruel captain never told us that, though undoubtedly he knew, for when he went back to Norfolk he carried the money, found the owner, paid him over the hundred dollars, and received back twenty-five as his reward!

Twenty-five dollars for a deed that no Modoc nor Apache Indian under heaven would ever have done! In cold, unprovoked blood—never!

Sunday was the fourth and last day of our convention, and not less than three thousand people were on the ground. Some estimated them at four thousand.

I learned all the facts I have just given, from the captain himself, early in the day. In the afternoon, when the crowd was the greatest, I made a full statement of the case, in words as fitting as were then at my command. Of course the effect on the audience was intense, but dependent on the estimate which different persons placed on the transaction between the captain and his helpless victim.

In the tumult, the captain came to the platform, and not having heard my statement, he demanded, in great wrath, who it was that accused him of stealing! He said somebody had just told him he had been accused of stealing. He was answered that his name had not been mentioned there ; and that nothing had been said about stealing. He said he had a right to be heard, and wished to be heard. We cheerfully accorded him the platform. He came forward, and in the frankest, blandest manner, stated his own case

in his own words.   When he concluded, we invited him
to a seat on the platform, which he accepted.

Stephen Foster spoke next.   He began in quite a
conversational tone to say : Mr. Chairman—We have
now heard from his own mouth, what our friend had
to say of the matter in hand.   And he confirms every
statement of Mr. Pillsbury, excepting one : he has not
told us that he is a member in good and regular standing of the Baptist church, as Mr. Pillsbury assured us
he was.   Now I wish to ask him if that is also true.
He admitted that with the rest,

Foster then opened his argument.   And those who
ever heard him can more easily imagine than I can
describe, its power.   Every eye kindled, every heart
throbbed, with admiration, or with rage and wrath.   I
had often heard him called "a *son* of thunder," before.
At that moment, he seemed *Father* of the seven thunders of Patmos, with all their bolts at command.   He
swayed those hundreds and thousands as prairie
cyclones, the vast fields of corn.   And yet the captain, really on trial, listened to every word with respect
and attention.   I knew he heard a voice within, louder,
more eloquent than the utterances of Foster, and
whose rebuke he could not resist.

The mob spirits now rushed for the platform, and
with oaths and curses of stunning power, called on
the captain to pitch him down to them.   Their number seemed legion ; and their nature and spirit like
that other *legion*, known of old.   The captain mildly
replied to them that he wished none of their interference nor defense.   He left the platform soon after,
and moved out of the crowd, and held a long conversation with some Boston abolitionists, who had come
down on purpose to attend the convention.   And he
very frankly told them that he had no fault to find

whatever with our treatment of the matter, nor of
him.   Nor did he ever after complain, that we heard.

Mr. Foster kept his feet and held the crowd at bay,
showing our religion to be falsehood and hypocrisy,
when a member of the orthodox church, who had just
come from his meeting, (and it was said from the sacrament), leaped like a lion on to the platform. His
eyes flashed fury if not fire ; his teeth and fists were
clenched, and he seemed a spirit from the pit, who
might have been commissioned to lead its myrmidons
in a deadly fray, for such a faith and such a church as
his, that a dozen years before had been proved by one
of its most eminent members,

"THE BULWARK OF AMERICAN SLAVERY."

He asked no leave to speak ; paid no respect to president or rules.   His first note was a shriek.   "It's a
lie ; what you say is a lie ; a damned lie ! and I'll defend the church !"

But he was immediately outvoiced by the yelling
troop, who leaped like tigers at his heels, as into the
arena, and added fearful deeds to his not less fearful
words.

What became of my platform companions I did not
see.   I was immediately seized, and with kicks, blows,
and dilapidated clothing, hurled to the ground.

There lay Captain Chase and Captain Smith, of
Harwich, both old men, who, with many others, had
sprung to our defense.   There the two lay, their faces
covered with blood ! They were both radical peace
men, and only remonstrated with our remorseless assailants.   But both of them would willingly have died
in our stead, or in our defense.   Truer, nobler men
never lived.

Havoc was soon made of our platform and what it contained. It was roofed over, but a temporary structure, for officers and speakers, and aged persons who sought its convenience and comfort. William Wells Brown, one of our eloquent fugitive slave lecturers, was roughly seized up and pitched over back of the platform by the infuriated crowd, down some six or eight feet, and left to his fate. Mr. Foster was rescued and taken away from danger—his Sunday frock coat rent in twain from bottom to top, and his body considerably battered and bruised.

Lucy Stone stood heroically with the rest of us, ready for any fate. But her serene, quiet bearing disarmed the vulgar villainy of our assailants, and she escaped unharmed.

I have seen many mobs and riots in my more than forty years of humble service in the cause of freedom and humanity, but I never encountered one more desperate in determination, nor fiendish in spirit, than was that in Harwich, in the year 1848.

And that mob was wholly, directly and undeniably in defense of the American church. "I'll defend the church," was the wild shout of the baptized ruffian who led the hordes, as he vaulted unbidden to our platform of moral and peaceful agitation and argument in behalf of our enslaved millions. "I'll defend the church," and his infuriated, yelling and blaspheming troop followed him, and commenced their fell work.

Yes, to save the church was that dire scene enacted. The church that Judge Birney had proved out of her own mouth was the "bulwark of American slavery in every one of her largest, most popular denominations!" Church, clergy, and theological seminary, every thing,

indeed, under ecclesiastical control. And Hon. James
G. Birney was surely among her choicest leaders and
brightest lights.

To my own account of this remarkable scene, perhaps should be subjoined at least an excerpt of the
official proceedings of the convention. The following is the close of it :

Parker Pillsbury related a fact illustrative of the
truth of the resolution under discussion of a sea-cap-
tain, of Cape Cod, a member of the Baptist church.

Immediately the captain's friends reported to him
that he had been slandered, upon the platform, and in
due time the captain presented himself and demanded
why he had slandered him, on that platform? He
was assured that his name had not been spoken by
any one on the platform, and that if he would wait
for the speaker to conclude his remarks he should
have opportunity to say all he wished.

Accordingly, when the speaker sat down, the captain took the platform, and stated the facts *precisely* as
Pillsbury had done, so it was manifest that there was
no slander, nor even contradiction between them.

S. S. Foster then proceeded to dissect the transaction, as stated by the captain himself, and to find its
moral quality. It was a process which he well understood, nor did he fail to expose the deformity of the
deed, and cause its infamy to stand out in fearful
blackness before that great assembly. The captain
said he had nothing to reply, and left the platform as
quietly as he had come upon it, saying he had not
come there to make any disturbance. Foster then
held up to the audience, in its true character, the religion, under whose cherishing influence such crimes
take root and grow, and asked who would defend
such a church? At that moment Captain Stillman
Snow, a member of the Congregational church under
the pastoral care of Rev. Cyrus Stone, (who we are
credibly informed, went about among his people and
advised them to stay away from our meeting), this
Captain Snow, steaming from his own meeting, rushed

through the crowd in front of Foster, screaming at the top of his voice, "I'll defend the church. What you say is a lie, a damned lie!" His lips trembled, his head shook upon its socket, like a leaf rattled by the winter tempest, while his countenance looked as if the genius of rage had his dwelling there. He made a leap at Foster, which was a signal for his allies. In a twinkling, there was a rush upon the platform. W. W. Brown, a fugitive slave, was seized and thrown over the high back of the platform, where he was trampled on by the throng gathered there. Pillsbury, with torn clothes, was dragged from the platform, receiving as he went, kicks and blows from those *behind* him. Those in front of him were harmless, awed by his fearless words, and undaunted look.

Again and again, some desperate spirits, with clenched uplifted fists, swore vengeance and destruction, but like the old Roman, Pillsbury calmly replied "strike, but hear me." While he was thus beset on every hand, S. S. Foster was assailed in another direction no less violently. At the first onset he hastened Lucy Stone from the platform, but had scarcely time to turn about, when the mob, thirsting for his blood, closed in around him, seizing him with desperate violence, wherever they could lay their hands upon him, and though they did not "part his garments among them," they quite divided his coat. For a few moments the most terrible confusion prevailed—all ran, without knowing whither they went—so great was the excitement that neither friends nor foes recognized each other. One friend would take hold of the arm of Foster for his protection, and another friend would pull him off supposing him an enemy.

One friend would step forward to stay an uplifted blow, and another friend would push him aside, supposing that he intended himself to strike. The scene baffled all description. At this juncture a shout was raised that they were riding Foster on a rail. This false cry was most opportune for Brown, who, during the whole time, had been dragged and trampled by the mob. Now his tormentors left him to see the ruin of Foster, and thus he made his escape, rifled by these

pious defenders of the nation's religion, of quite a
number of his *Anti-slavery Harp*. Foster, who had
been surrounded by the mob, showed no sign of fear
or fright. The man who had never quailed in peril's
blackest hour, was not the man now to tremble or flee.
But the friends, apprehensive for his safety, urgently
solicited him to leave the ground ; and when he did
not manifest a disposition to go, they took him, with
most unpleasant haste, outside the grove, aided by the
mob, who were pushing terribly in the rear, and on all
sides.

When Pillsbury ascertained that Brown and Foster
were safe, and that nothing more could be done, he,
too, left, taking the public road towards the house of
Captain Small, a well-known friend of the oppressed.
The mobocrats, who had returned to the grove howling and yelling in their rage and disappointment, that
Foster was out of their clutches, when they found that
Pillsbury was leaving, followed in hot pursuit, raising
the dust higher than the trees, filling the air with
demoniac screams and yells, which were heard at the
distance of more than a mile, and frighful enough to
make Pandemonium itself pale. They rushed on
headlong about thirty rods, and then, though Pillsbury was walking only a short distance in front of them,
for reasons best known to themselves, they turned back
to the grove, cursing as they went, and proceeded to
vent their rage upon the platform, which they soon
demolished.

While they were tearing up the planks they were
uttering most dreadful oaths, and vowing vengeance
on the lecturers, (should they ever make their appearance there again) who, they said, had assailed their
laws and their religion, which they were going to defend. The world will judge what kind of laws and
what kind of religion *need such* a defense. It was a
proud day for anti-slavery, and one which the friends
will long have occasion to remember with gratitude.
The lecturers were not particularly disturbed until all
had been said which they wished to say, until every
nail was driven in the right place, and then the mob
clenched them. They meant their violence for evil,

but God meant it for good. The dragon's teeth, which they were then unconsciously sowing, will yet come up, a host of true-hearted anti-slavery men and women, who will redeem Cape Cod from the false religion which now curses and enslaves it. Much praise is due to the friends, who are too numerous to mention, who so nobly stood by those whose lives the hungry mob were seeking. Nor would we fail to make suitable mention of others, who, during the day on Sunday, were active in exciting the mob spirit. Prominent among them was Henry C. Brooks, a merchant of Boston, of the firm of Crowell & Brooks, 38 Commercial street, son of Obed Brooks, Esq., of Harwich.

The good effect of the mob is already manifest in the increased activity and interest of the friends on the Cape, whose liberal contributions to the cause have been nearly doubled, and who see new reasons for girding themselves to more vigorous effort in behalf of human freedom.

ZEBINA SMALL, *President.*

CHARLES STEARNS,
LUCY STONE,
  Secretaries.

Only time, space and patience of readers prevent insertion of the whole of the able report of the secretaries of that phenomenal convention. Most of the names of the rioters mentioned in the extract given are suppressed.

No other mob or riot will be described in this work. Such as are given are but representative of many, very many ; some less destructive to property and harmful to person, and some others in those respects a great deal worse.

And now, wondrous to tell, with such records, *the church and clergy claim and boast that they abolished slavery !* The real, everlasting truth is, we had almost to abolish the church before we could reach the dreadful institution at all. We divided, if we did not destroy. Not to speak of the General Assembly of the

Presbyterian church at all, we did divide and even subdivided the General Conference of the Methodist Episcopal church. The slavery question certainly produced rupture in the American Board of Foreign Missions, the Baptist Board of Foreign Missions and the American Tract Society, as has been, or as will be shown. If it be said that it was their own internal heat that was consuming them, the answer would be it was not light and fire from heaven, the divine illumination of the Holy Ghost, or their differences would not have been so easily reconciled by surrendering the whole ground to the enemy ; the Northern Methodist Conference retaining thousands of slave-holders and tens of thousands of slaves, and six of the very largest of the slave states, besides Delaware and Maryland. The two missionary boards and tract society threatened at one time some separation or purification, but to what purpose will be made to appear

The institution at Oberlin, Ohio, was first to attempt a new standard for freedom in education and religion, irrespective of sex, complexion or race, with a professedly anti-slavery board of teachers and directors. But Oberlin was at once proscribed by the great bodies of ministers and churches, whose fellowship extended to the south. And even Oberlin never so much as contemplated any separation from our unhallowed union with slave-holders. Instead of it, under an assumed idea or pretence that the constitution was anti-slavery and not pro-slavery, an assumption that no president, congress nor supreme court nor state legislature nor court ever believed for an hour, Oberlin continued loyal to the government, swore by itself or elected rulers to support the constitution, and then kept the oath or made a virtue of perjury and violated it by refusing to return the fugitive slave.

And scarcely had the institution reached respectability in the estimation of more declared pro-slavery ecclesiastical associations, north and south, before the Infinite Patience was exhausted, and with the bolts of eternal justice stove down our already blood-besmeared idol, and buried it beneath the untimely graves of half a million men slain in a thousand battles, their massacred commander-in-chief and president of the nation with his own heart's blood, sealing the sacrifice !

CHAPTER XIV.

SOME ACTS OF THE PRO-SLAVERY APOSTLES—PERSONAL
ENCOUNTER WITH THE HENNIKER, N. H., CHURCH AND
SUFFOLK, MASS., ASSOCIATION OF MINISTERS—REV. DR.
BACON AND SON ON SLAVERY AND WHO ABOLISHED IT
—THE CHURCH AND CLERGY IN THE MEXICAN WAR.

It is time to draw this work to a close. It was un-
dertaken with extreme reluctance at the earnest solicitation of those whose wishes it is my delight to obey,
even at any cost of personal sacrifice of my latest
years, only if the cause of truth and the demands of
history be also subserved. And strict truth and justice to everybody concerned, has been, and shall be to
the end, my one constant study and care.

The next chapter may be called " Acts of the Pro-
Slavery Apostles," and will have respect mainly to the
connection of the church and clergy of the country
with the slave system. Their hostility to the anti-
slavery enterprise was not wakened into fierce and
general opposition till slavery was not only declared a
SIN ; *such sin* as that no slave-holder could be a christian, nor worthy to be fellowshipped as such, whether
south or north. The abolitionists insisted that every
church and pulpit dictating terms of sacramental communion should hold the man-stealer as just so much
greater criminal than the felon of the sheep-fold, as
a man is better than a sheep, remembering who He was
that asked, " How much better is a man than a sheep ?"
And our warrant for this judgment came from the
very highest evangelical authority the church could
furnish. Long before slavery had reached the pro-

portions of 1834, or developed half its prospective
cruelties, the General Assembly of the Presbyterian
church had officially and authoritively taught, citing
as their scripture basis, the first epistle of Timothy,
first chapter, ninth and tenth verses : " The law is
made for manstealers. This crime among the Jews
exposed the perpetrators of it to capital punishment.
Exodus xxi, 16 ; and the apostle classes them with
sinners of the first rank. The word he uses, in its
original import, comprehends all who are concerned
in bringing any of the human race into slavery, or in
retaining them in it. Stealers of men are all those
who bring off slaves or freemen, and keep, sell, or
buy them. To steal a freeman, says Grotius, is the
highest kind of theft. In other instances we only steal
human property, but when we steal or retain men in
slavery, we seize those who, in common with ourselves,
are constituted, by the original grants, lords of the
earth."

In 1791, Rev. Jonathan Edwards, D. D., declared
and published this :

" To hold any man in slavery, is to be every day
guilty of *robbing* him of his liberty, or of *man-stealing*.
Fifty years from this time (1791) it will be as shameful for a man to hold a slave as to be guilty of common theft or robbery." And John Wesley this :
" What I have said to slave-traders equally concerns
all slave-holders of whatever rank and degree ; seeing
men-buyers are exactly on a level with men-stealers !
Indeed, you say, 'I pay honestly for my goods ; and I
am not concerned to know how they are come by.'
Nay, but you are ; you are deeply concerned to know
they are honestly come by ; otherwise you are partaker with a thief, and are not a jot honester than he.
But you know they are not honestly come by ; you

know they are procured by means *nothing near so inno-cent as picking pockets, house-breaking, or robbery upon the highway.* You know they are procured by a delib-erate species of more complicated villainy, of fraud, robbery, and murder than was ever practiced by Mo-homedans or Pagans. In particular by murderers of all kinds ; by the blood of the innocent poured out like water. Now, it is your money that pays the African butcher. You, therefore, are guilty, princi-pally, of all these frauds, robberies and murders."

With abundance more of similar character and from the same high and representative sources, so that the abolitionists in their position and demand were only holding the church and pulpit to their own once de-clared and published principles on *slavery*, as well as always on every other acknowledged sin.

But every one of the great popular denominations apostalized as slavery grew in numbers of its victims and in the terrible crimes, cruelties, tortures and tor-ments, incident to the system, and became directly implicated, if not indeed the very chief of sinners, themselves.

What then could true christian abolitionists do, whether ministers or church members, but come out of such fellowship, to avoid the guilt of partaking in the sin ? Nothing in all scripture was more sublimely emphatic than the apocalyptic command, " Come out of her my people, that ye be not partakers in her sins, and that ye receive not of her plagues." And among the sins charged in that blood-guilty communion was, that its " merchandize " was "*in slaves and souls of men.*"

Some of those who composed the associations, who were known as " Come-outers," framed a course of proceedure for themselves, and rather excommunicated the churches than came out from them. To them the church was a principle, an idea, not a corporation or organization, voting members in or out by majorities, and in many of the sects forbidding women to vote at all on any question, though generally a majority, and frequently a large majority of the membership. To such Come-outers the visible church of the New Testament was christianity made visible in the life and character, whether of one or more, no matter how many, only let purity go before peace and liberty before charity. Conservatives held that "peaceful error was better than boisterous truth." But the other answered "Nay, not so. Peace if possible, but truth and right at whatever cost."

Our church in Henniker refused any forward step. Several withdrew from it altogether when a Kentucky slave-holder was invited to preach in the pulpit on Sunday, and administer the sacramental supper. Once when visiting in town a meeting was appointed for him all day on Saturday, in hope that two successive days of his preaching might produce a religious awakening and possibly a revival. No such result, however, followed. But an anti-slavery society was formed in the town, that did good and effective work, some joining from all the churches.

After absenting myself from the communion service a number of years, engaged constantly in the anti-slavery apostleship, I sent a letter to the church, excommunicating it from my christian regard and fellowship until it should repent of the sins and shames of slave-holding and bring forth fruits meet for repentance. No notice was taken of me nor my letter till in the autumn of 1846. Then, with a new pastor, who was also clerk of the church, an official order was sent me, signed and countersigned by the clerk, summoning me to appear, on a given day, to answer to the charge, not of absence from worship and communion table, but of denying the inspiration of the Bible.

I had labored with the church publicly and privately for years on the guilt and danger of slave-holding, or of recognizing as christians or christian ministers the southern slave-breeders or slave-holders, before sending my letter of solemn excommunication. But no similar step, nor any steps, had been taken towards me, by the church or pastor, till the formal call, couched in quite legal phrase, to come into court and plead guilty or not guilty, to a charge foreign as possible from the question, which for years had been in agitation between us. My only answer was the following letter, forwarded without unnecessary delay, to the minister, who was also clerk of the church:

MILFORD, N. H., Oct. 15, 1846.

FRIEND EDEN B. FOSTER—Yours of September 26th was duly received. In reply I would only say that I am not aware of the existence of any Congregational church in Henniker. Certainly none of which I am a member.

Four or five years ago there was an organization in that town known by that name, myself belonging to it. But that body I excommunicated for its grossly immoral character.

Since then the individuals comprising it, excepting a very few who have repented, have been to me as "heathen men and publicans," and so far as their conduct and their influence on the community are to be seen, my estimate of them must be pronounced eminently just.

I am still laboring for their reformation, and shall rejoice to see signs of penitence ; and to forgive with

all forbearance and charity so soon as I see hope of
genuine repentance and fruits meet for repentance.   I
know of no other business which concerns me and the
persons who once composed, with myself, the Congregational church in Henniker, and hasten to subscribe   Sincerely yours,

PARKER PILLSBURY.

What action was taken on this letter, if any, I never
knew.   If excommunication was voted, or other steps
taken, no copy or report was ever sent me, and so
there the matter rested.

But a controversy with the ministry, still more
grave, yet remained.   I was licensed to preach in
Boston by the Suffolk north association of divines,
after a pretty severe doctrinal examination, my certifi-
cate being signed by Dr. Curtis. president, and Dr. War-
ren Fay, secretary of the association, both then ministers in Charlestown.   My preaching was mainly in
New Hampshire and within the bounds of the Hopkinton association.   Only for remembering them that
were in bonds as bound with them, according to the
dictates of my own conscience and interpretation of
the divine will, I gave great offense to members of
the association.   But instead of calling on me in any
capacity, official or private, they made complaint to
the Suffolk association that granted my license.   This
led to correspondence between that body and myself,
of which the following letters are all that concern
either history or the present.   It will be observed by
dates of letters, that all this was some years before
my final encounter with the minister and people at
Henniker.   This whole affair to-day may seem trivial;
but to myself and wife, and other near and dear
friends, there was mighty meaning in every step, as
one after another had to be taken.

The summons before the Suffolk association was as
below :

MALDEN MASS., Feb. 3, 1841.

Mr. Parker Pillsbury :

DEAR BROTHER—At a meeting of the Suffolk north
association, held in Charlestown, Feb, 2d, 1841, the
following preamble and vote were unanimously
adopted :

Whereas, Certain communications have been received by this association, and are now on file, from
the Hopkinton association, of New Hampshire, and
Mr. Parker Pillsbury, a licentiate of this body, relative
to charges preferred by the Hopkinton association
against Mr. Pillsbury.   Therefore

Voted, That the case be assigned for consideration
and final action, to a meeting of this association, to
be held in Boston, at the house of Mr. Blagdon, on
Tuesday, the twenty-third day of the present month,
at nine o'clock, A. M., when the parties may be fully
heard ; and that a copy of this vote be communicated
by the scribe, both to the Hopkinton association and
to Mr. Pillsbury.

A true copy of record.

[Attest] A. W. McCLURE, *Scribe.*

To this arraignment, I immediately responded, to
the following effect :

CONCORD, N. H., Feb. 20, 1841.

To the Suffolk North Association of Congregational
Ministers in Massachusetts :

BRETHREN—Your communication of the third instant was duly received.   By it I learn that you have
appointed a time and place for consideration of
charges preferred against me by the Hopkinton, N.
H., association of ministers, and for " final action " on
the same.

On the course of the Suffolk association in this matter, I wish to be indulged in a few remarks.

In the first place, I was not a little surprised at your disposition to hasten the final action of a case so important to me and the parties concerned. In an "extra official" note, appended to your communication, your secretary says, "They [the association] thought it their duty to give you the opportunity to substantiate your allegations against the ministers of your region, on the truth of which allegations, you rely for defense against the charges filed against you by the Hopkinton association.,'

Now, you must have been aware that to go from town to town over any considerable part of the state, summon witnesses and assemble them at Boston, or to take affidavits and transmit them to the place of meeting, would be a work of much time and labor. You must also have been aware that in no other way could I attempt a defense. Had I not, then, good reason to be surprised that your communication informing me that "final action" was to be had on my cause on the twenty-third of February, was not mailed in Malden, Mass., till the fourth of the same month? Is such haste as this common in the courts of law?

But let me say farther, no charges as yet, have been specified against me. You say in your former communication that the complaint of the Hopkinton association is founded on an article from my pen, published in the *Herald of Freedom*, "printed at Concord, N. H., October 2d, 1840, containing charges against the clergy that are highly slanderous and unchristian." This is the indictment, and the whole of it.

Now, does the Suffolk association expect me to assemble witnesses at Boston, to prove every position in that letter touching the clergy? If not, why have they not *specified* the charges that are "highly slanderous and unchristian?"

But one word in relation to the general manner of procedure. We have heard much of late in this state of "Congregational usage;" and of "ecclesiastical usage;" and of "ministerial usage." But what shall I call that "usage" which (aside from considerations already noticed), permits a clerical body, to which I do not, never did, and never shall belong, and to which I am in no way, whatever, responsible, beyond that general relation which all christians bear to one another, to pursue a course towards one whom they do not regard as a brother in the ministry, such as the Hopkinton association have pursued toward me? Had they no individual duty to discharge to me alone? Or, had the association, in its organized capacity, none? Could they never, as individuals, nor collectively, administer one word of instruction, rebuke, nor correction? When they saw me wandering out of the way, was there no one venerable from age or experience, to warn my *iuexperienced* feet? Or, could not the body together give me one word of caution? Why should they, at the very outset, adopt a procedure which they knew must either condemn and banish me unheard, or subject me to such labor and expense for trial as I am utterly unable to meet?

But they acted as they saw fit; nor am I surprised nor grieved: I had no right nor reason to expect otherwise of a body of men, who, when a brother came before them with a complaint against one of their own number, to sustain which complaint, some six or eight of the best members of his own church stood ready, could deliberately vote in a moment after the presentation, to return it to its author, unread and unopened!

I have the best of evidence to show that the clergy, as a body, are determined to sustain each other in the crusade against the advocates of the rights of our enslaved fellow men. No unimportant part of that evidence is the fact that the Suffolk North Association have signified their intention to take "*final action*" on the complaint of the Hopkinton Association against me, irrespective of the manner or character of that complaint in three weeks after the determination was formed, and information of it transmitted to the parties concerned. I need not repeat here what has already been intimated, that you and the Hopkinton Association also must be aware of the utter impossibility for me to avail myself of the testimony requisite to a fair and full representation of the case, in so short a time.

But I ask for no continuance ; I am not anxious to prove to you that the great body of the clergy of this state are, and have been, deadly hostile to anything like efficient action for the overthrow of slavery. I deem it more important to establish that fact among those who support them; I mean their pastoral charges. And I am glad to know that the happiest success attends my labors, and those of my faithful coadjutors in the work.

You will not therefore be surprised to learn that I do not feel called upon to appear before you on the day you have specified for a hearing of my case. I might well say, in the words of Nehemiah to his adversaries, "I am doing a great work, so that I cannot come down. Why should the work cease while I leave it and come down to you ?" I should gain little, even could I do all that could be wished. The same work would still have to be done among the people which is required now, and by the same instrumentality, and through the same opposition.

I need not tell you that I have been compelled to excommunicate from my fellowship, most of the ministers of our land for the sin of conniving at American slavery; I do not regard them as christians, nor christian ministers. I regret to be compelled to add that even the *Suffolk North Association of Ministers,* are no exception; nor can I recognize them as vested with any authority to decide who shall, or shall not be licensed to preach the gospel. You have shown yourselves in various ways, to be the friends of the southern oppressor, rather than of the opprest. Not many of you have even established the monthly concert of prayer for the enslaved, to intercede with God on their behalf. You have done well for the heathen abroad, perhaps, but have neglected three millions of heathen at the doors of your own sanctuaries. Most of you oppose directly, the agitation of the subject of slavery, in any manner, among your people. You are in full fellowship and communion with the slave-holding ministers at the south, and their more guilty apologists at the north. For ten years we have been laboring to awaken an interest in the churches in behalf of the bleeding slave. Labor enough has been done in New England to have made every church, as a church, the inflexible foe of oppression, as it exists at the south, had it not been for the mighty opposition that has been constantly thrown in the way by the pulpit. It has come to be a mere truism that the firmest pillars of the bloody Moloch are the professed ministers of Jesus Christ; and in no part of these states have those ministers shown themselves more subservient to the will of slave-breeding and slave-holding ministers and others, than in Boston and vicinity. With your blood-stained feet on the necks of three millions of your prostrate brethren, you are deliberately talking of "*censure*" and "*resumption*" of my "*license*," because I have espoused faithfully their cause !

Recreant should I be to the interests of my Redeemer's kingdom, to recognize such men as ministers of Christ. I know full well how the warning will be received ; but still I warn you to *repent*. God has a controversy with you on this awful sin of enslaving millions of immortal beings as yourselves, compelling them into absolute heathenism, concubinage, adultery; robbing them of everything, wives, children, all the endearing relations of life, manhood, womanhood, with all else' only to gratify the cupidity of an unrighteous and cruel master-hood. Your christianity has less of humanity in it than has the religion of the Seminole savage! he befriends the slave and welcomes him to his wigwam : you, or most of you, and multitudes under your pastoral charge, are deaf as adders to his woes. Search the heathen world, ancient and modern ; you shall look in vain for a system of greater abominations, more horrible cruelties than American slavery ; and yet you baptise and sanctify it, and admit it to full sacramental communion and fellowship.

The ancient Romans with hearts of steel, had their god of war ; the ferocious Vandal had his god of vengeance ; but none of their high places ever shewed an altar to the fell demon of slavery. Never did the Nine Sisters hold fond dalliance with a fiend so foul ; never was Apollo's golden lyre tuned to his praise ; never did the wild harp of northern minstrelsy in all its long buried melodies, indite one hymn to the blood-swollen vampire. Never was altar reared to such divinity till the christian slave chain was forged, and the christian coffle formed ; till torturing evangelical thumb-screws were invented, and human flesh had hissed and broiled beneath the red-hot branding iron, and the one eternal God, in the person of his children, his own image and likeness,, was bought and sold in the shambles with the beasts that perish !

And now you, grave and venerable ministers, demand of me to fall down and reverence and worship your blood-besmeared idol, on pain of "censure," or resumption of the license with which you invested me as a preacher of the gospel ; and as logical consequence, expulsion from the church on earth, and the society of the redeemed in heaven ! Brethren, you know you can not deny what I say.

For three hundred years, your christianity has been tearing at the vitals of Africa, like vultures, snatching away from her bosom her poor sons and daughters in myriads, to supply the christian slave-markets of this and other nations. Her wailings have been borne on the trade-winds, on all the winds, to the ends of the earth. And yet to this hour, doctors of divinity dare doubt, dare openly deny that slavery is sin ! and even such as feign to believe it sin, make themselves, by a strange silence or open connivance, more guilty, if possible, or certainly more dangerous, than those who deny or doubt.

I repeat my denial that what is taught and professed by the great body of clergy in this nation as christianity is not christianity at all. I confine myself inth is letter wholly to slavery. To American chattel slavery. There are other accounts to be considered when slavery is overthrown. Let your intimated censure " and resumption of "license" be carried

into full execution.   I shall still preach the gospel of
Christ, and by his grace wash my hands from all participation in your guilt on the awful crimes and cruelties of slavery, and in the last day be a swift witness
against you, unless you repent.

Brethren, *regard this letter as my solemn excommunication of you*, and my work with you is done.

I go now to the lost sheep on the mountains to unfold to them the treasures of the gospel.   And I shall
tell them, as I have done before, except your righteousness exceed the righteousness of most of the professed ministers of Christ around you, you can in no
case enter into the kingdom of heaven.   And when
they, and you, and I, stand at the tribunal of God
with assembled worlds, the down-trodden and sorrow-
stricken slave in the vast congregation, it shall be
known who has served God and who has not.   And
justice shall be meted out to us all.

Yours, waiting that great event,

PARKER PILLSBURY.

At a subsequent meeting of the Suffolk North Association my "license" was resumed, as had been
before intimated and threatened.   But my higher,
more divine commission became to me from that time
more and more sacred and important.   Under it, I
have spoken the words of truth, righteousness and
freedom for more than forty years, to multitudes of
men, women and children in both the hemispheres, and
as I humbly hope and trust, not all in vain.

The first open, direct arraignment of the American
church and clergy as the guilty accomplices, north and
south, in all the crimes and cruelties, the sins and
shames of slavery, was a little pamphlet, entitled,
"The American Churches the Bulwarks of American
Slavery."   It was written by an American, though first

published in England in 1840. The last of similar import and purpose, was a larger work, published in 1847, entitled, "The Church as it is; The Forlorn Hope of Slavery."

The peculiarity of both these publications was, that the persons and parties whose character and conduct were to be considered, furnished all the testimony themselves. and the evidence was all direct, with no cross question nor quibble of any description, from the other side, so whatever conclusion might be reached, it would be wholly through their own words and works, as by themselves published to the world.

Since slavery was abolished, the clergy, as was always predicted they would, have claimed it as the result of their prayers, preaching and votes. But it was never expected that they or their children would boldly declare through pulpit and press, as well as by lips and lungs, that the abolitionists, even Garrison, did more harm than good; that "the final extinction of slavery was accomplished in pursuance of principles which Garrison abhorred, and by measures which he denounced;" that "he had but a heterogeneous following, charged with all the fanaticism of the times; and confined mostly to eastern Massachusetts and northern New England;" a "motley party; was only captain of a corporal's guard;" "his main principles were, down with the constitution, dissolve the union, denounce the churches and ministers, renounce the orthodox belief in the Bible; a man of headlong force, erratic, short-sighted and narrow, thought not of cleansing, but of crushing the temple of liberty, which would have made slavery perpetual and extinguished forever all hope of an American nation!"

A semi-centennial discourse, delivered in Cincinnati, Ohio, in April, 1881, contains most of these quota-

tions; and Rev. A. T. Rankin, in some published
essays, the present year, supplies part of the remainder. But it remained for Leonard Woolsey Bacon,
son of the late Dr. Leonard Bacon, of Connecticut,
to print such a life-size portrait of Garrison as will be
here subjoined. It is in a biographical sketch of his
father, in a popular magazine. Dr. Bacon's anti-slavery was worthy such a son, and to be by him celebrated in the manner it is in the notice furnished the
Century. It received many well-deserved scathings
when it appeared, and as anti-slavery had nothing to
fear from the father, so neither has the memory or
good name of Garrison anything to dread from the
contemptuous caricatures of the son. Both may be
safely trusted to history and to posterity. But here is
the Woolsey Bacon portrait:

In almost any assembly of crotchety people—long-
haired men and short-haired women—over a scheme
for the reconstruction of the solar system, you will
hear the appeal to "Remember Garrison, how he began with nothing and a printing-press against the
whole nation and the whole church, and how at last
he succeeded in bringing everybody over to his side."
It is really a matter of interest to public morals that
the ingenuous youth of America should know the truth
of this matter — that Mr. Garrison and his society
never succeeded in anything; that his one distinctive
dogma, that slave-holding is always and everywhere a
sin, was never accepted to any considerable extent
outside of the little ring of his personal adherents;
that his vocabulary, which had no word but man-
stealer and pirate for the legal guardian of a decrepit

negro, or for one holding a family of slaves in transit for a free state, with intent to emancipate them, never became part of the American dictionary; that the sophistry with which he spent a lifetime in trying to confuse plain distinctions had little effect except to give acrimony and plausibility to the defense of slavery; and that the final extinction of slavery was accomplished in pursuance of principles which he abhorred, by measures which he denounced, and under the leadership of men like Leonard Bacon, in literature and the church, and Abraham Lincoln in politics, who had been the objects of his incessant and calumnious vituperation.

And yet this bold calumniator has the grace to admit that "the brunt of my [his] father's arguments in the earlier stages of the slavery controversy, was directed more against the so-called abolitionists than against the advocates of slavery." Till the firing on Fort Sumter the abolitionists never knew that "the brunt of Dr. Bacon's arguments was ever changed in its direction," to any important purpose, to either side. Leonard Woolsey Bacon graciously thinks, however, that Garrison, now that slavery is abolished, may "be forgiven the great harm he did for the sake of the little good."

But all this aside from the main question in hand. The clergy to-day would have the world believe they were always opposed to slavery, and sought its overthrow. They were opposed to slavery just as was the government. No more; no less. And if the church and government were against slavery, why did they not put it out of existence? How could it have stood against them? If they were opposed to slavery why

were Louisiana and Florida bought for its extension ?
Why was Mexico robbed of Texas after a four years'
bloody and cruel, and fearfully unjust war on our part,
only to reinstate slavery where Roman Catholicism
a few years before had abolished it, as it hoped, forever ?

Whatever of slave-breeding, or slave-holding, or
slave-trading abroad, or slave-hunting at home the
government authorized and supported, the church
sanctioned and sanctified. So also of slavery extension. The clergy actually clamored for chaplaincies
in the atrocious Mexican war, knowing well its origin
and objects. The religious press, north and south,
shouted for the war, irrespective of denominational
differences. The *Presbyterian Herald* asked its readers," Do you pray for the Mexicans?" and answered :

There are good reasons why you should. They
have souls like other men. Is not this overlooked ?
They are not wild beasts, though like them. Why
pray for a Hindoo or a Hottentot ? Because he
has a soul of infinite value, but exposed to eternal
death. So has every Mexican. Because they are all
Papists. And will you pray for the conversion of
Romanism around you, and not for the conversion of
that one thousand miles off ?

The pope decreed the abolition of slavery in Mexico in 1829, " for the glory of God and to distinguish
mankind from the brute creation." Good reason why
slave-holding Presbyterians should " pray for the conversion of Mexicans as well as for Hindoos and Hot-
tentots." But the *Presbyterian Herald* had another
reason for praying for the Mexicans, verily this :

They are our enemies. This is one of the strongest
reasons. Does not the Savior so teach ? Matthew
v ; 44. This does not refer to private enemies only
—it extends to public foes also. It may be your duty
to fight them, to preserve the life and the liberty of

our countrymen—strictly in the defensive. But does that duty to our country exempt us from the other duty to them? Fighting and praying can go together. Jesus was a lion, yet a lamb—so his disciples.

The *Protestant Telegraph* viewed the war and its results, thus hopefully :

I have no fellowship with war, and deeply regret our present relations with our sister republic, Mexico ; yet I cannot but hope for some good from the conflict, and that good is, the entrance of the Protestant religion into the Mexican states. The Roman Catholic religion is now the religion of that nation ; none other is tolerated ; but it is utterly impossible that republican institutions can exist and flourish in connection with Romanism. The immense wealth of the churches in Mexico, now hoarded up in idolatrous images of silver and gold, (a petticoat of the Virgin Mary, estimated at half a million,) may be distributed among the people as a consequence of this conflict, or be laid out in the establishment of schools, in internal improvements, in efforts of various kinds, to exalt the people. "Great is the Diana of the Ephesians," is now the cry, but it may soon give place to "Great is the Lord our God."

But what shall be said of this from so eminent a Divine, as Rev. Joel Parker, D. D., in a sermon preached, and then published in the *Christian Observer?*

I was not an advocate for the present administration. I cast my vote for the opposing candidates, and my judgment is, that if they had been elected, the Mexican war would have been avoided, and the honor ot the country as well preserved as at present. But our present chief magistrate was duly elected. He is not the president of the democratic party ; he is the president of the nation ; he is my president and your president, and we are bound to treat him with the same deferential respect as if he had been the very man of our choice. Moreover, are we *absolutely* certain that he is not really laying a foundation for a

claim on our gratitude in this very matter of the
Mexican war? For one, I am free to confess that I
am not so well informed in respect to our relations
with Mexico, as to be sure that our executive could
have wisely avoided this collision. Perhaps I am as
well acquainted with the subject as the majority of my
hearers, yet I have no doubt that a bare three months
devoted to an investigation of our past and present
relations with Mexico, would secure to me tenfold the
amount of intelligence which I at present possess in
relation to the subject; and if it were left for me to
decide, whether that course of policy should be pursued which has involved us in war, I should not, with
my present limited knowledge, dare to assume the
responsibility of deciding against it !

Or this in the New England *Puritan*, from its
editor, Rev. Parsons Cooke, D. D.

The fact that this nation is earnestly engaged in
war with a neighboring nation, seems to be little real-
ized by the mass of the people, and especially by
christian people, who ought to take a deep interest in
the subject. But what shall christians do in the case?
The war will not be brought to a close the sooner by
bringing christian influence into antagonism with any
legal measures for prosecuting the war. We are in
the war by the acts of our government, and shall get out
of it, if we ever do, by the acts of the government and
none the sooner for any attempts to embarrass that
action. Our rulers have taken the responsibility of this
plunge, and we, in the exercise of a religious influence,
are not called upon either to justify or resist their action.
As citizens exercising the political franchise, at the
proper time, we with the rest, must make our opinions
felt, touching such important measures. But now the
simple question is, what can we do as christians, to
secure the favor of Providence and avert the storm?

The Rev. Evan Stevenson, editor of a monthly
magazine in Georgetown, Kentucky, hungered after
the righteousness of such a war as keenly as this
discloses :

While the war continues, we *cannot* and *will* not discuss the question of slavery, as we honestly feel more
like discussing roast beef and yams, or, if our service
is required, *national rights*, with our sword on the Rio
Grande. We entreat our correspondents that they
forward to us for publication no religious controversies
pending this conflict with Mexico. Let us drop our
denominational prejudices, "Fight the good fight of
faith, and lay hold upon *eternal life*."

Only two more of these excerpts, and one of them
very brief. The *Christian Observer*, a new-school
Presbyterian organ, of first-class, spoke in this tone,
and at such length, by a correspondent :

MEXICO IS OPEN !—Mexico is open to christian, as
well as commercial enterprise. Our countrymen
are protected in the prosecution of their lawful business, and so would our citizens be in the sale or gratuitous circulation of Spanish Bibles, tracts and bound
volumes. These books are on the shelves of our de-
positories. Why should they remain there, when now
they may be placed in the hands of the population at
Matamoras, Monterey, Tampico, Vera Cruz, Jalapa,
Perote, Puebla, etc., etc.? Will those whose obligations bind them to this circulation, answer this question ? *The sword has opened the way.* Our officers
and soldiers themselves need all the kindly influences
we can exert on them. They will gratefully receive
these publications, and bless their benefactors. Shall
we withhold them from the men *who fight the battles
of the country ? Many of the officers and soldiers, particularly among the volunteers, are church members,* and
will rejoice in such an enterprise. Colporteurs can be
found on the ground. Discharged volunteers will remain, and instead of shooting balls, will love to do
good, and communicate to the millions perishing
around them, the word of life. What is my duty as
an AMERICAN CHRISTIAN ? Let the hundreds of thousands of christian freemen in our land answer that
question. *If Captain Bragg gave "a little more
grape," and turned the victory, why may not the sons of
peace and righteousness* follow up that victory, with all

those missiles and weapons which are mighty through God to the pulling down of strongholds? It must be done. *It is the great movement of the present century.* Who will lead the advance?   J. C. S.

And this one more, from the Nashville, Tennessee, *Union* :

"At a *Missionary* meeting, held in the Methodist church, on Monday night, funds were raised for making General Taylor, Colonel Campbell, Colonel Anderson, Captain Cheatham, and Captain Foster, life-members of the Conference Missionary society. These compliments will be duly appreciated by the brave officers, who are *winning laurels* on the field of battle."

So did the government and the governing part and power of the church, coöperate in *fighting and robbing* to extend, as well as support slavery.

CHAPTER XV.

A long chapter this may be, though it is last but
one, and that one, readers may be glad to know, will
not be long. The charges against the church and
clergy may be sweeping and severe. All that is now
proposed is to submit their own recorded, printed,
published testimony in support of them. In scripture
phrase, "By their own words shall they be justified,
or condemned."

For convenience, the great representative ecclesiastical bodies will be considered separately, beginning
with the General Assembly of the Presbyterian church.
Notwithstanding its powerful testimony against slavery, so late as 1818, as has been shown, it grew to be
one of the boldest blasphemers against the holy spirit
of freedom the world has produced. And the *New-
school* assembly, after the memorable separation into
old and new schools, became quite as unscrupulous as
the other. Though slavery had little or nothing to do
in dividing the body, the new school was much the
strongest in the northern states.

In the new-school general assembly, in 1840, a motion was made, by a member, on the subject of slavery, when Rev. Dr. Cox, of Brooklyn, immediately

moved· its indefinite postponement.   On the motion
being carried, he exultingly exclaimed :   " Our Vesu-
vius is capped safely for three years," that being the
time for the next meeting.   And Judge Birney assures
us that Dr. Cox was at the first an abolitionist.

The clergy of the old-school were even more demonstrative in opposition to anything like hostility to
the " peculiar institution."   When the Richmond ministers held a meeting, expressly to wash their hands
clean before all the world, of any anti-slavery stain,
Dr. William L. Plummer was absent ; but on his return, he made haste to assure his acceptance and approval of the action taken, by a letter to the committee
of correspondence, from which these are extracts :

" I have carefully watched this matter from its earliest existence, and everything I have seen or heard of
its character, both from its patrons and its enemies,
has confirmed me beyond repentance, in the belief,
that, let the character of abolitionists be what it
may in the sight of the judge of all the earth, this is
the most meddlesome, impudent, reckless, fierce, and
wicked excitement I ever saw.

" If abolitionists will set the country in a blaze, it
is but fair that they should receive the first warming
at the fire.

"Abolitionists are like infidels, wholly unaddicted
to martyrdom for opinion's sake.   Let them understand that *they will be caught* [lynched] if they come
among us, and they will take good heed to keep out
of our way.   There is not one man among them who
has any more idea of shedding his blood in this cause
than he has of making war on the grand Turk."

To these instances of clerical devotion to the worship of the bloody idol, Judge Birney adds this ; a
letter from a reverend divine, announcing his inten-

tion to appear at the next session of the Presbytery, with important business, for which he would have everybody previously prepare. He opens thus ;

To the Sessions of the Presbyterian Congregations within the bounds of the West Hanover Presbytery :

At the appointed stated meeting of our Presbytery, I design to offer a preamble and resolutions on the subject of treasonable and abominably wicked interference of the northern and eastern fanatics, with our political and civil rights, our property and our domestic concerns.   You are aware that our clergy, whether with or without reason, are more suspected by the public than the clergy of other denominations. Now, *dear christian brethren,* I humbly express it as my earnest wish, that you *quit yourselves like men.*   If there be any stray goat of a minister among you, tainted with the blood-hound principles of abolitionism, let him be ferreted out, silenced, excommunicated, and left to the *public to dispose of him in in other respects.*

Your affectionate brother in the Lord,

ROBERT N. ANDERSON.

Mr. Birney farther gives us this individual expression of Rev. Dr. Spring, of New York.   He says : "At the anniversary of the American colonization society, held in Washington, in 1839, Dr. Spring was on the platform, as one of the speakers.   At his side was Mr. Henry A. Wise, a Virginia member of congress, a slave-holder and professional duelist.   In his speech, he had declared :   'The best way to meet the abolitionists is with cold steel and Dupont's best !'" [best gun-powder.]   And Mr. Birney adds :   "We were told that Dr. Spring spoke in sympathy with the southern sentiment, as evinced in the speech of Mr. Wise." Subsequently, Mr. Birney says : "The doctor preached and published a series of sermons on slavery in its scriptural relations, which were regarded by the pro-slavery party as highly serviceable to their cause."

If it shall be objected that these are only individual utterances, it may be said for that very reason they are given. But they are also the expression of the most eminent *pre*-eminent men in the denomination. Men of whom one is supposed to chase a thousand, and two to put ten thousand abolitionists to flight, even though "with cold steel and Dupont's best."

What follows shall be the expression of the very best of the general assembly, the new-school, and so late as the year 1846, when the American anti-slavery society had reached its sixteenth year, and when multitudes of church members had left the communion, when new and free churches had been organized and ministers settled over them, in the good name of anti-slavery.

At the session of 1846, the voice of protest against slavery was so much louder and stronger than ever before, that a report had to be made as nearly as possible in tune and tone with the protests. It was presented by Rev. Dr. Duffield, and read as follows :

The system of slavery, as it exists in these United States, viewed either in the laws of the several states which sanction it, or in its actual operation and result in society, is intrinsically unrighteous and oppressive, and is opposed to the prescriptions of the law of God, to the spirit and precepts of the gospel, and to the best interests of humanity.

The testimony of the general assembly, from the A. D. 1787, to A. D. 1818, inclusive, has condemned it, and it remains still the recorded testimony of the Presbyterian church of these United States against it, from which we do not recede.

We cannot, therefore, withhold the expression of deep regret that slavery should be continued and countenanced by any of the members of our churches ; and we do earnestly exhort both them and the churches, among whom its exists, to use all means in their power to put it away from them. Its perpetuation among them cannot fail to be regarded by multitudes influenced by their example, as sanctioning the system portrayed in it, and maintained by the statutes of the several slaveholding states, wherein they dwell.

But while we believe that many evils incident to the system, render it important and obligatory to bear tes-. timony against it, yet would we not undertake to determine the degree of moral turpitude on the part of individuals involved by it. This will doubtless be found to vary in the sight of God, according to the degree of light and other circumstances pertaining to each. In view of all the embarrassments and obstacles in the way of emancipation interposed by the statutes of the slaveholding states, and by the social influence affecting the views and conduct of those involved in it, we cannot pronounce a judgment of general and promiscuous condemnation, implying *that* destitution of christian principle and feeling which should exclude from the table of the Lord all who should stand in the legal relation of masters to slaves, or justify us in withholding our ecclesiastical and christian fellowship from them. We rather sympathize with, and would seek to succor them in their embarrassments, believing that separation and secession among the churches and their members, are not the methods God approves and sanctions for the reformation of his church.

While, therefore, we feel bound to bear our testimony against slavery, and to exhort our beloved brethren to remove it from them as speedily as possible, by all appropriate and available means, we do at the same time condemn all divisive and schismatical measures, tending to destroy the unity and disturb the peace of our church, and deprecate the spirit of denunciation and inflicting severities, which would cast from the fold those whom we are rather bound, by the spirit of the gospel, and the obligations of our covenant, to instruct, to counsel, to exhort, and thus to lead in the ways of God ; and towards whom, even though they may err, to exercise forbearance and brotherly love.

As a court of our Lord Jesus Christ, we possess no legislative authority; and as the General Assembly of the Presbyterian church, we possess no judiciary authority. We have no right to institute and prescribe a test of christian character and church membership, not recognized and sanctioned in the sacred scriptures, and in our standards, by which we have agreed to walk. We must leave, therefore, this matter with the sessions, presbyteries and synods—the judicatories to whom pertains the right of judgment to act in the administration of discipline, as they may judge it to be their duty, constitutionally, subject to the general assembly, only in the way of general review and control.

This was the exact position of the General Assembly New School in 1846. Briefly analyzed, it contains a fearful condemnation of slave-holding; then a re-statement of the old positions of the body, back in the former century and onward to 1818, and a hypocritical profession of adherence to them still; * * hypocritical, because regret is expressed in another place that, "slavery is still countenanced and continued by members of our churches;" which, if true, and slavery be such sin and shame, crime and cruelty, why were not the offenders dealt with long ago as other sinners, and so the church cleansed from such a curse? But the next propositition is a most unblushing attempt, weak too, as well as wicked, to excuse and extenuate the guilt of slave-holding, notwithstanding the previous stunning condemnation of it; while the last declaration is that "as a court of our Lord Jesus Christ, we possess no legislative authority, and as the general assembly of the Presbyterian church, we possess no judicial authority!" And so the abomination went on from generation to generation; growing with the nation's growth, increasing with the increase of the church!

Parodied in but a single word, this is the way these grave propositions would, a part of them, read :

First, the system of legalized *adultery*, as it exists in these United States is intrinsically unrighteous, and opposed to the law of God and the spirit and precepts of the gospel.

We cannot, therefore, withhold the expression of deep regret, that adultery should be countenanced and continued by any of the members of our churches. And we do earnestly exhort both them and the churches among whom it exists, to use all means in their power to put it away.

But while we believe that many evils incident to adultery, render it important and obligatory to bear testimony against it, yet we would not undertake to determine the degree of moral turpitude, *on the part of individual adulterers.* This will doubtless be found to vary in the sight of God, according to the degree of light and other circumstances pertaining to each individual.

While, therefore, we feel bound to bear our testimony against adultery, and to exhort our beloved erring brethren to remove it from them, as speedily as possible, by all available and appropriate means, we do at the same time condemn all divisive and schismatical measures, tending to destroy the unity and disturb the peace of our church, and deprecate the spirit of denunciation, and inflicting severities which would cast from the fold those adulterers whom we are rather bound by the spirit of the gospel, and the obligations of our covenant, to instruct, to counsel, to exhort, and thus to lead in the way of God ; and towards whom, even though they may *err*, to exercise forbearance and brotherly love.

Does not this change of a word throw light and *lightning* on the problem? Or suppose the words *sheep-stealing* and *sheep-stealers* had been substituted, taking the hint from him who exclaimed once, "How much better is a man than a sheep!"

And yet was not slavery both adultery and theft in all their most odious forms? That very church had quoted the eminent scholar, as well as priest and divine, Grotius, as declaring man-stealing to be the very highest kind of theft. But it was away back in 1794. The one unalterable truth was, the leading clergy never held slavery to be sin, in any such sense as even mere *heretical* offenses. Here is the general assembly, meekly and humbly confessing that it "possesses no judicial, no legislative authority to reach such "sum of all villainies" as slave-breeding and slave-holding, and drive it out of church communion and fellowship! Does anybody believe that if it were a question of robbing hen-roosts, instead of cradles and trundle-beds, a way would not have been made, had none existed, out of dilemma so dreadful, in all the years between 1794 and 1846? Church members and ministers have been expelled from the churches for denying or doubting the right or validity of infant baptism, where infant-stealers, where baby-breeders for the slave shambles, were welcomed to both pulpit and sacramental supper! Is it, then, too much to say, that denominational differences in the American churches have been deemed greater offenses and to be more severely and summarily punished than all the atrocities connected with the holding of slaves?

A. B. C. F. M.

The American Board of Commissioners for Foreign Missions was organized in the year 1810. It was com-

posed of ministers and members of the Congregational
and Presbyterian churches mainly, and its sole object
was to operate among heathen nations and tribes,
with a view to their enlightenment, elevation and cul-
tivation.   Its membership was gathered from north
and south, its missionaries, in one instance, Rev. John
Leighton Wilson, a slave-holder, (and according to
his statement there were others) as well as young ministers and their wives from non-slave-holding states ;
and its treasury was supplied from the northern and
southern states, the gifts of those whose wealth as well
as traffic, was in "slaves and souls of men," And
Judge Birney's tract contains an authentic account of
one legacy left to the Board, bequeathed for the benefit of the Indian mission, which for some reason was
in litigation in the Georgia courts.   And an advertisement copied from the Charleston, South Carolina,
Courier of February 12, 1835, was to this purport :

" FIELD NEGROES.

By Thomas Gadsden.   On Tuesday, the 17th inst.,
will be sold at the north of the Exchange, at ten
o'clock, A. M., a prime gang of

TEN NEGROES,

accustomed to the culture of cotton and provisions,
belonging to the Independent church, in Christ's
church parish.

February 6, 1835."

What was here but "trade in slaves and souls of
men ?"

In the United States the operations of the board
extended only to the Indian tribes, and to but few of
them, chiefly the Cherokees and Choctaws.   The
American board, like the general assembly, and at
about the same time, became greatly disturbed by the

agitation of the question of slavery. And like the general assembly, they referred the whole matter to committees for examination and report. In 1845, petitions and memorials against slavery were so many that the board seemed compelled to something more declarative than in preceding years in regard to them. Accordingly an august committee of nine was elected. all eminent men, Rev. Dr. Woods, of Andover Theological Seminary, chairman. Their report, of nine closely-printed octavo pages, is before me, but no change of former action is even recommended, either by the board itself or by its missionaries. The burden of complaint was that missionaries admitted slave-holders to the mission churches sustained by the moneys of the board, contributed by the churches. The charge was admitted, but justified thus :

The primary object aimed at in missions should be to bring men to a saving knowledge of Christ, by making known to them the way of salvation through His cross.   *   *   The missionaries acting under the commission of Christ and with the instruction of the New Testament before them, are themselves at first, and subsequently with the churches they have gathered, the rightful and exclusive judges of what constitutes adequate evidence of purity and fitness for church fellowship in professed converts.   *   * The indulgence of any *known sin*, and the neglect of any known duty, are to be decidedly discountenanced. *   * In respect to social and moral evils, with which missionaries are to come in contact in proscuting their work, it should be borne in mind that they are by no means few or of limited territorial extent. The evils of slavery will probably be met in some form in nearly every part of the great missionary field. *   * Should it be found, as the result of experience, that souls among the heathen are in fact regenerated by the Holy Spirit before they are freed from all participation in the social and moral evils, and that

25

convincing evidence can be given that they are regenerated, then may not the master and the slave, the ruler and the subject, giving such evidence of spiritual renovation, be all gathered into the same fold of Christ?   *   *   In proceeding on these principles the missions, under the care of this board and the churches gathered under them, are no otherwise connected with slavery than they are with every other evidence and result of imperfect moral renovation in their converts and church members. And they no more really give their sanction to the one than they do to all the others.

It may be well to show here what some of those social and moral evils are, which are enumerated in this report. Next to slavery castes in India come ; then " unrestrained exactions made in the form of revenues ;" then "military or other service connected with a species of feudalism," and lastly, and later in the report, " Polygamy ! "

Exactly how many wrongs are required to make one right, or to justify one wrong, the board does not show. It seems to plead guilty to sanctifying so many at the outset. But paying taxes and performing military service are not counted " social and moral evils," nor yet "results of imperfect moral development" in the United States nor Great Britain. But even should the mission converts be compelled to most oppressive taxation, in whatever form, they surely are never required to *perpetrate* slave-holding nor polygamy, for both of which the missionaries of the board were called to account, and were not only proved, but, to a limited extent, actually *pleaded* guilty. But to return to the report :

Your committee believe that no established system of involuntary servitude prevails among any tribe of North American Indians where the missionaries of this board are laboring, except the Cherokees and Choc-

taws. *   *   The following statements will therefore relate to the Cherokee and Choctaw missions,
*   *   Negro slaves appear to have been introduced among those Indians by white men, who removed into their country from sixty to eighty years
ago, and to have gradually increased in number, till
the missions were established among them in 1817
and 1818. By a census taken in 1820, Cherokees
were holding five hundred and eighty-three slaves.
*   *   The number now owned by both tribes
may probably be not far from two thousand ; while
the number of Indians in both tribes is thirty-eight
thousand. *   *   That slavery should exist at
all in these tribes who have suffered so severely from
the violation of their own rights by their white neighbors, is deeply to be regretted. And all should earnestly pray that as social improvement and christian
knowledge are advancing rapidly among them. they
may rapidly exemplify the spirit of the true philanthropy as well as the gospel law of love, by showing
that they duly appreciate the rights and welfare of
the whole race of man.   *   *
* " Relative to the principles on which converts were
to be received to the churches, all the missionaries of
the board among the Cherokees and Choctaws, seem
to have been perfectly unanimous, Both masters and
slaves," says Mr. Buttrick, " I receive on the same
principle, viz., on the ground of their faith in the Lord
Jesus Christ." Mr. Worcester says : " The general
principle on which I have voted for the reception of
members is that all are to be received who desire it,
and give evidence of a change of heart." Mr. Wright
says : " When any, whether masters or servants, have
given evidence of a change of heart, of repentance
and faith in the Lord Jesus Christ, they have been received."   *   *   *
*   *   *   " The whole number of the
Cherokee tribe is about eighteen thousand, and the
number of slaves owned by them is probably about
one thousand. The whole number of church members in this tribe is two hundred and forty, of whom
fifteen hold slaves, and twenty-one are themselves

slaves. The Choctaw tribe, including the Chickasaws, is about twenty thousand. The whole number connected with our churches there is six hundred and three, of whom twenty hold slaves, one hundred and thirty-one are slaves, and seven are free negroes.
*   *   *   Mr. Byington says : " We give such instruction to masters and servants as are contained in the epistles, and yet not in a way to give the subject a peculiar prominence, for then it would seem to be personal, as there are usually but one or two slave-holders present. In private, we converse about all the ills and dangers of slavery." Mr. Wright says : " The instructions, public and private, direct and indirect, have been such as are found in the Bible.   *   *   *
*   *   *   " Strongly as your committee are convinced of the wrongfulness and evil tendencies of slaveholding, and ardently as they desire its speedy termination, still they cannot think that in all cases, it involves individual guilt, in such manner that every person implicated in it can on scriptural grounds be excluded from church fellowship. In the language of Dr. Chalmers, ' Distinction ought to be made betwixt the character of *a system*, and the character of the persons whom circumstances have implicated in it.'   *   *   *
*   *   *   " Such, substantially, are the views of your committee ; and the more they study God's method of proceeding in regard to war, slavery, polygamy, and other kindred social wrongs, as it is unfolded in the Bible, the more they are convinced that in dealing with individuals implicated in those wrongs, of long standing, and intimately interwoven with the relations and movements of the social system, the utmost kindness and forbearance are to be exercised, which are compatible with steady adherence to principle.   *   *   *   Some of the slave-holders have been known to require their slaves to attend meetings and other opportunities for obtaining religious instruction, and all are believed to favor their doing so. Before it was forbidden by law, in 1841, numbers of their slaves were taught to read, in Sab-

bath and week-day schools. And such instruction is still, to some extent, given in private, and seven out of fourteen slaves in Fairfield church, in the Cherokee country, can read, and one can write.   *   *   * One who has been occasionally employed as a helper in missionary work, highly esteemed for intelligence and exemplary piety, has been left by the will of his master, manager of his property, and virtually guardian of his orphan child and heir.   *   *   *

*   *   *   "That the missionaries among these Indians have been faithful in their work, seems evident, not only from their own statements, but also from the fact that the holy spirit has most remarkably owned and blessed their labors, the hopeful converts among the Choctaws being proportionately more numerous than those in any other mission connected with the board, except that at the Sandwich Islands."

Finally, the report closes with this remarkable confession, without proposing any change, or system of operations that would tend to remove the atrocious slave system, or ameliorate the condition of one of its victims. Here is the conclusion of the report, the names of the committee appended to it :

"There can be no prospect of benefiting the slave, in a slave country, without the consent of the owner. The only hope we can have of benefiting either the one or the other, is through the influence of the gospel ; and the gospel, to be effectual must be conveyed in the spirit of meekness and love."

LEONARD WOODS,
BENNET TYLER,
REUBEN N. WALWORTH,
THOMAS W. WILLIAMS,
CALVIN E. STOWE,
BENJAMIN TAPPAN,
DAVID SANFORD,
JAMES W. MCLANE,
DAVID GREENE.

The American board is occupying much space, but it must be remembered that it represented the Congregational and Presbyterian church and clergy of

the country at that time, both as to religion at home
and as sent to the heathen abroad. Abolitionists
charged that it was a pro-slavery religion, and in no
sense anti-slavery.   None denied that there were honorable exceptions ; but as in the state, so in the
church, the governing influence, and power upheld
and extended slavery, and so slavery continued, and
its victims were multiplied.

The report underwent long discussion, and scanty
extracts of the arguments are here given. Rev. Dr.
Tyler, president of a Connecticut theological seminary, said :   "The apostles admitted slave-holders to
the church, and for this board to decide against it
would be to impeach the apostles."

Rev, Dr. Bacon, another Connecticut divine, said :
"The board ought to make a distinction between *slavery and slave-holding*, a distinction that I deem extremely obvious.   The master does not make the man
a slave, but the laws and constitution of society."
Readers will remember that Dr. Bacon was before us
not very long ago, with his anti-slavery.   He was
famous at *definitions*, and stating and adjusting *issues*,
not one of which I think he declared " raised by Garrison, was ever accepted."   But here was a definition
to be admired, a distinction to be remembered ; a
"distinction between slavery and slave-holding."   A
distinction between horse-stealing and stealing horses.
"The master does not make the man a slave."   To be
sure, he takes him, works him ; takes her, works her,
and if there be children, the laws say "they shall follow the condition of the mother !"   Not the father.
There was often a too striking resemblance between
the owner or overseer, and the children, for that.   So
the children followed the condition of the mother.
And thus Dr. Bacon's innocent slave-holder enjoyed

all the profits of the outrageous robbery and wrong, from generation to generation, and the "laws and constitution of society" suffered the perdition which otherwise the thief and robber must meet.

Dr. Stowe, of another theological seminary, said : " I would sooner die, than say our missionaries ought to enter their open protest against all the evils with which they may come in contact.   *   *   * Jacob lived with four women at once. Had there been an organized church then, must Jacob have been excluded ? "   *   *   *   " These examples are for our instruction, and give us just the light we need in this matter."

And Dr. Beecher said : " Masters and slaves existed in the primitive churches, and it was allowed by Christ and his apostles. Slavery is an organic sin, made by law, and therefore not dealt with as other sins."

"Organic sin." That was good. That was worthy of Dr. Bacon. I remember a wicked wag who asked, on reading it, " Could not the laws and constitution of society *organize* all the sins ? and then we could rush in the millennium as by spontaneous combustion."

The report was thus severely criticised, and how earnestly was shown in the strange fact that, on taking the vote, there was not one dissenting voice !

And it is certain that most of the churches, and doubtless many ministers, were ignorant that one of their own missionaries was owning slaves at home while preaching to the Africans in their own native land. Nor did they know what laws the Choctaw and Cherokee Indians enacted to protect themselves in slave-holding, after the missionaries went among them. The Indians had heard of the abolitionists, and doubtless feared, if they did not suspect the missionaries themselves.

The secretaries and directors of the board knew all about those slavery-protecting enactments, as well as did their missionaries ; but they did not disclose all they knew. They did not for a long time tell that John Leighton Wilson, one of their African missionaries, was himself an owner and holder of slaves. The Boston *Recorder* did, and the Congregational *Observer* said : " The secretaries have not acted with their usual judgment in suppressing the letter of Mr. Wilson, for six years "—a letter as was said, announcing that he, and even other missionaries, owned slaves.

Here are a few examples of Indian legislation to protect the holding of slaves in the nations :

" Be it enacted by the national council, that from and after the passage of this act, it shall not be lawful for any person or persons to teach any free negro or negress, not of Cherokee blood, *nor any slave*, belonging to any citizen or citizens of the nation, to read or write." The annexed penalty is "fine not less than one hundred, nor more than five hundred dollars, at the discretion of the court."

Another statute prohibited slaves from "owning any horses, cattle, swine, or fire-arms." The reason assigned for such legislation was, that the ownership of such property by slaves, " has become a nuisance to the master, and a temptation to theft."

In 1836, the Choctaws enacted : " That from and after the passage of this act, (and it was almost twenty years after the mission had been established), if any citizen of the United States, acting as a missionary, or a preacher, or whatever his occupation may be, is found to take active part in favoring the principles

and notions of the most fatal and destructive doctrines of abolitionism, he shall be compelled to leave
the nation, and forever to stay out of it.

"And be it further enacted : That teaching slaves
how to read, to write, or to sing, in meeting-houses or
schools, or in any open place, without the consent of
the owner, or allowing them to sit at table with him,
shall be sufficient ground to convict persons of favoring the principles and notions of abolitionism."

And this one more, enacted on the 15th of October,
1846, almost at the very moment of the meeting of
the board when the report of the committee of nine
was made, now under our consideration :

" Be it enacted ;   That no negro slave can be
emancipated in this nation, except by application, or
petition of the owner to the general council.   And
provided also that it shall be made to appear to the
council, that the owner or owners, at the time of application, shall have no debt or debts outstanding
against him, her, or them, either in or out of this nation.   Then, and in that case, the general council
shall have power to pass an act for the owner to
emancipate his or her slave, which slave, after being
freed, shall leave this nation within thirty days after
the passage of this act.   And in case any such slave
or slaves shall return into this nation afterwards, he,
she, or they, shall be exposed to public sale for the
term of five years, and the proceeds of such sale shall
be used as national funds."

And now the most remarkable word of all remains
to be spoken.   The A. B. C. F. M. held its anniversaries regularly ; made annual and most elaborate reports ; some of them showing frightful pictures of the
slave system among the Cherokee and Choctaw
churches and church members.   But in the year 1859,

the board reported its work *done* in the Choctaw nation, and in 1860, in the Cherokee, and gave its legitimate, logical reason : "The Cherokees are a christian people."   *   *   *

     *   *   *   "The committee have arrived at the conclusion that it is time to discontinue its expenditures among the Cherokees. To prevent all misapprehension, it should be stated at the outset ; First, *that this is not owing to the relations of our work among those Indians to the system of slavery.*" The Choctaw mission was similarly closed, in 1859.

O, no ! "Slavery had nothing to do with it !" The board found slavery among the Indians in 1817, accepted it as of divine appointment, and compelled its missionaries to accept it, and they did ; as did the churches and pulpits that sustained them, When the anti-slavery agitation reached to the churches, and protests were sent up against a slave-holding religion, supported at home, and sent abroad to the heathen, the Board refused to interfere. And once when the Sandwich Island missionaries sent home a most powerful remonstrance against slave-holding in the churches as a hindrance to their missionary work as well as false to the true christian faith, the Board *suppressed their testimony*, and by solemn resolution duly adopted, recorded and published, virtually imposed silence on the subject, at every missionary station under its patronage. When the interest on the subject began to threaten loss to the treasury, then the Board by its Secretaries attempted, by argument to justify slavery as supported by scripture ; by patriarchal practice and apostolic approval, the very chiefest apostle actually, as was claimed, voluntarily restoring a runaway slave to his owner. From 1817 to 1860, more than forty years, did the Board conduct the religious and moral education of those Indian tribes, gathering them into churches : masters and slaves alike, with this law in full force :

No slave, or child of a slave, is to be taught to read or write, in or at any school, by any one connected in any capacity therewith, on pain of dismissal and expulsion from the nation.

And now one thought more, and the Board and all its work shall be discharged from further consideration.

In 1860 the Cherokees, and in 1859 the Choctaws, were graduated by the Board from paganism to christianity with full credentials, as no longer in the darkness of the heathen world. In 1861, the war of Rebellion set the country on fire. The Indian tribes were early awake to the situation. The New York *Evangelist*, on the 21st of March of the same year, 1861, said ; "the Cherokee, Choctaw, and other Indian tribes of the south-west, nearly all of them slave-holders, are evidently under the influence of the secessionists. The principal Choctaw chief hastened to convene the local legislature   *   *   *   and recommended a general council of the Chickasaws, Creeks, Seminoles and Choctaws to be held at a central point for the purpose of adopting some line of policy necessary to their security.

In August following, the New York *Journal of Commerce* announced that : " The Choctaws, Creeks, Seminoles and Chickasaws have given their adherence to the Confederates, and probably the Cherokees are divided on the question."

Of the rest, we know enough. How well and truly was it said at the opening of the war of Rebellion, "in the forty-two years of the maintenance of the Cherokee and Choctaw missions, by the American Board, they have *connived* at slavery, avoiding, by various dishonorable and dishonest means and contrivances, the hard duty of reformation. Now they go a step further, spontaneously and publicly vouching for slaveholding churches as *christian* churches, and for a nation upholding the worst form of slavery, as "*a christian people.*"

And between four and five thousand armed Indian warriors, led by an able Boston-born general, the tallest, handsomest officer in the rebel army, at the battle of Pea Ridge, fighting in a war waged by slaveholders and waged wholly for slavery, and nothing else, was a spectacle worthy the American Board of Commissioners for Foreign Missions !

THE BAPTIST CHURCH.

Or if we turn to the Baptist denomination with its vast proportion in the slave states, the record will not improve ; and in that again we can learn its spirit and position through its great national Foreign Missionary Association known in early anti-slavery days as *The Baptist Triennial Convention.* The harmony in it seems never to have been disturbed by the slavery problem till broken by the tocsin of the abolitionists. For so late as the year 1834, Rev. Dr. Bolles, of Boston, one of its Secretaries of correspondence in an official paper, said :

There is a pleasing degree of union among the multiplying thousands of Baptists throughout the land.
* * * Our southern brethren are generally slave-holders, both ministers and people. .

And another Boston Baptist doctor of divinity, Rev. Daniel Sharp, wrote under date January 21st, 1840 : "There were undoubtedly both slave-holders and slaves in the primitive churches ; I therefore for one, do not feel myself at liberty to make conditions of communion which neither Christ nor his apostles made.   I do not feel myself wiser nor better than were they ;   *   *   *   and I believe that a majority of the wisest and best men at the north hold to these sentiments."

In 1841, at the Triennial convention and by appointment, a slave-holder presided, another slave-holder performed the devotional exercises, and a third slave-holder preached the Triennial sermon ; and the Rev. Elon Galusha, of New York, an earnest, outspoken anti-slavery man, was removed from the Board of Management, partly, or principally, from demands like this of the Camden, South Carolina Baptist church :

Resolved,   That we view with contempt, the advice, opinions, menaces and declarations of Elon Galusha and his coadjuutors contained in their address to southern Baptists.

Resolved, That we recommend to our associations to use their influence to have Elon Galusha expelled from his office as Vice-President of the Board of Foreign Missions.

The fifth, sixth and seventh, ran thus :

Resolved,   That we extend to northern Baptists who are opposed to the abolitionists, our warmest affection and fraternal regard.   They will ever have an interest in our prayers.

Resolved,   That the address of Elon Galusha be returned to him, with request that he will never again insult us with an address of any kind.

Resolved,   That these proceedings be published in the *Christian Index, The Biblical Recorder, Religious Herald, New York Baptist Advocate, and Camden Journal.*

C. M. BLEEKER, *Chairman,*
E. G. ROBINSON, *Secretary.*

And as already told, Mr. Galusha was removed. All the proceedings appeared to have been in keeping with such expulsion ; for the meeting closed with the sacramental supper and singing :

> Lo, what an entertaining sight
> Are brethren who agree !

A member writing to the *Biblical Recorder and Southern Watchman*, thus rejoices :

Our meeting was truly delightful. The spirit of the gospel prevailed, and gave a tremendous shock to the abolitionists. Let us be thankful to God, and give him the glory. And now, if we of the south and they of the north, whose sympathies are with us, shall be mild I am satisfied that abolitionism will go down among Baptists. All our " principal men" are sound to the core on this *vexed question*.

The Triennial Convention exhibited a noble spectacle of moral grandeur. About two hundred and fifty men from the various parts of our extended country were engaged in a long and arduous session, that tried the temper and put into requisition all the intellectual energy which they possessed. And all this in connection with a most exciting subject. And yet, self-possession, calmness, the christian spirit, predominated throughout the whole scene. No tumult, no angry feeling, no harsh expression had place in our deliberations and conclusions. At the communion board on Lord's day the scene was overwhelming. In view of the *cross* the hundreds that participated were all *one*. No test, other than that of our dear Lord's requirement, was thought of. To God be all the glory, Amen and Amen.

But such dissatisfaction arose among the *now* " principal men" in the convention that before the next Triennial gathering a division occurred. A new but small rival society was formed. One principal reason assigned being that gifts of slave-holders should not mingle with northern contributions in the missionary treasury, since God had said " I hate robbery for a burnt offering."

But the extent of principle and height of integrity of this new and sublimated movement, was seen in the fact, that when, just afterwards, the old board sustained a loss by a failure in India, there was an immediate appropriation of five hundred dollars voted to it, with all its slavery, out of this purified treasury. The following is the official record of the proceeding :

Whereas, The Foreign Mission Board have recently sustained a heavy loss, by the failure of their banker at Calcutta, and thus appropriated supplies are cut off from the missionaries in Asia ; therefore

Resolved, That the treasurer of this committee be instructed to forward, as soon as possible, five hundred dollars from funds now in the treasury, to the relief of the missionaries, "to be expended under the direction of Dr. Judson and Mr. Vinton."

[Signed]   S. G. SHIPLEY, *Chairman.*
C. W. DENISON, *Secretary.*

The new association seems to have been short lived, for at the next meeting of the old board, all parties, old and new were present, and the proceedings were as unanimous almost as before slavery had ever disturbed them. The president, a North Carolina slaveholder, declined a reëlection, on the ground that, as for more than thirty years the chief officer had been selected from the slaves states, it was time the boon should be conferred on the north. Accordingly, the Rev. Dr. Wayland, of Providence, on the second ballotting, was elected to that office.

The subject of Slavery was introduced and disposed of by the passage of the following resolution, ONLY TWO voting in the negative :

Resolved, That coöperating together as members of this convention in the work of foreign missions, we disclaim all sanction, either express or implied, *of slavery or anti-slavery*; but as individuals we are free to express and promote our view on this or other subjects, in a christian manner and spirit.

Rev. Mr. Davis, of New York, [neighbor of Elon Galusha] then remarked with much exultation, if not *exaltation*, that the convention had passed *a stupendous crisis*, and moved a season of devotional exercises. The season was voted, a northern minister, Mr. Webb, of Philadelphia, gave thanks, and they closed with singing the Doxology, by the congregation,

" Praise God, from whom all blessings flow."

In view of the passage of the above resolution, the editor of the *Boston Christian Reflector*, a professedly anti-slavery journal, most complacently remarked :

" It will be seen by the passage of the resolution on Friday, that we are no longer required to fellowship slavery or slave-holders, as such, in the work of missions."

But had the business related to *infant sprinkling* instead of infant stealing, or on *immersion* as baptism, instead of *sprinkling*, the whole past history of this immense denomination throughout christendom proves it would never have been so easily nor so amicably adjusted.   In 1846, a new association was incorporated under the name of "The American Baptist Missionary Union," and the old *triennial* was no more. The first article of the new constitution designates the name, the second the object of the society.   The third provides that *"persons," without reference to place*, " may be life members, by the payment at one time of not less than one hundred dollars."   The twenty-first article declares that the officers and missionaries of the association " *shall be members in good standing of regular Baptist churches."*   No north nor south any more.

It has been contended that this association was formed with particular reference to a separation from slavery.   I was so informed *by an officer of the board.*

But there was no such intimation, either in the act of incorporation or the constitution. Among the life members were persons from Missouri, Mississippi, Delaware, and Georgia; and the first meeting of the board of managers was organized by the choice of a president from a free, and a secretary from a slave state. The first meeting of the union was opened with prayer by the Rev. Nathaniel Colver, of Boston. All these proceedings, and others, are appended to the annual report of the old Baptist convention for 1846.

But enough about the mission movements as between south and north, or between slavery and anti-slavery. The Baptist denomination, like the others, had hosts of anti-slavery men and women; but the *ruling power* was for slavery, or the system could not have survived as it did, till stove down by the avenging bolts of eternal wrath.

METHODIST EPISCOPAL CHURCH.

Coming now to the mighty Methodist denomination it would be a relief and joy if a far better record could be given. But to write history, not make it, is the work still in hand.

Two copies of the Methodist Book of Discipline are before me, of different dates, but both contain an address "To the Members of the Methodist Episcopal Church," signed by the bishops, in which it is declared: "We wish to see this little publication in the house of every Methodist. And the more so, as it contains the articles of religion, maintained more or less, in part, or in whole, by every reformed church in the world. Far from wishing you to be ignorant of any of our doctrines, or any part of our discipline, we wish you to read, mark, learn, and inwardly digest the whole. You ought, next to the word of God, to procure the articles and canons of the church to which you belong." One chapter of the discipline is entitled : " General Rules and Reception of Members." On one page this is found :

There is only one condition previously required of those who desire admission into these societies ; a desire to flee from the wrath to come and to be saved from their sins.

But wherever this is really fixed in the soul it will be shown by its fruits. It is, therefore, expected of all who continue therein that they should continue to evidence their desire for salvation ;

First, by doing no harm, by avoiding evil of every kind, especially that which is most generally practiced ; the taking of the name of God in vain ; the profaning the day of the Lord ; drunkenness ; buying or selling spirituous liquors, or drinking them, unless in cases of extreme necessity.

And then the next, for some reason, to this writer inexplicable, is printed in italics, and reads thus :

The buying and selling of men, women and children with an intention to enslave them.

There are many more of these requirements of larger or less importance, and then the section closes thus :

If there be any among us who observe not these rules, who habitually break any of them, let it be known unto them who watch over that soul, as they who must give account. We will admonish him of the error of his ways. We will bear with him for a season. But if then he repent not, he hath no more place among us. We have delivered our own souls.

So much for text. Now for commentary. In less than half a century from the enactment of that magnificent rule and testimony against slavery, against " the buying and selling of men, women and children, with intention to enslave them," printed in the discipline in italics, from the first, the slaves of Methodist, ministers, elders and deacons holding them with the rest, numbered tens of thousands, and those numbers rapidly increasing in every slave state. And before the Garrisonian anti-slavery agitation was seven years old that stupendous organization in general conference, convened at Cincinnati, Ohio, anno domini 1836, by vote of a hundred and twenty to only fourteen, solemnly resolved that they "are decidedly opposed to modern aboliitionism, and wholly disclaim any right, wish, or intention, to interfere in the civil and political relation between master and slave, as it exists in the slave-holding states of this Union."

He is a close student of history who can parallel in brazen audacity and effrontery such action as this. By vote of a hundred and twenty to fourteen, on motion of Rev. A. J. Few, D. D., of Georgia, the conference solemnly declared they had "*no wish nor intention*" to fulfil what they have so often declared to the world was a most important part of their covenant vows.

One of the rules specified in the section of rules and requirements reads :

"By doing good, especially to them that are of the household of faith, employing them preferably to others, helping each other in business, and so much the more because the world will love its own, and them only." Now observe how this rule was respected. In southern and some northern states, colored people were never allowed to testify in any court against any white person in any case. Any outrage on any colored woman or man could be perpetrated by any white ruffian with perfect impunity, were none but colored witnesses at hand. And scenes and instances of shocking cruelty went often unpunished on that account.

And now·behold the Methodist General Conference wrestling with a problem like that. There were at that moment more than eighty thousand colored Methodist communicants, and Ohio and several other non-slave-holding states enacted them all as unfit to give testimony under oath in any court of justice within their jurisdiction. They might do for Methodist churches, might even be fit for heaven, but they were not worthy to be trusted under oath to speak the truth.

Now, what was to be done ? The conference was equal to the occasion. In 1840, in general conference assembled, this resolution was adopted, and become Methodist law :

Resolved, That it is inexpedient and unjustifiable *for any preacher to permit colored persons* to give testimony against white persons, in any state where they are denied that privilege by law.

So ran Methodist brotherly " preference " toward their " own household of faith," as required by the "rules of admission to fellowship." The state pronounced colored testimony ùnfit for courts of civil law and justice against white offenders, no matter what the crime. And the Methodist General Conference, in 1840, sanctified the impious proscription by extending it over their own church trials, as well.

Thus they unblushingly confessed to man and God that they had in fellowship over eighty thousand members, redeemed by sacrificial blood, enrolled in the " Lamb's Book of Life," as they believed when they baptised and received them ; eighty thousand fit to shine and reign for ever and ever in heaven, and yet not worthy to testify any more in an ecclesiastical court held before their own sacramental altar, than at any civil tribunal ! While the veriest blasphemer, the

vilest profligate who ever scoffed at the mention of
religion, if covered with a white skin, even though
purpled with drunkenness and debauchery, might be
legal and competent testimony in both, to any extent,
whatever the crime.   In view of a proceeding so monstrous, an eloquent writer of the time thus justly per-
tinently said :

By this rule, which is now a part of the discipline of
the church, eighty thousand of its colored members
are denied the right to testify against a *white* brother
or sister in any case whatsoever.   No matter what the
crime may be, or how aggravating the circumstances.
The reverend mover of the resolution might now violate the chastity of the colored members of his church
with entire impunity.   He is no longer in any danger
of being censured and silenced by his more fortunate
brethren, as was a late Massachusetts doctor of
divinity.   Should he unfortunately be " overtaken in
a fault," the church has "provided a way of escape."
And an ample provision it is, even for the *chiefest* of
sinners.   Neither the reverend doctor, nor any of his
coadjutors, could desire greater liberty—or *privilege*,
as they might term it.   The lips of their victim and
her friends are now hermetically sealed up, both in
the church and in the civil tribunals !

Dr. Adam Clarke, the eminent Methodist scripture
commentator, says, on Ephesians vi, fifth :   " In
heathen countries slavery had some sort of excuse.
Among christians it is a crime for which perdition has
scarce adequate punishment."   But Dr. Adam Clarke
had hever heard nor read of slavery in heathen countries more horrible than the slavery thus supported,
sanctioned and sanctified in the Methodist church !
What would he have said to this resolution of Dr.
Few ? Thrilling protests were offered against it in
the conference but to no purpose.   One of them contained words like these :

The adoption of such a resolution has inflicted, as we fear, an irreparable injury upon eighty thousand souls, for whom Christ died. Souls, who by this act of your body, have been stripped of the dignity of christians, degraded in the scale of humanity and treated as criminals, for no other reason than the color of their skin !

The protest, which was wholly in the tone of these pathetic words, was, as Judge Birney shows, " handed to the bishops, but was never read to the conference."

Why need it have been even handed to the bishops ? One had already declared, *ex-cathedra*, " The right to hold slaves is founded on this rule ; all things whatsoever ye would that men should do unto you, do ye even so unto them." That was Bishop Hedding, whose home was in Lynn, Massachusetts.

And the " pastoral letter " of the general conference of 1836, closed its solemn exhortation on the whole question of slavery in a strain like this :

From every view which we have been able to take, and from the most calm and dispassionate survey of the whole ground, we have come to the conclusion that the only safe, scriptural and prudent way for us, both as ministers and people, to take is, wholly to refrain from this agitating subject.

And Bishop Soule had declared, " I have never yet advised the liberation of a slave, and I think I never shall."

Rev. Wilbur Fisk, D. D., President of the Wesleyan University in Connecticut, declared : "the relation of master and slave may, and does, in many cases exist under such circumstances as frees the master from the just charge and guilt of immorality. * * * The New Testament enjoins obedience upon the slave *as an obligation due* to a present *rightful* authority."

And Moses Stuart, of Andover Theological Seminary, had published a tract, to prove that slavery was not in itself an evil ; and had said in so many words, "slavery may exist without any violation of the christian faith." ⁕ And it was in view of American slavery that he wrote. And Dr. Fisk endorsed Stuart thus : " This doctrine of Professor Stuart will stand, because it is Bible doctrine."

But the *impertinent* and persistent meddling of some ministers and many of the laity of the Methodist body, in time had its disastrous effect ; and in the year 1843, a sufficient number of individual ministers and separate churches had withdrawn from conference jurisdiction, to warrant a new Methodist organization. So in May, 1843, a convention was held in Utica, New York, and inaugurated *The Wesleyan Methodist Connection of America*. This mightily increased the agitation in the parent body. It was now certain that something decisive must be done, that had not yet even been contemplated. The next year, 1844, the general conference met in New York, where it was shown, to the terror of the most pro-slavery, that one of the bishops had, by recent marriage, become a slave-holder ! An agony of strife was wakened which lasted day after day. In the hope of appeasing the opponents of slavery, the Baltimore annual conference voted with them on a *censure* ; but not *expulsion* from church nor office. The censure was only to the extent that "Bishop Andrew be requested to suspend the exercise of the duties of his office, while his impediment should exist, but that his name may stand in the hymn book and book of discipline, and his salary be continued, just as in the past !"

Our travelling agents were constantly disputed by Methodists as to the conference action on Bishop Andrew as a slave-holder. I myself had meetings broken up by mobs, for the sole offense of speaking the truth, and only the truth, on that most remarkable proceeding in the Methodist general conference. After one of these riotous demonstrations, I published in the *Liberator* of January 28, 1848, the following letter, which readers must pardon me for producing here :

DEAR FRIEND GARRISON—A short time since, as I was addressing a large assembly on the connexion of the Methodist church with slavery, a minister of that denomination rose up and charged me with bearing false witness, and added, with much earnestness, that *the church had even deposed one of its bishops, only for marrying a lady who held slaves.* A similar declaration has been often made, and I find the church generally believes it. It may be that the ministers know no better ; though it is a defense of their hearts at great cost to their heads to suppose it.

I have before me the official proceedings relative to Bishop Andrew, in the general conference of 1844, and will give a few very brief extracts. They were published by the church at the conference office in New York.

After the subject had been many days under discussion, and no prospect of an adjournment had appeared, the four bishops, beside Andrew, issued an address to the conference, in which they say, (page 185)—

At this painful crisis, we have unanimously concurred in the propriety of recommending the postponement of further action in the case of Bishop Andrew, until the ensuing conference.

It was not done, however, and the discussion proceeded. At length, the following resolution was passed, as the sense of the conference, (pp 191–2)—

Whereas, the discipline of our church forbids the doing of any thing, calculated to destroy our itinerant general superintendency; and whereas, Bishop Andrew has become connected with slavery, by marriage and otherwise, and this act having drawn after it circumstances, which, in the estimation of the general conference, will greatly embarrass the exercise of his office as an itinerant general superintendent, if not in some places entirely prevent it ; therefore,

Resolved, That it is the sense of this general conference, that he desist from the exercise of this office, so long as this impediment remains !

The yeas and nays were taken, and the resolution was adopted, 111 to 69.

After some further discussion, the bishops issued another address to the conference, proposing the three following questions—p. 214 of records :

First—Shall Bishop Andrew's name remain, as it now stands in the minutes, hymn-book and discipline, or shall it be struck off of those official records?

Second—How shall the bishop obtain his support ? As provided for in the discipline, or in some other way ?

Third—What work, if any, may the bishop perform? and how shall he be appointed to that work ?

It was moved to refer the question to a committee of three, but the motion was afterwards withdrawn.

The following, from page 216 of the Record of Proceedings, tells the rest :

Mr. Mitchell proposed the following resolutions, in reply to the inquiries of the bishops :

Resolved, First, as the sense of this conference, that Bishop Andrew's name stand in the minutes, hymn-book and discipline, as formerly.

Resolved, Second, that the rule in relation to the support of a bishop and his family, applies to Bishop Andrew.

Resolved, Third, that whether any, and in what work Bishop Andrew be employed, is to be determined by his own decision and action, in relation to the previous action of this conference in his case.

*   *   *   *   *   *

The ayes and noes were called on the first resolution. For it, 154 ; against it, 18 For the second resolution, ayes 141, noes 14.

Dr. Winans said he should go against the third resolution. The discipline of the church knew no discretion in an officer of recognized standing, to withdraw himself from the duties of his office. By the two votes just passed, it was clear and unequivocal, that Bishop Andrew had an unquestioned standing as a bishop of the M. E. church, by a vote of a large majority of that church, and the provisions of the discipline; and he congratulated the south on the fact that they had now a recognized slave-holding bishop, whose name appeared on all their records, after being known as a slave-holder, and that Bishop A. has no right to elect, whether he would serve, or in what way he would serve.

Mr. Cartwright thought his brother Winans shouted before he was happy.

Mr. Winans—I was happy.

Dr. Cartwright—Yes; but the brother was only happy in the false fires of his own warm imagination.

The ayes and noes were then taken on the third resolution. Several asked to be excused, some retired; and the result of the vote was, ayes 103, noes 67.

Such, then, was the expulsion of Bishop Andrew. A subsequent report of the conference, adopted by a vote of 116 to 26, declares on page 232:

The action of the general conference was neither judicial nor punitive. *It neither achieves nor intends a deposition—nor so much as a legal suspension!* Bishop Andrew is still a bishop; and should he, against the expressed sense of the general conference, proceed to the discharge of his functions, *his official act would be valid!*

And yet the Methodist clergy tell the people, and make them believe it, and have often done it in my meetings, that Bishop Andrew was expelled as a bishop, for the crime of owning slaves.

Yours, to expose such lies and hypocrisy,

PARKER PILLSBURY.

Slavery was sometimes called "the peculiar institution;" the "patriarchal institution." An old cotton

king, of Boston, visiting the south, talked softly to
slave-holders about their "unenlightened labor."
But it remained for the general conference of the
Methodist-Episcopal church to refine on that, putting
it in one single word, and that a less offensive word,
than *labor* and *unenlightened* labor, too.   Slave-holding
in Bishop Andrew was but an *impediment!* and not
serious, at that, as it neither deprived him of the honors, nor emoluments of his office ; only relieved him
from its labors and responsibilities.

But the southern Methodists were no more happy
than before.   Nothing short of the terrible penalty
inflicted on Bishop Andrew, would placate the north,
and that with the south seemed only to complicate
matters more and more.   Division,   disruption,
threatened—last year, six or seven thousand church
members and nearly a hundred ministers, had seceded
and formed the Weslyan Connection of America, all
in the good name of anti-slavery.   So that was never
part of the general conference.   It was now the slave-
holder's turn.   Nor did they hesitate.   The south seceded, and from that day (1844), onward to and
through the war of the rebellion, there were both a
southern and northern general conference.

But the new Utica movement found no place in
either, neither desired it.   And so there seemed more
need of it than ever.   And yet, from the day of the
separation, many in the northern conference, ministers and people, proudly plumed themselves as a
strictly anti-slavery church, that had shaken off the
pollutions of slavery.

But two stern denials must ·be made of any such
virtue.   The northern conference never left the southern, still less excommunicated it.   The south abandoned the north in part, only in part, for the sake of

peace, not the north for the sake of purity. But both were disappointed. The south found no peace, the north surely purchased no purity, as most stubborn facts more than prove. This history is only written, not made ; and the testimony is all furnished by the parties most concerned themselves.

The following extract from the proceedings of the first meeting of the southern general conference, shows how far there had been any change of heart on either side, as concerning the sin which John Wesley had designated as "the sum of all villainies," and Dr. Clark had declared, "Perdition had scarcely adequate punishment," for such as logically proved themselves the sum of all villains. But here is the extract :

After the formal adjournment on Monday, Bishop Soule requested the members to tarry a few minutes, Dr. Winans then read an expression of his feelings and that of many of his brethren, who had passed through the bounds of a portion of the "northern church," for the very kind and affectionate treatment they had received from their northern brethren on their way to this city. It expresses the hope that, although a separation has taken place, whenever a southern brother, in the providence of God, shall be called to visit a northern city, or place, where there is a Methodist pulpit. he may find it open to his ministry, and assuring the northern brethren that the like christian courtesy shall be always extended to them. The document was unanimously adopted and ordered to be signed by a committee of the conference.

And why should it not be ? for the very next year but one, we find one of the largest annual conferences, the Baltimore, of the north, adopting this resolution :

Resolved, That this conference disclaims having any fellowship with abolitionism. On the contrary, while it is determined to maintain its well-known and long-established position, by keeping the traveling preachers composing its own body, free from slavery, it is also

determined not to hold connection with any ecclesiastical body that shall make non-slaveholding a condition of membership in the church ; but to stand by
and maintain the discipline as it is.

And now for the one overpowering fact of all ; a
fact which for years after the separation of 1844, convicted multitudes of Methodists, ministers with the
rest, of an ignorance the most remarkable, or hypocrisy and falsehood the most fearful ever known in all
the annals of human weakness or wickedness.

*Not only did not the northern hemisphere of the con-
ference sunder itself from the southern to rid itself of
the sin and guilt of slavery, but instead, when the south
withdrew, the north contrived to retain seven or eight
Annual conferences whose territory was mainly or wholly
in the slave states in which dwelt four thousand Methodist slave-holders, owning more than twenty-five thousand
slaves !*

And that was a body to set itself before men,
angels and God as an anti-slavery church.   Everywhere, in New England and New York, as well as at the
west, the anti-slavery agents encountered that
astounding boast and pretension among the Methodists, both ministers and people.

I could not myself believe, till I went to the Methodist book concern in Boston, and purchased the
book of discipline, now on my desk, and read the
boundaries of those annual conferences, with my own
eyes.   "Border territory" it is called in the official
records of that time, but it included Delaware, most,
or all of Maryland and Virginia, the whole of Kentucky, Missouri, Arkansas and Texas.

To the resolution of the Baltimore conference just
cited to show what northern conference anti-slavery
was worth as testimony against slave-holding sin,

shame and crime, let this be added, and the argument shall close : the extracts are from the "Address of the Philadelphia annual conference, to the societies under its care, within the bounds of the Northampton and Accomac circuits."

Whereas, the discipline says, "Virginia conference shall be bounded on the east by Chesapeak Bay and the Atlantic Ocean ; " and "Philadelphia conference shall include the eastern shore of Maryland and Virginia"—the Chesapeake Bay, an arm of the ocean being between them ; therefore, Resolved, that in our administration, we will regard the "eastern shore of Maryland and Virginia" as not being "border" work in the sense of the "plan of separation."

We cannot, therefore, but regard all the Methodist societies within the peninsula, as under our pastoral jurisdiction, according to the provisions of the plan of separation.

If the plan of separation gives us the pastoral care of you, it remains to inquire whether we have done anything as a conference, or as men, to forfeit your confidence and affection. We are not advised that even in the great excitement which has distressed you for some months past, any one has impeached our moral conduct, or charged us with unsoundness in doctrine, or corruption, or tyranny in the administration of discipline. But we learn that the simple cause of the unhappy excitement among you is, that some suspect us, or affect to suspect us, of being abolitionists. Yet, no particular act of the conference, or any particular member thereof, is adduced, as the ground of the erroneous and injurious suspicion. We would ask you, brethren, whether the conduct of our ministry among you for sixty years past, ought not to be sufficient to protect us from this charge ? Whether the question we have been accustomed for a few years past, to put to candidates for admission among us, namely, *are you an abolitionist?* and without each one answered in the negative, he was not received, ought not to protect us from the charge. Whether the action of the last conference on this particular matter, ought not to satisfy any fair and candid mind that we are not, and do not desire to be, abolitionists.   *   * * * We cannot see how we can be regarded as abolitionists without the ministers of the Methodist Episcopal church south, being considered in the same light.   *   *   *

Wishing you all heavenly benedictions, we are, dear brethren, yours, in Christ Jesus,

J. P. DURBIN,
J. KENNADAY,
IGNATIUS T. COOPER,
WILLIAM H. GILDER,
JOSEPH CASTLE,
Committee.

Wilmington, Del., April 7, 1847.

Such was American Methodism in 1836, and onward to 1847, and the Philadelphia conference of that year. Such was Methodism as held, represented, inculcated by the bishops, elders, and rulers in the high places of power in that immense spiritual dominion, alike in the northern and the southern states.

But such was not Methodism in the day, nor in the mouth of John Wesley.

On February twelfth, 1772, he wrote in his Journal : I read a book of an honest Quaker on *that execrable sum of all villanies,* called the slave trade ; I read nothing like it in the heathen world, whether ancient or modern ; it infinitely exceeds in every instance of barbarity, whatever christian slaves suffer in Mohamedan countries."

And a word more from the same hand, shall close this too extended chapter on Methodism and slavery. He wrote : "What I have said to slave-traders, *equally concerns all slave-holders, of whatever degree or rank.* The blood of your brother crieth against you from the earth. O, whatever it costs, put a stop to that cry ! Your hands, beds, houses, lands, furniture, are stained with blood.   Surely it is enough !

THE PROTESTANT EPISCOPAL CHURCH.

The anti-slavery character of this denomination is pretty clearly set forth in a pamphlet, entitled, "Thoughts on the duty of the Episcopal church in relation to slavery," by the late William Jay, one of its most illustrious members :

Alas ! for the expectation that she would conform to the spirit of her ancient mother. She has not only remained a mute and careless spectator of this great conflict of truth and justice with hypocrisy and cruelty, but her very priests and deacons may be seen ministering at the altar of slavery ! Offering their talents and influence at its unholy shrine, and openly repeating the awful blasphemy that the precepts of our Savior sanction the system of American slavery ! Her northern, free-state clergy, with rare exceptions, whatever they may feel on the subject, rebuke it neither in public nor in private. And her periodicals, far from advancing the progress of abolitionism, at times oppose our societies ; impliedly defending slavery, as not incompatible with christianity, and, occasionally withholding information useful to the cause of freedom.

As why should they not, or, rather, it might be asked, how could they have done otherwise ? pulpit, or press, with instructions like the following, issued by the oldest bishop in the United States, for their instruction and guidance, though directed, as will be seen, to a far more august dignitary than the bishop himself :

JUBILEE COLLEGE, ILLINOIS, N. A., ⎱
August 1, A. D. 1846.   ⎰

To the Right Rev. Samuel, Lord Bishop of Oxford, England :

VERY DEAR BROTHER IN THE LORD JESUS—Allow me, the oldest bishop of the "Protestant Episcopal church" in the United States, to address your lordship on the subject of a pamphlet, entitled "A Reproof of the American Church," which "reproof" is said to be contained in copious "extracts" from your lordship's lately published history of said church.

Never having read this work from which the said "reproof" is drawn, yet from many years' acquaintance with your lordship's excellent character, I can say, with full confidence, that the *acerbity* which is spread over the pages of this pamphlet cannot be approved by your lordship.   *   *   *

In the deepest sorrow of heart do I lament the melancholy effects produced by the circumstances before me. Alas! what do I see? The bishops and clergy of America censured for that of which they are not guilty, and of which they are not the cause, and those who censure them evidently unconscious both of the evils which their mistaken censure produces, and of the extent of the evils which must follow from the weight of their character and opinion.

Before I proceed, I beg leave to state, that, in endeavoring, by my feeble means, to shield the Protestant Episcopal church in the United States, I crave to be understood as not assuming political ground. The Episcopal church in America did in no wise originate slavery. She always, in connection with other benevolent persons of the day, raised her voice against its introduction into the then British colonies. Nor is she now, in any competent sense, a part of the civil government to cure its temporal evils. Her bishops are not, as the English prelates are, admitted to a seat in the halls of legislation, nor are they allowed to "rise in their places" to plead the cause of humanity. All she can do is by her prayers and the preaching of the gospel, and teaching the blessed doctrines of christianity, to endeavor to ameliorate the condition of the slave; but, like the primitive christians, amidst the evils that surround her, she does not think herself called upon to eradicate at once the evil. She rather finds herself commanded, as were the servants in the gospel, to exercise caution, "lest in eradicating the tares, they root out the wheat also." Let both grow together, saith our Lord. Let the *evil* be borne for the sake of the *good* that may be done to the souls of the poor slaves.

The tenor of these remarks falls in with the example of St. Paul. The gospel through his mouth and the power of the divine Spirit had converted the noble Philemon from the slavery of sin to the freedom of the Son of God. This Philemon's "*runaway slave*" enjoyed the same benefit at the hands of the same apostle, some time after, while a prisoner in the city of Rome. His name was *Onesimus*, and while ministering to the necessities of the holy apostle, he heard the word of God, and like his master, believed. It now becomes a matter of great importance, in relation to the subject of this letter, to know what directions the apostle gave to the converted slave of Philemon, when he sent him back to his master. Was it that he was a freeman in the temporal sense, and must maintain his rights as a part of "a whole gospel," Was it that as a freeman he was to go back and claim the privileges and immunities of this his temporal freedom, as it is now understood by the abolitionists? Was it that henceforth he was to consider himself as having a right to propogate his sentiments and "preach the whole gospel? That is to say that he had a right to creep into his former master's kitchen and fill the heads of all the bond servants with the ideas of their temporal rights according to this creed, thereby exciting them to rebellion, and if resisted, (and resisted they certainly would be) to murder their kind master and take possession of his estate.

Far, very far, from so wicked an estimate of the holy religion unto the blessings and privileges of which the apostle had admitted him, this now converted servant of the pious Philemon, that he sent the former immediately back to serve the latter as heretofore. Not a word of *abolitionism* was uttered in the presence of *Onesimus*, or intimated by the apostle. He entreats Philemon to receive his servant back again as a brother beloved of Christ, though still a servant, and as such, if required, engages to pay the losses he had occasioned his master by his leaving him. "If he hath wronged thee aught, put that to my account, I Paul have written it with my own hand, I will repay it." How different this from the language of modern abolitionism. Yet this, my Lord, is a part of our Holy Bible.

Hence it is clearly to be inferred that the relations of political society are to continue, be they what they may, notwithstanding the most intimate ties of christian fellowship.

Here is another singularly illustrative act, furnished, too, as is all the testimony introduced by the church herself. In 1836, Rev. George W. Freeman delivered two sermons in Raleigh, North Carolina, that were published under the imposing title of "The Rights and Duties of Slave-holders," with the following imprimatur from Bishop Ives, of the diocese:

RALEIGH, NOV. 30, 1836.

REV. AND DEAR BROTHER—I listened with most unfeigned pleasure to the discourses delivered last Sunday, on the character ot slavery and the duties of masters And as I learn a publication of them is solicited, I beg, from a conviction of their being urgently called for at the present time, that you will not withhold your consent.

Your affectionate friend and brother in the Lord,

L. S. IVES.

In South Carolina, the "Society for the Advancement of Christianity," made up of clergymen and laymen, the bishop at the head of it, seized upon the sermons, imprimatur and all, and published them as religious tracts, for gratuitous distribution.

An extract from the sermons read thus :   "No man, or set of men in our day, unless they can produce a new revelation from heaven, are entitled to prouounce slavery wrong. *   *   Slavery, as its exists at the present day, is agreeable to the order of Divine Providence."

And now one more witness, perhaps most valuable of all, and a late bishop, too.   On my table is a work with this imposing title :

Sermons addressed to masters and servants, and published in the year 1743, by Rev. Thomas Bacon, minister.

of the Protestant Episcopal Church in Maryland, now republished with other tracts and dialogues on the same subject, and recommended to all masters and mistresses to be used in their families. By the Reverend William Meade. Winchester, Virginia. John Heiskell, printer.

In his preface, Bishop Meade remarks : "The editor of this volume offers it to all masters and mistresses in our southern states, with the anxious wish and devout prayer that it may prove a blessing to themselves and their households. He considers himself most happy in having met with the several pieces which compose it, and could not with a quiet conscience refrain from affording to others the opportunity of profiting thereby."

The title of this work shows its miscellaneous character. The sermons are in two series, the first, doubtless, by Mr. Bacon published in 1743. Then succeed two others, author not named, but presumably by Bishop Meade himself, and always so assigned while he lived. And from them the following excerpts are taken. He first shows that God appointed, for great and wonderful ends, several offices and degrees in his family, making some masters and mistresses, some kings and rules, some merchants and sea-faring men, some tradesmen, husbandmen and planters and laboring men to work for their own living, and some He hath made *servants and slaves* to assist and work for their masters and mistresses who provide for them. And as God hath sent each of us into the world for some or other of these purposes, we are all obliged, from the king to the poorest slave, to do the business He hath set us about. And while you whom He hath made slaves are honestly and quietly doing your business and living as poor christians ought to live, you are serving God in your low station as much as the greatest prince alive.

With more in the same strain, but not one duty
specified, not one grace, not one emotion nor aspiration
that rises above, or relates to any power or person,
only the master and mistress and their service and
adoration, as what follows, in the recent bishop's own
words, abundantly shows:

When people die, we know of but two places they
have to go to, and one is heaven, the other hell. Now
heaven is a place of great happiness, which God hath
prepared for all that are good, where they shall enjoy
rest from their labors. And hell is a place of great
torment and misery, where all wicked people will
be shut up with the devil and other evil spirits, and be
punished forever, because they will not serve God.
If, therefore, we would have our souls saved by
Christ, if we would escape hell and obtain heaven, we
must set about doing what he requires of us, that is,
to serve God. Your own poor circumstances in this
life ought to put *you* particularly upon this, and taking
care of your souls.   *   *   Almighty God hath
been pleased to make you slaves here, and to give you
nothing but labor and poverty in this world, which
you are obliged to submit to, as it is his will that it
should be so. And think within yourselves what a
terrible thing it would be, after all your labors and
sufferings in this life, to be turned into hell in the
next life; and after wearing out your bodies in service
here, to go into a far worse slavery when this is over,
and your poor souls be delivered over into the possession of the devil, to become his slaves forever in hell,
without any hope of ever getting free from it. If,
therefore, you would be God's freemen in heaven, you
must strive to be good and serve him here on earth.
Your bodies, you know, are not your own; they are at
the disposal of those you belong to; but your precious
souls are still your own, which nothing can take from
you, if it be not your own fault. Consider well, then,
that if you lose your souls by leading idle, wicked
lives here, you have got nothing by it in this world,
and you have lost your all in the next. For your idle-
ness and wickedness are generally found out, and your

bodies suffer for it here ; and what is far worse, if you
do not repent and amend, your unhappy souls will
suffer for it hereafter.

Having thus shown you the chief duties you owe to
your great master in heaven, I now come to lay before
you the duties you owe to your masters and mistresses
here upon earth. And for this you have one general
rule, that you ought always to carry in your minds,
and that is, to *do all service for them, as if you did it for
God himself*. Poor creatures ! you little consider
when you are idle and neglectful of your master's
business, when you steal and waste, and hurt any of
their substance, when you are saucy and impudent,
when you are telling them lies and deceiving them, or
when you prove stubborn and sullen, and will not do
the work you are set about without stripes and vexation, you do not consider, I say, that what faults you
are guilty of toward your masters and mistresses, are
faults done against God himself, who hath set your
masters and mistresses over you in his own stead, and
expects that you will do for them just what you would
do for him. Pray, do not think I want to deceive you,
when I tell you that *your masters and mistresses are
God's overseers*, and that if you are faulty towards
them, God himself will punish you severely for it in
the next world, unless you repent.   *   *   You
are to be obedient and subject to your masters in all
things. And christian ministers are commanded to
exhort servants to be obedient unto their own masters
and to please them well in all things. You are to be
faithful and honest to your masters and mistresses ;
not purloining nor wasting their goods and substance,
but showing all good fidelity in all things. Do not your
masters, under God, provide for you ? And how shall
they be able to do this, to feed and to clothe you, unless you take honest care of everything that belongs
to them ? Remember, God requires this of you ; and
if you are not afraid of suffering for it in this world,
you cannot escape the vengeance of Almighty God.

Turning now to the next sermon, page 116 of the
volume, the bishop expounds, reasons, and argues to
this effect :

"*All things whatsoever ye would, that men should do unto you, do ye even so unto them;*" that is, do by all mankind just as you would desire they should do by you, if you were in their place, and they in yours.

Now, to suit this rule to your particular circumstances; suppose you were masters and mistresses, and had servants under you, would you not desire that your servants should do their business *faithfully* and *honestly*, as well when your back was turned as while you were looking over them? Would you not expect that they should take notice of what you said to them? That they should behave themselves with respect towards you and yours, and be as careful of every thing belonging to you as you would be yourselves? You are servants, do, therefore, as you would wish to be done by, and you will be both good servants to your masters, and good servants to God, who requires this of you, and will reward you well for it, if you do it for the sake of conscience, in obedience to his commands. * * * Take care that you do not fret, or murmur, or grumble at your condition; for this will not only make your life uneasy, but will greatly offend Almighty God. Consider that it is not yourselves, it is not the people you belong to, it is not the men that have brought you to it, but it is the will of God, who hath by his providence made you servants, because, no doubt he knew that condition would be best for you in this world, and help you the better towards heaven, if you would but do your duty in it. So that any discontent at your not being free, or rich, or great as you see some others, is quarreling with your heavenly Master, and finding fault with God himself. * * * There is only one circumstance which may appear grievous, that I shall now take notice of, and that is CORRECTION.

Now, when *correction* is given you, you either deserve it, or you do not deserve it. But whether you really deserve it or not, it is your duty, and Almighty God requires that you bear it patiently. You may, perhaps, think that this is hard doctrine, but if you consider it right, you must needs think otherwise of it. Suppose, then, that you deserve correction, you cannot but say that it is just and right, you should meet with it.   Suppose you do not, or at least, you do not deserve so much or so severe a correction for the fault you have committed ; you perhaps have escaped a great many more, and are at last paid for all.   Or suppose you are quite innocent of what is laid to your charge, and suffer wrongfully in that particular thing, is it not possible you may have done some other bad thing which was never discovered, and that Almighty God, who saw you doing it, would not let you escape without punishment one time or another ?   And ought you not in such a case, to give glory to Him, and be thankful that he would rather punish you in this life for your wickedness, than destroy your souls for it in the next life ?   But suppose that even this was not the case, (a case hardly to be imagined,) and that you have by no means, known or unknown, deserved the correction you suffered, there is this great comfort in it, that if you bear it patiently, and leave your cause in the hands of God, he will reward you for it in heaven, and the punishment you suffer unjustly here, shall turn to your exceeding great glory hereafter.

So much for Bishop Meade ; his whole volume is a wonderful exposition and illumination of the whole slave system, as related to, or rather sanctified by the American church, almost irrespective of denomination. Judge Birney, might have reproduced these extracts in his luminous tract on slavery and the church, and on them alone, so far as the Episcopal body is concerned, have rested his case forever.

The whole volume of Bishop Meade contains two hundred and fifty pages of solid apology for, and justification of slavery as then existing at the south, in the name of the christian religion, its Christ and God.

No other copy of it has ever come to my knowledge. For it, I was indebted to the kindness of my excellent friend, Mr. Samuel Brooke, a native Virginian himself. He was born a Friend or Quaker, one of a family of four or five brothers, all excellent men who early

removed into Ohio and became earnest, working abolitionists, eminently hospitable to anti-slavery lecturers,
both men and women ; besides being large proprietors
in the underground rail-road ; and frequently running
its *nightly* and well loaded trains, themselves.   And
my friend, Samuel Brooke, who gave me Bishop Meade,
was long an active anti-slavery agent, and for a number of years, general agent of the Western Anti-Slavery Society, and since slavery was abolished, an officer
in the revenue department of the government service.

But a word more on the Protestant Episcopal church
and its defense and reverend defenders of the terrible
slave system.   For besides Bishop Meade, another
eminent divine has left us his volume of sermons, now
on my table.   It contains twenty-six discourses, and
the title-page reads thus :   "Sermons preached on
plantations to congregations of negroes, by the Rev.
Alexander Glennie, rector of All Saints parish, Wac-
camaw, S. C., Charleston, S. C.   Published and sold
by A. E. Miller, number 4 Broad street, 1844.

In his preface, Dr. Glennie says :   "The following
sermons were written for the benefit of the colored
portion of my flock.   As the want of simple sermons,
suited to the capacity of negroes, is frequently spoken
of, I have made this selection from among those which
I have been writing for several years past, and publish them in the hope that catechisists and religious
masters may find them of use."

The fourth sermon of the twenty-six is precisely in
tone and sentiment like the quotations from Bishop
Meade.   Readers, therefore, could not be interested
in them.   Let this one exclamation suffice.   The text
is :   "With good will doing service as to the Lord
and not to men."   The first utterance is in two lines :
"In this part of the word of God, servants are taught

with what mind they should do their service." And then this exclamation : "What a blessed book the Bible is, my brethren ! "

And the law of the state at that moment, punished with twenty lashes any slave found in any assembly convened for mental instruction, held in any secret place, though in presence of white persons. And an older law, never repealed, punished with fine of a hundred pounds, any person who should teach a slave to write. In North Carolina, to teach a slave to read or to sell, or give a slave any book, Bible or tract not excepted, was thirty-nine lashes, if the offender were a free negro ; or, if a white person, a fine of two hundred dollars. The reason given for this law was stated in the preamble, and read, in part, thus : That "teaching slaves to read and write tends to excite dissatisfaction in their minds and to produce insurrection and rebellion."

More time and space have been given to the Episcopal church than was intended. Not by any means because that was more culpable than the other denominations ; but the nature of the testimony adduced, appeared to throw more and clearer light on the relation between master and slave, and between both and the church, than almost any other, making incontestably certain that in church and clerical estimation, slaves had no religious rights which white saints were bound to respect here ; nor any salvation hereafter, but such as must be worked out with "literal fear and trembling," in wholly secular service for such masters and mistresses as "God had set" to wield the lash over them. To just such, and there were then three millions of them, and a fourth million being born, could Rev. Dr. Glennie, with deep devotion, exclaim : "What a blessed book, my brethren, is the Bible ! "

But let one more Episcopal bishop come into this court of inquiry and investigation; "the Right Rev. George W. Doane, bishop of New Jersey." For there may be worse, as well as better men than Dr. Glennie and Bishop Meade, and northern men, too. In 1857, or near, there was published in Philadelphia, an edition of the Episcopal "book of common prayer," marked by the authentic *imprimatur* of Bishop Doane. At that time no works of religious art were more admired than those of Ary Scheffer, and not one of his more than his wonderful and deeply affecting "Christus Consolator." The New York *Tribune* shall tell the rest, in an article copied into the *National Anti-Slavery Standard*, of January 2d, 1858 :

All of our readers, we will venture to assume, are familiar with the engraving of Ary Scheffer's famous picture, entitled "Christus Consolator." They will remember that the Savior is seated with the emblems of his divine compassion around him, in the persons of the wretched beings whose diseases he had cured, or whose sorrows he had ministered unto. There is the mother laying her dead infant at the sacred feet, the sick man imploring the healing of the Almighty touch, the maniac just restored to reason, with his broken chain in his deliverer's grasp, the negro slave holding out his fettered hands for help and deliverance. Everybody that has seen it will recall it all. Well, the Philadelphia publishers of the prayer-book have selected this conception of Scheffer's as an appropriate ornament of its title-page. And, surely, they might have looked very far for a more fitting one ; but they thought it needed some emendation and expurgation before being put before the eyes of dainty christians in this land of churches and of cartwhips. The imploring face and the eloquent manacles of the slave might, perchance, disturb the devotions of southern saints, and even make the cotton-stuffed hassocks of many northern brethren uncomfortable to their knees. So, to remove this cause of offense out of the way, the prudent publishers, while they left all the other monuments of Christ's compassion, *most carefully expurged the negro.* Perhaps they thought it was derogatory to the divine character of Jesus to suppose him capable of sympathizing *with a nigger.* Perhaps they belong to the sect of the philosophic (and we dare say pious) John Randolph, of Kansas, who denies that negroes have souls any more than horses or oxen. More likely, their prophetic souls told them that the black face and those chained wrists would stand in the way of the mercantile transaction they were engaged in with the church. We have seen many and base concessions to slavery and pro-slavery on the part of publishers at the north, but we think that *this mutilation of an artist's ideal, to suit the prayer-book to the state of the slave-market, is rather the meanest, paltriest and dirtiest of them all !*

We would not be understood as implying that either the Episcopal church or the prelate who gave his sanction to this edition of the Book of Common Prayer is responsible for this worse than shabby trick. Whatever faults may have been attributed to Bishop Doane we believe that he was always in favor of the admission of the colored churches to equal right of representation in the conventions of the church, during the long struggles of Mr. John Jay (erroneously printed William on page 426) to effect what justice and canonical regularity alike demanded. And we believe, too, that the section of the Episcopal church usually distinguished as the high church, in this city and in Boston, and perhaps generally in the free states, set an example of christian spirit in this regard, which their dissenting opponents might well follow. In the city of Boston, we happen to know, while a prominent Baptist church *makes it a condition in the deeds of the pews that they shall be forfeited if sold to a Baptist with a colored skin,* the Church of the Advent, embracing many persons distinguished for genius, culture, refinement and wealth, not only admits black men and women to a perfect equality of sittings, but actually seeks them out to invite them to come in. And we believe the same christian spirit of equality before God prevails among the high churchmen of this city, also. This sneaking act of servility we attribute solely to the publishers, and we have told of it merely as a proof of the all-pervading influence of slavery, and of the opinion of the Philadelphia printers as to its supremacy in the church. The sensitive nerve of the pocket answered to the sensibility of the slave-holding conscience, and hence this despicable toad-eating, even in the presence of God himself.

No southern sect was more zealous in giving what was called "religious instruction" to slaves than the Episcopalians. And by many, as has been shown, it was held that the slaves should be taught to read the book, to see for themselves that it was God and not man, the Bible not the laws nor constitution that authorised and ordained slavery! And so why should Ary Scheffer's picture contradict the doctrine and impertinently disturb the consciences of the slave-holding bishops and christians in *New Jersey* or in the southern states?

Of the lesser denominations composing the American church or churches, it may be sufficient to say that generally they supported the dominant political parties and their policy toward slavery, including, as has already been shown, the execution of the fugitive slave law to the end. The one exception was the old school Scotch Covenanters, few indeed and extremely sectarian, but their doctrine and practice on war as well as slavery, were always respected and honored by the abolitionists.

The Friends, or Quakers, permitted no slave-holding among members. But neither the duelling, slave-holding, nor other known vices of Henry Clay, nor the bloody and barbarous war record of Zachary Taylor, besides being a very large slave-owner, prevented a large proportion of the Quakers of the country from supporting them as candidates for the presidency of the United States. The Unitarians and Universalists denied the sacramental fellowship to none, deeming the table their Lord's and not their own. So a slave-holder might presume to approach unforbidden. But it was ever the opinion of at least one anti-slavery apostle, that if a persistent horse thief or notorious counterfeiter had made too bold approach, that, were it only for the decency and respectability of the thing, the question of expediency and propriety would not have been deemed irrelevant or out of order. But abolitionists as such never interfered with any denominational doctrines or doings, only so far as they might affect favorably or unfavorably the emancipation of the slaves.

The Free Will Baptists, too, like the Quakers, claimed exemption from the guilt of slave owning, and in 1839, at Coneaut, Ohio, refused to ordain a slave-holder to the ministry, and voted that "with sorrow of heart we learn that slavery is tolerated, defended and practiced in the christian church." But the whole truth soon disclosed that they could do much more than call slave-breeders, slave-traders and slave-holders the "Christian church." In New Hampshire and Maine, where their great strength lay, they reviled the anti-slavery movement, and expelled both ministers and members for anti-slavery fidelity. This very hour I spoke with one of them, a man of most unspotted christian character, and to this time, a faithful and able minister of the New Testament. No democracy in slavery's darkest days was too foul for Free Will Baptist embrace. The democratic party long ruled Maine and New Hampshire, as it could not have done but for the vote of that denomination. One of its ministers insolently boasted to me that every voting member in his church belonged to the democratic party, and ,he himself had held distinguished civil office as a working member of the party. In all these denominations just named, I knew many, or some most honorable exceptions, to be sure not many in all, and among the very best and bravest, some were leading clergymen.

Of the Campbellites or Disciples, not so good account can be given. They were little known in New England or New York. But where they were found generally, though not quite always, they were on the side of the oppressor. Their principal leader, if not founder, was Rev. Alexander Campbell, and he was also editor and controller of the *Millennial Harbinger*, the denominational organ. In that, Dr. Campbell wrote thus :

" Is the simple relation of master and slave necessarily and essentially immoral and unchristian, as that for example of the adulterer and adulteress ? *We are clearly and satisfactorily convinced it is not.* It would be, in our most calm and deliberate judgement, a sin against every dispensation of religion,—Patriarchal, Jewish and Christian,—to suppose that the relationship of master and slave was, in its very nature and being, a sin against God and man."

In May of the same year he declares further :

" There is not one verse in the Bible inhibiting slavery, but many regulating it. It is not, then, we conclude, *immoral.*

" *The discipline of the church is the only discipline under which christian slaves can be placed by christian masters.* If they will not faithfully serve their christian masters, who 'partake of the benefit' of their labors, then are they, after proper instruction and ad-

monition, to be separated from the church, and to be
put under whatever other discipline a *christian* master
under the existing laws of the state, may inflict." * *
* * "To preserve unity of spirit among
christians of the south and of the north is my grand
object, and for that purpose I am endeavoring to show
that the New Testament does not authorize any interference or legislation upon the relation of master and
slave, nor does it, either in letter or spirit, authorize
christians to make it a term of communion.

"Every man who loves the American Union, as
well as every man who desires a constitutional end
of American slavery, is bound to prevent, as far as
possible, any breach of communion between christians
at the south and at the north."

So far Dr. Campbell. Dr. Shannon, president of
Bacon college, an eminent Disciple authority, also
wrote a Bible argument for slavery, with this conclusion :

"Thus did Jehovah stereotype his approbation of
domestic slavery, *by incorporating it with the institutions
of the Jewish religion, the only religion on earth that
had the Divine sanction.*"

In paying attention to the Free Will Baptists it
seemed proper to refer to their democratic tendencies at a time when that party ruled supreme and
slavery enjoyed the full benefit. The Campbellites
were similarly *patriotic*, and appear to have so continued, even to the very last presidential election, as
the following passage from the famous "Dorsey-Gar-
field correspondence" proves :

On August 30, 1881, Mr. Garfield wrote thus : "If
we carry Indiana in October, the rest is comparatively
easy. We shall make a very serious, perhaps fatal,
mistake if we do not throw all our available strength

into that state.   I have taken great pains to ascertain the situation of the parties there, not from extensive correspondence alone, but I have sent intelligent and trustworthy observers to various parts of the state to make special enquiries on various aspects of the contest.   *   *   From twenty-five thousand to thirty thousand voters of Indiana are members of the denomination of Disciples, and at least half of them are democrats !   A quiet, but very earnest movement, wholly outside the state committee, has been organized, and is being vigorously and judiciously pushed, with the strongest probability that at least two thousand five hundred changes of votes in our favor will result. *   *   I went over the whole ground with Senator Dorsey when he was here *en route* for Chicago, and his letters since his arrival there strongly confirm my opinion.

No comment is needed here.   My own experience among "Disciples," not only in Indiana and Ohio, where they were very numerous in the hottest days of the anti-slavery conflict, but in other parts of the west, induced me to believe that not only were "at least half of them democrats," but that they were very far from being of the highest order even of the democratic party.

One personal encounter I well remember.   My traveling companions and myself, three or four in all, went on a beautiful October Saturday to Hiram, the seat of the college of which Mr. Garfield was principal and head, to commence in the afternoon a strictly moral and religious anti-slavery meeting to hold over Sunday.   But in the afternoon a crowd of the pupils got possession of the house, and behaved in so vile and vulgar a manner as to prevent our being heard, and before night we were glad to leave the place.

28

The *Millennial Harbinger* was law and gospel there to all intents and purposes, coming fresh from Virginia, then the land of whips, chains and red hot branding irons, and all the frightful paraphernalia and appointments for slave-breeding and slave-trading, as well as slave-holding. Virginia, where so late as 1849 a law was enacted making it criminal to teach any slave or free colored person to read or write. Virginia, where the kind-hearted Margaret Douglass was imprisoned for teaching some free colored children to read only the New Testament and catechism. Virginia, under whose soil ran the roots of Preceptor Garfield's *Hiram college*, whose students, studying under the afterwards President Garfield, could, and did, wantonly, wickedly, maliciously, under a bright October sun, enter, break up and scatter a strictly moral, peaceful, religious, anti-slavery convention, and compel those who had come to hold it, to leave the town !

THE AMERICAN BIBLE SOCIETY.

This society was organized in 1816, its object being " to encourage a wider circulation of the Bible without note or comment," using only the then accepted version, and its field was the world, as opportunity and resources permitted. The slave states had some auxiliary societies, though in most, if not every one of them, a sixth part of the people were prohibited, under heavy penalties, from being taught to read. True the slaves were held amenable to the law, and seventy offenses which they might commit were punishable with death ! And in the election of president and members of congress the masters were permitted to count three-fifths of the slaves as free men and cast their votes for them accordingly ; and in the year 1837, many millions of surplus revenue were distributed among the states on the same unjust and unrigh-

teous principle, giving six slave states nearly seven
million dollars ; while Pennsylvania, with a free population larger than all six of them, received less than
four million dollars.

But the parent Bible society never reckoned even a
fractional humanity in slaves. So far as reading and
writing were concerned, it just plunged the whole
slave population down to the dead level of brute
beasts, as will be shown. Strange confusion would
sometimes result from a state of society so unnatural,
so monstrous. In 1841, a little Bible auxiliary society existed in New Orleans, and one of its distributing agents was overheard asking a group of slaves if
they could read or write, or wanted a Bible ? He was
immediately arrested as an incendiary and carried to
court. His name was Chauncey B. Black, and the New
Orleans *Picayune*, of August 12, 1841, gives a minute
account of the trial. The accuser was William H.
Avery ; the magistrate was Mr. Recorder Baldwin,
and Mr. Maybin, Mr. Lowndes, Mr. Stevens, Mr.
Goodrich, and Rev. Mr. Wheaton, (good Massachusetts names) were summoned to testify.

The accused stated that he was agent of the Bible
society, and that he was appointed by Mr. Lowndes,
one of the prominent members of it. He said he was
then engaged in taking the names only, of such persons as stood in need of the Bible and would accept
it from the society, and entered on his list indiscrim-
inately white and colored, free persons and slaves.

The witnesses admitted their organization and objects; had raised a thousand dollars already, and
ordered books from the parent depository in New
York to that amount ; some in German, French and
Spanish, as well as in the English language, but they

declared "it never for one moment entered into the mind of the society *to present one single Bible to a slave.*"

Mr. Lowndes distinctly stated, and impressed it strongly on the mind of the court, "that before any Bibles were distributed to those whose names might be taken by the accused, the list was to be first submitted to him. And as it was opposed to his own feelings, and contrary to the intention of the society, he would certainly furnish no Bible to any slave."

"The strongest, most satisfactory evidence was given that the accused bore an excellent character ; and that in speaking to the slaves at all he acted from a misconception of the instructions of Mr. Lowndes, and an ignorance of his duties as an agent of the Bible society."

A Mr. Micon was counsel for the accused, and made a good and successful defense.

"The Recorder briefly addressed the prisoner, told him he highly approved the laudable work of distributing the Bible, in which he was engaged. But while executing that duty, he must be cautious not to infringe on other rights which are *as sacred to this community as religion itself.* Believing that in speaking to the slaves he was actuated by no evil intention, he would discharge him, bidding him God-speed in his religious career, and cautioning him against ever bringing himself in contact with our institutions."

The latest Louisiana enactment on the teaching of slaves letters which I can find was in 1830, to this purport :

"Any person who shall attempt to teach any free person of color or slave to spell, read or write, shall, upon conviction thereof, be imprisoned not less than one, nor more than twelve months."

But what shall be said to this provision for *oral* instruction, in that same Louisiana ?   According to Judge Stroud, quoting First Martin's Digest, 610 : "It shall be the duty of every owner to procure for his *sick* slaves all kinds of temporal and *spiritual* assistance which their situation may require."

Here truly was death-bed repentance contemplated, distancing in extremity that of the thief on the cross. But there were many at the south, as has already been intimated, who believed that the slaves should have the Bible, and be taught to read it.   The reason given was that it would tend to *make and keep them contented with their lot in bondage*, to know that it was all by divine appointment !

In the year 1854, at the Abbeville, South Carolina, district Bible society anniversary, this subject was agitated, and had earnest and extended discussion. This society was organized in 1823, and had, in 1854, seven working auxiliary associations.   At the anniversary of that year, a principal address appears to have been delivered by Robert A. Fair, Esq., and published in the society proceedings, under this heading :

"The christian duty of placing the Bible in the hands of the negro, and teaching him to read it."

A few passages from that discourse will be both instructive and interesting :

If the teachings of holy writ were at war with the institution of slavery, and we were struggling to maintain it in opposition to those teachings ; or if the proposition were to put the slave in possession of a knowledge of the arts and sciences—to confer a high degree of intellectual culture—fully to educate him, we might be disposed to yield the point.   But how stands the case ?   Why, that the teachings of the Bible are not only not unfriendly to the institution of slavery, but that in those teachings, the institution is most amply recognized. It is upon them that we triumphantly rest its defense.

That question being settled beyond dispute, the ingenious orator proceeds*:

We would not be startled at the announcement of the fact that two-thirds of our slave population do not know or believe that the subject of slavery, or their condition, is ever alluded to in the Bible—that two-thirds of them are ignorant of the authority by which we essay to hold them in bondage, or demand at their hands obedience and service. To such, how galling is the yoke! How bitter is the bondage!

So much for the slaves and the Bible. Now for the masters. For the humane, Mr. Fair does not forget to deal *Fairly* by both parties. As, for example:

Nor would we be startled at the announcement of the fact that many masters are ignorant of any scriptural view of the subject — ignorant of the true grounds upon which to place the institution and the duties of masters; which ignorance betrays them into many errors and abuses, the tendency of which is to *undermine the institution.* Now, relieve the minds of both parties of their ignorance and darkness, and thoroughly educate and indoctrinate them into clear, sound, intelligent scriptural views of the whole subject, and of what an immense weight will the institution be relieved! and of what a burden will the bosoms of slaves, and the minds of masters be relieved!

Here are the motives, reasons for teaching both masters and slaves the scriptural doctrine of chattel slavery. That both may know that God and the Bible were at the bottom of the whole horrible system.

But what said the parent organization, "the American Bible society," now under our consideration, to such reasoning and such religion? It said, through its secretary, and the *Monthly Record*, organ of the society, just this:

This subject of furnishing Bibles to slaves, is one of vast importance and will receive more of the attention of our southern auxiliaries than heretofore. I find that the recent *excellent address*, delivered in South Carolina, and reprinted in part in our February *Record*, has been widely read, and so far as I have learned, meets the approval of the christian community.

But the *Southern Presbyterian* reviews Mr. Fair with great severity—disagrees with him altogether, thus :

We insist that the laws are imperiously demanded by a regard to the public safety. Is there any great moral reason why we should incur the tremendous risk of having our wives and children slaughtered, in consequence of our slaves being taught to read incendiary publications ? * * * Mr. Fair seems to be uninformed of the fact that the scriptures are read in our churches every sabbath day. And these very passages which inculcate the duties of masters and slaves, in consequence of their textual connection, are more frequently read *than other portions of the book.*

It is worthy of note that Mr. Fair is not a clergyman. Possibly, the editor of the *Presbyterian* is not. But he evidently belongs to the church *militant*, and holds statute law forbidding slaves to read such "incendiary publications" as Isaiah, and the sermon on the mount, as absolutely needful for the safety of "the throats of the wives and children of slave-holders."

Such, at that time, was the American Bible society and its auxiliaries, judged by the declarations and testimonies of its organs and officers. Its own friends, and no others.

THE AMERICAN TRACT SOCIETY.

And now we touch bottom, if ever, in sounding the depths of clerical devotion to slavery. To the Tract society, ministers, always its controlling, governing influence, especially in the publication department, the

slave-holder could well have sung, in the strain of
King Solomon :

"Many daughters have done virtuously,
But thou excellest them all."

The Bible society could say it was instituted for one
sole, specific purpose, to disseminate the scriptures,
"without note or comment." The tract society was
chartered :

"To diffuse the knowledge of our Lord Jesus
Christ as the redeemer of sinners, and to promote the
interests of vital godliness and sound morality, by the
circulation of religious tracts, calculated to receive
the approbation of all evangelical christians."

And so, when asked to testify in one little sheet,
against slavery, as was asked by thousands of church
members and contributors to its funds, were it "only
so much as quotations from scripture, bearing on the
various elements of oppression which enter into slavery, it dared to refuse, on the simple ground that all
tracts were to receive the approbation of all evangelical christians." And how could slave-holders approve even scripture protest against their *patriarchal*
institution ?

Indeed, the time came, when not only whole
churches and their ministers protested against the
course of this society, but even state ecclesiastical associations earnestly petitioned, as well as solemnly
protested, in relation to the subject. It was the general association of Michigan that asked, with but a
single dissenting vote, for the scripture tract against
slavery. For only "so much as the naked Bible texts
against it." In one instance, the answer was soured
with an insolence worthy the plantation itself. "If
the southern churches remain evangelical churches,
and southern christians are evangelical christians, it

is their right, *and your duty*, to abstain from publishing *even truths*, the publication of which, they would not approve.

But instead of dwelling on the controversy, which for a long time only *worried* the society, and its nearly harmless opponents, and which would neither expiate the tediousness nor reward our toil, let us glance a little at some of the society action in various ways to shield the bloody idol from the attacks of the earnest, upright and downright abolitionists, whose word and work were always, not only respected by the south, but greatly feared ; as our New York and Boston anti-slavery anniversaries always showed, to the very last.

Besides tracts, the society published, for cheap sale or gratuitous distribution, many bound volumes, and sometimes they contained sentiments quite blasphemous to the worship of the slave-holding Moloch. These were always, with wondrous prudence and foresight, suppressed. Some of these works were English, and copy-righted, too. But that made no difference. They were not only "pirated," as it was called, but most unrighteously perverted (and for most piratical purposes, too), from the author's meaning. Instead of denying, the publishing committee defended what they did : they defended it in one of their annual reports, thus : "We do expunge whatever the christians of the south would regard as untruthful, harsh, or denunciatory."

Here, now, is an instance. The well-known work, by the eminent Dr. Harris, of London, on covetousness, entitled : "Mammon," a prize essay, was thus seized and published by the tract society, with this slight, but, to slave-holders, terribly significant omission. The author, showing the immoral influence of covetousness, said : "Its history is the history of slavery and oppression, in all ages." "Evangelica christians at the south," might stand "oppression," but "slavery," never. And so "oppression" was retained, but not "slavery."

Another English work, republished by the society, was entitled, "Habitual exercise of love to God," by Joseph John Gurney, an eminent preacher of the society of Friends. It was remarkable that the society should have taken up a work of such an arch heretic as a Quaker preacher. But so it did, and mutilated it to this extent. On page 142, the author reaches a conclusion thus :

Had this love always prevailed among professing christians, where would have been the sword of the crusader? where the African slave trade? where the odious system which permits man a property in his fellow man, and converts rational beings into marketable chattels?

The tract society makes this sentence read like this : Listen !

If this love had always prevailed among professing christians, where would have been the sword of the crusader? where the *tortures of the inquisition?* where every system of oppression and wrong by which he who has the power revels in luxury and ease, at the expense of his fellow men?

Another foreign book was "Life of Mary Lundie Duncan, of Scotland. On one occasion, she had listened with youthful ardor and sympathy, to the eloquence of the distinguished orator, as well as abolitionist, and, subsequently, member of parliament, George Thompson. She afterwards wrote this, which the tract society suppressed from her work :

We have lately been much interested in the emancipation of the slaves. I never heard eloquence more overpowering than that of George Thompson. I am most thankful that he has been raised up. O that the measure 'soon to be proposed in parliament, may be successful ! "

Later, when he was about to visit the United States, at the earnest desire of Garrison and other abolitionists, to plead the cause of the American slave, Mrs. Duncan addressed him as, "George Thompson, the eloquent pleader for the abolition of slavery ; " and closed her communication with these strains :

> " Yet go, heaven-favored hero, go !
> Pursue your glorious plan ;
> Abridge the weight of human woe,
> And raise the slave to man.

> " Heaven bless your cause ! Your country's prayers,
> Attend you o'er the sea !
> Go break the chain that slaverv wears,
> And bid the oppressed go free ! "

All this, and much more was most unrighteously suppressed by the mendacious publication committee of the Tract Society !

Mrs. Lundie was in New York when this memoir of her daughter was already in the hands of that committee ; and it was well understood that she was called upon by one of the secretaries and modestly asked, even urged to consent to the mutilations. But she persistently declined ; the lines being peculiarly precious to her for their sentiment, and for her dear daughter's sake. The shameless omissions were however made, reckless of all truth and right, regardless of a mourning mother's feelings, and tenderest love !

One other of these marvelous changes, and monstrous omissions, is all for which time, space, and patience can permit.

Dr. Cotton Mather, so well known in Puritan history, among his voluminous writings, left one entitled, *Essays to do good*," and here is a passage :

O that the souls of our slaves were more regarded by us ; that we might give a better demonstration that we despise not our own souls, by doing what we can for the souls of our slaves ! How can we pretend to christianity, when we do no more to christianize our slaves ?

But the Tract Society carefully, prudently, printed the word *servants*, instead of *slaves !*

And the following whole paragraph was most wickedly suppressed :

But if any servant of God may be so honored by Him as to be made the successful instrument of obtaining from a British Parliament, an act for the christianizing of the slaves on the plantations, then it may be hoped something more may be done, than has yet been done, that the blood of souls may not be found in the skirts of our nation. A controversy with heaven and our colonies may be removed, and prosperity may be restored ; or however the honorable instrument will have unspeakable peace and joy in the remembrance of his endeavors. In the meantime, the slave trade is a spectacle which shocks humanity.

> " The harmless natives basely they trepan
> And barter baubles for the soul of man.
> The wretches, they to christian climes bring o'er,
> To serve worse heathen than they did before ! "

Such were the suppressions and changes made by the Tract Society in reproducing the " Essays to do good," more than a hundred years after they were written. One other fact should be stated here which even adds to the audaciousness of the whole proceeding. For a long time the work was out of print. It was afterwards reissued in England ; and slavery having already been abolished there, the allusions to it were for that reason omitted. But the editor in a foot note, stated what they were, and why they were omitted. That edition was followed in this country ; but not the notes ; the English editor omitting the

passages because they were inapplicable to his country, and giving his reasons; the Tract Society omitting them because they were applicable, in dreadful
sense, and saying nothing about it !

For some of these startling statements and facts, I
am indebted to a masterly letter of remonstrance sent
by the unanimous vote of the Fourth Congregational
church in Hartford, Conn., to the officers and directors of the American Tract Society. The letter was
prepared by a committee consisting of the pastor of
the church, Rev. Wm. H. Patton, John Hooker, Esq.,
an eminent lawyer of Hartford, husband of the well,
and widely known Mrs. Elizabeth Beecher Hooker,
and Mr. Milo Doty. It was published in a tract form
of thirty-four closely printed pages, and circulated to
the number of several thousands. In 1855, the stereotype plates were generously presented to the American
Tract Society, and the work was immediately adopted
as No. 16 of its tract publications.

But to the old Tract Society, the mighty appeal was
of small account; it had already received thousands of
similar substance and disposed of them after its pleasure. It is only too certain that its officers knew very
well the quality of the remonstrants, especially their
leaders and directors. I have already more than
intimated that they were not of formidable or dangerous character to the slave-holding communion, and
their northern allies and abettors. When the American churches were proved "the bulwarks of American
slavery," and its "forlorn hope," indeed, by testimony
immovable as earth's foundations, the abolitionists
came out of them as their only escape from the sin
and its plagues. But the "new organization" anti-
slavery as it was called, did not come out from among
the slave-holders ; and the American Tract Society

knew it, and knew they had no intention of such separation. The directors of the American board of foreign missions knew it, and the Baptist board, and the general conference of the Methodist Episcopal church, There were some pretended separations, and we have seen to what purpose. The tract society saw to what purpose, at the time, and knew just what to expect ; and the society was not disappointed.

There was a seeming separation among the supporters of the American Tract Society.

It should be said here that the original tract society was organized and incorporated in Massachusetts with head quarters at Andover. In 1823, its name was changed from New England Religious Tract, to American Tract Society. In 1825, the American Tract Society was incorporated in New York under a new charter, the Massachusetts society becoming a branch of it : but surrendered all its stereotype plates and publications to the new society, with agreement that it should be furnished with all the publications it required, at cost not greater than it had been before. This union continued till 1859 ; then, in consequence of the dissatisfaction of many members, and some officers, (expressed like the Hartford and other letters,) because the society would not publish tracts disapproving of American slavery, the Boston society withdrew and resumed its former independent position. And what readers must desire to know is, exactly what position did the Boston department assume and sustain towards the parent stock at New York, from which they had sawed themselves off, and that had been deliberately guilty of the outrages just revealed and exposed, and which the remonstrants themselves urged with such power as motive and reason for their final withdrawal.

Among the many writers, whether as editors of periodicals or authors of reports of societies, or of conventions, or of tracts, or larger works on slavery and kindred themes, the anti-slavery conflict produced no one of finer quality, everyway, especially for patient, untiring industry and perseverance, clear, calm and ever conscientious judgment of men and of parties, whether political or religious, than Mr. Charles K. Whipple. To his sterling faithfulness, energy and perseverance, editors, lecturers and other writers and workers were often indebted for facts, statements and statistics, inevitable to their success. His exhaustive work on the relations to slavery of the American Board of Commissioners for Foreign Missions, in nearly two hundred and fifty large pages, closely printed in fine type, compiled wholly from its own annual reports and other official documents, was a labor greater than has made the fame and fortune, too, of many authors of our day.

And his invaluable tract of twenty-four well-filled pages on the two Tract societies after the separation, and their relations towards each other, should have covered with blushes of shame the faces of all who pretended to anti-slavery character, only in consideration of such repentance and reformation as that fully and faithfully disclosed. The dissenters were numerous, and doubtless many were earnest and sincere. Thirty auxiliary bodies, thirteen being states, or their equivalent, could not all have been pretended. But we shall see into what they were led, and out of what they unfortunately were not led. They did at last compel the parent society to lend an ear to their petitions and protests, and a committee of fifteen, ten being ministers, and nearly all well-known friends of the society and approvers of its former unrighteous courses,

was appointed to make inquiry and investigation into
what too many already knew. And all who did know
should have been ashamed.

Subsequently that committee reported to this effect :

Resolved, That the action of the executive, as reported, *be approved.*

A long debate ensued. Various substitutes and
amendments were offered and rejected, and finally
the original resolution, which was presented by Bishop
McIlvaine, was adopted, by a vote of the great majority of the members and directors present.

And immediately following this action of entire approval of their former course, in the completest possible manner, the whole board of officers was re-
elected :

And now the question is as to the course of the remonstrants, " Thirty auxiliary bodies in all, thirteen
of them representing states or other large districts."

Their first resolution at their meeting in Boston
directed the executive committee to report *next year*
on " the expendiency of dissolving the connection between this society and the National Society at New
York." No hurry, it seems. " Next year " will do.
And then the inquiry will only be as to " the expediency " of the step. And now for their fourth resolution to this purport :

Resolved, That we entertain the highest respect for
the wisdom, judgment and sincerity of the special committee of fifteen, appointed by the American Tract
Society of New York, at the annual meeting of 1856,
and do heartily adopt the resolutions reported by
them, and declare our purpose to carry into effect the
principles embraced in those resolutions.

Why not then have held their peace and kept to
their work ? Entertaining " the highest respect for
the wisdom, judgment and sincerity of that committee

of fifteen," why not have let them alone ? How would that committee have looked turning round and passing a like admiration "for the wisdom, judgment and sincerity," especially *sincerity* of those dissenters? But to give facts, not comments on them, is our present business.

Here is another of the declarative resolutions of the disaffected :

Resolved, That the *political* aspects of slavery lie entirely without the proper sphere of this society and cannot be discussed in its publications ; but that those moral duties which grow out of its existence, as well as those moral evils which it is known to promote, and which are condemned in scripture, and so much deplored by evangelical christians, do undoubtedly fall within the province of this society, and can and should be discussed in a fraternal and christian spirit.

One more quotation will be sufficient, and more than sufficient for the purposes of this work.

Passing over much which might be cited from this annual report of the Boston society. [its forty-fourth] take the following from the official " Address of the executive committee to the friends of the society, in the following July, a few weeks after their anniversary. They say :

It may be well to state that the organic relations of this society to the New York society have not been materially changed by the above resolutions. This society may therefore be made the channel for the contributions of all persons who, for any reason, may prefer our position or our policy to that of the other society. * * We invite no separation from that society, but under present circumstances we believe the greatest amount of good will be done by each society occupying the whole country as its field. We are not an anti-slavery society, but simply a religious tract society. We earnestly entreat the churches of our Lord Jesus Christ no longer to permit this important enterprise to decline because of divers views on the various questions arising out of the slave system, the time and occasion for that having passed ; as two societies now offer their facilities for conveying the gospel of Christ in this form to those who so much need that gospel.

And this voluminous and tedious testimony is but a specimen of what might be adduced ; and to what then do all these confessions amount ? In the first place the new association of dissenters declares in so many words, " We are not an anti-slavery society, but simply a religious tract society." Only that, and nothing more. And what was the New York Society, but just that, and nothing less ?

Another confession is : "The organic relations of this society to the New York, have not been materially changed." And another : " We invite no separation from the New York society." And this one more, most remarkable of all, explaining why neither is, nor should be an anti-slavery society, nor pretend to be ; as it is only "certain moral duties which grow out of the existence of slavery, as well as those moral evils which it is known to promote, that lie within our proper sphere." What is this but flat denial that slavery in itself is sin at all? Drunkenness, in itself, is no evil. Is it? Nor adultery, any more than marriage. Is it?

The *old* tract society published testimonies solemn as judgment, heaven and hell, against intemperance, novel-reading, card-playing, horse-racing, theater-going, and chewing and smoking tobacco. But to degrade men and women to brute beasts, goods and chattels, and then treat them accordingly, as did the Bible and tract societies, not counting them as families at all, that was no sin. Both societies proposed to supply states or counties, cities or towns, as the case might be, with their works, "every family willing to receive them." And reported every family so supplied, when they knew, and everybody knew, that to sell or give a Bible or tract to any slave, and in some states, to any free person of color, was a penal offense and sure to be sorely punished by the statute law! The old society knew it had nothing to fear from the new, and trusted it accordingly. Dr. Nehemiah Adams, of Boston, had published two volumes of most unblushing vindication of slavery, one of over two hundred, the other almost three hundred pages, and he was one of the most prominent and influential officers in the publication department of the tract society, and never endangered the sale of his works by printing tracts or protests against his favorite institution. The declared object of the tract society is, in part : "To diffuse the knowledge of our Lord Jesus Christ, as the redeemer of sinners, and to promote the interests of vital godliness and sound morality."

And it was no violation of "sound morality" to establish, support and sanctify, generation after generation, a slave system, that converted every slave cabin into a brothel of prostitution, or a hovel or sty of beasts, where marriage and parentage were unknown, not one marriage of all the millions of slaves ever sanctioned by law, not one mother ever made legally secure for one hour in the possession of her babe ; no, not one ! Not one slave girl, no matter how beautiful, had the slightest protection for her virtue, though dearer to her, as was thousands of times proved, than life ; no, not one ! The whole slave code was declared in one terse utterance :

"If any slave shall presume to strike any white person, such slave may be lawfully killed." Killed, of course, on the spot !

In all this, there was no outrage on " sound morality," nor " vital godliness," in tract society estimation ;
in one society, more or less, than in the other. " We
are not an anti-slavery society." No, truly not. You
need not have said it.

Herodotus tells us that the Babylonians and
Cyprians had a law or custom, compelling every
woman, once in her life, to visit the temple of Venus,
and prostitute herself to the honor of that unclean
divinity. But Babylonians and Cyprians were not
christians. They were not even Jews. They were
pagans. And then, their women need go there but
once. The slave girl or woman never went anywhere
else. "Vital godliness," and "sound morality," in
Bible and tract society sense, sent her there, kept her
there all her life, and the people, excepting a few abolitionists, said amen and amen. The great ecclesiastical organizations wielded a power in shaping and
controlling their character and destiny, second only to
omnipotence. The commission of the faithful, uncompromising abolitionists, was unmistakable : "Go
and speak my words unto them, whether they will hear
or whether they will forbear.　*　*　And they,
whether they will hear or whether they will forbear,
(for they are a rebellious house), yet shall they know
that there hath been a prophet among them." And
the faithful among them spoke that divinely inspired
word, crying aloud and sparing not, showing the
southern slave-holder his transgressions, and his
northern abettor and apologist his sins, till the dying
agonies of Bull Run and over a thousand other battles and bloody encounters, answered for them, mag-
nified and made honorable their ministrations, and
showed to the whole world that there was yet a God
in Israel !

THE FUGITIVE SLAVE LAW.

In the early part of this work allusions were made to that "bill of abomination," known as the fugitive slave law of 1850. That law was often executed, and sometimes in Boston, with peculiar atrocities and aggravations, the navy yard near by, furnishing ample facilities for the necessary military force. Once, however, troops were ordered from the interior of Massachusetts, and quartered in Faneuil hall, till the poor victim was sent back to his whipping post and branding-iron. Honest men and women were beggared by imprisonments and heavy fines, for harboring and concealing, or refusing to aid in the blood-hound work of pursuing and capturing fugitive slave men and women in their nightly flight to Canada. Massachusetts pulpits, even Andover theological seminary, ably defended the diabolical business. On the 7th of March, 1850, Daniel Webster nearly stunned, not only his constituency, but the whole north, by his speech in the United States senate, in advocacy of that direful enactment. The old federal and whig party succession of Massachusetts, had bowed low and long to the despotic slave power before. All the compromises in the constitution had been exacted and enforced, unrighteous and unjust as all of them were, from the first. Then, even against constitutional restriction, Florida and Louisiana had been purchased for slave states. The Seminole and Mexican wars ensued, as a first consequence, continuing on through a dozen years and more, all "red with uncommon wrath," in many of the atrocities perpetrated on the poor Indians; but now new vials of slave-holding indignation, as well as power, were to be uncorked upon the north. The people of the northern states had long violated the solemn command to "remember

them that were in bonds as bound with them," and
now a stern decree came up from the slave power, to
go and be bound with them in chains more ignoble than
the shackles of the slaves themselves! Robert
Toombs, of Georgia, had prophesied that he would yet
"call the roll of his slaves on Bunker hill." And now
he did so, and in Faneuil hall as well! Slaves armed
to protect the lordly slave-holder in recapturing, in
Boston streets, their fellow slaves, who had been at
least brave enough to attempt escape to Canada, land
of kings and queens, where they could be free!

So was it when Professor Stuart sat down in the
sacred shades of Andover, and wrote a work all ablaze
with blasphemy against liberty, entitled, "Conscience
and the Constitution, with remarks on the recent
speech of Daniel Webster, in the senate of the United
States, on the subject of slavery ; " a work in large octavo, of about a hundred and twenty pages. It was
not the first time the venerable professor had drawn
his pen in defense of his friend, Mr. Webster, in some
of his official acts, as the history of the Tyler administration revealed.

From Professor Stuart's hundred and eighteen
pages, less than one will here be given, the first part
bearing directly on the return of fugitive slaves. On
page sixty, he asks :

What, now, have we here? Paul sending back a
christian servant, who had run away from his *christian*
master.   *   *   *   He enjoins it upon Onesimus
to return to his master *forever*. This last phrase has
respect to the fact that Paul supposed that the sense
of christian obligation which was now entertained by
Onesimus, would prevent him from ever repeating the
offense. And all this, too, when Philemon, being an
active and zealous christian, would in a moment have
submitted to any command of Paul, respecting Onesimus. Why, then, did Paul send him back? There

is only one answer to be given, viz., that Paul's christian *conscience* would not permit him to injure the vested rights of Philemon.   *   *   *   Paul's conscience *sent back* the fugitive slave ; Paul's conscience, then, like his doctrines, was very different from that of the abolitionists.   Theirs, *encourages him to run away*, and then protects him in the misdeed.   The conscience of Paul sends him back the fugitive without any obligation at all on the ground of compact ; theirs, encourages and protects his escape, in the face of the most solemn national compact.   And all this for *conscience's* sake.

Some of the states, Massachusetts among them, had enacted state laws or measures, contravening in some respects, the demands of the slave law.   On that subject, Professor Stuart wrote :   "To the position our honored legislature in their recent resolves, viz.: That the case of the fugitive shall be tried 'by jury, in the state where the claim is made,' *I am unable*, highly as I respect their motives, *to yield my assent.*"

And, in summing up, the professor says, and this closes the citations from him :

I have done with this subject.   The brief result, as it strikes my mind, is, that *the Constitution* in respect to fugitives held to service or labor, *must be obeyed*.   It is useless to talk about *conscience* as setting it aside.   It is an imputation on the men who formed our government.   It is holding them up to the world as having neither justice nor humanity.

In these extracts the italicizing and capitalizing are the professor's own.   Let them speak for themselves. I will only say, they are but samples of his whole work.

President, Nathan Lord, D. D., of Dartmouth College, soon after the appearance of "*Conscience* and the *Constitution*," wrote to the author, Professor Stuart, a reply in a pamphlet letter of two and forty pages octavo, correcting, not the doctrine, or morality of his work, but some statements of fact relating to Puritan history and slavery. Professor Stuart wrote on page 109 : " In looking back on the history of slavery in our country, whence do we find it to have originated ! From Great Britain, and from her alone ; all the colonies fought pitched battles against it ; but the king and parliament defeated them. North and south were united on this question—united before the Declaration of Independence, and united for a long time after it."

These statements of the learned Professor, the more learned President Lord refutes in masterly manner ; he shows that slavery existed in all the British colonies with exception of Georgia for a short time and with a power of erudition and argument proves it, and apparently, *approves* it too. He even implicates the Rhode Island, New Jersey and Pennsylvania Quakers with the rest. The President says :

A foggy sort of notion is beginning to prevail, that from their origin, at any rate from their settlement in this country under William Penn, the Quakers as a denomination, have been opposed to slavery. This position if true, would only prove that among many wild and visionary theories which distinguish them as a sect, they adopted that of abolition. But the notion is not true ; opposition to slavery sprang up among them at a comparatively recent date. William Penn lived and died a slave owner. There is a letter on record from T. Matlack, an aged Friend, to William Findlay, which gives account of the rise and progress of this idea among them. The letter says :

The practice of slave-keeping in New Jersey and Pennsylvania, commenced with the first settlement of the province, and certainly was countenanced by William Penn.   *   *   *   Penn left a family of slaves behind him.   *   *   *   Slave-keeping of course, became general among Friends.

President Lord says Penn attempted to legislate, not for the abolition of slavery, but for the sanctity of marriage among slaves, and for their personal safety ; but he also declares, "there is no more reason to suppose George Fox was an abolitionist, than that Governor Winthrop was an abolitionist. And by Rees's Cyclopedia, by Sir Edward Coke, Sir William Temple and Lord Campbell, he establishes the fact of practical slave-holding and slave-trading, and shows that slaves could neither acquire nor hold any property in land nor goods, and children always followed the condition of the parents ; and further, that the renowned Sir John Hawkins first opened and established the African slave trade with Queen Elizabeth, a ready accomplice. So President Lord argues that it was natural and reasonable that Puritans in the colonies should hold and trade in slaves as they did, even " *branding them on the shoulder,*" and exporting cargoes of their Indian prisoners to the West Indies. At the close of King Philip's war, he says, " a great many of the chiefs were executed in Boston and Plymouth, and most of the rest of the prisoners were shipped for slaves to the Bermudas and other parts." This, he says, and truly, " *was an affair of state.*" And then whole pages more, which must not only have enlightened the mind of Professor Stuart, but greatly gladdened his heart ; as showing that even the Puritans, always regarded as only very little, if any, lower than the angels, were not only slave-breeders, and traders, but exalted the red hot branding-iron as part of the paraphernalia of the diabolical business.

President Lord's own estimate of slavery is directly given in two other pamphlets, now on my table, beside the long letter to Professor Stuart. In one, entitled "A True Picture of Abolition," he says (page 8, 9) :

The south is slave-holding. It is so constitutionally and legally. Slavery enters into, the structure of its society, not a thing of accident, possibly not everywhere of preference, but an inheritance according to the common law of earth ; a providential order, without which, in view of necessarily, that is naturally and statedly existing diversities of race, culture and condition, the social state could not have been constituted at all, and "life, liberty and happiness" would have been insecure to a christian people, who had just bought them at so great a price. Slavery was not, indeed, the corner stone, but the practical condition of the Union, the constitution and the laws.   *   * It had existed in the usages of nations.   It was common law ; it was incorporated into the civil institutions of Moses ; it was recognized accordingly by Christ and His apostles. They regulated it by the just and benevolent principles of the New Testament. They condemned all intermeddlers with it.   *   * Wherever it was subsequently abolished its want of physical adaptation and consequent inconveniences, not its essential wrongfulness, were mainly the reasons for its abolition.

On page ten the president continues :

So it stood till a generation arose that comprehended none of these living realities ; that honored not God and the Father, and for His everlasting word of natural and revealed religion, substituted *a higher law*. Among them were born the abolitionists, who are now, officially, supreme over the land. They were at first a small class of speculative enthusiasts, intoxicated by the airy pantheism of France and Germany, which had covertly breathed its spirit into the "glittering generalities" of the Declaratien of Independence, and by that instrument insensibly affected the public mind. They were men of no mark nor figure ; inflated visionaries, mistaking their own fancies for another gospel, which is not another.

With almost two pages octavo of similar if not even worse.

Of the doings in congress he wrote : " Calhoun and Webster at the head, or such men as *Brooks* (Bully Brooks) *and Sumner at the tail*, could never have contended greatly to the public detriment, till congress let in subjects of discussion which concerned more immediately the government of gods. That was our original mistake.   *   *   Common mistake of all countries, as virtue declines.   *   *   *   Till we made that blunder the country was united, prosperous and happy. There had been no such instance in the history of the world."

One quotation more. Would that space and patience of readers, would permit insertion of the whole pamphlet. On pages twelve and onward the president proceeds :

Abolitionism became an institution, organic and vital, body and soul ; a working power. It was envious at God's appointed orders. It labelled the constitution, " A covenant with death, an agreement with hell."   *   *   Gaining confidence as it acquired ascendency over the simple, the curious, the fearful, imaginative, the undisciplined, the dispassionate, it aspired to popular control and revolutionary distinction. But to that end it must become religious. It was ready for the occasion.   *   * It appealed to scripture, now twisted by improved versions, arbitrary criticisms and fantastic commentaries from its literal, direct and scientific meanings, till it was made as subservient and as obscure as a Delphic oracle.   *   *   To the same end it must also be political. It affected the well-being of the state. It studied intrigue and finesse. It became an expert. It disciplined its ranks. It found the balance of party power and then sold itself to the progressive party. The price was the government of the country. The object was the dissolution of the Union, and then the introduction of the New Jerusalem.   *   *   Such is the moral record of abolitionism, brought down to the date of presidential proclamations.   *   *

So we speak, for so we make good our cause. Abolitionism is at fault. It is false and wrong. It destroys the ancient landmarks. It obliterates the old paths. It puts its heel on constitutional relations. It sunders what God has united, and unites what God had sundered.

So much, and surely very much, for Nathan Lord, D. D., president of Dartmouth college. Readers may remember, about the college mob we had there twenty years before this pamphlet was written. For this did not appear till 1863. This was penned amid the battle thunders and dying shrieks and groans of the war of the rebellion—over the graves of thousands and hundreds of thousands already dead! With such presidents of colleges as Dr. Lord, and such theological professors as Moses Stuart, what wonder that we had our pro-slavery riot and tumult at Dartmouth! What wonder that we had such general assemblies of the Presbyterian church! And such missionary, Bible and tract societies! And what wonder that slavery, with its inevitable attendant horrors, so supported, so sanctified, continued so long!

But to return to the fugitive slave law and its ecclesiastical sanctification. The two volumes of Dr. Adams, of Essex-street church, Boston, published in 1854, and 1861, are before me. The whole soul and spirit of them both is summed up in these few words, in the volume of 1851, and with these few, readers will be glad to have done with them:

"Unless we choose to live in a perpetual state of war, we must prevent and punish all attempts to decoy slaves from their masters. Whatever our repugnance to slavery may be, there is a law of the land, a constitution to which we must submit, or employ suitable means to change it. *While it remains, all our appeals to a higher law are fanaticism.*"

And Dr. Adams was, for many years, a prominent member of the publication committee of the American tract society.

The last fugitive slave bill was signed by acting President Millard Fillmore, and became a law, September 18th, 1850. Its execution soon began, but, everywhere, was attended with difficulties ; was sometimes resisted even unto blood. The pulpit soon came to the rescue ; Boston sure to be in the van.

On the first Thanksgiving day, Dr. Sharp, of the Baptist church, and Rev. Mr. Rogers, of the Congregational, gave each a sermon, which was subsequently printed, from which a few extracts will now be given. Of the Essex-street pastor, Dr. Adams, nothing need be adduced after the passage from his South-side view of Slavery," just presented.

Dr. Sharp said :

It is our duty to submit to the government extending over the region in which we dwell, and to obey the magistrates under whose jurisdiction we are. The condition of our obedience is, that they who claim to govern us, have legal authority for doing do. With these facts well established, our obedience is not to be measured and graduated by our estimation of the wisdom or folly of the laws under which we live ; their partiality or impartiality, their justice or injustice. With one exception, while any given law exists, although it may operate upon our interests unjustly and oppressively, we must, nevertheless, submit to it. * * *

* * * To bring this subject nearer home, let us consider the duty of subjection to the powers that be, as applicable to the fugitive slave law. And in what I would say, I would have it understood that I discriminate between slavery and multitudes of excellent persons who hold slaves. Before

the colonies became independent, or the union of the
states was formed, slavery, that system of injustice,
oppression and wrong (as it appears to me), was so
interwoven with all the habits, interests and worldly
hopes of the people at the south, that they had not
the courage, the faith, the disinterestedness, to set the
slaves free. And yet they feared that their slaves,
hearing of the freedom of their own race in other
states, would attempt to escape. The southern members, therefore, of the convention that framed the national compact called the constitution of the United
States, insisted on a clause securing the return of
fugitives from labor, on legal evidence of the fact
being presented. This engagement became part of
the constitution. I regret its existence, but there it
is.   *   *   *

*   *   * The question then arises, are
you willing to enjoy the benefits of the great national
compact, but to violate its conditions? How much
there would be of high-mindedness in such a course,
I leave it to you to determine.   *   *   *

*   *   * Much less can the free citizens
of the United States, living under the protection, and
enjoying the benefits of our blessed laws, with all the
advantages of the national compact, be justified in
encouraging poor fugitive slaves to acts of resistance,
in putting forth the fist, or unsheathing the sword of
rebellion. In this state, world-wide renowned for its
steady habits, no one should allow himself to have the
hardihood and unseemliness to say that a law of congress cannot be here enforced.   *   *   *

*   *   * Our country, extending from the
Atlantic to the Pacific, having a coast and an interior
unparalleled in the world's history, is the new Canaan,
the land of promise, to which the poor and the tax-
ridden, and they who have yet something left, are
coming from the decaying institutions and over-stocked
millions of older lands. But it will be a Canaan no
longer than we prize the union, revere the constitution, and obey the laws, *wise* or *unwise*, right or *wrong*,
until we can modify or change them from unwisdom
to wisdom, from wrong to right, by the only process
that is justifiable, the process of legislation.

So held and taught Dr. Sharp. It is easy to remember, if hard to accept the words of those brave men, who, eighteen hundred years before, had said : "Whether it be right in the sight of God, to hearken unto you more than unto God, judge ye?"

But Dr. Sharp held with Dr. Adams, that "appeal to any higher law than the constitution, while that was in force, was *fanaticism!*"

But we must hasten to Mr. Rogers, of the Winter-street Congregational church :

Within the limits of this broad land, the citizen of the United States is everywhere at home ; the soil of his country beneath his feet, the flag of his country above him, and the protection of its laws around him, he is nowhere an alien and a stranger in this commonwealth of our Israel. * * * And yet with peace in our borders, with plenty in our store, with every privilege and opportunity open to all men for development of mind, for appreciation of all the benefits pertaining to air, to earth, to sea ; and yet with all of good we have, and can have, there are differences among us : there are dissensions ; and bitter words are uttered, and bitter words are retorted, and men speak of resistance to law ; some men speak of the nullification of the constitution. Men speak of disunion, horrible as it is, and it has thrilled every nerve in my soul! Horrible as it is, these words have become as familiar as household words. It has been proclaimed : " Law or no law, constitution or no constitution, the hands of the law and of the people should not execute the behests of the court, within the precincts of this commonwealth.

It is one of the articles of the constitution, that a person held to service or labor in one state under the laws thereof, shall be delivered up on the claim of the party to whom such labor is due ; I say that it is one of the articles of the constitution ; for you might readily gather from the popular cry, and from the tendency of the popular feeling, that the whole of the constitution of the United States was nothing but an

instrument for the oppression of the slave, in utter
forgetfulness of every other right and every other duty.
It is one of the articles of that constitution ; being one
of the articles of that constitution, then I gather that
whatsoever party is in power, it makes no difference
what the name, what the principles they affirm before
or after election, whatever party is in power, in their
place in congress, if there were no law already made,
pursuant to this article of the constitution, they would
be bound to make a law, and a law which should carry
out this provision and restore the fugitive to the claimant upon due proof of that claim and that service to
be rendered in another state.

Do you say, no ? do you say that it would be wrong ?
that it is sinful, thus to do ? but I ask you to consider
as an honest man, with a consciousness that your representative had called the God of heaven to witness
that he will maintain the constitution of these United
States, would you have him perjure himself and refuse
to carry out the constitution ? Leave it to an infidel
christianity to teach such morals, but when you ask
counsel of God, expect no such answer.   *   *
*   * The fugitive asks us to interpose ; when he
does so he asks us to do what the people of the
United States, or a majority of them, have said we
shall not do ; he asks us to do precisely what we have
agreed not to do.   We are under bonds to the millions
of this country to keep the peace, and to make this a
government of law, and not a government of force.
Oh, it is a miserable alternative in which we are placed
*by the mistakes, by the guilt of our fathers beyond the
waters,* in bringing this curse upon us, and leaving us
to decide between what seems the voice of charity and
mercy, and a law vigorously severe, to which nevertheless we must bow. If the slave ask us to stand
between him and the marshal armed with the power
of the people, for his arrest, what can we say to him,
but make the miserable confession that we have dispossessed ourselves of the power to stand between
the oppressor and the oppressed ?

Then it follows, and should be distinctly understood,
that if a fugitive from bondage come to our common-

wealth, and abideth here, he does it on his own responsibility, and does it with a knowledge that those among
whom he lives, have dispossessed themselves of all
power under the constitution and the law to stand
between him and his master.   This we can do for him,
but, when the question is presented to us, shall we
obey the law? and the answer is, nay, but resist it ;
what do we, but nullify the constitution of which the
law is but the practical working? What do we but
make void the organic law of the country? What do
we but that which South Carolina has attempted in
the days of her nullification, and seems likely to repeat
in this second case of her madness? Ah ! we said bitter things against South Carolina in those days.   We
told her there were·bayonets enough and men enough
in the old Bay state to put her in her place and keep
her there.   If we were right then, we are
wrong now, But it is said we are wiser now
and we may have been right.   Then the law is a sin
against God, and the constitution a law organic in the
life of the nation.   Well if it be so, then it seems to
me the inference is very plain.   This confederacy
ought not to exist an hour ; if it be so, then those men
who voted for the admission of California as a free
state into this confederacy, were very wicked men.   It
was voting the admission of that commonwealth
into a confederacy against the God of heaven.

But when the slave asks me to stand between him
and his master, he asks me to do something more than
free him ; and here is the difficulty.   Could you separate the question of the slave's freedom or bondage,
from those difficulties with which, under the law, it is
involved ; would you make it a clear question here
upon this soil, whether he should be a free man or a
slave, there is not a hand or heart within the limits of
the commonwealth, but would go at once for freedom.
We must be false to our fathers, false to ourselves and
to the spirit breathed into the soul of the word of
God, if we could even have any other sympathy than
sympathy with the oppressed, against the oppressor,
the bondman rather than the bond master.   But when
the slave asks me to stand between the marshal and

himself, what does he ask me to do? simply to free
him? no, that is not all ; he asks me to substitute
force for law ; anarchy for government. He asks me
to overturn the tribunals of justice, to break into fragments the power of a nation overshadowing all, and
protecting all. He asks me to do him right by wrong-
ing twenty millions of men ! The question comes
home to my soul ; I am not at once ready to answer ;
I pause ; I reflect ; I meditate ; if I resist that law, I
nullify the constitution ; in doing it, I am righteously
held to answer for all the natural and proper consequences of my conduct. When the slave asks me to
stand between him and his master, what does he ask ?
He asks me to murder a nation's life ; and I will not
do it, because I have a conscience, and because there
is a God.

Then I say unto you, as a minister of the Lord
Jesus Christ, the conviction of my conscience is that
upon the ground of reason, there is no safety for us,
no better hope for the slave, than for the time, the
carrying out of the constitution and laws of the country ; and that as a question of conscience, God
requires this at our hand.

But if the spirit of sedition and rebellion become
rampant in the land ; if the ordinary strength of the
magistracy cannot countervail it, if there be treason, if there be rebellion ; if needful, to defend the
constitution of the fathers, the magistracy call you
to arms, arm ! If they call you to the field of battle,
stand in your ranks as your fathers stood, shoulder to
shoulder ; *if to take human life, take it ; and if you fall,
your memory shall be hallowed with those whose bones
moulder on the slopes of Bunker Hill !*

Verily, verily ! Had Mr. Rogers lived in Babylon,
or Cyprus, with what alacrity would he have despatched
his daughters in all their maiden modesty, and virgin
purity, to the foul embraces of Mylitta's horrible rites !
"As a minister of the gospel" he demanded "obeying
the constitution and the laws."

This is what he says. " When my daughter asks
me to save her from such foul pollution, what does

she ask ? simply that I save her ? no, that is not all ;
she asks me to substitute force for law ; anarchy for
government.   I pause ;   I reflect ; I meditate.   If I
resist the law, I nullify the constitution !   *   *
*   When my daughter asks me to stand between
her and the law, what does she ask ? she asks me to
murder a nation's life ; and I will not do it, because
I have a conscience, and because I believe there is a
God ! "

And that was Rev. William Rogers, of Winter street
Congregational church in Boston, in the one thousand
eight hundred and fiftieth year of christian grace !
And of the Independence of the United States, the
seventy-fourth ! Change only the civil fugitive slave
law for the sacred prostitution act of Babylon and
Cyprus, and the parallel is complete ; is perfect.
With only this tremendous difference in favor of
Babylon and Cyprus ; that there, one visit to the temple sufficed forever.   But return to American slavery,
under its fugitive law was crossing that awful "bridge
of sighs," over which was inscribed,

"All hope abandon ye who enter here !"

And now this protracted argument is done ; not for
lack of material, but only out of respect to space and
time.   For be it ever remembered, all that has been
adduced, and surely it is much, is but specimen of
whole volumes which yet remain.   For instance, the
masterly argument of Mr. Whipple, on the American
Board of Commissioners for Foreign Missions, is a
book of nearly two hundred and fifty pages, closely
printed in fine type, and made up entirely from the
annual reports and other official literature of the board
itself.   And his work might have been extended to
two or three times its present size ; and the same substantially, could be said of the sources from which the

information and evidence have been derived on the American Bible and Tract societies, and on the great leading, controlling, religious sects and organizations that represented the religious sentiment of the country at the beginning, and in the progress of the great anti-slavery conflict. And what must be the conclusion from it all ? Judge Birney answered early : "The American churches the bulwarks of American slavery." Stephen S. Foster replied later, in tones of thunder, ". The Brotherhood of thieves ; or a true picture of the American church and clergy." Then came a ringing voice from the west : "Slavery, and the slaveholder's Religion ;" by Samuel Brooke, of Ohio, and still later : "The Church as it is : the Forlorn Hope of slavery," a larger pamphlet than the others. Nor were these all. And all pursuing the same course, which was to permit the accused to furnish all the testimony; not half, nor a part, but the whole. Nor was there any cross questioning, nor inferential evidence, from beginning to end.

What more could church or clergy have asked, unless in the language and spirit of those who demanded of the great teacher of Nazareth : "*What have we to do with thee ? let us alone !*" Or what can this generation ask of us to-day ? the very few of us who yet remain on earth ? and in justice to ourselves and our cause, what less, or otherwise, could, or should we abolitionists, have done ?

CHAPTER XVI.

Returning now to the acts of the anti-slavery
apostles, it should be explained that this long digres-
sion to the acts of another order of apostles became
necessary after the work was begun, and extends it,
too, beyond my original design. Within the past
year, the enemies of the anti-slavery enterprise, or
their children, have not only renewed their old calumnies against the faithful and uncompromising friends
and advocates of that enterprise, but they have urged
them with augmented aggravations. Their language
need not be here reproduced. They themselves have
given it to history and to posterity, and they and the
sure years, will render a true and just verdict.

But though the book has grown already beyond my
purpose at the outset, it shall not close without at
least some fraternal and friendly allusions to a few
faithful men and noble women with whom I became
acquainted in the lecturing field, each single one of
whom deserves a volume of finer strains than mine.

The Burleigh brothers, Charles C., and Cyrus M.,
came to the field almost in their boyhood, but valiant,
vigorous as the young knights of chivalry, equal always to any encounter. Had Charles C. Burleigh
pursued the profession of the law, as was his intention, there was no eminence he could not easily have
reached. On the platform, in argument, he had no

superior and few equals. We always felt safe when
Burleigh came to the stand. He never rose but when
he had something to say. And, generally, when he
had spoken, not much more was needed on the question in hand. With his pen, when he did write, he
was not less mighty, as his " Thoughts on the Death
Penalty," away back in 1845, proved. N. P. Rogers
wrote of it in the *Herald of Freedom :* " I have gone
over the ' Thoughts ' as particularly as I am able to a
book, and can witness to its being all that the reader
has right to expect from the power of the writer. It
is arranged with great judgment and order, and winds
about the poor old gallows tree an uninterupted
chain for its destruction. Chain lightning, I wish it
might prove, to strike and splinter it to its very roots,
as I have seen a white pine, that had been just visited
by one of these touches from the clouds. *   * A
trimmer, abler, more masterly argument, has not been
put together in words. Burleigh's antagonist is Dr.
George B. Cheever. Burleigh doesn't leave a rag of
his parson's gown on his back. Nobody makes an argument perfect and unanswerable but Charles Burleigh. Give him a good cause at the bar, as good as
he has here, and let him speak first, and the adversary
council would never reply. The court wouldn't let
him. His client wouldn't let him, not if he had common sense. The counsel wouldn't himself, for he
wouldn't find an inch of ground left to start on. I
never knew so *absolute* an arguer as Burleigh. And
he has displayed himself completely in this work."

A younger brother, Cyrus M. Burleigh, was an
earnest, faithful worker in the lecture field, but fell an
early victim to consumption. Amiable, gentle, com-

panionable, simple and sincere, he was ever well received, and most beloved and respected, where best
known.

Abby Kelley Foster and Lucy Stone both achieved
enviable success in their anti-slavery work, not to
speak of their ever abounding labors since in the
cause of woman suffrage, to well fill a volume. And
each has a brilliant and cultivated daughter, too,
every way equal to its production. Mrs. Foster was
in the lecturing field when I entered it, in 1840, and
had been for a number of years. And she is the last
survivor of those I found there who continued constantly in the conflict till the battle was won. She
early entered to conquer or die, and nobly and bravely
she kept her vow. Lucy Stone came later, but came
not less with the spirit of hero and martyr, and came
long before the period of peril, as well as of sacrifice
and severe suffering was passed. I have seen her in
truly ferocious mobs, that knew no distinction of sex
nor color, race nor religion. I once saw her hit on the
head with a large Swedenborgian prayer-book, hurled
across the hall with a velocity and force worthy other
cannons than the "sacred *canons*" of "holy church."
A less severe blow, on a vital spot, has taken life. The
mob was in a hall, used on Sundays for Swedenborgian
worship ; and in a town famous in that day for the
manufacture of cotton gins, for southern trade, and
so was an offering to slave-holding customers, as well
as a tribute to religion and worship.

Charles Lenox Remond earned a place in anti-slavery history worthy a monument, as well as extended
biography. Salem, the place of his birth and resi-
dence during most of his life, never knew him, never
will, to do any justice to his memory and worth. But
he achieved a reputation, both in his own country and

Great Britain, that might well be coveted, and doubtless was, by thousands who knew him in Salem,
and all over Massachusetts and New England ; but
who scorned him and his race, not more for their
color than condition in slavery, down to which so
many millions of them were consigned by the republicanism, the religion and the unhallowed prejudice and
hatred of the nation.   Many times I have myself gazed
on him with admiration, when before the best Boston
audiences, he acquitted himself with a power of
speech, argument and eloquence, which rarely, if
ever, thrilled a house of congress or legislative hall.
And I would often wonder how many young men of
Salem, how many in Massachusetts, who had enjoyed all
the advantages of grammar school, high school or academy, from which his color drove him away, could come
there and occupy and fill his place—not occupy, merely,
but fill his place !   How many !   Alas ! how few, how
very few, could do it !   We hear much, talk much of
"self-made men."   But who ever thinks of how scant
material our codes, customs, constitutions, schools and
churches permitted the colored people, a half-century
ago, to set up the business of "self-made men"
making !

And then I had not been long in the lecturing field
before fugitive slaves began to appear on our platform.   Among the earliest, as well as most eminent,
were Frederick Douglass and William Wells Brown.
And what had they out of which to create a "self-
made" manhood, or any manhood ?   I was to-day
reading two advertisements, and feel inclined to copy
them to answer that question.   The first was from the
Charleston, S. C., *Courier*, of February 12th, 1835, and
was headed :

"Field negroes—by Thomas Gadsden. On Tuesday, the 17th instant, will be sold at the north of the Exchange, at ten o'clock, A. M., a prime gang of ten negroes, accustomed to the culture of cotton and provisions—belonging to the *Independent church, in Christ church parish.*"

The other was this, taken from the Savannah, Ga., *Republican*, one item only given here, as below :

Also, at the same time and place, the following negro slaves, to wit : Charles, Peggy, Antoinnett, Davy, September, Maria, Jenny, and Isaac—levied on as the property of Henry T. Hall, to satisfy a mortgage fi. fia. issued out of McIntosh superior court, in favor of the board of directors of the theological seminary of the synod of South Carolina and Georgia, vs. said Henry T. Hall. Conditions, cash. C. O'NEAL,
Deputy-sheriff, M. C.

And right at hand was another, which has just fallen under my eye, and will help to answer this question about self-made manhood :

On the first Monday of February next, will be put up at public auction, before the court house, the following property, belonging to the estate of the late Rev. Dr. Furman, viz : A plantation or tract of land, on and in the Wateree swamp. A tract of the first quality of fine land, on the waters of Black river. A lot of land in the town of Camden. A library of a miscellaneous character, chiefly theological. Twenty-seven negroes, some of them very prime. Two mules, one horse, and an old wagon.

The Declaration of Independence reads : "All *men* are created equal." So all *men*, at creation, have equal elements to make up into manhood. But Rev. Dr. Furman had another breed of men, seven and twenty of them, and two mules and one horse ; or twenty-nine in all, and all "created equal." And "one old wagon," just as "equal" as the rest. And the Independent church in Christ's church parish, had ten more. And, then, a "South Carolina theological seminary" had in litigation, eight. Now, it is not probable that Frederick Douglas was any one of these. But he, and every slave who makes himself a man, sets out from that dead level. Who ever thinks of it? "Two mules, a horse, and an old wagon, and twenty-seven negroes, *some of them very prime.*" Nothing said of the mules, not a word of the horse. But the wagon is "old," and only part of the negroes are *prime.* Probably some of them may be older, more dilapidated than the wagon. Frederick Douglass began there, as an old wagon ; one of a gang of "twenty-seven negroes, two mules, a horse, and an old wagon." Some of the negroes not "very prime." Does any mortal man, or woman, comprehend all the tremendous meaning of these words? If there be, such must have read more and deeper than Rev. Dr. Furman's "library of miscellaneous character, *chiefly theological,*" advertised with the rest of his property. Finally, if the average Salem, or Massachusetts boys, with all their advantages of school, below the university, cannot rival Charles Lenox Remond, who, though never a slave, nor son of slaves, yet had none of their advantages in youth nor manhood, what will they say of Frederick Douglass, as he stands to-day, in the national capital, spurning the lingering evolutionary processes of Darwin, and mounting, as in an instant, from the deep dead level of mules, horses and old wagons, to the very proudest manhood yet achieved in the nineteenth century ! When, or where in all the historic, or traditionary years of the past, shall the self-made man be found to measure with such a phenomenon as this?

And there were many others in the field, doing noble anti-slavery work, when I entered it, who were not agents of anti-slavery societies for any length of time, and perhaps never at all. Among these were Dr. Hudson, Henry C. Wright, Edwin Thompson and James N. Buffum. The last, Mr. Buffum, has been named before among these pages, and in a way greatly to his credit, and by one, too, who could appreciate genuine anti-slavery service, no matter by whom performed. And besides much good work well done, Mr. Buffum's house was for forty years, not only a safe and well-patronized depot of "the under-ground railway," but a hotel of unlimited, as well as elegant hospitality extended by himself and family with utmost cheerfulness, not only to the anti-slavery apostles, but the faithful, earnest workers in every other department of real progress and reform. But beyond the good work done in his own country, Mr. Buffum also rendered valuable service to the anti-slavery cause in Great Britain; particularly in Scotland, with the churches there- In 1845, it was found that the Free church had sent delegates to the United States, Dr. Candlish and Dr. Cunningham, to solicit money to aid their branch of the Scottish church. And by consorting with American churches, north and south, fellowshipping slave-holding ministers and others as christians, and by silence, or open avowal, approving of the slave system, with all its attendant horrors, they obtained and carried home three thousand pounds, or about fifteen thousand dollars. Some of it they acknowledged was even obtained from slaves. At that time, it so happened that Frederick Douglass and Henry C. Wright, as well as Mr. Buffum, were in Great Britain; and, joined by George Thompson, then in his full power and prime, they entered Scotland and commenced a system of anti-slavery conventions and operations which soon set the country ablaze, as the journals expressed it, with excitement and agitation. The battle-cry was, "Send back that blood-stained money!"

And the slogan of William Wallace and his valliant Scottish chiefs and knights, was not more terrible among the highlands, seven hundred years before, when southern hosts invaded them, than were the voices of Thompson and his three American friends, one then a young fugitive slave, (and a Douglass, too, worthy his namesake who followed Wallace), demanding, day and night, in city, town and country, of that heartless Free church and its unscrupulous priesthood, to return that blood-besmeared gold and come out from the fellowship and communion of a slave-breeding, slave-trading and slave-holding church, and its northern abettors in the United States of America, and thus rebuke, instead of partake in their cruelties and crimes. Before me are full reports of some of those meetings, and for earnestness, as well as argument, eloquence, pathos, and intense responsive feeling in many crowded audiences, the cause might well have been proud of them in either hemisphere. And from every account given, it is certain that Mr. Buffum acquitted himself nobly wherever he spoke or labored, during his year abroad. And when seven years afterward I visited Great Britain, no American was mentioned with more respect, or inquired about with more apparent interest, than James N. Buffum.

In the New Testament "Acts of the Apostles," mention is made of "honorable women, not a few." These *Acts* could register great numbers of such, who went everywhere preaching the anti-slavery word. Sarah and Angelina Grimke emancipated their slaves in South Carolina, and in their youth abandoned affluence and elegance at the south and came to the north

and gave the remainder of their long lives to the
cause of freedom and humanity.   Later, came Sallie
Holley, daughter of Hon. Myron Holley, of New York,
graduate, with Lucy Stone, of Oberlin College, who
seems like a true Sister of Mercy to have consecrated
her whole life to the outcast Ethiopian.   For so soon
as slavery was abolished, she, with her invaluable and
inseparable companion, Caroline Putnam, removed to
Lottsburg, Virginia, and established themselves as
teachers among the freed people, where they still continue in their truly millennial work, making the wilder-
ness to bud and blossom as the rose, and the old
deserts of slavery to shout and sing for joy.   Susan
B. Anthony was early in the temperance and anti-
slavery, as well as woman suffrage work.   Jane Elizabeth Jones and Josephine S. Griffing performed labor,
made sacrifices, encountered sufferings at the west,
not known, probably never will be known, to the
world.   Lucy N. Colman went from Massachusetts
and for several seasons did excellent service and
encountered the incidents sometimes not easy to face,
of pioneer work.   Sarah P. Remond, sister of Charles
Lenox Remond, went to the west, and with her brother
did service above all praise — removing prejudice
against their complexion and winning fast friends
wherever they came.   Sarah subsequently went to
England, studied medicine in London, went to Italy,
married, and settled in large medical practice in
Florence.   But most wondrous of all was the Ethiopian Sybil, Sojourner Truth, still living, a centenarian
and more.   These all it was my pleasure and privilege to meet as best of friends, as well as co-workers
in that mighty moral and peaceful struggle for humanity and liberty which made the middle of the nineteenth century memorable amid the ages.

It is impossible for me to do justice to the services of not a few others whom I met on the field of conflict, should I even mention their names. Oliver Johnson was among the first to place his young Green Mountain manhood bravely by the side of Garrison. And his recently published work entitled " Garrison and His Times," has been of important use to me in the compilation of these chronicles.

The faithful, most invaluable services of Samuel May as general agent of the Massachusetts Anti-Slavery Society for many years, and for a time, before and during the rebellion, of almost the whole Eastern States movement, would if truthfully written be nearly a history of the anti-slavery enterprise for its last quarter of a century.

And Andrew T. Foss was another minister who abandonded his pulpit and profession, and for a dozen years was among the bravest and best of the Anti-Slavery apostles, never faltering till the last slave was free.

George W. Putnam, poet as well as lecturer, accompanied George Thompson in one of his brilliant lecturing tours through the country. And the surpassing genius of the orator so inspired the poet and singer that his impromptu songs, given in connection with the lectures, added greatly to the interest, enthusiasm and success of the campaign.

Captain Jonathan Walker, of the " Branded Hand," published a small volume of his sufferings and sacrifices in a vain attempt to carry a cargo of escaping slaves across from Florida to the nearest British West India Islands. Narrowly escaping with his life, he returned to his home on Cape Cod, where, joined by Loring Moody, he entered the lecturing field. The account of his terrible sufferings in a Florida prison,

besides being branded on the palm of his right hand
with a red hot iron, for the dreadful crime of doing
as he would be done by, and "remembering them
that were in bonds as bound with them," was heard
with profound attention, interest and sympathy, by
many large audiences all over New England. He
subsequently removed to Michigan, where he died in
1878, at the advanced age of seventy-nine years. A
handsome monument of Hallowell granite, costing
about seven hundred dollars, and generously presented by Rev. Photius Fisk, of Boston, marks the
place of his burial. The city of Muskegon, near which
he lived and died, honored itself by presenting and
preparing a commodious lot in its principal cemetery,
where his body lies entombed. And on the first of
August, (a memorable day in British anti-slavery history,) 1878, the monument was unveiled with appropriate ceremonies, in the presence of the Mayor and
city government, besides many state officials, and a
concourse of fully ten thousand people. The procession, with three bands of music, the marshals
mounted, a part of them colored men, in special compliment to the deceased, extended nearly from the
city hall to the monument.

Mr. Moody continued in the anti-slavery service,
was at one period general agent of the Massachusetts
Society, till the opening of the war of the rebellion.
He was afterwards secretary of the Society for the
Prevention of Cruelty to Animals, and still later of a
similar association in behalf of poor children. His
reports proved conclusively his earnestness and faithfulness and consequent usefulness in his work. His
last labor was doubtless most important of all in his
life of nearly seventy years. He originated and organized *The Institute of Heredity*, perhaps, viewed in all

its aspects and relations, the most important enterprise to universal human well being of the nineteenth century. And while its secretary, treasurer, and almost sole working element, he faltered and finally died early in the year 1883.

Among the later, younger comers into the antislavery vineyard were E. H. Heywood, graduate of Brown University, at one time general agent of the Massachusetts Society, Joseph A. Howland and Aaron M. Powell. But in the early Christian years, seventy apostles were at one time ordained and sent forth to do all the works and wonders of the very chiefest apostles, whose names were not even recorded, with or without divine inspiration. And yet they all returned and reported that even the very devils had been subject to their command and control. So there were many unnamed and unknown to-day, who on the antislavery field of moral, even of mortal, combat, "wrought righteousness, stopped the mouths of lions, quenched the violence of fire, escaped the edge of the sword, waxed valliant in the fight and turned to flight the armies of the aliens."

ADMISSIONS AND CONFESSIONS.

In concluding these acts and chronicles, two considerations present themselves : one as admission, the other confession. In the severe arraignment of the American church and ministry as the bulwark, and finally as the forlorn hope of slavery, it was not always easy, if indeed necessary, to make explicit exceptions. Though the sect known as come-outers, particularly in the second decade of the Garrisonian movement, was numerous, it was not true that all came out of the churches who deserved the good name of abolitionists; many remained in the churches

under the plea or pretense of reforming them ; they
did so after the churches had been proved the accomplices of actual and practical adulterers at the south ;
and the churches at the south, worse than the houses
of ill fame in New York ; worse than the temples of
the obscene goddess, Mylitta, in Cyprus and Babylon.
Worse in at least two particulars ; one visit to the
abominable worship of Mylitta was all that the law
required of women in a lifetime.   But in the southern
churches, marriage was utterly unknown among
slaves in all their lifetime.   Out of that dreadful condition there was no escape but into the cold embraces
of death ; and the victims were born into their condition ; they did not enter it voluntarily, as do the
wretched inmates, the dens of infamy in New York.
They are not born into them ; no law, no custom,
no religious observance forces them there ; they enter
when they will ; they can leave when they choose.
And more than that, there are many Magdalen
associations and female moral reform societies whose
special mission it is to tempt them from those dread
abodes, by promise of every assistance to return to
the paths of purity and virtue, with no penalty for the
past, no rebuke, no reproach, only the gentle word of
Him who said to one of the same unhappy class, " go,
and sin no more."   All this was urged on the consideration of church members who would not leave
their adulterous slave-holding communion and fellowship, with this appeal ; could you recommend to the
inmates of no worse place than the house of ill repute
in New York, to remain in it to reform it ? Could you,
would you, though you believed such reformation
possible ?

And not unfrequently, such church abolitionists
were zealous members of the so-named liberty, or

31

free soil party, and had left the whig and democratic parties with stern self assumed integrity, and would not vote in them, nor for them, nor their candidates, for any office in the public gift. Thousands of times such have been seen on Sunday, at the sacramental supper, with the wickedest whigs and democrats who ever voted for slave-holders, or caught and returned fugitive slaves; but on Monday, at the polls, they would spurn all such from their presence as unclean; would no more vote for them, nor their candidates, than for the Prince of Darkness. Then, to whichever of the three parties they belonged, they were members of a slave-holding union and government, and sworn by themselves or their elected officers, to support the constitution, which over and over again had been decided by the supreme court of the country, to require the return of fugitive slaves, as well as to hold the slave claimant secure against any insurrection among his slaves. Even Senator Sumner never forgot those obligations. In his letter accepting the office of senator of the United States, he wrote: "I accept, as the servant of the union; bound to study with equal patriotic care the interests of all parts of the country; and to oppose all sectionalism, whether it appear in unconstitutional efforts by the north to carry so great a boon as freedom into the slave states, or in unconstitutional efforts by the south, aided by northern allies, to carry the sectional evil into the free states." Such were the "solemn guaranties" to the slave power as declared by John Quincy Adams, as accepted by Senator Sumner on his election to the United States senate, in 1851. In 1861, ten years later, Mr. Lincoln came to the presidential chair. He began, not only where Mr. Adams left off, where Senator Sumner left off, but where the whole democratic party left off ; and in his very *inaugural address* said, in reference to those same "solemn guaranties" and their binding force ; " I understand a proposed, *amendment* to the constitution has passed Congress to the effect that the Federal Government shall never interfere with the domestic institutions of the states, including that of persons held to service. To avoid misconstruction of what I have said, I now depart from my purpose, not to speak of particular amendments, so far as to say, that holding such a provision to now be *implied* constitutional law, I have no objection to its being made *express* and *irrevocable !*"

So much for President Lincoln. And only a little more than one month before he passed through Ohio on his way to Washington and his inauguration, a slave woman and her unborn babe were sent back from Cleveland to Virginia, under circumstances, recital of which in the city papers should have chilled all human blood. Referring to the sickening transaction, Mr. Garrison said : " Several columns of our paper are occupied with a heart-moving but most humiliating account of the legal rendition of a fugitive slave girl in Cleveland, *and by republican hands*, as a peace offering to the traitors and brigands of the south. Hear what Judge Spaulding, *a high professing anti-slavery man* of many years standing, said in his concluding speech at the trial :

"While we do this in the City of Cleveland, and permit this poor piece of humanity to be taken PEACEABLY through our streets and upon our railways back to the land of bondage will not the frantic south stay its parricidal hand ? Will not our compromising legislators cry, hold ! enough ? . . . We are this day offering to the majesty of constitutional law a homage that takes with it a virtual surrender of the finest feelings of our nature ; and is, I almost said, the contravention of a christian's duty to his God "

And that was Judge Spaulding, an eminent free-soil man and republican of many years ! And what was the answer of his fratricidal south, to now " stay her fratricidal hands ? " He obtained his answer not many weeks after, from the brazen throats and blazing lips of Carolina cannon around Fort Sumpter, shaking the sea and land ; and followed by the bloodiest slaughter of human ·beings that this poor world has mourned in all the christian centuries !

Now this one word about "sweeping charges," and making no exceptions, or too few, so constantly and universally preferred against the abolitionists. We saw the very best men in church and state with no exception, in the three great political parties, solemnly sworn and pledged to observe all the compromises of the federal constitution, and religiously keeping the obligation. Every man they sent to congress was thus sworn. Through their agents they kept the oath ; or violating it they were guilty of legal and moral perjury. This the abolitionists saw, and hence their obedience to the demand issued from Patmos : " Come out of her, my people, that ye be not partaker in her sins, and that ye receive not of her plagues."

And so where should we begin to make *exceptions* of such as remained in connection with the state, or in fellowship with the church fulfilling their obligations and requirements ? But we made exceptions. We made too many, not too few. Our charity covered not only a multitude of sins, but of sinners, too.

And now the final consideration relates to ourselves, the abolitionists. And, as already intimated, it shall take the form of confession.

Through all these many pages, to patrons and readers, too many perhaps, no word has been spoken of differences or disagreements among ourselves, any more or less among leaders than others, men or women. For among the abolitionists, though there were women in goodly numbers on the platform of speech and in the field of work, we knew no male nor female, no high nor low.

In the great apostacy of 1840, which resulted in the formation of what was known as new organization, one principal grievance, especially among the more orthodox sects, was what they termed the "woman question." With that came the cry against our " no voting theory," that we were opposed to all government among men and nations, as though there were or could be no government but our government, no church but our church.   With all these questions or quibbles, the abolitionists made short shrift and went on with their work.

But being intensely human, abolitionists were intensely individual.   And so they proved true what a great man once wrote, that for any considerable number of persons to profess to think just alike on any important problem was simply to confess that they did not think at all.

Abolitionists did think, and deeply too.   And they felt as intensely as they thought.   And so how could they but differ ?   And there were disagreements that were not all reconciled before death sundered the parties to meet on earth no more.   But they lived and died with their faces ever towards freedom, justice and love.   A little more toleration, a very little more remembrance of our difference of temperament, of power of perception, of inherited tendencies, of possible material, mental or moral infirmity in ourselves,

for which we should be scarcely responsible in the
least degree, might have preserved from many a dis-
cordant note that seemed to ring on down to the gates
of the grave. It was not anger, it was not hate.
It was rather the result of intensity of love. At least
it was so among some of our very truest, bravest, best,
whose natures could but love, could never hate.

> "Alas! they had been friends in youth!
> But whispering tongues can poison truth:
> And constancy lives in realms above:
> And life is thorny, and youth is vain:
> And *to be wroth with those we love*
> Doth work like madness in the brain."

To the last, there were differences of opinion. On
the question when to cease our operations as an anti-
slavery organization, there was much earnest debate.
Some contended that our distinctive work was not accomplished till the slave was made equal to the master at the ballot box, and in the government. And
that this was all the more important since it was only
by the slaves' valor on the battle-field, that the masters had been defeated and their rebellion suppressed.

As my last printed speech was on that subject, at
the last anti-slavery anniversary I attended, it may be
pardonable to present it here, as showing somewhat
the temper and spirit of the discussion, as well as the
nature of the subject then in hand. It is, however,
only pardonable because from the beginning it has
been my constant care to be myself as little obtrusive
as the nature of my work would warrant consistently
with exact truth and right.

The anniversary exercises were held in the church
of the Puritans, whose walls had often shuddered
with the truly terrible eloquence of Dr. Cheever, from
Sunday to Sunday, in rebuke and denunciation of the
southern oppressor and his not less guilty abettor

and accomplice in the north, in church and pulpit, as well as in the state. In the later years of the anti-slavery conflict, after he had been anathematized by the pulpit and almost driven from the pale of the church, only for his faithfulness to the cause of free-dom and humanity, for his orthodoxy, as well as pri-vate virtues were high as heaven above suspicion, he seemed to speak as by permission and power of Him who "touched Isaiah's lips with hallowed fire," and to superadd at times all the terrors of Patmos as well. No other voice penetrated the dark, deep recesses of the pro-slavery church and pulpit, the American Bible, missionary and tract societies, as did his. For to his faith and virtue, he added a perfect knowledge of all their works and ways. My resolution at that last anniversary, read as below :

Resolved, That the objects of the American anti-slavery society, as announced in its constitution and declaration of sentiment, are, "the entire abolition of slavery in the United States," and "the elevation of "all persons of color, who possess the qualifications of others, to the enjoyment of the same privileges, and the exercise of the same prerogatives as others." And while we joyfully welcome, and will heartily co-operate with every new auxiliary in this vast field of action and effort, under whatever name, we can never lay down our own distinctive apostleship, until all those high purposes are fully accomplished.

Though we had come to the last day and session of our meeting, I had not spoken before. We met at an early hour in the forenoon, and it was now nearly three in the afternoon, and we had not even taken a recess ; but I ventured to obtrude myself at that unseasonable hour, and was heard with most respect-ful attention in the following remarks :

MR. PRESIDENT—This is the first time I have pre-sumed on the attention of this convention, and now I know full well it is too late to ask to be heard. But it seems to me something might be said which has not yet found utterance, and I will not be long. I quite agree with our excellent friends who have said that this society has been four years virtually dead, though it seems to me a most humiliating confession to make. And I think, that although they insist that this is no time for a funeral, still, if the society has been really four years dead, it is time it should be buried out of sight. It has certainly been inactive, though I trust it has only slept. And I have hoped that to-day a voice would be uttered that should be effective, say-ing, "Lazarus, come forth!"

Four years ago it was announced on our platform that slavery was dead—that our anti-slavery efforts were no longer needed—that General Scott was now our general agent in place of Mr. May, and that the Amer-ican army was now the American anti-slavery society. Well, that new anti-slavery society, under General Scott and others, prosecuted its conflict with such suc-cess and disaster as we now know. And the war dragged its slow length along, through nearly four dreary, desolating years. And slavery was still able to compete valiantly, if not successfully, with the mightiest armies that ever gathered in the field of bloody fight. For though we began with but seventy-five thousand, and they enrolled only for ninety days, before that period expired, we had summoned sud-denly a half-million more, for a three years' service. And in less than four years, our army had reached the stupendous muster-roll of more than two and a half millions, and nearly the half-million had already "fought their last battle, slept their last sleep!"

Last month, we were wakened early one Monday morning, to celebrate what we presumed to be the complete triumph of our northern hosts and vanquishing of every southern foe. Richmond had surrendered, General Lee was our prisoner, and his forces with him, and we fancied that then, indeed, our work was done. There lay the monster slavery writhing in death agonies at our feet, his head not bruised only, but severed from his scaly form. And the whole free north burst into a joy unseen, unknown before since we were a nation. And that was a full week of jubilation. We thought the great red dragon was dead, our work done, and already *reconstruction* was under way. The president had made that last speech of his on the question, and the press of the country had given in its adhesion to his fatal doctrine.

I well remember that on our Massachusetts Fast-day, our friend, Mr. Spaulding, of Salem, who addressed us so earnestly this morning, invited me to occupy his pulpit. And let me say for him, that although pastor of one of the largest churches in that state, he has been so faithful as to have driven what is known as "the copper-head element," pretty much out of his congregation, and dared still to invite me to give the fast-day discourse. So, occupying the desk, I presumed the prerogative of minister and selected a text from the scriptures, and spoke of the goodness and forbearance of God to the nation. The text was this, from the Hebrew prophets: "What could I have done for my vineyard that I have not done in it? Wherefore when I looked that it should bring forth grapes, brought it forth wild grapes?"

In the course of remark, I referred to that speech of President Lincoln, and said it appeared to me highly proper that we observe a day of fasting and prayer, for we had to treat with an evil spirit, which, though we fancied he was dead, and were celebrating our conquest and victory, was one that went not out after all, but by prayer and fasting. In the afternoon of that day, I went into the Salem Athenæum and read every daily newspaper of New York and Boston there, and every one, I think, with no exception endorsed its doctrine.

I had a lecture in a neighboring town that evening, and went to it with a heavy heart; for I felt that it would be my duty to tell my audience that our joy was ill-timed, and would be vain; that our rejoicing, I was sure, would be turned into mourning. For in our very hour of triumph and of victory, as we thought, we were not doing justice; and were ready to reconstruct the government on the basis of white suffrage and citizenship, and that also disloyal; rejecting the bravery and loyalty that God had made the salvation of the country! I went to my lecture, you may be sure with heavy, desponding heart. I told my audience it seemed to me we were lost. I said: you have all called me "blue, blue-black, and bilious," and I know not what else, from the beginning of the war, but we are inevitably lost! For God has visited us in judgment; and in the last hour, when He seems to have left nothing undone that he could do for His vineyard, we still forget justice and judgment; none calling for justice, nor any in the high places of government pleading the cause of the poor, the very poorest of the poor! It was a sad meeting; well might it have been sad; it continued till a late hour in the evening; and a sadder audience. I never addressed, and a sadder heart in that joyous week, probably could not be found, than was mine. But in four and twenty hours from that time, God did appear, and in most mysterious manner, and showed that there was at least one thing more possible to be done in his vineyard, that had not been done. The solemn, mourning drapery which darkens this temple to-day, answers the question of our text; "what more could have been done for my vineyard than I have done in it?"

And so we closed our week of joy. I thought of the lines of Byron on Bonaparte, when he sung of his greatness and his fall :

"O who would soar the solar height
To set in such a starless night!"

Yes, Mr. President, that was a sad week for us. Our enemy was not slain ; for while we exulted over his fall, and triumphed in what we presumed his everlasting discomfiture, the quivering monster gathered enough vitality to swing around his envenomed tail, and in an instant to sting our almost idolized chief magistrate to death, before our very eyes !

I felt then, that there was more work for me to do ; and I have felt all through this meeting, that there was more work yet to be done by this grand old antislavery society, and I thought if we were indeed to cease from our good old apostleship, and our association was to be sacrificed here, it was fitting and well that we had this funeral drapery hanging here about us. But it seems to me that such a deed as our disbandment and dissolution would better become Ford's theatre than "the church of the Puritans," crape-darkened as it is for the dreadful tragedy which long yet must the nation mourn !

No, Mr. Chairman, no ; our work is not yet quite done ; at least mine is not done, nor will it be done till the blackest man has every right which I, myself enjoy. I cannot prove that I love my neighbor as myself till he stand by my side. And I honor my friend, Senator Wilson, for standing here to-day, and asserting it as his life purpose, to labor in private and in public, for the accomplishment of that glorious end. And I dare tell you my friends, that when slavery is abolished, we shall all know it, for it will be as though "Death and Hell gave up the ghost!"

When we comprehend the malignity, yea, the "uncommon wrath" of the fell demon we have to face and overcome, and the terrible power and tenacity of life he has acquired, we shall all realize that our warfare is no pastime, no children's play; and that however freedmen's aid societies, and christian associations may operate in their fields, they will every one of them, need the old polar star to guide them in their new, untried and dangerous way.

Charity of readers may be trusted to forgive the egotism of inserting this address, in part for its sad historical reminiscences, but more especially for the other reasons already intimated. In methods and measures, abolitionists, even of clearest vision, spiritual as well as mental, could not always see eye to eye; though ready to live and die in defense of their common cause. But let the temper and spirit which breathe in this utterance, remarkable only that it was my last on our great subject ever given to the public through the press; let this witness, that even in our differings, we were still in heart and spirit friends in all which that divine word can be made to mean.

And now this work is done. Would, that it could be as truthfully said, "well done." But nearly three score and fourteen, is too late in life to be engaged in such a service; especially when it is remembered that authorship has been no part of all my public labors of three and forty years.

Truth in statement, justice and right towards all persons and parties interested in any way in these chronicles, have been constantly, carefully, kept in view, alike towards foe and friend. In soul, spirit, purpose, I have known no foes ; no sun has risen nor gone down on any wrath of mine.

Most of my early comrades in the field-service, have gone, some of them long since gone to their well earned rest and reward. It is mine yet to live and guard watchfully their graves, and with tenderest affection to cherish their memory, and to shield it from any unjust reproach to the full extent of my power and to my latest breath.

Of the great west and my many dear ones there living, or dead, I have scarcely spoken. And yet, nearly twenty of my autumns, and several winters were spent in most laborious service in the western states ; and many there became not only faithful co-workers, but life-long and devoted friends. A volume much larger than this and greatly better every way would not suffice to do any justice to their exalted worth. But I live in unshaken faith and expectation of a glorious re-union awaiting us all.

Nor with my present vision, could I desire sublimer felicity in such re-union, than to become more and more divinely endowed with celestial wisdom, knowledge and power ; and then, in the same spirit of love and good will to men, to all men, appealing ever only to the highest, divinest elements in the human nature, to continue our work and service till the whole race shall be restored and redeemed, and sin and death, the last great and only real enemies, shall together give up the ghost.

48339